T0313839

Contracts and Deals in Islamic Finance

The Wiley Finance series contains books written specifically for finance and investment professionals as well as sophisticated individual investors and their financial advisors. Book topics range from portfolio management to e-commerce, risk management, financial engineering, valuation and financial instrument analysis, as well as much more. For a list of available titles, visit our Web site at www.WileyFinance.com.

Founded in 1807, John Wiley & Sons is the oldest independent publishing company in the United States. With offices in North America, Europe, Australia and Asia, Wiley is globally committed to developing and marketing print and electronic products and services for our customers' professional and personal knowledge and understanding.

Contracts and Deals in Islamic Finance

A User's Guide to Cash Flows, Balance Sheets, and Capital Structures

HUSSAIN KURESHI
MOHSIN HAYAT

WILEY

Cover image: top: ©iStock.com/asikkk; bottom: ©iStock.com/JLGutierrez
Cover design: Wiley

Published by John Wiley & Sons Singapore Pte. Ltd.

1 Fusionopolis Walk, #07-01, Solaris South Tower, Singapore 138628

Other Wiley Editorial Offices
John Wiley & Sons, 111 River Street, Hoboken, NJ 07030, USA
John Wiley & Sons, The Atrium, Southern Gate, Chichester, West Sussex, P019 8SQ, United Kingdom
John Wiley & Sons (Canada) Ltd., 5353 Dundas Street West, Suite 400, Toronto, Ontario, M9B 6HB, Canada
John Wiley & Sons Australia Ltd., 42 McDougall Street, Milton, Queensland 4064, Australia
Wiley-VCH, Boschstrasse 12, D-69469 Weinheim, Germany

Library of Congress Cataloging-in-Publication Data is on file

ISBN 9781119020561 (Hardcover)
ISBN 9781119020578 (ePDF)
ISBN 9781119020585 (ePub)

This book is dedicated to the memory of my father, the late Muhammad Azam Kureshi, who left this world too soon, and my grandfather, Ali Muhammad Baloch. Both men served their countries and not their pockets—a rare breed.

—Hussain Kureshi

To my mother, who held my hand and took me to the library; to my father, who writes every day and first encouraged me to write; and to my wife, a beautiful writer who keeps focusing and championing me.

—Mohsin Hayat

Contents

Foreword

It is difficult to describe the pride with which I commend the reading of this fine piece on Islamic finance. Hussain Kureshi came into contact with OCBC Al-Amin (and thus me) through our scholarship program with INCEIF, of which he is an inaugural recipient. Hussain duly completed his CIFP with distinction and went on to engage with us as a research assistant. We certainly did not expect him to also come out with a book on Islamic finance. But that is exactly what his trail-blazing approach and academic prowess have produced. Doubtless, he has set the standard, no, raised the bar, of expectations from future scholars.

Islamic finance, or offering *shariah-compliant* financial products to clients, is no longer confined to the domain of Muslim customers anymore. We at OCBC Al-Amin have experienced strong demand for *shariah*-compliant products from numerous non-Muslims as well, evidently because the structures offered to them at the right price make sense.

Islamic finance has gone beyond the stage of just making the headlines; it is now making money and attracting the attention of issuers of credit notes and investors. With countries like Luxembourg, the United Kingdom, and Hong Kong announcing issues of *sukuk*, we feel that a book that clearly spells out the process flows inherent in the structures and contracts has become necessary for the education of industry participants and aspirants alike. No book has covered aspects of process flows, accounting treatments, risk analyses, and *shariah* analysis in a single volume. Not until now. Hussain and Mohsin have an easy writing style, which mitigates the inevitable technicalities that come with this type of book, gently walking the reader through the contracts and structures step by step. The net result is a painless ride for individuals not familiar with the religion or the language to understand the contracts and the products.

We are already looking forward to the sequel to this work, which I understand will focus on Islamic derivatives and structured products. For now, you will certainly have more than enough to digest and ponder when you turn the page. I hope you enjoy this book as much as I did.

Syed Abdull Aziz Syed Kechik
Director and CEO
OCBC Al-Amin Bank Berhad

Preface

Contracts and Deals in Islamic Finance is a unique idea for which I have my professors and industry peers to thank. It is a collaborative effort between two conventional bankers with Islamic roots and aims at addressing some basic fundamentals of Islamic finance and banking and explores complex enhancements to traditional contracts that are the pillars of Islamic banking.

This work we hope will be of use not only to students, beginners, and practitioners, but banks, central banks and governments that are trying to get a grip on this subject.

This work has been designed keeping in mind the cynic and the skeptic who feels that Islamic finance is a mere twisting of legal terms to achieve ends that replicate loans. To such a cynic we can only ask him or her to read the book. The coauthor of this book, who approached the subject of Islamic finance with equal skepticism, however, at one point had to question his own assumptions and expectations.

One key aspect that is explored is what do we as Muslims expect from Islamic financial institutions (IFIs)? If we expect IFIs to finance us with money and then forgive the resulting debt obligations later on, then this is an unrealistic expectation, as we see later that IFIs are not financing borrowers using their own money, but that of their depositors. If we expect IFIs to offer loans on "generous" terms, on terms that make losses for the IFI, then this is also incorrect as Islam allows a Muslim a right to profit making within certain conditions. If we expect IFIs to finance us money and only ask to be repaid when and if we as borrowers generate profits from investing the mobilized funds, then this expectation can be accepted but provided the debtor fulfills certain covenants of contracts and acts with a sense of responsibility as well.

Is it the purpose of Islamic finance to reduce poverty, or to extend money to poor people? This expectation can be addressed, but fundamentally, this depends on the type of IFI concerned. If the IFI is engaged in microfinance, then the answer would be yes, but if the IFI exists for commercial reasons, in that it exists to make a profit, then an IFI can no more be expected to give loans to the poor with high risk of default than a shoemaker can be expected to sell shoes at cost price to the poor.

In essence, IFIs exist not to make benevolent loans, to give charity, or to eradicate poverty, but to generate profits for shareholders and capital providers from providing financing through *shariah*-compliant financial products.

IFIs are as entitled to profit as any other commercial enterprise within the *halaal* industry. They are a component of a *halaal* economy and play the role of financial intermediaries.

The world of finance is rather different than the world of service providers, trading, or manufacturing. In the world of manufacturing, inventors evolve into entrepreneurs and raise funds through different means, either from banks or by selling shares in their businesses. The created entity, the firm, however, uses its own funds to manufacture goods and then sells them at a profit. Traders purchase goods from one market at a cost price and sell them in another market at a profit, at times in different countries and in different currencies. Service providers also use their capital to set up certain infrastructures to enable them to operate and then charge customers a price for the services they render.

Financial institutions are unique in that they are set up by shareholders who combine their capital to set up a retail bank, a commercial bank, an investment bank, an asset management company, a brokerage firm, a mutual fund, a finance company, or an insurance company. But shareholders do not lend their money to borrowers in the case of the banking model.

Shareholders provide capital to set up a conventional bank and then mobilize deposits from households, businesses, corporations, governments, and international investors, and lend these monies to households, businesses, corporations, governments, and international borrowers. Banks, if they mean to refer to shareholders, do not lend their own money; they leverage on their own capital to borrow from surplus economic units and lend to deficit economic units, making a spread between the income earned from financing activities and the expensed paid as cost of mobilizing deposits. Islamic banks do no different, but perform these same functions using *shariah*-compliant contracts for mobilizing profits, extending financing, recording profits, and sharing profits and expenses.

The principles of the *shariah* govern how these activities are conducted, but the core activity of an Islamic bank and a conventional bank are the same. Depositors in essence give their consent to bankers to extend financing with their moneys out to qualified borrowers provided that the customer has no exposure to the risk of losing capital or expected profit from the borrower's default. If we were to look at the concept of risk sharing, this would not be much different from conventional depositors and requiring guarantee on their principle amounts. More on that later. Islamic bankers like conventional bankers must have the expertise in identifying suitable candidates for financing, and must have the expertise in mitigating all the risks involved in credit finance and other aspects of managing money.

Asset management firms raise funds from investors and invest these funds in financial assets for a return. Asset managers have the expertise in raising funds and in knowing how to invest them in different market circumstances to get a positive return on investments. Fund managers perform this function either on a principal and agency basis, or on commission basis. Islamic fund managers do the exact same thing except they must mobilize funds from *halaal* sources and invest them in *shariah*-compliant assets. Scholars have established various criteria for determining whether a certain asset is *shariah*-compliant.

Investment bankers and Islamic investment bankers fulfill the same roles in an economy. Islamic investment bankers may have fewer assets at their disposal due to the restrictions on investments in derivatives. However, Islamic investment bankers help companies raise money through initial public offerings, underwrite issuances of *sukuk*, raise funds from investors, sell financial products, and make investments in various assets to earn returns. Islamic investment bankers, however, must perform all these functions according to contracts and processes permitted by *shariah*.

Similar to insurance companies that underwrite risk, *takaful* companies underwrite risks as well. Insurance companies factor their cost of insuring risks into the premiums they charge by a simple formula, "probability of event occurring × sum assured." *Takaful* companies underwrite risks in a similar fashion but use different contracts of *tabarru* and *wakala* to perform the same function.

Islamic brokerage firms must adapt to trading practices that are *shariah*-compliant, but in every other way are similar in their roles to conventional brokers.

Islamic banks use the same methodologies of financial mathematics, econometrics, and financial modeling to develop models of risks and returns as conventional banks and also use a benchmark interest rate to discount future cash flows to a present value. These elements are part and parcel of the Islamic financial system. Islamic financial institutions use the same T-accounts methods of accounting that we are all familiar with. Assets, liabilities, equity, debt, income, expenses, and so on, are all parts of an IFI's balance sheets. However, how different economic events are recorded to be *shariah*-compliant can be unique in many cases.

Islamic banks recognize entries such as "unearned income," "constructive liquidation," future income, and so on, much in the same fashion as conventional banks.

One may, therefore, rightfully ask, "What is the difference between Islamic banking and conventional banking?" An initial response would be that the vision to date behind Islamic banking has been to provide conventional financial products in a *shariah*-compliant manner. So there has been no incentive so far to be different; the incentive has to only be *shariah*-compliant.

Is there a difference between a wedding contract in a Christian church and a wedding contract in a mosque? One may well argue that both contracts contain positive and negative covenants that assign rights to each party of the contract and impose simultaneous limitations on each party to the contract. On the surface, both contracts of a Christian marriage and a Muslim marriage may well be similar, but Islam allows certain things that Christianity may not allow and Islam may forbid certain rights to either party that the Christian worldview may allow. Both contracts would require two parties having the legal capacity to contract, an offer, an acceptance, certain terms and conditions imposed by one party over the other, and some terms and conditions imposed by the worldview of the religions in question. The differences would be minor but yet are differences nevertheless. This is the kind of subtlety of differences that lies in the discussion of some of the broader issues in Islamic finance, such as risk sharing and equity.

Our approach to the subject must be built carefully, without emotion, without preconceived assumptions (no bank is sponsoring the authorship of this book), and with an open mind. If the reader wishes to explore the texts and do further research to substantiate his or her understanding of the subject material, we would feel well satisfied in having sparked the curiosity of an intelligent mind.

The models offered are by no means perfect. The Muslim world is just beginning to wake up from the slumber of colonialism and is trying hard to find its identity in an ever-changing world. Archives of records lie buried deep within many libraries all over the Muslim world and need to be explored to create better alternatives to trade and financial intermediation than what we have been able to develop so far.

For the time being, the reader must appreciate and accept the realities: the world is dominated by Western powers, it is dominated by debt, interest-bearing contracts dominate the world of finance, and scholars are trying to tap into the world of finance with the best possible contracts they have at their current disposal. As much as Islamic banking can serve as an alternative to conventional banking in certain ways, it still has some ways to go to be robust enough to replace it completely.

So, having laid the ground rules and expectations at the outset for this book, we say *Bismillah* (In the name of Allah the Beneficent, the Merciful).

Acknowledgments

It is part of the traditions of Islam to acknowledge one's teachers. To honor this tradition I have to recognize the team at International Centre for Education in Islamic Finance (INCEIF) in Kuala Lumpur, Malaysia. I thank Professor Yusuf Saleem for encouraging me to write my first paper on salaam, which was published in the *ISRA Journal* of 2014; Professor Ezamshah for his eloquent explanation of risk and how to price risk; Professor Rosly, who painstakingly answered every question I had; Professor Azam, who is as elegant as he is knowledgeable; Professor Razak for dropping the one pearl of wisdom that the rate of *zakat* should be the minimum profit rate applied to a credit financing contract; Professor Pisal for his humorous anecdotes; and last but not least, Professor Yusuf. I also thank Mohammad Ghaith Mahaini for urging me to write in the first place.

I would be doing an injustice if I did not extend a word of thanks to all my fellow students who tolerated me for a year, when I asked question after question, hogging the professor's attention. Izzaty, Nur Fatin, Tariq, and all the rest, thanks for putting up with me. I also congratulate INCEIF for providing students from all over the world a platform to study Islamic law and finance. Few places are left in the Muslim world where one can "argue" on *shariah* in a nondogmatic environment. Professor Ahsenne has to be congratulated on that.

The face of INCEIF for me has been Dr. Abbas Mirakhor, Dr. Al Habshi, and the famous D. Vicary to whom I am indebted for the wonderful institution they have set up.

I acknowledge the warmth and hospitality of the peoples of Malaysia who gave me and my family a home and an environment conducive for me to finish my program.

I give a warm acknowledgment to the support of my mother, Mrs. Bilquise Azam Kureshi, who patiently mentored me through the challenges of going back to school at the age of 42. I acknowledge "team oomi zoomi," which consists of Inaya, Azam, and Sophiya, who were forced to be separated from their homeland and loving grandparents, Mamajaani, Mamo, and Dado, to keep me company while I finished my studies and the book. Finally, I cannot thank Hannah, my wife, enough for putting up with missing out on her career and my mood swings. I am indebted to you for that.

A final word of acknowledgment to Septya Iriani Mukhsia, whose input was invaluable and without whom the book possibly would never have been finished. I also acknowledge OCBC AL Amin Bank Berhad for affording me a scholarship to finish my studies. They have not supported the book directly but their financial help certainly made it possible for me to continue my research.

I thank Moorad Choudhry, who is possibly one of the most prolific writers on banking and finance. To him I owe a word of thanks for the encouragement. Gladys and Jeremy at John Wiley & Sons, thank you for patiently taking all my calls, and then again, where would you find a writer who submits material weeks before deadlines?

—Hussain Kureshi

I acknowledge my family, which has always been supportive of my projects. Even though my two boys, Zidaan and Araz, would rather play with me, they understand the value of work. I also acknowledge my colleague and office manager, Nasir Rabbani, who for many years has organized, documented, researched, MS "Excel-ed," and made available anything and everything upon request. His work has always been invaluable.

My thoughts and ideas have evolved through people I've met along the way—friends, restaurant owners, entrepreneurs, emerging market CEOs, financiers, investors from New York, Hong Kong, Kuala Lumpur, Islamabad, Karachi, London, Singapore—people such as Glen Taylor, Yee Hui Wong, Punit Khanna, Kaman Leung, Iqbal Latif, and many more.

And last but not least, I acknowledge my coauthor, who did the heavy lifting for this project. Hussein is passionate, thoughtful, and driven by what he believes.

—Mohsin Hayat

Product Offerings

RETAIL ASSET PRODUCT OFFERINGS	
RETAIL PRODUCT	**RELEVANT CONTRACT**
PERSONAL FINANCE	BAI BITHAMN AJIL, BAI AL INAH TAWARRUQ IBRA
PURCHASE OF COSNUMER GOODS	BAI BITHAMN AJIL, BAI AL AL INAH TAWARRUQ IBRA MURABAHAH MURABAHAH BY PURCHASE ORDERER IJARA SALE AND LEASE BACK
CREDIT CARD	BAI BITHAMN AJIL, BAI AL AI INAH TAWARRUQ IBRA MURABAHAH
CAR FINANCING	BAI BITHAMN AJIL, TAWARRUQ IBRA MURABAHAH MURABAHAH BY PURCHASE ORDERER IJARA MUSHARAKAH MUTANAQISAH
HOUSE FINANCING	BAI BITHAMN AJIL, TAWARRUQ IBRA MURABAHAH MURABAHAH BY PURCHASE ORDERER IJARA MUSHARAKAH MUTANAQISAH

COMMERCIAL ASSET PRODUCT OFFERINGS	
COMMERCIAL PRODUCT	**RELEVANT CONTRACT**
WORKING CAPITAL	BAI BITHAMN AJIL, BAI AL INAH TAWARRUQ IBRA MURABAHAH WORKING CAPITAL
TERM FINANCE	BAI BITHAMN AJIL, BAI AL AL INAH TAWARRUQ IBRA MURABAHAH IJARA SALE AND LEASE BACK
PROJECT FINANCE	BAI BITHAMN AJIL, BAI AL AL INAH TAWARRUQ IBRA MURABAHAH IJARA SALE AND LEASE BACK ISTISNA
LETTER OF CREDIT	WAKALAH
LC - SIGHT	WAKALAH
LC-USANCE	WAKALAH MURABAHAH
LETTER OF GUARANTEE	KAFALAH

LIABILITY PRODUCT OFFERING	
LIABILITY PRODUCT	**RELEVANT CONTRACT**
CURRENT ACCOUNT	WADIAH QARD WAKALAH
SAVINGS ACCOUNT	WADIAH QARD WAKALAH HIBAH
FIXED DEPOSIT	COMMODITY MURABAHAH MUDHARABAH

Introduction

The authors of this work would like to develop the understanding of the concepts of *shariah* and Islamic finance as the book progresses so that readers make up their own mind about the conclusion we offer. We encourage active reading and analyses and not passive reading, as we have been fortunate enough to have had mentors and teachers who encouraged learning, questioning, and understanding and not mere dogmatic rote learning.

The reader must understand that within the universe of Islamic finance money cannot be lent from one party to another with the intent of making a gain on the repayment of the loan. Conventional finance is built on the permissibility of this transaction whether it takes place between a depositor and a bank or it takes place between a borrower and a bank. To date, the aim of Islamic Finance has been to replicate the cash flows that take place in disbursing and servicing a loan with a sequence of sale contracts. For the best part of financial engineering in the industry, spot sales are combined with deferred payment sales to construct cash flows that resemble those of a loan. The underlying "sales contracts" must involve a permissible asset and the sale contract must abide by the laws of contracts of *bai*. Thus, much of the discourse in Islamic finance is a legal discourse based on the rights and obligations imparted to various parties in various contracts under varying circumstances.

Before proceeding further we therefore wish to highlight some salient features and legal maxims that affect the conduct of affairs of trade in Islam. As we have all learned our religion from our mothers, fathers, and tutors, whose memories are very sacred to us all, we do not want to tread on any sensitive grounds without giving due warnings.

We request the reader to consider what rules, if any, other than the rule of *riba*, apply to commercial transactions in Islam. The first "rule" that may come to mind is to be "fair" in one's dealings.

The texts offer no specific standards of "fairness," but offer stories that give guidelines or parameters of what can be deemed fair. We discuss the rule of one-third in due course as well as to expound on it. The texts have been very specific, to the decimal place on one commercial transaction, which is that of inheritance, where detailed methodologies of calculation are ordained for the distribution of wealth of a deceased. Specific workings are also offered for the calculations of *zakat*. The texts, however, do not offer specific calculations of how a merchant, trader, or manufacturer may calculate his or her profit margin on goods or services rendered, so the discussion of *riba* is not about excessive interest or unfair interest, it is about interest in its absolute sense of the term, which is money returned in excess of money borrowed.

There are other parameters of legal rulings within the discourse of Islamic commercial law, and this extends to three or four additional prohibitions. *Shariah* discourages elements of uncertainty in contracts, or *gharar*, and it forbids speculation and gambling, or *maysir*. The texts also admonish hoarding of goods, admonish purchasing goods from caravans outside the city limits before they enter the city to inflate prices, and prohibit the circulation of wealth among the few. Some can argue that these five or six principles are sufficient to develop a judicious and fair economic system.

The Muslim world has manifested various economic models in various times in history. In peace time, there seems to be a preference for free markets, and in war time, there seems to be preference to command economic policies, especially in the distribution of wheat.

This work does not tackle the topic of using fiat money in an economy and having a gold-backed currency, as this is the work of currency experts and monetarists, both of which we are not.

To revert back to our legal maxims, we have identified four core legal maxims and two supplementary ones, which are *all* that is available for a believer to follow in order to develop an economic system of which a financial system is a part.

The reader should be aware that Islam stipulates specific conditions under which an individual has a right to earn a profit. These conditions are that an individual may be either a provider of capital, or a provider of labor, or assumes certain liability for events (or assumes risk) in order to be entitled to any profit from any economic venture. We discuss this in detail in subsequent chapters.

The reader should be additionally aware of the prohibition of certain trade practices, like selling what one does not own. This was a prohibition identified in the texts by the Prophet Muhammad (saw), but the Prophet (saw) extended exceptions to this condition for certain specific kinds of transactions that involved agricultural goods and made-to-order goods. The sale contracts of *salaam* and *istisna* are exempt from this condition.

The reader should be additionally aware that Islam limited the sale of certain goods to be on spot basis. These goods are referred to as *ribbawi* items. Such goods can only be bought or sold in a spot transaction where buyers and sellers are present.

The reader may be unaware of the permissibility of the difference between a spot price and a credit price or a deferred price. This permissibility allows a seller of goods to charge a price *X* for the sale of goods if the buyer pays the full purchase price on spot, and allows the seller to sell the same goods at a price *Y*, which is greater than *X*, if the buyer pays in installments in the future or via a balloon payment, but takes immediate possession of the goods at time of contract initiation.

Another prohibition is that two contracts cannot be part of one contract, or that one contract cannot be conditional on another. Party A cannot sell a good to Party B on the condition that he sells another good to Party A or even to Party C.

These prohibitions are not chronologically organized in the texts, nor are they neatly arranged in a chapter of any handbook. These prohibitions have been passed on by the Law Giver in different situations and within specific circumstances. The historical background and context of these rulings are touched on where necessary.

The reader may have discovered that certain assumptions may not be adequate. A Muslim in general may think that there are specific criteria for calculating profit over a cost price; after all, we are always bargaining with sellers in the bazaars, but yet none exist. However, several other legal maxims exist of which the ordinary Muslim of today may not have heard.

To be fair to all Muslim readers of various backgrounds and levels of education we examine the contracts that are the fundamental pillars of Islamic finance. We examine their classical structures (as they were used in the time of the Prophet [saw]), and we shall identify the "enhancements" made to these contracts to adapt to the modern economic times of today. We leave it up to the reader to decide if these enhancements defeat the purpose of prohibitions, circumvent them to achieve impermissible outcomes, or are beneficial innovations that are for the good of the *ummah* (Muslim Community). The reader may also conclude that the amendments made are necessary to achieve the goals of modern economic life, but may question whether the goals of modern economic life are worth striving for. Let us say at the outset, that discussion is beyond the scope of this work.

We begin our discussion with the most controversial contract in Islamic finance, that of *bai al inah*, but before we do, here is a word on who the Law Giver is today. In 620 A.D. the Law Giver was Allah (swt) who spoke through Muhammad (saw) and appointed him as another Law Giver for mankind. No Muslim contests that there is no other primary source of law in Islam. But how many laws did the Law Giver actually spell out? The reality is very few. As times changed, situations changed, the Prophet (saw) left our world, as did His companions, the successors of his companions and the successors of successors. New dominions came under Muslim rule, and Islamic law evolved over time. In the case of selling what one does not own, the enhancements came by the original Law Giver himself.

The question to ask is who is the rightful Law Giver today? Every Muslim country is today either a democracy or a monarchy with Iran being the only official theocracy. Within democracies, elected members of Parliament pass laws in a country. If these members of Parliament are Muslims, it can be expected that they will pass laws within the guidelines set by the *shariah*. In a monarchy, the monarch is the Law Giver and in a theocracy, the cleric. In the space of Islamic finance certain bodies have been set up that are funded by the various Muslim countries, and these bodies have gathered together a bodice of *shariah* scholars who now issue legal guidelines or *fatwas*. They assemble in an *ijmah* and pass certain rulings based on their research and understanding. Whatever we as authors of this work are commenting on is not based on *fatwas* we have individually devised.

A reader can also argue: Who gave *shariah* scholars the authority or the right to pass *fatwas*? The answer is no one. These *fatwas* are not binding legislation of all member countries, although some are; however, the infrastructure of developing a sound education system of developing *shariah* scholars and having benchmarks for their qualifications is sadly missing from the Muslim world and we acknowledge that. Any reader of Islamic finance should view the websites of the following entities:

Accounting and Auditing of Islamic Financial Institutions (AAOIFI)
Islamic Financial Services Board (IFSB)
Islamic Development Bank
International *Shariah* Research Academy
Organization of Islamic Countries Fiqh Academy
Bank Negara Malaysia *Shariah* Advisory Council
Shariah boards of the Central Banks of various countries
Dow Jones Islamic indices

We also advise the reader to download a version of *Sahih Muslim* and the *Holy Quran* in his or her language to keep as a reference.

CHAPTER 1

The Islamic Finance Space

As a historical religion, Islam has been in existence for 1,400 years. The word *religion* comes from the Latin word *religio*, which means to bind oneself.[1] Religious principles bind mankind to a way of life that is meant to be pleasing to God. Human history provides enough evidence that mankind has not always followed religious principles in their true spirit and has had to pay the consequences from time to time.

Finance has been around as long as man has inhabited this earth. The most basic form of finance in prehistory was money lending and remains so today. All the Semitic religions of Christianity, Judaism, and Islam warn mankind against the practice of usury, which allows interest to be the reward for money lent. Islam is not the only religion to forbid the taking of interest. The word used in the Quran is *riba*,[2] and has been interpreted by scholars as taking of any excess money from a borrower when a loan is repaid. A loan is specifically defined as a contract whereby one party lends money to another party for a specific period of time, for example, borrowing $1,000 for 90 days and repaying $1,200.

Finance was also an integral part of the Muslim empires of the Ummayads, the Abbasids, the Fatimids, the Mamlukes, the Seljuks, and also of

---

[1]Wilfred Cantwell Smith, *The Meaning and End of Religion* (Minneapolis: Fortress Press, 1991 edition).

[2]Verses from the Quran regarding the prohibition of *riba*:

30:39: "The usury that is practiced to increase some people's wealth, does not gain anything at God. But if you give to charity, seeking God's pleasure, these are the ones who receive their reward many fold."

4:161: "And for practicing usury (interest), which was forbidden, and for consuming the people's money illicitly, We have prepared for the disbelievers among them painful retribution."

3:130: "O you who believe, you shall not take usury (interest), compounded over and over. Observe God that you may succeed."

the Ottomans. Islam dawned on Arab traders (most previous Prophets were either craftsmen or farmers). The Prophet ([saw] peace be upon him) himself was a trader. Trade has such an importance on the fabric of Islam that the Quran itself endorses trade or *bai*.[3]

What kind of trade did Islam permit? Certainly Islam permitted certain trade practices and forbade others, like hoarding of goods,[4] inflating prices by meeting merchants outside city walls and buying their goods before they come to market,[5] or selling goods not in one's ownership.[6] These obligations had an impact on the trading practices endorsed within the Muslim world. Principles of fairness, keeping one's oath, fulfilling terms of contracts were endorsed not just in conversation but in the Quran itself.[7]

Much of the Muslim world remained an agriculture-based economy, with a monarchical political system of rule. The Muslim world is famous for its *bazaars*, where traders came from across the globe to trade wares and to be exposed to this new religion that had shown its face on the pages of history. Although much of Orientalist literature[8] focuses on the military conquests of the Muslim rulers, little is talked about of the impact of trade with the Muslim world, or the institutions of trade. Scholars such as Donald Quateart are working on archives found in the libraries of Istanbul to give a more clear picture of what life was like in the most recent episode of Islamic history, that of the Ottoman Empire.

In an empire as vast as the Ottoman Empire with Istanbul being the center of trade for much of the civilized world, trade and finance must have

---

[3]Legality found in the Quran, surah Al-Baqarah verse 275, "However, God permits commerce, and prohibits usury (interest)."

[4]This is mentioned in the Quran, chapter 3, verse 180: "Let not those who withhold and hoard God's provisions think that this is good for them; it is bad for them. For on the Day of Resurrection they will carry their hoardings around their neck"; and also in a hadith, which narrates the saying of Prophet (saw): "Nobody hoards except the wrongdoer." Al-Qazveeni, Muhammad bin yazeed, sunanibn-e-maajah, Berut: Dar-ul-fikr, 1999, H:2153.

[5]Abu Huraira (Allah [sat] be pleased with him) reported the Prophet (saw) as saying: "Do not meet the merchant in the way and enter into business transaction with him, and whoever meets him and buys from him that when the owner of the goods comes into the market, he has the option to declare the transaction null and void."

[6]Muslims are prohibited in selling goods before possessing them. The Prophet (saw) mentioned, "Whoever buys cereals shall not tell them until he has obtained their possession."

[7]The Holy Quran, 17:34, "Come not nigh to the orphan's property except to improve it, until he attains the age of full strength; and fulfil (every) engagement, for (every) engagement will be enquired into (on the Day of Reckoning)."

[8]Edward Said, *Orientalism* (New York: Pantheon Books, 1978).

gone hand in hand. There is no evidence of the existence of modern-day banks in Istanbul; certainly, however, the oldest banks and banking families belonged to Italy and lived in the 1500s. There is also no concrete evidence of cooperatives, or benevolent funds that could be the prototype of modern-day insurance. We would have to wait until the libraries of Istanbul reveal these secrets to come to any conclusion.

However, with vast stores of grain coming from different parts of the Empire where different currencies were employed it is not difficult to imagine that some informal structures of commodity exchanges must have existed, some mechanisms must have been developed to hedge risks of price volatility, and some mechanisms must have existed to raise capital and borrow capital. Development comes in times of peace, and unless one were to buy Kinross's version of Ottoman history, the Empire offered its citizens a period of respite for close to 500 years. Media headlines tend to focus on atrocities alone, but that is another matter. Another element of genius within the fabric of the Empire was that Christians, Jews, Indian Muslims, Arab Muslims, Italians, and Venetians alike were allowed to serve the Empire and to develop trade, commerce, and institutions of law in a manner not seen at any other phase of at least Islamic history. Humans, whether Muslims or non-Muslims, must have developed innovative commercial contracts, mechanisms of trade, financial products, and even derivatives over a period of time within the boundaries of the Empire. It is no surprise therefore that the first formal codification of commercial law is found in the *Mejelle*, which was a Hanafi document developed in the seventeenth and eighteenth centuries within the Ottoman Empire.[9]

So, how far back does Islamic finance go? One can say the contracts of sale of *murbahah, bai al inah, bai al wafa, bai al dayn*, or *bai al sarf* even predate Islam. Islam just eliminated certain features of these contracts and retained others depending on whether certain features contradicted any legal maxims. The application of these sale contracts to financial intermediation in a fractional reserve system is far more recent and can be first seen in the 1970s in places like Egypt, Sudan, Iran, and other pockets of the Muslim world.[10]

However, one must note that the past 200 years for every Muslim country has been one of colonial domination, with many countries gaining formal political independence in the latter half of the previous century, and all after World War II. As such, almost all Muslim countries have inherited

---

[9]David P. Forsythe, *Encyclopedia of Human Rights*, vol. 1 (New York: Oxford University Press, 2009).

[10]Natalie Schoon, "Islamic Finance—A history," *Finance Services Review*, 2009.

legal systems from the times of their colonial rulers, and other institutions of rule, government, and commerce. We must not forget that much of the Muslim world did not experience the Industrial Revolution in the manner that Europe and the United States did, nor could many wonderful inventions and advancements in the sciences be attributed to a Muslim world that still predominantly had pockets of agricultural economies and trade-based economies. The Muslim world also inherited a dollar-based and an interest-based global financial system.

The need for oil in the twentieth century put the Muslim world into prominence again with much of the natural resource being found under the sands of the ancient cities that were once home to peoples of prehistory.

It is also important to keep in mind that the Muslim world is divided in its interpretations of the religion and in the social structure of their societies, with certain countries adopting monarchies, or constitutional monarchies, and others adopting a democratic form of government. Military dictatorships have been common in the Muslim world until the recent demise of such figures as Saddam Hussein and Qaddafi. Iran has a unique theocratic form of government, where religious clerics are key stakeholders in the running of the government. Some Muslim countries have a large percentage of non-Muslims as their citizens as well. All these factors influence not only the exchange of ideas within the Muslim world but also the development of any consensus of issues of importance within the sphere of political and commercial life. Needless to say there is need for convergence and unity among the Muslim countries in their understanding of the religion and in coordinating efforts to serve the needs of close to 1.3 billion Muslims across the globe.

MODERN PHASE OF ISLAMIC FINANCE

The modern phase of Islamic finance may have been the brainchild of political ideologists that saw the post–World War II world economic system built on the principles of interest. Efforts were made to develop in theory and in practice an economic and a financial system that did not depend on *riba*, but any such attempt could only meet with limited success when the currencies of each Muslim country were pegged to the U.S. dollar. The U.S. dollar system is based on interest. Had the Muslim world adopted a more isolationist attitude to international trade the results may have be different, and ironically two economies, China and India, that during the 1970s and 1980s had turned their back on international trade are now leading exporters on the global economic stage.

Nevertheless, the Muslim world developed institutions to collaborate, the first of its kind being the Islamic Development Bank (IDB), which possibly embodies the aspirations of many Muslims in fulfilling the goals of a

Muslim society.[11] The IDB is unique in that its capital is provided by its member states, which are Muslim countries, and it funds projects related to infrastructure development, poverty alleviation, access to education, and clean water and such. The IDB is dedicated to providing funding on a sustainable basis to various segments of the Muslim world to improve the well-being of the *ummah* in general. One may think of it as a world bank for Muslim countries. The existence of IDB created a unique problem of providing funds to member countries not on an interest basis but on *shariah*-compliant basis, and it is likely that within the halls of IDB meetings the first financial products were developed.

Institutions such as Accounting and Auditing for Islamic Financial Institutions sprang up when the idea of offering *shariah*-compliant financial products took germ as a commercially viable proposition for the private sector to adopt. Since 1971, when IDB was set up, other countries, like Pakistan, Malaysia, and Indonesia, also took the mandate to move their financial systems away from a *riba*-based structure to a more *shariah*-compliant alternative. *Shariah* advisors were placed within central banks and other regulating bodies to come up with a framework for "Islamic Banking and Islamic Insurance." No other country took this task more seriously than Malaysia, which saw it as an opportunity to become a global hub for Islamic finance. Malaysia is surrounded by some of the major financial and business capitals of the world, such as Shanghai, Singapore, Hong Kong, and Tokyo, cities that are destinations of billions of dollars of foreign direct investment and international capital flows. Malaysia saw an opportunity to be the routing point for the flow of capital within the Muslim world and made great strides in making necessary changes in its regulatory system by acts of Parliament, changes in its taxation system and its legal system to bring Islamic finance in the mainstream of financial transactions. Capital markets were restructured and a methodology of *shariah* screening of asset classes was developed. The first *shariah*-compliant index was proposed in Kuala Lumpur.

The Malaysian government funded research institutions to develop the infrastructure of Islamic banking products and also to set up training institutes to train its own bankers and those around the world in what it believed was a viable alternative to conventional banking and insurance.

Bank Negara Malaysia, Securities Commission Malaysia, soon to be followed by Bank Indonesia, and Securities Commission Indonesia made formal announcements of issuing licenses to Islamic Banks, *takaful* companies, and Islamic asset management companies, and slowly the rest of the Muslim world followed.

[11]Islamic Development Bank, www.isdb.org, accessed June 26, 2014.

Malaysia followed a prudent approach to developing Islamic banks allowing existing banks to first begin with Islamic windows. Windows operations offered customers *shariah*-compliant asset and liability products as part of a conventional banks framework. The window operation functioned with its own balance sheet, but shared the infrastructure of the conventional bank to save on costs. The Islamic banking window had to have a team of *shariah* advisors to endorse products and processes. These products had to be approved by a *shariah* board placed at the central bank. The window operation was phased into subsidiaries, which had to maintain separate economic capital and report separate financial statements. Foreign banks were given the leniency to maintain Islamic banking divisions where a limited product menu was on offer, and capital only had to be lien marked in the bank's balance sheet to fund the assets of the Islamic banking business.

Similarly, changes were made to the capital markets and rules were developed for screening asset classes and for offering *shariah*-compliant securities and products on the stock exchange. A *shariah* board at the securities commission was put in place to regulate the issuance and sale of *shariah*-compliant capital market instruments such as *sukuk*. Malaysia masterfully maintains a dual-banking system in which conventional banks and Islamic banks operate simultaneously.

Undoubtedly, Malaysia enjoyed the position of being a thought leader in the sphere of Islamic finance and generously shared its understanding of *shariah*-compliant products and principles not only with the rest of the Muslim world but with the non-Muslim world as well. Institutions such as J.P. Morgan, Citibank, Barclays, and HSBC all have Islamic banking divisions catering to either investment banking or wealth management. HSBC offers the brand of HSBC Amanah and Standard Chartered took pains to develop the brand of Standard Chartered Sadiq. International rating agencies such as Moody's and Standard & Poor's have worked with industry professionals and developed mechanisms of rating *shariah*-compliant institutions and financial instruments. International fund managers and hedge funds now have in place methodologies of screening asset classes for *shariah*-compliance for their clients. Dow Jones has in fact developed a *shariah* index for all the major indices it develops, including FTSE 100 and Nikkei 225 index, the BRIC index, and the GCC index, thus facilitating *shariah*-minded investors in guiding their capital in a manner that fulfills certain *shariah* guidelines. In post–September 11 times, for financial institutions to adopt the word *shariah* in their brochures is quite an achievement.

These are no minor achievements to say the least, but has Islamic banking provided a viable alternative to conventional banking? As many architects of Islamic banking were likely attached to the Islamic Development Bank, there is also a strain of disillusionment that Islamic banking has gone astray, or gone commercial. IDB was and is a public policy institute funded not by shareholders but by governments. Its aim is to fund projects and make a nominal return on the financing provided. The technology of Islamic banking was transferred to the commercial sector, and to compare an Islamic bank driven by the aims of maximizing returns to the IDB is like comparing J.P. Morgan to the World Bank. Both entities exist for different purposes. One can argue that there are not enough Islamic micro-finance banks, or Islamic venture capital firms, or Islamic SME fund houses, but that is not the fault of the concept of Islamic banking. Capital providers or investors must see the light and allocate capital to such enterprises; academics and scholars cannot do so.

Islamic financial institutions therefore offer financial products using *shariah*-compliant contracts. The "impact" of these products is the same on a client or an investor, in that if an Islamic bank facilitates the purchase of a new car, the beneficiary of the purchase must pay the bank back with profit. There is no free lunch. IFIs rely on the same model of financial intermediation that conventional banks, insurance companies, and asset management companies do, and that is the "pooling of funds." Islamic banks collect funds from customers using *shariah*-compliant contracts, and use these funds to finance assets or make investments. The capital of the Islamic bank is not used to fund assets, but is used as a buffer to cushion losses. All profits generated are shared with depositors. Conventional banks absorb losses in entirety, whereas Islamic banks in some circumstances pass on losses to their customers.

Takaful companies also pool in funds of participants. Participants contract to contribute to a pool of funds that will be used to indemnify the participants if they suffer losses from specific events. Participants do not buy insurance policies from insurance companies; they seek to protect themselves and each other against adverse events. In practice no participant in a *takaful* plan knows any other participant, so such claims may only be interpreted as being cosmetic. *Takaful* operators are then hired to manage the underwriting process for a fee.

Fund managers also work on a contract of agency or *wakalah* and are compensated by investors for above-market performance by healthy commissions like in conventional firms. The road thus far shows the Islamic financial services industry converging toward the conventional industry and many critics feel this does not in any way fulfill any broader goals of Islam. Critics have a point, but we leave it up to the readers to determine that during the course of reading this book.

The Islamic financial services industry is built around 16 or so fundamental contracts. We first study these contracts and then later see how they are reengineered or modified to develop financial products. The criticism of the modifications is left up to the reader.

CHAPTER 2

Bai al Inah

We do not attempt to overwhelm the reader with a plethora of Arabic words and we translate every relevant word in English for ease of understanding. Bear in mind that in a study of Islamic laws, sciences would have previously been impossible without a knowledge of Arabic and we thank all those scholars who have made efforts to translate works into language of everyday use or the language of trade, which is English today.

This chapter focuses on the controversial contract of *bai al inah*, a construct of a sale and buyback between two parties that creates cash flows that resemble a loan structure.

DEFINITIONS OF *BAI AL INAH*

Bai means sale, *tijarat* means trade, and *ribbh* means profit on a sale. *Bai al inah* or *inah* is a sale contract that existed in the time of the Prophet (saw).

Bank Negara Malaysia defines *bai al inah* in the following manner: "*Bai' 'inah* refers to an arrangement that involves sale of an asset to the purchaser on a deferred basis and subsequent purchase of the asset at a cash price lower than the deferred sale price or vice versa, and which complies with the specific requirements of *bai al'inah*."[1]

The International Financial Services Board, a standard-setting body for Islamic banks, defines *bai al inah* as follows: "A contract involving the sale and buy-back transaction of assets by a seller. A seller sells an asset to a buyer on a cash basis and later buys it back on a deferred payment basis where the price is higher than the cash price. It can also be applied when a seller sells an asset to a buyer on a deferred basis and later

[1]Bank Negara Malaysia (BNM) (2013), Tawarruq (Shariah Requirements and Optional Practices) Exposure Draft December 2013, www.bnm.gov.my/documents/SAC/13_Tawarruq.pdf, accessed July 2014.

buys it back on a cash basis, at a price which is lower than the deferred price."[2]

Bai al inah refers to an arrangement that involves a sale and buyback. An asset is sold by a seller to a counterparty on a deferred payment basis, creating a debt obligation on the said counterparty. Immediately, the original seller buys the asset back for a spot price. This second leg of the transaction creates the cash flows that resemble disbursement of a loan. As *bai al inah* is a sale contract, it must follow the requirements of contract law for sale and purchase transactions. A sale contract requires 14 conditions:[3]

1. Presence of two parties, a buyer and a seller.
2. Both parties must be sane persons.
3. Both parties must have the legal capacity to contract.
4. There must be in existence a subject matter of the sale, an asset or a good.
5. This asset must be a permissible asset.
6. The underlying economic activity behind the sale must be permissible.
7. There must be an agreed purchase price of the asset and an agreed mode of payment.
8. The seller must disclose all features of the asset involved.
9. The buyer must have the right to inspect the asset.
10. There must be an offer (to sell from the buyer) and there must be an acceptance (to purchase).
11. Once the sellers have sold the asset they have surrendered all claims of ownership to the asset in exchange for the purchase price, whether the purchase price is paid on spot or on deferred basis.
12. Even if the buyers fail to pay for the asset if the purchase was made on credit terms, the sellers do not have the right to repossess the asset, they only have a right over the purchase price.
13. The seller may obtain a collateral from the buyer under the contract of *rahn* (to be discussed later), to ensure a deferred payment is fully settled. If the buyer fails to make full payment, the seller may liquidate the asset held as collateral and recover any unpaid portion of the purchase price and return any excess to the buyer.
14. The asset must be in existence at the time of the sale.

These rules apply to almost all the sale transactions and must be borne in mind by the reader. These rules are simple enough, so now let us revert

[2]Islamic Financial Services Board, www.ifsb.org, acessed June 10, 2014.

[3]Muhammad Yusuf Saleem, *Islamic Commercial Law* (Hoboken, NJ: John Wiley & Sons, 2013).

to the exclusive sale contract of *bai al inah*. We explain the sale by using illustration for ease.

Bai al Inah in essence is a combination of *bai mu'ajjal* and *bai haal*, a sequence of a deferred sale followed by a spot buyback. These terms will be clearly explained in the subsequent chapter.

BAI AL INAH PROCESS FLOW

We illustrate the process flows in *bai al inah* by using a simple example involving two parties, A and B.

Party A wishes to use his asset of value $10,000 but wishes to convert the asset into cash of $10,000 and at the same time does not wish to surrender ownership rights to the asset.

Parties A and B agree to a spot sale price of the asset of $10,000, and a deferred sale price of $12,000 if the payment is made in 90 days.

Step 1. Party A sells the asset to Party B on a deferred payment basis. Party B pays undertakes to pay Party A, $12,000 in 90 days and Party B now enjoys full ownership rights over the asset. Party B can sell the asset to another Party C, enjoy the usufruct of the asset, or sell the asset back to A.

Step 2. Party A instantaneously buys the asset back from Party B at a spot price of $10,000. The asset is transferred back to ownership of Party A, who has his or her original asset back, and has in receipt an **obligation from Party B to pay Party A, $12,000 in 90 days.** The sale contract concludes with asset remaining with the ownership of the original party and the **creation of a debt obligation due on B to A.**

FIGURE 2.1 Parties to the Contract

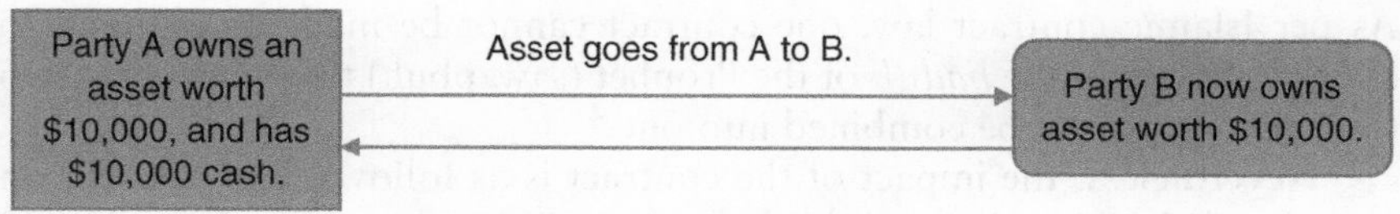

FIGURE 2.2 Step 1—Party A Sells to Party B

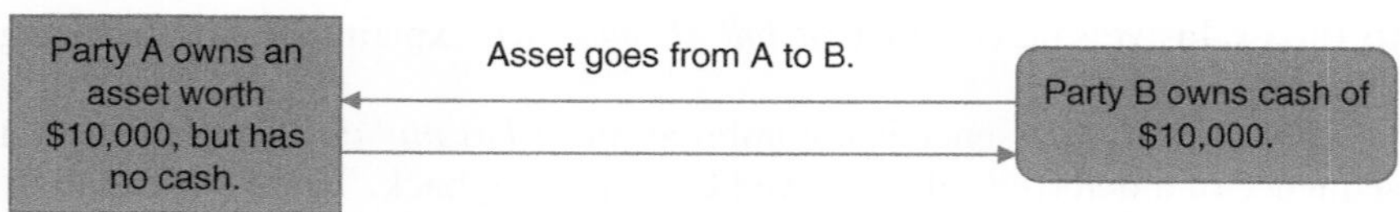

FIGURE 2.3 Step 2—Party A Buys Back from Party B

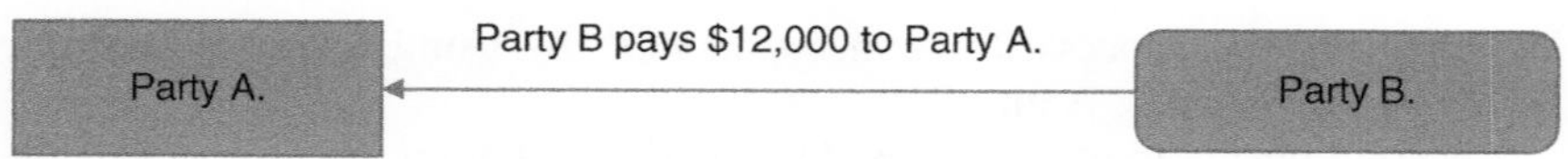

FIGURE 2.4 Step 3—Party B Pays Deferred Price to Party A

Step 3. At contract conclusion Party B pays the deferred price of $12,000 to Party A.

The previous sequence of transactions treated separately are merely two sales transactions between two parties, but for a credit price and for a spot price. However, when they are combined they resemble a granting of a loan from Party A to Party B of $10,000 with a repayment of $12,000 in 90 days. There is no questioning that the two sales contracts combined have developed a suspicious likeness to a loan with an interest repayment and hence *riba*.

It seems quite judicious to question the intentions of both Party A and Party B. It seems that Party B has no real intent (however, it may remain undisclosed) to own the asset that is the subject matter of the "sale." At each stage of these transactions the ownership of the asset is transferred from A to B; there is also no payment of any sales tax as in reality these transactions are just paper-based. Although there is a transfer of ownership from one party to another via sale and purchase agreements, there may not be any transfer of possession.

Another area of controversy lies in the fact that the first sale transaction is conditional on the second sale. A will sell the asset to B for $12,000 on the implicit or explicit condition that B will sell the asset back to A for $10,000. As per Islamic contract law, one contract cannot be made conditional to another, based on the *hadith* of the Prophet (saw, pbuh) that states that two transactions cannot be combined into one.[4]

Nevertheless, the impact of the contract is as follows: Party A sells an asset for $12,000 and buys it back for $10,000, making a profit of $2,000

[4]Sunan Al-Tirmidhi 2/514.

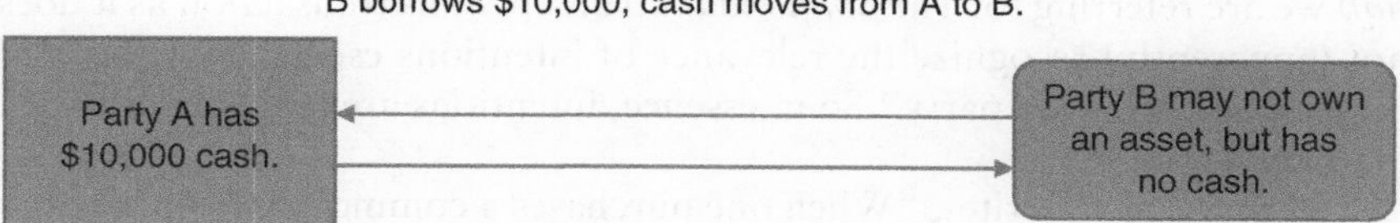

FIGURE 2.5 *Riba* Contract

over a period of 90 days and Party B is able to raise $10,000 of funds for 90 days with committing to repay $12,000 in 90 days.

Let us look at a *riba* contract in Figure 2.5.

Can the reader observe any substantial difference between both the contracts? One is a set of contracts of sale, where an asset is sold and then bought back. The other is a contract of lending, where A lends B money. Money here is treated as the sole subject of exchange; one nominal amount is exchanged for another nominal amount over a period of time. The architects of Islamic finance do not recognize the exchange of money in this fashion, where an excess amount is repaid. The excess repayment is considered to be *riba*.

LEGAL ISSUES WITH *BAI AL INAH*

Proponents of theories on Islamic finance do recognize the difference between a spot price for an asset and a deferred price for an asset. *Shariah* scholars recognize that the deferred price of an asset can be greater than the spot price of an asset in a sale transaction. They also recognize that a seller can repurchase an asset sold to a buyer and vice versa, but do comment on the combination of two sale contracts between a buyer and a seller that result in cash flows that resemble a loan disbursement and repayment with interest. There is no difference between *bai inah* and *riba* in essence, but there is considerable difference in form as the former is a sequence of sale contracts and the latter is a contract of lending. In essence it seems that a sequence of legal sales has resulted in a transfer of money for money. This is referred to as "legal means to illegal ends."[5]

Can the element of the intentions of both parties be taken into consideration? Here arises a fundamental question of what *madhab* (school of thought) we are referring the judgment to and what methodology of *usul ul*

---

[5]Muhammad Ayub, *Understanding Islamic Finance* (Hoboken, NJ: John Wiley & Sons, 2007).

fiqh we are referring to. The *Shafi madhab* accepts this transaction as it does not (apparently) recognize the relevance of intentions especially if they are undisclosed by either party.[6] So in essence, intentions are left to be between man and God.

Imam Al Shafi writes, "When one purchases a commodity from another and takes its delivery, and the price happens to be on deferred terms, it is not objectionable for him to sell it to the person from whom he had purchased it or to someone else, for a cash price less than his purchase price or higher, or on credit, or against another commodity."[7]

Many scholars, however, feel that this saying has been taken out of context, and Imam Shafi did not refer to the contract of *inah* by name. Were two parties contracting merely to create cash flows that replicate loans, and "the second sale is considered to be conditional on the first, by virtue of custom, thus resulting in both contracts being invalid"?[8]

The *Shafi madhab* also does not recognize *saad ul dhariah* as a source of *shariah* law. *Saad ul dhariah* means to block legal means to result in illegal ends and as an approach to law is a secondary source of law in *shariah*.[9] The Shafiis would contend that if each sale contract were to fulfill the requirements of a sale contract, they cannot be termed invalid.

Nevertheless, the contract of *bai al inah* remains controversial to this date and is accepted in Malaysia, but is frowned on in the Gulf Cooperation Council, or GCC, Saudi Arabia, Pakistan, and other Muslim countries.

Taken as a financial transaction, it is also implied that the original sale is based on the condition that A will buy back the asset from B and the second offer and acceptance is already agreed on. Would it make any difference if the deferred price was not calculated by either party but was merely the market price for a heavily traded asset, like wheat, for instance? What are the risks that Party A is exposed to? Party B could in essence sell the asset to Party C, or decide to hold the asset and enjoy its usufruct. The rapid sequencing of both these sales mitigates this risk. Party A is also exposed to credit risk, in that Party B may be unable to make the required payment in 90 days. Party A can demand that some other asset be held as collateral with Party A to ensure repayment. The asset here plays a crucial function.

---

[6]Abu Ishaq al-Shatibi, *Al-Mufawaqat fi usul al Shari'ah*, vol. 4, 435–436. (Cairo: al-Maktabah al-Tijariyyah al-Kubra, 1983).

[7]Imam Shafi–Al–Umm. Extracted from *Shariah Rules in Financial Transactions* course SH1003, 2013, INCEIF.

[8]*Shariah Rules in Financial Transactions*, course SH 1003, 2013, INCEIF.

[9]Muhammad Yusuf Saleem, *Islamic Commercial Law* (Hoboken, NJ: John Wiley & Sons, 2013).

If this transaction seems charged with controversy for the reader, let it be no surprise as it has been so for more than 1,200 years. Scholars have seen it as an attempt to circumvent the contract of *riba*; others have seen it as an alternative to *riba*, depending on the intentions of the parties involved. This contract, however, if deemed permissible, allows economic units short of liquidity but with an availability of fixed assets to use their assets to raise funds or liquidity. This need is fundamental in any business, no less a bank that is in a perpetual state of asset/liability mismatches.

BAI AL INAH AS A FINANCIAL PRODUCT

The contract of *bai al inah* can be applied to a liability product as well as an asset product.

Asset Product

The sequencing of sales contracts can occur between an Islamic bank and a customer, with the Islamic bank being Party A and the customer being Party B. Islamic Bank A would sell an asset that the bank owns to Customer B for say $10,500 via a sale agreement. The customer would be required to pay this price in 90 days; thus, this price will be referred to as the *credit price*. Islamic Bank A would then immediately buy back the same asset from the customer via a purchase agreement for $10,000 on spot basis; $10,000 would then be referred to as the *spot price*. The Islamic bank would pay the customer $10,000 in cash. The net effect of the two sales transactions would be that the customer receives $10,000 in cash on the spot and has to pay the Islamic Bank A $10,500 in 90 days. In essence, Party B would be a borrower of funds for 90 days with a 5 percent interest payment, but in form, A and B would have only entered into a sequence of sale and purchase transactions.

This application of *inah* is valuable for developing such retail products as credit cards, cash lines, personal finance products, or any element of extending liquidity to a customer or unrestricted funding.

Liability Product

Another variant of the *inah* contract would be where Party B being a customer approaches an Islamic bank, with an asset in the Bank's possession. Bank A sells its asset to party B for a deferred price $10,500 and then buys it back for a spot payment of $10,000. In essence, Party B has just placed a fixed deposit with the Islamic Bank A, in the shape of a spot purchase price of $10,000 for the asset, and will receive $10,500 from the Islamic bank in 90 days. The same sequence of cash flows is initiated, one of a spot price at contract initiation and a deferred price in the opposite direction at contract conclusion.

This application of the contract is used in developing fixed deposit liability products in the Islamic finance space, where moneys are placed for a fixed term with an Islamic bank for a preagreed period of time, and a predetermined rate of return. In both the liability and asset version of the product the profit rate, which is used to determine the credit price, becomes comparable to interest rates on loans or fixed deposits.

TRANSFER OF OWNERSHIP

Assuming the *inah* contract is permissible, we will examine the two sale contracts in detail. One sale is a spot sale, which is straightforward. Ownership of the asset is passed on from Party A to Party B. Here we refer to the enhancements we have mentioned earlier. Accordingly, the *shariah* sale is effected when either purchase price is transferred from buyer to seller, or the asset is delivered from one party to the other. The selling party must have ownership of the asset before entering into a sales contract for that particular asset.[10] One may question that since there is no "actual" sale, or that the seller buys back the same asset instantaneously, then is it really necessary for the asset to be in existence at the time of the first sale, need it be in the possession of the seller? Is there any actual transfer of ownership of the asset via transfer of title of ownership for any period of time? Proponents of *bai inah* feel that the fundamental feature that distinguishes the *bai al inah* sale contract from a contract of *riba* is the sale of the underlying asset. So scholars feel that the asset must be in existence at the time of the sale and must be in the ownership of the seller.

The second issue is whether there is transfer of title of ownership from A to B and then back to A. In practical implementation of the contract, the answer is no. Although both parties enter into separate sale and purchase agreements for each leg of the transaction, there is in essence no sales tax paid,[11] nor is the transfer of ownership of the asset recorded in any legal Registrar's office.

[10]Taqi Usmani, *An Introduction to Islamic Finance* (India: Idara Isha'at-e-Diniyat (P) Ltd., 2005).

[11]See "Malaysia—The Tax Haven for Islamic Finance," by Naim S. in *Islamic Finance News Magazine*, October 2010; Stamp Duty (Exemption) (No.2) Order 2000, PU(A) 16/2000; Stamp Duty (Exemption) (No.2) Order 2004, PU(A) 19/2004; Stamp Duty (Exemption) (No. 3) Order 2004, PU(A) 20/2004.

DOCUMENTATION INVOLVED

One may well inquire then what documents are used in this transaction. The first sale requires a sale and purchase agreement, and the second sale also requires a separate sale and purchase agreement.[12] However, neither of the sale and purchase agreements can make reference to the other sale and purchase agreement, otherwise the transaction comes under the clause of one contract being conditional on another and therefore becomes invalid. There is a sale and purchase agreement with payment of price on a deferred price. In this contract the buyer undertakes to pay the price in the future and at this point the buyer takes on a debt obligation.

RESOLUTIONS ON *BAI AL INAH*

The *Shariah* Advisory Council of Bank Negara Malaysia resolved that *bai al inah* is permissible subject to the following two conditions: that the transaction must follow the mechanism accepted by the *Shafii* school and that the subject matter in the contract is not a *ribawi* item.[13] Notwithstanding this ruling, the SAC recognizes the fact that this is still an issue among *shariah* scholars from different jurisdictions. Consequently, in 2006, the Council in the Regional *Shariah* Scholars Dialogue resolved that the *bai al inah* concept is still necessary with regard to the development of Islamic banking, keeping in mind that its application is to be backed with sound operational process and documentation, yet it is more desirable that IFI limits the use of this concept in its products.[14]

However, apart from the Malaysian SAC, most of the other jurisdictions prohibit the use of *bai al inah* concept. For instance, related to the resolutions on *bai al inah,* AAOIFI set out *shariah* parameters in the application of *tawarruq* so as to avoid *inah*, which was ruled to be strictly prohibited.[15] As mentioned previously, the use of the concept is not permissible in the other Muslim countries, where the *tawarruq* concept is more popular and widely used.

---

[12] Applied *shariah* in financial transactions, INCEIF, 2006.

[13] Ribawi items refers to six items that can be classified into two categories: medium of exchange (currency), such as gold and silver; and staple food, such as wheat, barley, dates, and salt.

[14] Bank Negara Malaysia (BNM) (2010), *Shariah Resolutions in Islamic Finance: Second Edition,* http://www.bnm.gov.my/microsites/financial/pdf/resolutions/shariah_resolutions_2nd_edition_EN.pdf, accessed July 2014.

[15] AAOIFI Standard No. 30, Article 4/5.

CONCLUSION

Bai al inah is seen as a controversial sale and buyback contract. However, if one were to adopt the business of banking, which by its very nature borrows short and lends long, *bai al inah* offers a contract structure that supports liquidity needs on a short-term notice. Banks have to finance long-term assets with short-term funds, and at times when short-term funds are not available, the only way to structure short-term banking notes is through the mechanism of *inah*.

One may conclude by saying that total income from *inah* contracts on a bank's balance sheet must be less than 33 percent, and the contract should be used in the interbank markets only as a necessity.

CHAPTER 3

Murabahah, Bai Mu'ajjal, and *Bai Bithman Ajil*

This chapter looks in detail at the contract of *murabahah, bai bithman ajil*. We also briefly address the underlying issues involved, and briefly look at the concepts of business risk and financial risk to determine whether it is justified to use the word *sale* in a banking environment.

The contract of *murabahah* may well be the backbone of much of Islamic banking. Simply put, *murabahah* is a "cost plus" sale, where a seller discloses to a potential buyer the cost at which a certain asset was sourced or purchased and whereby the seller and buyer subsequently negotiate on the profit margin at which the good or asset is sold to a final buyer.

Bai Murabahah is merely a contract of sale where a seller must disclose the cost price for the subject matter. *Bai Musawamah* is a contract of sale for a subject matter between a buyer and a seller, where no disclosure of the sale price is required. The asset must be delivered on spot in both transactions, and payment can either be on spot (*bai fawri*) or deferred (*bai mu'ajjal*). *Bai fawri* is also known as *bai hall*, and is simply a contract of sale and purchase where the subject matter of the sale is delivered on spot and the purchase price is paid on spot. In a contract of *bai mu'ajjal*, the subject matter of the sale is delivered on spot, and the purchase price is paid in the future. The purchase price may be paid in installments, or as a balloon payment at some time in future or according to any schedule agreed upon between the buyer and the seller. In a contract of *bai bithman ajil* the purchase price is paid in installments over a predetermined period of time.

Murabahah involves similar conditions as *bai al inah*, including the presence of two parties, and the existence of an asset or a good that is the subject of sale between the two parties. The two parties are simply a buyer and a seller. The seller in this case must, however, disclose to the buyer the cost at which a certain asset was sourced. The buyer then has the right to negotiate on the profit margin at which a subsequent sale can be executed. In an initial stage a seller purchases an asset from a third-party source at a particular cost from say a wholesale market. The seller then attempts to sell this asset to a buyer at cost plus profit in the retail market. If this sale is executed through a *murabahah* contract, the seller must disclose the cost at which the asset was sourced. If the seller does not disclose the cost price, the sale is based on a contract of *musawamah*.[1]

In contracts of sale, four scenarios may occur.

- **Scenario 1:** Where a buyer and seller exist, the subject matter of the sale, an asset exists, and a price is agreed on at the time of the sale. The buyer pays for the asset in full at a spot price, and the seller transfers ownership of the asset to the buyer with immediate delivery.
- **Scenario 2:** All of the conditions above prevail, except that the buyer does not pay the purchase price on the spot, and instead agrees to pay a deferred price or a credit price in the future. The seller, however, transfers ownership of the asset immediately to the buyer. The buyer enjoys the ownership of the asset prior to having paid the purchase price, and enjoys the usufruct of the asset. The seller and buyer agree to a deferred payment mechanism where purchase price is paid in full at a future date in lump sum or is paid in installments over a specific period of time. This deferred price is typically higher than the spot price of the asset. The payment of the purchase price is a debt obligation on the buyer.
- **Scenario 3:** All the conditions of Scenario 1 prevail, except the asset is not in existence at the time of the sale. The buyer agrees to buy an asset that may require to be grown (as in agricultural goods) or manufactured (as in industrial goods), and pays the purchase price in full to the seller. The seller contracts to source the asset that is the subject of sale and delivers to the buyer at an agreed time in the future. The buyer purchases the asset by making full payment of the purchase price. Typically, this purchase price is lower than the spot or market price of the asset as in essence the buyer is financing the manufacture or production of the asset in question.
- **Scenario 4:** A buyer and seller agree to transact in the future. This is a forward sale, where a buyer agrees to purchase an asset of specific description and quantity at a specific price from a seller, but payment of price and delivery of the asset will be executed at a future date.

In a *murabahah* sale, the asset may be purchased with payment of a spot price or a deferred credit price. The buyer pays the full price of the

[1] Muhammad Ayub, *Understanding Islamic Finance* (Hoboken, NJ: John Wiley & Sons, 2007).

asset and then subsequently takes delivery, or the buyer may make payment of the purchase price in installments or in lump sum at a future date. The deferred price is higher than the spot price. This is accepted in the *shariah*.[2] The rationale for this is, however, not provided, as this element of a sale on deferred payment basis resembles a loan obligation and offers a contract readily usable by IFIs.

MURABAHAH SALE/CREDIT SALE/CREDIT

We illustrate our point using a simple example. Two parties exist, Party A and Party B. Party A owns an asset worth $1,000 that Party B wishes to purchase but does not have the required moneys. There can be two solutions to resolving this predicament and facilitate the transaction.

Party A lends Party B $1,000 in cash, using the contract of *qard* or loan and Party B purchases the asset from Party A on spot basis. Under the obligations of the contract of *qard*, Party B must repay the $1,000 borrowed after a specified time, but Party A cannot demand any payment in excess of $1,000 as this will constitute *riba* or interest. The Quran, in many injunctions, advises Muslims to repay their debts.[3] Party B, however, on repayment of the loan, at his or her own discretion and under no legal obligation, rewards

---

[2]Majority of *shariah* scholars are of the view that the fundamental principle in transaction is permissibility (*harus*), hence the deferred price can be higher than the spot price as there is no prohibition to do so from both the Quran and Sunnah. *See* Taqi Usmani, *An Introduction to Islamic Finance* (India: Idara Isha'at-e-Diniyat (P) Ltd, 2005); and Muhammad Yusuf Saleem, *Islamic Commercial Law* (Hoboken, NJ: John Wiley & Sons, 2013).

[3]Quranic verses with regard to settlement of one's debt:

> 4:58: "Allah (sat) doth command you to render back your trusts to those to whom they are due; and when ye judge between man and man that ye judge with justice: Verily, how excellent is the teaching which He giveth you! for Allah (sat) is He who heareth and seeth all things."

> 4:12: "In what your wives leave your share is a half if they leave no child; but if they leave a child ye get a fourth; after payment of legacies and debts. In what ye leave their share is a fourth if ye leave no child; but if ye leave a child they get an eighth; after payment of legacies and debts. If the man or woman whose inheritance is in question has left neither ascendants nor descendants but has left a brother or a sister each one of the two gets a sixth; but if more than two they share in a third; after payment of legacies and debts; so that no loss is caused (to anyone). Thus is it ordained by Allah (sat) and Allah (sat) is All-Knowing Most Forbearing."

Party A for lending the money by giving Party A a gift using the contract of *hibah*. Under this contract, B may reward A with an additional repayment of $20 along with the $100 loan, but is under no obligation to do so.

Alternatively, Party A can sell the same asset to Party B on a deferred payment basis and can in fact charge a higher deferred price of $1,020, for instance. The financial implications of this closely resemble a loan and repayment of interest, but *murabahah* is a contract of sale and not a contract of lending money, or *qard*. These are delicate subtleties of the legal framework of the *shariah* and we request the reader to take these subtleties into consideration. In essence the repayment by Party B of $1,020 is permissible by the *shariah* as long as the **sale of an underlying asset is involved and the amount is reflective of a purchase price.**[4] Alternatively a repayment by Party B of $1,020 is not allowed by the *shariah*, if the payment is not for an asset, is not the purchase price of an asset, and is only repayment of a loan.

What justifies the element of the payment of a deferred price of $1,020 is that the underlying transaction is a transaction of sale, otherwise the transaction resembles a loan or *qard*, where a payment of any excess amount cannot be guaranteed. The *shariah* also requires therefore that the seller must own the asset before selling it to another party.[5]

ENHANCEMENTS TO *MURABAHAH*

Islamic banks appoint a customer as their agent under the contract of *wakalah* to purchase on the bank's behalf any (permissible) asset that the customer wishes to purchase. The customer identifies such an asset as a house, car, or even industrial goods or raw materials, or may also make a nominal downpayment for the asset. The customer then furnishes the Islamic bank with the invoice of the purchase and the Islamic bank pays the seller (vendor) the balance of the purchase price. The Islamic bank purchases the asset on behalf of the customer, but does not record the asset in its books, and instantaneously sells the same asset to the customer on a deferred payment basis. This is illustrated in Figure 3.1.

Note the quotation marks around the words *buys* and *sells*. When the customer makes a downpayment to the vendor, in actuality the vendor

[4] Ash Shawkani, Muhammad, *Nayl al-Awtar Sharh Muntaqa al-Akhbar*. Volume 5.

[5] The Majelle Art. 365: "In order that a sale may be *nafiz*, it is a condition that the seller should be the owner of the property sold, or agent, or natural or appointed guardian of the owner of the property, and that there should be no right in any one else."

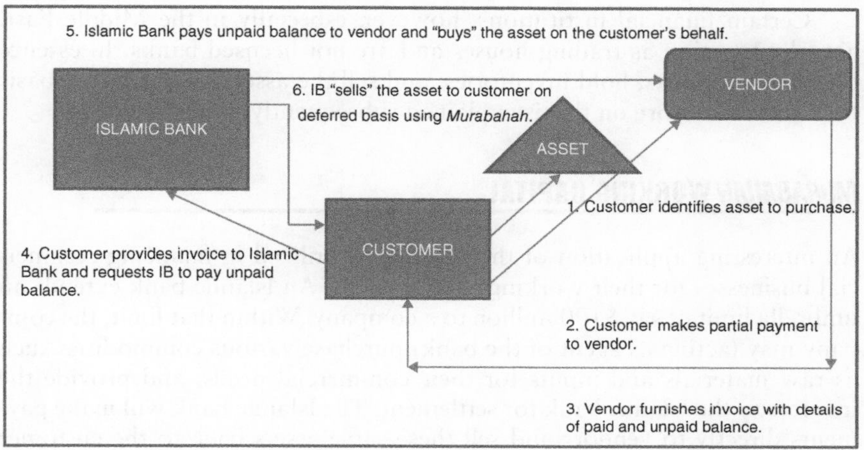

FIGURE 3.1 *Murabahah* to Purchase Orderer Process Flow

initiates the process of transferring the title of ownership of the asset to the customer.

The customer is likely to pay a sales tax on the purchase. When the customer approaches the Islamic bank to pay the unpaid balance or in essence "buy" the asset on the customer's behalf, there is no transfer of title from the vendor to the Islamic bank. The Islamic bank subsequently also pays a tax on the purchase of the asset's unpaid price and then resells the asset to the customer.

At this final stage there is no payment of tax again. In essence the transfer of title happens straight from the vendor to the customer and not from the vendor to the Islamic bank and then to the customer. This would make the sale a bona fide sale or a true sale, but would make the transaction costs very high as transferring title involves payment of various stamp duties as well. If the sale was a true sale, the Islamic bank would pay a sales tax when buying the asset from the vendor, the bank would bill this tax to the buyer or customer, and the customer would pay an additional tax when the Islamic bank sells the asset to the customer.

A true sequence of sales would involve double taxation as first the Islamic bank would buy the asset and then sell it to the customer in question. The above model is therefore an imperfect one and allows the bank to finance the purchase of an asset under the guise of a sale. However, in essence the contract resembles one more of a loan for purchasing an asset than one of selling an asset.

Certain financial institutions, however, especially in the Middle East, actually function as trading houses and are not licensed banks. In essence they acquire assets, hold inventories, and sell the assets on a deferred basis to customers. More on this is explained subsequently.

MURABAHAH WORKING CAPITAL

An interesting application of the contract is utilized in financing commercial businesses for their working capital needs. An Islamic bank extends an umbrella limit of say $100 million to a company. Within that limit, the company may (acting as agent of the bank) purchase various commodities such as raw materials and inputs for their commercial needs, and provide the invoices to the Islamic bank for settlement. The Islamic bank will make payments directly to vendors and sell these same assets back to the customer on a deferred basis. Each deferred price will constitute what is known as a subfacility within the umbrella facility. The customer will retire each facility according to a separate amortization schedule. Upon full payment of a particular subfacility the customer will be able to make additional purchases.

CREDIT-BASED SALE/MARKUP OR *RIBA*

Often Muslims in particular wonder why *riba* is forbidden. Many come up with their conclusions, such as it implies a predetermined rate of return on financing, or any economic activity, that *riba* or the contract of lending money treats money as a commodity or asset on its own, which is not recognized by Islam. Let us establish that there is no consensus on any approach to how money should be treated, whether as an asset or not. Further, if it is an asset, it can appreciate in value or depreciate in value. A contract of loan requires repayment of principal and interest and therefore does not recognize or allow the value of money to depreciate or the value of a loan contract to depreciate. These explanations are incomplete, and we have no alternative.

The *murabahah* contract can be a debt-based sale contract by combining it to *bai mu'ajjal* as the buyer is indebted to repay the purchase price to the seller. The purchase price includes a cost component and a built-in profit rate component, which is predetermined at the outset of the sale. If the buyer falls on hard times and is unable to repay the credit price, the seller may call in any collateral held in its custody to settle the outstanding balance. To this point the *murabahah* sale resembles a conventional loan. There are some differences, though. In the event the buyer defaults on payments, the seller of the Islamic bank cannot charge a fee for late payment, and second, the seller cannot increase the purchase price at any time. Unlike in a conventional loan arrangement, where a bank compounds the interest payments owed to it by a borrower, an Islamic bank cannot do the same. If an Islamic bank liquidates any collateral, it must refund any excess over the outstanding amounts back to the customer after recovering its sale price. This feature is unique to Islamic banking.

There is an added risk mitigant to this contract. As the financing is disbursed directly in favor of the vendor, this arrangement controls the behavior of the customer. In essence, the Islamic bank is able to ensure that moneys raised through financing are being utilized for the purposes disclosed by the customer and not leaked into any other business venture or enterprise.

BONAFIDE *MURABAHAH* TRUE SALE

Bank Negara Malaysia describes Islamic banking as the business of banking that does not contradict the rulings of Islam.[6] We explore the concept of the business of banking.

Islam permits bai and forbids riba.[7] We use this verse of the Quran to illustrate the true function of a bank.

Islam permits trade. Trade has some underlying economic principles attached to it that involve the factors of production. It is the recommended economic model where a unit of labor, either employed by a third person, or in his own employ, produces more than his immediate necessities by engaging in some craft or labor and subsequently trading the surplus for other goods with other parties. This concept is a precursor to the concept of specialization of labor, division of labor, competitive advantage theories, and other concepts that are common in contemporary literature on microeconomics. However, before a good can be traded, it must be manufactured. Manufacturing goods is certainly not the function of banks. After manufacturing a good, it is sold from a farm or factory in large quantities to a wholesaler, which on taking delivery may resell it to other traders in varying quantities and at various prices. These traders then sell these goods to end users. Banks may finance any stage of these processes, and serve as intermediaries,

---

[6]Bank Negara Malaysia, "Islamic Banking & Takaful," www.bnm.gov.my/index.php?ch=fs_mfs&pg=fs_mfs_bank, accessed June 14, 2014.

[7]The Holy Quran, Surah Al-Baqarah verse 275: "Those who charge usury (interest) are in the same position as those controlled by the devil's influence. This is because they claim that usury is the same as commerce. However, God permits commerce, and prohibits usury (interest). Thus whoever heeds this commandment from his Lord, and refrains from usury, he may keep his past earnings, and his judgment rests with God. As for those who persist in usury, they incur Hell, wherein they abide forever."

but their core function is neither trading nor manufacturing. Each component in this cycle from production to selling of goods to end users takes on the **risk of doing business** or *business risk*. At any stage production processes may fail, demand for products may change, prices may change, trends may change, costs of inputs may change and may cause loss of capital to the entity undertaking these activities. Banks are not involved in these economic processes. Banks only **finance** the purchase of these products if end users are unable to pay for them in full at the time of purchase. These goods may include such large-ticket items as houses, cars, and may also include such small items as a microwave. Banks therefore only absorb the **credit risk** inherent in the business of repaying borrowed money. They incur additional risks because the money they lend out is also **not their own** but borrowed from the public in the shape of deposits. Therefore, banks take on market risk and liquidity risk among other risks as well. Business and financial risks are illustrated in Figure 3.2.

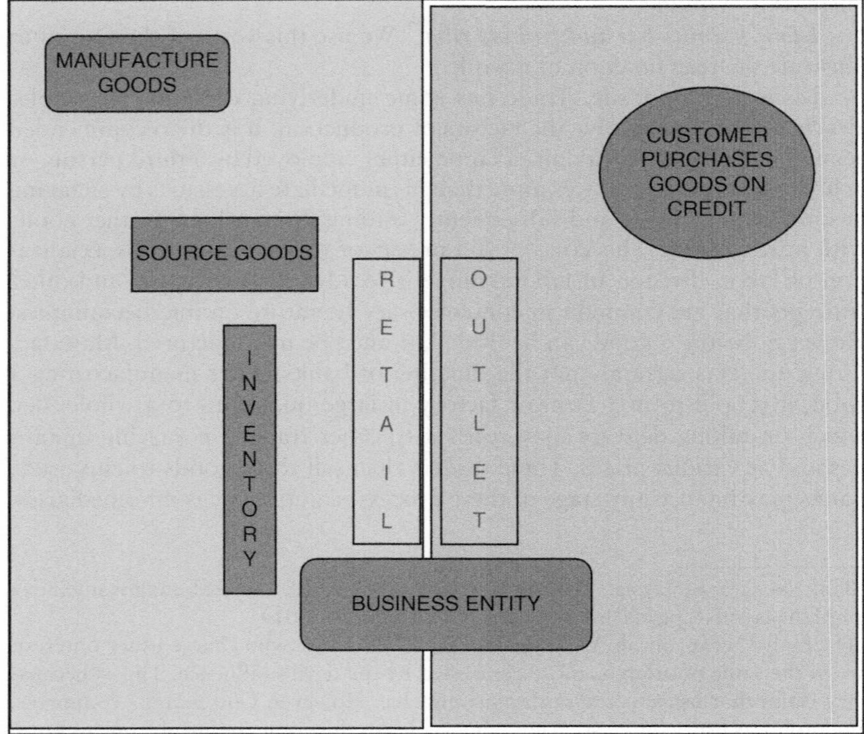

FIGURE 3.2 Business Risk and Financial Risk in a Bona Fide Sale

Islam, however, only recognizes *bai* in its texts, and therefore recognizes the accompanying business risk. It allows an economic entity to earn a profit as a reward for incurring business risk. The Arabic word for profit is *ribbh*. Islam does recognize financial risk, and enjoins followers to repay debt, but does not clearly spell out how to reward financial risk. In the context of conventional lending the reward for financial risk is interest or *ribah*.

Banks participate in financing a sale transaction. They enter the picture when a customer has already agreed to purchase a particular asset from a seller. Banks do not maintain inventory of goods in warehouses or maintain retail outlets waiting for customers to walk in the door to purchase goods from them, which they will then finance. Banks function as financial intermediaries, and only get in the game when the sale has been decided and the buyer needs money on credit to make the purchase. In fact as per the requirements of Basel, banks are penalized for holding such assets on their books.

What distinguishes an Islamic bank in the way it provides credit financing is that it does not offer customers a loan contract but a deferred sale contract. One may ask whether Islamic banks own goods, inventories in warehouses, and the answer is no. They use a cleverly-thought-out sequence of contracts to **circumvent** having to take on business risk, or the risk of doing business. We leave it to the reader to decide if this solution is creative or distortive. However, this is an enhancement to the *murabahah* contract that makes its application to the role of banking efficient within the context of banking.

TRADING HOUSE MODEL

The trading house model has been adopted by some Islamic institutions and offers a unique alternative to a banking model. We can illustrate this application by using the following example. A developer approaches a cash-rich institution for funds to help develop a residential area of 1,000 villas. The cash-rich unit provides the developer the funds in exchange for 300 units of the villas under an *istisna* contract. The cash-rich unit then onward sells these villas to third parties on a deferred sale basis. This transaction is a pure sale, where the cash-rich unit actually has possession of the asset it wishes to sell. One imperfection in this scenario would be if the cash-rich unit would sell these villas to third parties before they are completed. This is typically the case and again leads to the problem of selling something not in one's possession. However, the cash-rich unit has provided capital to the developer not as a loan but as a purchase price as part of a sale/purchase transaction.

In this model, the cash-rich unit, or capital provider, actually behaves as a trader in real estate and not a bank.

FINANCIAL SERVICES DIVISION OF A MANUFACTURER OR RETAILER

This model is in use, however, outside the Islamic Banking Space and is employed by manufacturers of cars such as Mercedes, BMW, and Toyota. Each of these companies have set aside capital and established a financial services wing to facilitate the purchase of their cars by providing in-house credit facilities. Customers who wish to purchase a car by cash can do so by paying a market price. Customers who wish to pay in installments can obtain financing from the manufacturer only. In this scenario, the manufacturer is selling an asset that it owns on a deferred payment basis albeit using the contract of *riba*. If the same contract is executed using *murabahah*, then it becomes *shariah*-compliant.

Retailers of consumer goods may also use the same model, as may developers of real estate. Dubai-based Emaar offers financing for purchase of its properties and department stores like Sears, and Aeon offers customers credit cards or layaway plans to help make purchases in easy installments. Layaway plans, or in-house store installment plans, are perfect examples of the implementation of *murabahah*. Companies that adopt this model incur business risk as well as credit risk, however, through two subsidiaries of the same overall group.

BAI BITHMAN AJIL

Bai bithman ajil refers to a sale where the purchase price is paid in installments. If the cost price is disclosed by the seller, the contract is a combination of *murabahah* with *bai bithman ajil*. The deferred credit price can be repaid as per any schedule of payments agreed on between the buyer and the seller. The purchase price will have two components, one of the principal repayment or payment of the cost price and one of the profit payments. The principal and profit payment can be combined in an installment or profit payments may be paid on monthly or quarterly payments and the principal can be repaid in lump sum at maturity, much like the payments in a conventional bond.

BBA WITH *INAH*

The combination of contracts in Figure 3.3 has been very common in Malaysia.

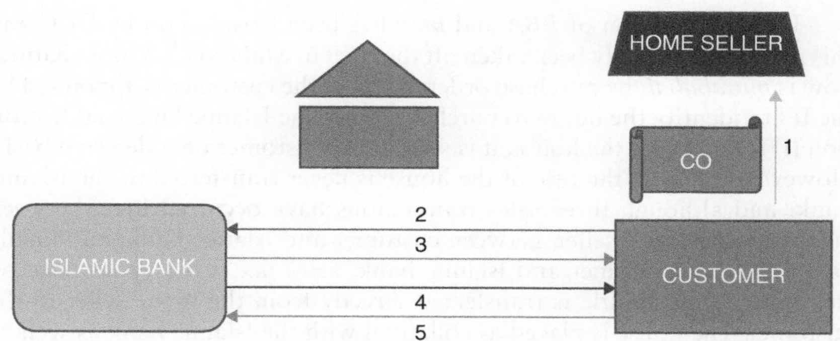

FIGURE 3.3 The Combination of *BBA* with *Inah*

The combination of *BBA* with *inah* has been applied to finance the purchase of houses. A customer interested in purchasing a home identifies a property for purchase. The property is worth RM 100,000 and is referred to as the *purchase price*. The customer makes a downpayment of say 10 percent or RM 10,000 of the purchase price to the home seller (1). This deposit can be made under the contract of *urbun*. Upon such payment, Malaysian Law (for instance) recognizes that the customer has obtained "beneficial ownership" of the property.

The customer then approaches an Islamic bank and sells the house to the Islamic bank for the balance owed to the original home seller, which in this case is RM 90,000 (2). Bear in mind that the customer does not have complete ownership of the property and it is questionable if he or she has the legal capacity to sell the house to the bank.

The Islamic bank makes the payment of RM 90,000 to the customer (stage of disbursement of financing amount), and the customer settles all outstanding amounts owed to the home seller (3). At this point, note the sequence of transactions. The customer makes a downpayment or *urbun* to the home seller of RM 10,000. The customer then sells the house to the Islamic bank for RM 90,000 and uses this money to pay the home seller. In essence the customer sells the house to the Islamic bank without having paid the full purchase price of the house to the original seller.

Finally, the customer then buys back the house from the Islamic bank for a deferred price, RM 200,000 (4), which is to be paid over a period of 20 years (5). The end result of this sequence of transactions is that the customer is able to raise RM 90,000 from the Islamic bank, which he or she repays over a period of 20 years with a profit component of RM 110,000.

This combination of *BBA* and *inah* has been frowned on by GCC and this product has slowly been taken off the shelf in Malaysia.[8] A more natural flow is *murabahah* by purchase orderer, where the customer is appointed by the IFI to identify the house to purchase. Once the Islamic Financial Institution (IFI) purchases the house, it is sold to the customer on a deferred basis. However, note that the title of the house is never transferred to the Islamic bank, and although three sales transactions have occurred here, between customer and home seller, between customer and Islamic bank, and finally again between customer and Islamic bank, sales tax is only paid once on the house, and the title is transferred directly from the home seller to the customer. The house is placed as collateral with the Islamic bank as well.

The matter is further complicated when the customer identifies a house that is still under construction or is still being worked on by a property developer. In that case the property developer essentially sells a house that does not exist. Such a sale contract cannot happen under a *murabaha* contract but can be facilitated through the *istisna* contract.

Related to the enhancements of *murabahah*, there is another contract that is also widely used, not only in Malaysia, but also in the GCC countries,[9] and we discuss this in the following chapter.

CONCLUSION

We have discussed *bai al inah*, *bai bithman ajil*, and *murabahah*, and we have pointed the reader's attention to the controversy surrounding some of these contracts. *Inah* itself is controversial in that parties to the contract do not have any apparent intent to trade in goods, just in money. *Murabahah* is a simple contract of sale, but becomes complicated when Islamic injunctions require a seller to own the asset prior to entering a sale contract. Islamic banks, as we discussed, are not in the business of trading, of holding goods, and then selling them. Islamic banks are in the business of financing purchases, and we see how using a sale contract can create controversy. *Murabahah* by purchase orderer is a combination of *wakalah* and *murabahah* and as such is "engineered" to develop a banking product. Whether such enhancements, modifications, or engineering tools are valid is up to readers to explore further.

[8]Al-Zaquan Amer Hamzah and Bernardo Vizcaino, "Malaysia Tightens Rules on Divisive Islamic *Bai Inah* Deals," Reuters, May 21, 2014, www.reuters.com/article/2014/05/21/us-islamic-finance-malaysia-idUSBREA4K0FM20140521, accessed June 15, 2014.

[9]Tijani, I. M. (2013), "A Snapshot of Tawarruq in Contemporary Islamic Finance," *International Shariah Research Academy Monthly Publication*, September 2013 edition.

CHAPTER 4

Tawarruq

We look at the development of cash flows through a sequence of tripartite sales. This chapter is an extension of the chapter on *inah*, which is a sequence of sales between two parties. The reader is introduced to the idea of using commodity sales on an independent exchange to construct these cash flows and how such sales can be arranged to develop either asset products or liability products.

In Bank Negara Malaysia's most recent exposure draft, *tawarruq* is referred to as "an arrangement that involves sale of an asset to the purchaser on a deferred basis and subsequent sale of the asset to a third party on a cash basis to obtain cash or vice versa."[1] It is named as such as there is no intention of the buyer to actually utilize the asset, but rather more of the intention of obtaining cash.[2]

Illustration of three sales in sequence: A sequence of tripartite sales is executed between 3 or more parties creating cash flows that resemble disbursing a loan amount and being repaid an amount in excess of the original loan. The original loan is the spot price of an asset or commodity and the repayment amount is the deferred price or credit price of an asset or commodity. The sequence of transactions can construct a fixed deposit instrument or a financing instrument depending on whether the customer is buying the commodity or is selling the commodity.

---

[1]Bank Negara Malaysia (BNM) (2013), *Tawarruq (Shariah Requirements and Optional Practices) Exposure Draft December 2013*, www.bnm.gov.my/documents/SAC/13_Tawarruq.pdf, accessed July 2014.

[2]Bank Negara Malaysia (BNM) (2010), *Shariah Resolutions in Islamic Finance: Second Edition,* http://www.bnm.gov.my/microsites/financial/pdf/resolutions/shariah_resolutions_2nd_edition_EN.pdf, accessed July 2014.

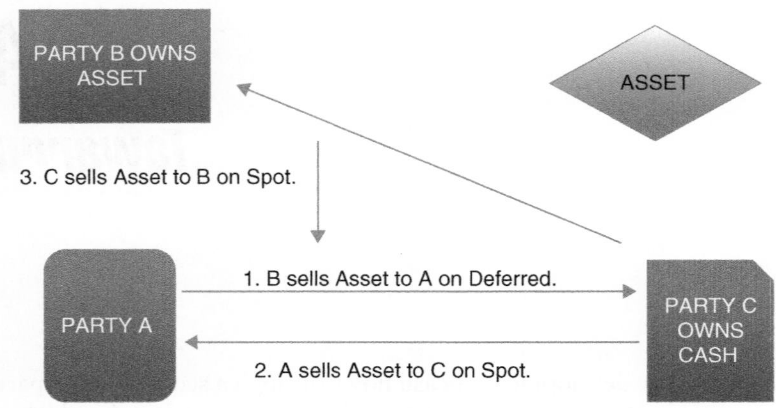

FIGURE 4.1 Tripartite Basic Process Flow

For a simple illustration of *a sequence of sales*, we look at a scenario in Figure 4.1 with three parties, A, B, and C. As 3 parties are involved we refer to the sale as a *tripartite sale*.

Party A is in need of liquidity, or in simple terms, of cash. Party B owns an asset and Party C owns cash. In a conventional financing scenario, Party A would simply approach Party C to borrow money and would contract to repay Party C with principal plus interest.

Within a tripartite sales transaction, Party A approaches Party B and buys an asset from Party B on a deferred payment basis, say for $150,000. Party B will pay the purchase price of the asset either in three easy installments of $50,000 or in one lump sum payment or balloon payment in 90 days.

Party B has sold an asset to Party A for cash to be paid in the shape of a deferred purchase price. Hence Party B enters into a debt-based sales contract with Party A, and transfers ownership of the asset to the latter in exchange for a deferred purchase price.

After the asset is transferred to the ownership of Party A, A sells it to Party C for a spot payment of $100,000.

In other words, Party A obtains ownership of an asset without making any spot cash payments. A then sells the asset to Party C for a spot payment. A has executed two transactions, one of purchase without making any payment (with Party B) and has entered into a sale contract (with Party C) while receiving the sale price in cash. Party A must mobilize these funds in such a manner that he or she is able to generate $150,000 in 90 days and pay the debt owed (in the shape of a deferred payment or credit price) to Party B.

Party C has parted with $100,000 and has acquired an asset. Party C decides that it does not want to retain ownership of the asset and **sells it back to Party B.** Party B retains ownership of the asset in question and is due a deferred payment price from Party A for the same.

ISSUE OF PRICE FIXING

This tripartite sale is a form of *tawarruq*, one that is highly discouraged in current usage. So far the sequences of sales contracts are independent and unrelated to one another. An issue arises now at what price Party C will sell the asset to Party B, for there are three sale contracts here of the asset.

The first sale is a deferred sale at a deferred price. The second sale is a spot sale at a spot price.

The third sale is also a spot sale and the price of the commodity in the third sale is equal to the spot price in the second sale. The same sequence of sales transactions may also have different scenarios.

Scenario 1

In the third sale, Party C sells the asset to Party B for $90,000; Party C will make a loss of $10,000 as Party C paid Party A $100,000 for the same.

Party B would have sold the asset to Party A for $150,000, and bought the asset back from Party C for $90,000, having made a profit of $60,000 on the two transactions, deferred payment sale and spot purchase. However, Party B would be exposed to credit risk of default on Party A.

Scenario 2

Party C could sell the asset to Party B for $110,000, making $10,000 profit on the two transactions. Since Party C bought the asset from Party A for $100,000 and sold it to Party B for $110,000, Party B would make a profit of only $40,000 as Party B would have sold the asset to Party A for $150,000 and bought the asset back for $110,000.

Scenario 3

Party C could sell the asset to Party B for $100,000, making no profit on the sale transactions and yet Party B would make a profit of $50,000 as the difference between the spot price and credit price of the asset.

If the reader looks carefully at the sequences of transactions on a standalone basis they are all just sale and purchase transactions. However, when combined, the cash flows created resemble a loan transaction, **especially if Party C sells the asset back to Party A for $100,000.** It is evident then that no party has the intent to purchase the asset under question, and the combined sequences of sale transactions simply facilitate Party A borrowing money from Party C using an asset owned by Party B to create a **sequence of sales transactions.**

Let us also examine the incentives behind each party's actions. Party B owns an asset, and sells it to Party A, fully expecting Party B to sell the asset to Party C. Party B will then buy the asset back from Party C. If Parties B and C **collaborate together,** where Party B convinces Party C to buy the asset from Party A for a specific price ($100,000) and then Party B agrees to buy the same asset from Party C for an agreed price, this is referred to as organized *tawarruq*. This is a sequence of sales with preagreed prices, and in essence Party A convinces Party C to buy the asset from Party A.

Party C is incentivized by a resale price offered by Party B, not by the desire to own the asset.

This organized sequence of sales transactions is called *tawarruq* Munazzam and deemed impermissible by OIC as they replicate a loan transaction.[3] As in the case of *inah*, Malaysia follows the Shafi school of thought, which looks at the form of transactions and not the substance.

As per this approach the sales contracts are all valid in their own right, as long as there is no express intent that the sale contracts are fictitious in nature. Party B earns a spread equal to the difference between the spot price for the asset in Party B's ownership and its credit price. Party B creates the exchange of cash flows, Party C finances the sales transactions, and Party B is able to mobilize funds for a specific period of time.

TRANSFER OF TITLE

An important element to understand here is that although there is transfer of title or ownership risk of the asset within each sale, there is no real intent to buy and hold the asset at any given time. When Party B sells the asset to Party A, this is executed through sale/purchase agreements, and there is actual transfer of title. A now bears all ownership risks and responsibilities of the asset but immediately sells the asset to Party C. Finally, when Party C sells the asset back to Party B, there is also actual transfer of ownership. In fact throughout the sequence of transactions, the asset remains in legal ownership of Party B.

[3]See OIC Fiqh Academy Resolution no. 179 (19/5); AAOIFI, 2010, Shariah Standard No. 30, Article 4/5.

PAYMENT OF SALES TAX

If this asset is the underlying asset of all three transactions, and three separate distinct sale transactions occur between Parties B and A, A and C, and C and B, then a sales tax should apply to each transaction. The fact that no sales tax is levied in jurisdictions where these contracts are permissible further adds relevance that these are fictitious sales transactions.

In fact a legal hurdle for implementing Islamic banking in any legal jurisdiction lies primarily on the tax treatment of these "sale transactions."

We have seen how a sequence of sales transactions can construct cash flows that resemble a loan structure. The sequence of sales transactions can involve 3 parties, 4 parties, or 2 parties and a central commodity exchange.

What is important to realize is that if these sales transactions are prearranged such that the two spot prices are the same, and that the seller in each case is willing to accept the offer made by the buyer without any modifications, then these transactions are not deemed natural. The sequence of transactions effectively resembles a financial product if there is a willing buyer for the commodity at every stage of the sale and vice versa.

The abovementioned sequence of sales transactions can take the shape of a financial product in the following manner. One party to the transaction is a customer with $100,000 that is to be placed in a fixed deposit. The customer, instead of placing funds with an Islamic Bank, appoints an Islamic Bank to purchase a certain quantity of commodity on the customer's behalf. Thus, when a customer places $100,000 in an Islamic Bank as a fixed deposit, the Islamic Bank actually transfers the funds to a commodity broker to purchase (say) 1,000 tons of commodity on the customer's behalf. There may not be a willing seller for 1,000 tons of commodity at that particular instance in time. Just saying the bank will arrange to sell or purchase a commodity at a market price does not mean there is a willing seller at that price. This transaction may be an Over-the-Counter Transaction or an Exchange-Based Transaction. Subsequently, the Islamic Bank will purchase the commodity from the customer for a deferred price, say $110,000 payable in 90 days. This is an Over-the-Counter Transaction between the Islamic Bank and the customer. In the final leg of the transaction, the Islamic Bank then sells the commodity back to a broker on an exchange for $100,000. The Islamic bank may not find a willing buyer in this case and is thus stuck with an inventory of commodity for which it will have to pay storage charges and insurance and incur opportunity cost of tying up its liquid funds into commodity holdings. For the structure of three sales to resemble a fixed deposit, the Islamic Bank must be able to ensure there is an available and willing buyer or seller for the required commodity at each stage of the transaction.

Three Sales and *Tawarruq*

We shall now look at the three forms of the *tawarruq* transaction, *tawarruq fiqihi*, *tawarruq munazam*, and the form practiced today.

Tawarruq fiqihi is a structure where all three sales transactions occur in a natural market; each sale is executed on the basis of a natural demand and supply of the underlying commodity. All the parties to the sale may or may not know each other, the sales transactions may or may not have a time lag between them, and there may well be a change in the spot prices of the commodity.

Tawarruq munazam is a structure where all three sales are prearranged. Thus, if A buys an asset at spot price SP1, and sells it to B at a deferred price of DP1 allowing B to sell the asset to party C (or D) at a spot price of SP2, it will be a prearranged sequence if SP1=SP2. If prices are made to be the same in two sales transactions, the participants to the trade have preagreed on terms and conditions and thus such a market is not deemed to be a real or natural market.

Specialized Trading Platform

Certain jurisdictions have developed a trading platform whereby there is always an availability of a specific commodity, and willing sellers and buyers that are willing to transact in commodity to replicate financial transactions. Critics feel that this platform does not do enough to distance itself from *tawarruq munazam*.

APPLICATIONS OF *TAWARRUQ* IN BANKING PRODUCTS

The basic concepts remain the same. However, tripartite sales can be used to construct asset products or liability products depending on the role played by each party to a tripartite sale.

Asset Products

With one party being a banking customer and the other being an Islamic bank, the customer who requires funding will approach an Islamic bank for a financing facility as in Figure 4.2.

When a customer approaches an Islamic bank for a facility of $100,000, the IFI buys a certain commodity from a commodity broker, Broker A, for $100,000. The title of the commodity is not actually transferred to the IFI, nor is actual delivery made to the IFI. The IFI now sells this commodity to

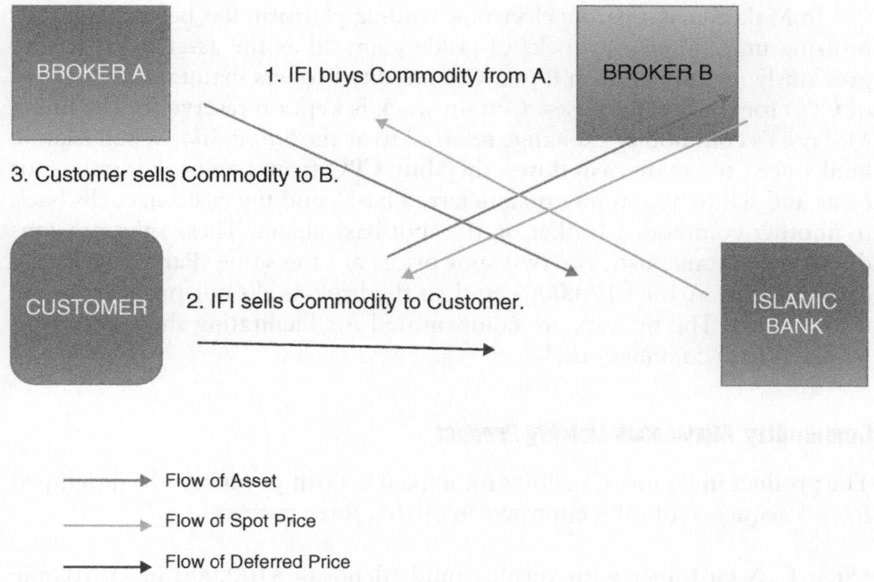

FIGURE 4.2 Tripartite Sale Asset Product

the customer for $120,000, which is to be paid in 90 days. The actual title of the commodity is not transferred to the customer, nor is there any actual delivery of the commodity made.

The customer now sells the commodity to another commodity Broker B for $100,000, who is part of this "arrangement." Brokers A and B are compensated by the IFI with a commission fee, which is built into the deferred price of $120,000 charged to the customer. The previous sequence of sales allows the customer to raise $100,000 for 90 days from an Islamic bank while committing to repay $120,000 at maturity.

In essence the customer then receives the funds from Broker B; the facility is not disbursed by the IFI crediting the account of the customer, but by Broker B crediting the customer's account with the spot price for the commodity.

The financing is repaid by the customer to the bank via a mechanism or vehicle of the deferred sale price, which is settled directly between the customer and the IFI.

Essentially, Broker A and B can be the same; in this case this would be an organized *tawarruq* transaction.

In Malaysia, a separate electronic trading platform has been created for utilizing unencumbered stocks of crude palm oil as the asset to create the previously mentioned cash flows. Commodity brokers maintain inventories of CPO for trading purposes. Certain stock is kept on reserve for the Bursa Malaysia's commodity exchange referred to as the *Suq-a-Sila*. When Islamic banks need to create cash flows, they buy CPO from one broker on a spot basis and sell to a customer on a deferred basis, and the customer sells back to another commodity broker on the spot basis again. These sales are conducted instantaneously, the two spot prices are the same (Party C sells the asset to Party A for $100,000), and so the brokers do not profit from the transactions. The brokers are compensated for facilitating the transaction by being paid commissions.[4]

Commodity *Murabahah Liability Product*

The product in Figure 4.3 allows for a fixed deposit product to be developed from a sequence of sales contracts involving three parties.

Step 1. A customer with surplus funds deposits $100,000 in an Islamic bank.
Step 2. The customer appoints an Islamic bank as an agent to buy palm oil from a commodity Broker A for $100,000.
Step 3. The Islamic bank buys the commodity on the customer's behalf.
Step 4. The customer sells oil to the bank on deferred basis for a price of $150,000, which has to be paid in 90 days.
Step 5. The Islamic bank sells the commodity to Broker B for a spot price of $100,000.

The net effect of the sales transactions is that the customer deposits $100,000 in an Islamic bank and the Islamic bank pays the customer $150,000 in 90 days. The cash flows resemble a fixed deposit. The Islamic bank is able to mobilize funds with a predetermined cost of fund for a specific period just as in a fixed deposit structure.

This product was launched in Malaysia in 2007 and Islamic banks mobilized millions of Ringgits worth of funds; it has proven to be extremely popular in Malaysia.[5] However, certain scholars look down with scorn at *tawarruq* and *inah*. For instance, related to the usage of *tawarruq*, AAOIFI

[4]For more, see Bursa Malaysia, www.bursamalaysia.com.
[5]Islamic Interbank Money Market, "Information: About IIMM," http://iimm.bnm.gov.my/index.php?ch=4&pg=4&ac=22, accessed June 16, 2014.

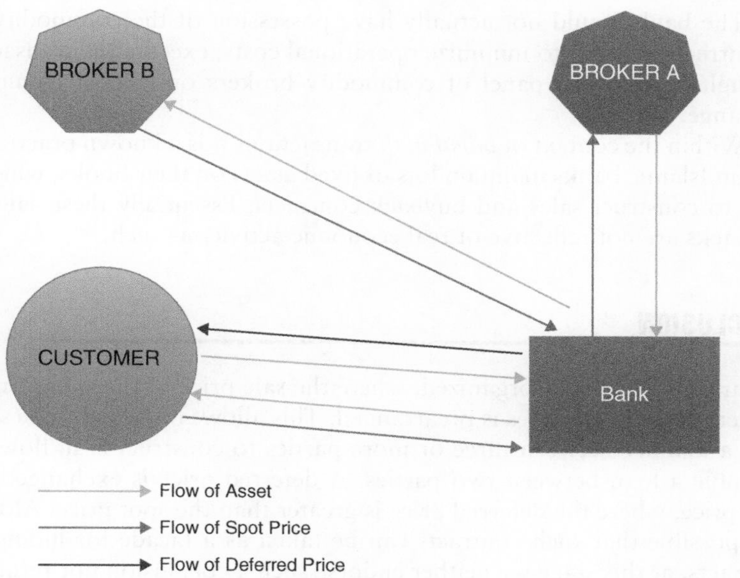

FIGURE 4.3 Tripartite Sale Liability Product

listed down the parameters in which the *tawarruq* concept can be applied. This is to ensure that the transaction does not lead to *riba*.[6]

REAL ECONOMIC ACTIVITY

One of the claims of Islamic finance is that it deals with the real economy and financing real transactions. In contracts of sale and buyback of an asset, whether executed between two parties or three, an asset is used to merely structure a sequence of sales transactions, and one asset can be used to structure several transactions. For instance, in the context of commodity *murabahah*, a bank may acquire 10,000 tons of a commodity with a market value of $100,000 and use the same lot to structure several cash flows. If a bank receives funds worth $1,000,000 in a day to place in a fixed deposit, the bank can use the same lot of 10,000 tons 10 times to structure buy-backs and book 10 fixed deposit contracts that have an aggregate value of $1,000,000.

[6]AAOIFI, Shariah Standard No. 30, Article 4/6; 4/7; 4/8; 4/9; 4/10; 5/1; 5/2 (2010).

The bank would not actually have possession of the commodity, and for further ease and to minimize operational costs, execute the transactions through a registered panel of commodity brokers on a local commodity exchange.

Within the context of *bai al inah* transactions it is a known practice that certain Islamic banks maintain lots of fixed assets on their books, which are used to construct sales and buyback contracts. Essentially these sales and buybacks are not reflective of real economic activity as such.

CONCLUSION

Tripartite sales can be organized, where the sale price of the subject matter at every stage of the sales is prearranged. This allows one asset to be sold in such a manner between three or more parties to construct cash flows that resemble a loan between two parties. A deferred price is exchanged for a spot price, where the deferred price is greater than the spot price. Although it is possible that such contracts can be taken as a façade for hiding loan contracts, at this stage we neither endorse such a conclusion nor refute it.

CHAPTER 5

Deferred Payment Sale or Credit Sale

In the previous chapter, we referred to the *bona fide murabahah* transaction when a bank actually owns the asset to be the subject of sale on its books. We demonstrate in this section how a deferred sale transaction can be recorded in the books of an Islamic bank. A deferred payment sale is referred to as *bai mu'ajjal*. For illustration purposes we work through a simple example involving Bank A and Customer B, starting with the data in Table 5.1.

Islamic Bank A has capital of $200, and no deposits at this stage. The Bank purchases an asset for $100 from its capital and keeps $100 in cash on its balance sheet with the remainder. Islamic Bank A is approached by Customer B, who wishes to purchase the asset from A for a credit price of $120, payable in 90 days. Islamic Bank A would earn a profit of $20 on the sale. Customer B contracts to make monthly payments to Islamic Bank A of $40, which would include a partial principal repayment of $33.33 and a partial profit payment of $6.66 (Table 5.2).

At contract initiation, Islamic Bank A sells the asset to Customer B and the asset is removed from the balance sheet of the bank. The bank in turn records a financial asset in its place, known as *murabahah financing*, for $120, which reflects the purchase price that B has to pay the bank. Islamic Bank A also records an entry for unearned profit of $20 as a contra entry.

Upon each payment made by the customer, which includes a $33.33 payment of principal amount and $6.67 of profit, the Islamic bank records an increase in cash by $40 and reduces its *murabahah* financing asset by $40. The bank records income of $6.66 and reduces its unearned profit also by $6.66. A subtle point to note is that the *shariah* allows the bank to record profit in installments, before the receivable is recovered. There seems to be no dispute on this issue.

Although this is not a work on accounting for Islamic banking or sales transactions, we want to highlight some salient features. One is that *shariah*

TABLE 5.1 Islamic Bank A's Balance Sheet

Islamic Bank A's Balance Sheet	
Asset	
Cash	$100
Asset subject to buy and sale	$100
Liability	$0
Equity	$200

TABLE 5.2 Accounting Entries for Deferred Sales Transaction

Islamic Bank A					
Contract Initiation		**DR**		**CR**	
Islamic Bank sells asset to B	Balance sheet			Asset	$100
Islamic Bank A books a *Murabahah* financing asset for $120	Balance sheet	*Murabahah* financing	$120		
Islamic Bank A records unearned income of $20 on the sale	Balance sheet			Unearned income	$20
Customer B pays first installment of $40	Balance sheet	Cash	$40	*Murabahah* financing	$40
Islamic bank recognizes income of $6.667	Income statement	Unearned income	$6.667	Income	$6.667
Customer B pays second installment of $40	Balance sheet	Cash	$40	*Murabahah* financing	$40
Islamic Bank A recognizes income of $6.667	Income Statement	Unearned income	$6.667	Income	$6.667
Customer B pays third installment of $40	Balance sheet	Cash	$40	*Murabahah* financing	$40
Islamic Bank A recognizes income of $6.667	Income statement	Unearned income	$6.667	Income	$6.667

Note: For a detailed review of treatment of accounting entries for deferred sales transaction, please refer to AAOIFI FAS 20—Deferred Payment Sale.

scholars have no objection to using modern accounting techniques to record transactions, but with some exceptions that are unique to the nature of Islamic contracts. In essence, therefore, in this treatment of recording data, an Islamic institution is permitted to record unearned income and receivables. The $120 due to Islamic Bank A is therefore treated as a "receivable" by the bank and is therefore an "asset." This is exactly how a loan is treated in conventional banking—it is considered a receivable, whether it is in the shape of a loan to purchase a car, or a house, or a business loan.

With each installment, the *bona fide murabahah* financing is reduced until it becomes 0, and the bank converts its asset worth $100 into cash worth $120, thereby earning a profit of $20 in its income statement.

What is unique about the above transaction is that the Islamic bank owns the asset under question. In a *murabahah by purchase orderer* transaction, however, the Islamic bank never really records ownership of the asset to be the subject of sale. In principle, a customer identifies an asset to be purchased, the bank purchases the asset on behalf of the customer, and then instantaneously sells it to the customer on a deferred payment basis. If the Islamic bank were to actually take ownership and delivery of the asset, the bank would incur additional operational costs and incur tax charges on the purchases. Further, as per Basel III rules, were the bank to record the purchase of the asset on its book, as assets held for sale, the Islamic bank would incur an additional capital charge and assign a risk-weightage charge to the asset.[1]

ACCOUNTING ENTRIES FOR *MURABAHAH* BY PURCHASE ORDERER

In a *murabahah by pay orderer* sale, the entries that are reflected on the books of the Islamic bank are as follows:

Although all entries remain the same in Table 5.3, the first entry is recorded as a cash outflow of $100. This $100 is used by the customer to purchase the asset that is the subject matter of the deferred sale transaction. With the initial transaction being one of a cash outflow, in the manner that this transaction is recorded, there is no difference from the disbursement of a loan. In its recorded form, it becomes a transaction of a sale of money for money, as on the books of the bank there is no mention of the asset.

The entries in Table 5.3 would apply to the deferred payment sale part of an *inah* contract, a *BBA* contract, or a *tawarruq* contract. An *inah* contract

[1]Capital Adequacy Framework (Basel II—Risk Weighted Asset).

TABLE 5.3 Accounting Entries for *Murabahah* by Purchase Orderer

Islamic Bank A					
Contract Initiation		**DR**		**CR**	
Islamic Bank finances purchase of asset—Cash outflow	Balance sheet			Cash	$100
Islamic Bank A books a *Murabahah* financing asset for $120	Balance sheet	*Murabahah* financing	$120		
Islamic Bank A records unearned income of $20 on the sale	Balance sheet			Unearned income	$20
Customer B pays first installment of $40	Balance sheet	Cash	$40	*Murabahah* financing	$40
Islamic bank recognizes income of $6.667	Income statement	Unearned income	$6.667	Income	$6.667
Customer B pays second installment of $40	Balance sheet	Cash	$40	*Murabahah* financing	$40
Islamic Bank A recognizes income of $6.667	Income Statement	Unearned income	$6.667	Income	$6.667
Customer B pays third installment of $40	Balance sheet	Cash	$40	*Murabahah* financing	$40
Islamic Bank A recognizes income of $6.667	Income statement	Unearned income	$6.667	Income	$6.667

would have to initially reflect the sale and buyback of an asset; an Islamic bank would have to record the ownership of the asset in its balance sheet.

ACCOUNTING ENTRIES FOR A *BAI AL INAH* CONTRACT

Table 5.4 illustrates the accounting entries of a *bai al inah* sale. The entries for the repayment of the deferred price are similar to the illustration above and not repeated.

Once the deferred sales price is settled, its payment becomes a debt obligation on the customer and a financial asset for the Islamic bank. The financial asset is a set of receivables, which in this simple case are three monthly

TABLE 5.4 Accounting Entries for a *Bai Al Inah* Contract

Bai Al Inah Contract			
		Debit	Credit
Islamic Bank A purchases an asset for $100 in cash	Cash		$100
	Asset	$100	
Islamic Bank A sells asset to B for credit price of $120 and books a financing contract for $120	Asset		$100
	Inah financing	$120	
Islamic Bank A buys back the asset from B for spot price of $100; financing disbursed	Asset	$100	
	Cash		$100

cash payments of $40. In this illustration we have ignored the recognition of profit entries.

PRICING OF DEFERRED SALES UNDER *MURABAHAH, BBA, INAH,* AND *TAWARRUQ*

We examine some features of a credit sale or a deferred payment sale. The deferred payment sale is a component of the *bai al inah contract, tawarruq contract, murabahah contract, bai mu'ajjal contract (bai bithman ajil) contract*, and *commodity murabahah contract.*

Modes of Payment of Spot Price and Deferred Price

A sale of an asset with immediate transfer of ownership of an asset from seller to buyer with payment of purchase price in future is a credit sale and is an essential component of Islamic financial engineering. For our discussion we simply explore the payment of a deferred price where a Party B must pay $120 for an asset in 90 days. As in our example in *bai al inah*, Party A sells an asset to Party B, where the cost of the asset is $100; as this asset is sold on a deferred payment basis, the deferred price is $120. The profit thereby is $20.

Can Party B pay this deferred price in installments over 90 days? Remember the profit component of the sale price of $120 is $20, and the cost price is $100. Using banking terminology, $100 is the principal and $20 is the markup.

Can Party B pay this amount in installments of say $40 per month or after every 30 days, or can Party B pay the deferred price of $120 at the end of 90 days in what is referred to as a *balloon payment*?

The answer is yes to both questions. If Party B pays the sale price in installments, the mode is referred to as *bai bithman ajil*, which refers to a sale contract where the price is paid in installments. There is no *shariah* issue with that. Party B can also pay the $120 in lump sum at maturity depending on the payment terms agreed between both parties.

What is important to understand is that once Party B has entered into a purchase agreement with deferred payment, Party B has initiated a debt obligation on itself, and Party A has booked a receivable in its financial records. The payment of $120 is a liability on Party B, and is an asset for Party A.

How Is the Deferred Price Calculated?

We have not addressed the issue of how the deferred price of $120 is computed. It can be arbitrarily agreed on by both Parties A or B. Or it can be *benchmarked* to the deferred price of a related asset with matching tenor. This mechanism can be employed if the asset under question is a heavily traded commodity on an exchange. The deferred price can also be benchmarked against the rates of *riba* or *interest rates* on 90-day deposits or money market transactions or loans. This element of benchmarking does not in the eyes of scholars make the deferred sale a contract of a loan. Benchmarking the deferred price against interest rates is another enhancement in pricing mechanisms that the reader should understand has been acknowledged by *shariah* scholars.[2] Comparing *ribbh* or profit rates to interest rates on *ribah* does not change a sale contract into a loan contract and any student of law can verify this statement. The pricing of financial products is dealt with in detail in subsequent chapters.

Is Profit Mechanism Fixed or Floating?

This is also another issue of consideration, especially if the repayment period is extensive, for example, three years. Can an Islamic bank change the sale price after the contract is signed? The clear response on this is no. As such, using the terminology of Risk Management, the *inah* receivable is a fixed rate asset, and changes in prices and inflation expectations must be anticipated

[2]Ethica Institute of Islamic Finance (2013), *Ethica's Handbook of Islamic Finance (2013 Edition)*. Dubai: Ethica Institute of Islamic Finance.

when computing the selling price, as once it is calculated and imputed it cannot be revised.

A fixed profit rate greatly limits the flexibility needed in pricing long-term financial assets. However, product developers have developed an ingenious method of allowing for a floating profit rate using the contract of *ibra* or discounts. Islamic Bank A enters into a contract where the bank purchases an asset on behalf of a customer and sells the same asset to the customer and expects a return of $120 in one year. The profit rate computed for simplicity purposes is therefore 20 percent and is to be paid every four months. The Islamic bank computes a maximum sale price of the asset, of $125. This price reflects a maximum possible return of 25 percent on the asset. The bank, however, intends to earn only 20 percent on the asset as its current cost of funds is only 15 percent (hypothetically speaking). The bank does not expect costs of funds to increase, and so offers a discount every quarter to the customer, such that total payments add up to $120. This is illustrated in Table 5.5.

However, if cost of funds increases to 17 percent, and in order to still earn a spread of 5 percent, the Islamic bank would have to charge a revised price of $122 on the asset. The price of $122 is within the ceiling price of $125, but the bank will adjust its quarterly discounts accordingly. This is illustrated in Table 5.6.

The Islamic bank will adjust the discounts offered every quarter to the customer so that the total selling price is revised to $122. With a return of 22 percent on the asset and facing an increased cost of funds of 17 percent, the Islamic bank continues to enjoy a spread of 5 percent on its assets.

This mechanism has helped product developers in Islamic banking engineer floating rate financial assets. This is critical to the survival of Islamic banking as, in this manner, Islamic banks can incorporate changes in cost of funds into their assets.

TABLE 5.5 Mechanism of *Ibra* (1)

Maximum Selling Price	125	Discount Offered (%)	Prevailing Profit Rate	In $	Actual Installment Paid
Equal monthly installment	31.25				
Installment 1 due	31.25	4.70	20.3%	1.47	29.78
Installment 2 due	31.25	3.65	21.35%	1.14	30.11
Installment 3 due	31.25	3.65	21.35%	1.14	30.11
Installment 4 due	31.25	4.00	21%	1.25	30.00
Total receipts	125.00			3.75	120.00

TABLE 5.6 Mechanism of *Ibra* (2)

Maximum Selling Price	125	Discount Offered (%)	Prevailing Profit Rate	In $	Actual Installment Paid
Equal monthly installment	31.25				
Installment 1 due	31.25	2.70	22.3%	0.84	30.41
Installment 2 due	31.25	1.65	23.35%	0.52	30.73
Installment 3 due	31.25	2.65	22.35%	0.83	30.42
Installment 4 due	31.25	2.61	22.39%	0.82	30.43
Total receipts	125.00			2.19	122.00

Discounting Receivable of a *Murabahah* Financing Contract

Adhering to our original example, Party A is owed a receivable of $120 from Party B to be paid in 90 days. Can Party A approach Party C and sell this receivable to another party at discount, at par, or at a profit? From the point of view of the scholars, once Party B has signed a purchase agreement to buy the asset for $120 on a deferred payment basis, this amount becomes a debt *due* on Party B, and becomes a *financial asset* or *a debt owed* to Party A. As the receivable is a debt, as per the current legality pertaining to sale of debt, the debt can only be sold at par.[3] It means that if Party A wishes after the second installment to recover as much money as possible to invest in another transaction and Party B owes Party A another $80, Party A can only sell this debt to a third party such as Party C for $80. This gives Party C no incentive to take over this debt. If Party C could *buy this debt* at a discount for say $75, and then recover $80 from Party B, then Party C would have an incentive to take over the debt at a discount.

Once a buyer enters into a deferred payment *murbahah* contract with a seller, the purchase price owed to the seller becomes a debt and thereby a financial asset. Conventional banking has developed tools of packaging such receivables, also known as *collateralized debt obligations* (**CDOs**), and then selling these receivables at a discount to a third party. This would be from a *shariah* point of view a contract of the sale of debt or *bai ul dayn*. From the point of view of the majority of *shariah* scholars, in Islam, debt can only be sold at par, not at discount or at a premium.[4] This calls into question the

[3]Usmani, Taqi Muhammad. (2005), *An Introduction to Islamic Finance*. New Delhi: Idara Isha'at-e-Diniyat (P) Ltd.

[4]This is also the condition set by the Maliki *madhab* pertaining to the legality of sale of debts.

ability of Islamic banks to discount the receivables owed to them in their *murabahah* financing portfolio to a third party.

The subject of *bai ul dayn* is discussed separately.

Can Collateral Be Taken by the Seller?

Can Party A obtain any assurance from Party B that he or she will fulfill the required payments made in the future? Party B can offer his or her personal guarantees for payment of the deferred price, or can also offer an additional asset to be placed with Party A of equivalent value as collateral under the contract of *rahn*. In the event that Party B fails to make payments on the deferred payment cycle and defaults, Party A can liquidate the collateral and only recover the amount of the sale price due to him or her.

Party B can also obtain a third-party guarantee from a third party, whereby the guarantor in this case will pay any unpaid balances to Party A in case Party B defaults on his or her payments. This can be done using the contract of *kafalah*. The contracts of *kafalah, ibra*, and *rahn* are acceptable by Islamic law and are dealt with in detail in subsequent chapters.

RISK TREATMENT OF DEFERRED PAYMENT SALES

As this is a credit-based sale, all the technical tools of credit analyses are applied in screening customer's requests for financing. This includes analyses of repayment capacity, capital, credibility, existing facilities, feasibility of business projections, certainty of future cash flows, and value of collateral among other things.

Credit Analysis and Credit Risk

An Islamic bank does take on the credit risk associated with a customer defaulting on payments, and therefore must develop a risk management strategy to deal with the risks and to price these risks accordingly. Deferred sale–based contracts involving *BBA, inah, tawarruq*, and *murabahah* all expose a seller to credit risk on the buyer. The seller (in our case an Islamic bank) transfers ownership of an asset to a buyer (a customer) for a credit price that is to be paid in the future. If the customer defaults on the payments, the Islamic bank cannot repossess the asset as all rights of ownership are surrendered at the time of contract initiation.

The Islamic bank would only have recourse to liquidate collateral obtained from the customer to recover any overdue amounts. A detailed analysis of credit risk is offered on the chapter on risk management.

Risk-Weightage Charges and Expected Losses

Islamic banks in the developed markets of Malaysia and the GCC comply with Basel rules and treat assets booked under deferred payment sale according the rules applied to collateralized loans.[5] *Bai al inah*–based sales, *Murabahah*-based sales, or *tawarruq*-based sales are all assigned risk weightages using the formulas provided below.

$$\text{Risk Weightage} = \text{Probability of Default} * \text{Exposure at Given Default} * \text{Loss Rate Given Default} * \text{Tenor}^{6}$$

where probability of default offers a quantitative measure of the risks associated with a financing contract. This measure is calculated using historical data.

We can offer a simple illustration of this concept using an example. Table 5.7 offers data on the number of car loans extended in a community by an Islamic bank. It segregates loan categories into different brackets, with Bracket 1 being good-quality loans extended to individuals with high creditworthiness and 5 being poor-quality loans extended to individual with low creditworthiness.

An Islamic bank extends 30,000 Tier 1 loans to customers, of which it is found that 1,000 defaulted. Therefore, the probability that a Tier 1 borrower will default is only 3.33 percent. The probability of default for Tier 5 borrowers, on the other hand, is 9 percent. The column for current outstanding amounts is referred to as *exposure at given default* and simply refers to the outstanding amount due at default.

Loss rate given default (LRGD) is calculated as (EAGD – value of collateral)/EAGD, and adjusts the exposure on the basis of any amount recoverable by liquidation of collateral.

Expected loss (EL) is calculated as probability of default × EAGD × LRGD. For the Tier 2 portfolio of car loans the bank should maintain reserves of $4,200,000, and of $4,050,000 for Tier 4 loans, and $900,000 for Tier 5 loans. The bank need not maintain reserves for Tier 1 loans and Tier 3 loans as the recoverable amount from sale of collateral exceeds the financing amount outstanding.

The risk weightage of a *deferred payment* contract is higher the longer the tenor of the deferred payment and the lower the value of the collateral

[5]IB2002 Risk Management of Islamic Financial Institutions module book (INCEIF, 2013).

[6]Capital Adequacy Framework (Basel II—Risk-Weighted Assets).

TABLE 5.7 Data on Car Loans Extended by an Islamic Bank

	Number of Loans Extended in 2005	Number of Loans Defaulted	Probabilty of Default (%)	Average Loan Size	Original Loan Disbursed	Current Outstanding (EAGD)	Current Market Value of Collateral/Cars	Loss Rate Given Default (%)	Number of Years until Maturity	Expected Loss
1	30,000	1,000	3.33	40,000	1,200,000,000	720,000,000	960,000,000	−33	6	(8,000,000)
2	20,000	1,200	6.00	35,000	700,000,000	420,000,000	350,000,000	17	4	4,200,000
3	15,000	1,300	8.67	30,000	450,000,000	270,000,000	315,000,000	−17	5	(3,900,000)
4	10,000	900	9.00	15,000	150,000,000	90,000,000	45,000,000	50	3	4,050,000
5	5,000	450	9.00	10,000	50,000,000	30,000,000	20,000,000	33	2	900,000

offered. It is also a function of the credit risk profile of the customer or party that is obligated to make the deferred payment. All deferred payment sales contracts expose the seller to credit risk, which is calculated using the earlier formula.

Each class of auto loans can be assigned a risk weightage based on its respective probability of defaults, EAGD, LRGD, and tenor.

$$\text{Risk Weightage} = \text{Probability of Default} * \text{Exposure at Given Default} \\ * \text{Loss Rate Given Default} * \text{Tenor}$$

A detailed discussion on risk is provided in later chapters.

Risk Concentration

The *murabahah* contract lends itself easily to a bank's function of credit financing as it is a debt-based sale contract. The imperfections in its application lie in the fact that Islamic banks do not truly own the assets they sell on deferred basis. Given the scale of modern economies and their components, one can well question that to place both business risk and financial risk on one business entity would be burdensome. After all, in the Toyota Financial Services Model, we discover that although Toyota is in the business of manufacturing cars, not financing their purchase, revenues from financing purchases of cars exceeds the revenues from mere sales. Dividing the risk of doing business and the risk of financing purchases may be a more equitable approach to dividing risk among the various components of an economy, and greatly justifies the role of financial intermediaries.

This argument also then leads to justifying the enhancements or modifications made to the *murabahah* contract to facilitate Islamic banking. A consequence, however, is the easy flow of credit and a society addicted to debt. Here we may add that the ratios of leverage we witness in today's economies by governments, corporations, and households are unjustified and unhealthy for any society. Islam may permit debt, but discourages a reliance on it. Today's businesses run more on debt than shareholders' capital, many governments are running on debt and repaying debt by incurring more debt, and households are addicted to debt as well. Debt is then further securitized and sold to a third party, absolving the originator of loans from any prudent screening of loans, as was the case in the subprime mortgages scandal.

As can be witnessed on most Islamic banks' balance sheets, there is a predominant exposure to *murbahah*-based assets and therefore to credit-based financing. This exposure is further aggravated by a considerable percentage of this exposure being in the areas of consumer financing. Home purchases and vehicle purchases dominate the *murbahah*-based financing, leading one to believe that Islamic Banks are following the same paths set out by conventional banks.

FIXED INCOME PORTFOLIO

For any Islamic bank, its portfolio of *murabahah financing* or *BBA financing* is considered a fixed income portfolio as the profit payments are predetermined within the purchase price. The schedule of payments is also predetermined. The purchase price may incorporate a floating price mechanism as discussed earlier or it may incorporate a fixed profit rate mechanism. This is deemed as a secured portfolio as Islamic banks usually obtain sufficient collateral from their customers to cover their exposure and usually the asset purchased under these contracts is placed under lien, mortgage, pledge, or hypothecation with the Islamic bank.

Figure 5.1 shows the cash flows experienced by an Islamic Bank, financing the purchase of a $100,000 house for 10 payment periods. The customer agrees to pay a repurchase price of $150,000, with a $5,000 profit payment every payment period, and settling the facility with full repayment of the $100,000. The bank ends up with $150,000 in cash after 10 payment periods. Each payment period may be a 3-, 6-, or 12-month period, depending on the contract periods.

Figure 5.2 shows the same facility but with a slightly different repayment schedule where the customer repays an equal installment every payment period, which includes a partial principal repayment and partial profit payment.

Initial cash outflow	CF0	−100,000
subsequent cash inflows	CF1	5,000
	CF2	5,000
	CF3	5,000
	CF4	5,000
	CF5	5,000
	CF6	5,000
	CF7	5,000
	CF8	5,000
	CF9	5,000
	CF10	5,000
	CF10	100,000
	TOTAL	150,000

−100,000	5,000	5,000	5,000	5,000	5,000	5,000	5,000	5,000	5,000	105,000
0	1	2	3	4	5	6	7	8	9	10

FIGURE 5.1 Repayment Period for a Loan

			Profit	Principal
Initial cash outflow	CF0	−100,000		
subsequent cash inflows	CF1	15,000	5,000	10,000
	CF2	15,000	5,000	10,000
	CF3	15,000	5,000	10,000
	CF4	15,000	5,000	10,000
	CF5	15,000	5,000	10,000
	CF6	15,000	5,000	10,000
	CF7	15,000	5,000	10,000
	CF8	15,000	5,000	10,000
	CF9	15,000	5,000	10,000
	CF10	15,000	5,000	10,000
	TOTAL	150,000		

−100,000	15,000	15,000	15,000	15,000	15,000	15,000	15,000	15,000	15,000	15,000
0	1	2	3	4	5	6	7	8	9	10

FIGURE 5.2 Repayment Period for a Loan with Equal Installments

Conventional banks are able to strip the profit payments from the principal payments and sell them at discounts to other banks. As this would involve selling debt, Islamic banks are to date not allowed to avail themselves of this facility.

If an Islamic bank is able to book 10,000 houses with financing contracts of \$100,000 each, it would have receivables of \$1,500,000,000 over 10 years, a considerable portfolio with long-term exposure to the housing market. As long as the value of the collateral remains at \$100,000 per house, the Islamic bank is safe from risk of nonrecovery.

CONCLUSION

The reader must walk away with some key deliverables. One major point is that *shariah* scholars recognize a deferred credit price, or a receivable, as an asset. Second, *shariah* scholars allow Islamic banks to record income against payments received on receivables while part of the receivable remains outstanding. These two accounting treatments for payments are crucial to the business of conventional banking and lending. A deferred credit price is treated for credit risk in much the same manner as an outstanding loan and thereby a credit price "behaves" in the same manner as a loan. Collateral can be secured by the seller for extending a credit "facility" and, in some jurisdictions, receivables linked to the payment of a deferred price can be sold to a third party at a discount. This allows for credit sale origination and disposal (or *securitization*).

CHAPTER 6

Bai al Wafa

Bai al wafa is a transaction of sale and buyback, where the prices in both sale contracts are the same and payment is made on spot. The *Majelle* defines this contract as "a sale of asset with the condition that if the seller pays back the price of the asset, the buyer shall return the asset to the seller."[1] A *bai al wafa* contract must follow all the requirements of a sale contract as discussed in previous chapters. There must be the existence of two parties that have the legal capacity to contract, there must be a subject matter of sale in existence at the time of the transaction, there must be an offer to sell the asset at a spot price, and there must be an offer to buy the asset at the spot price.

The *bai al wafa* process flow is illustrated in Figure 6.1.

Party A sells the asset to Party B for a spot price of $100,000. The ownership of the asset is transferred to Party B, but this ownership is somewhat restricted. Party B can enjoy the usufruct of the asset, place it as *rahn* to a third party to obtain financing, or simply keep the asset in custody. Party B pays Party A the purchase price of the asset, $100,000.

At some point in the future, Party A pays Party B $100,000 and buys the asset back from Party B. Party B is required to return the asset to Party A and recover the purchase price of $100,000. Party B is unable to charge a premium from Party A as this would then be tantamount to *riba*. The limitation on this contract that the two purchase prices must be equal limits the usage of this contract in treasury repo contracts.

A *shariah* issue here is with all sale and buyback agreements, which is the inter-conditionality of two or more sale contracts. The first sale cannot be made on the condition of the second sale. There can be no express intent when contracting that the original sale is conditional on the buyback. It is

[1] *The Majelle: Being an English Translation of Majallah al-Ahkam-l-Adliye and a Complete Code of Islamic Civil Law*, translated by C.R. Tyser, D.G. Demetriades, Ismail Haqqi Effendi, article 18 (Kuala Lumpur: The Other Press, 2003).

FIGURE 6.1 *Bai al Wafa* Process Flow

permissible to contract the first sale as a spot transaction with a promise or undertaking to enter into the second sale at a specified time in the future. This latter transaction would be a forward sale. The two parties can enter into both contracts at the same time, the spot sale and the future sale contract, but the second sale cannot be conditional on the first sale.

FINANCIAL ASSETS AS SUBJECT OF SALE

A version of *bai al wafa* is used in conventional repo transactions, where banks sell equities or bonds to other banks at a discount and then buy them back at market price at a specified time in the future. Any dividends or coupon payments, however, are payable to the original seller. Any difference between the discount purchase in the first sale and the repurchase at market prices is referred to as the *repo rate*. The conventional concept allows for there to be a price differentiation between the two sales, whereas *bai al wafa* would not allow for such treatment.

BAI AL WAFA AND SALE OF EQUITIES

Financial assets may be the subject of *bai al wafa*. Party A may sell, for instance, 10,000 shares in company XYZ to Party B for, say, $100,000, with the understanding that Party A will buy back the 10,000 shares at $100,000 in 30 days. The motivation for Party B may be too cover a short-sale position, or to place the shares as collateral in another transaction. Party B may also sell the shares to Party C as long as Party B is able to furnish Party A with 10,000 shares of XYZ in 30 days.

BAI AL WAFA AND SALE OF *SUKUK*

Party A may sell 10,000 *sukuk* to Party B with the understanding that Party A will buy back instruments in 30 days for the same price. These *sukuk* have a rating of AAA and a maturity of 10 years with a coupon rate of 4 percent. Party B may sell these assets to Party C. Party B will then be bound to furnish Party A with AAA-rated Islamic bonds, with a maturity of 10 years and a coupon rate of 4 percent, that is, bonds with similar features, not the exact same instruments Party A originally sold to Party B. The issuer of these instruments may be another entity, or even the same entity.

CONCLUSION

Within the scope of financial assets the applications of *bai al wafa* are very broad and possibly largely unexplored. A major reason for this is that with considerable intellectual work being done on Islamic finance in Malaysia, which predominantly follows the Shafi school, the contract of *bai al wafa* is recognized to be valid by the Hanafi school only.[2]

In a country like the United States where there are trillions of dollars of U.S. Treasury bills in circulation, Parties A and B can transact in various series of U.S. Treasury bills. However, obviously the financial asset that can be transacted in *bai al wafa* cannot be an interest-based asset.

[2]See Dr. Mohd Daud Bakar's article on "*Contracts in Islamic Commercial and Their Application in Modern Islamic Financial System,*" n.d., also *The Majelle*, article 58–59.

CHAPTER 7

Salaam and *Istisna*

Deferred Delivery Sale

The contracts of *salaam* and *istisna* are sale-based contracts between two or more parties that involve the sale of an asset that does not exist at the time the contract is negotiated. It is a sale contract for goods either that are not in the possession of the seller but are available from another vendor, or that need to be either grown or manufactured. If the reader recalls, the Prophet ([saw] peace be upon him) laid restrictions on sale contracts requiring the seller to own an asset before selling it to a third party. In general, therefore, the Prophet (saw) laid restrictions on future sales or spot sale of goods not in the possession of the seller. The Prophet ([saw] peace be upon him), however, offered exceptions to this rule for agricultural goods, and goods that by their very nature are made to order.[1]

Although *salaam* and *istisna* contracts are similar to each other, we deal with them separately.

SALAAM

The contract of *salaam* requires all of the conditions of a normal sale contract except that it does not require the existence of the asset or good at the time of the creation of the contract. A seller wishing to sell an asset that is not in the sellers' possession would enter into a *salaam* contract with a buyer. The buyer would pay in full the negotiated purchase price of the asset on spot, and the seller would contract to deliver the said asset at a specific date to the buyer at a specific location in the future. The performance of this act

[1]This is based on the *hadith* narrated by Ibn Abbas (mAbpwt), which states that the Prophet (saw) had said to the people in Medina, "Whoever pays in advance the price of a thing (fruits or grains) to be delivered later should pay for it for a specified measure at specified weight for a specified period." See M. Muhsin Khan, *Sahih-al-Bukhari* 3 (book 35, no. 2240).

becomes an obligation on the seller, and the seller is indebted to the buyer to deliver the goods as the seller has already received the purchase price of the asset in question. To ensure the seller performs as required by the contract terms, the buyer can in fact obtain collateral from the seller in the shape of another asset under the contract of *rahn*. As in effect the buyer makes a payment in advance to the seller, and awaits for delivery in the future, the buyer in essence finances the seller in acquiring the goods and is exposed to performance risk. Therefore, the negotiated price in a *salaam* contract is typically lower than the spot market price of an asset.

To summarize, payment is made in full at the time of contract initiation and delivery of the asset is made on a deferred basis. The good or asset is defined in terms of quality, quantity weight, and so on, and is agreed on between the seller and the buyer at the time of contract initiation. What is important to understand is that the seller is bound to deliver the asset as per the terms and conditions of the contract on delivery date. The seller is not required to manufacture the good with the proceeds of the purchase price, or source the asset immediately, either. The seller may use the proceeds of the purchase price to engage in any other economic activity, and hedge in a purchase price for the asset with a third party using various forward sale contracts. The seller would then have to ensure sufficient liquidity to purchase the asset from the third party and make delivery to the buyer on the delivery date.

The traditional usage of *salaam* was in the agricultural sector. Farmers unsure of market prices of their harvest would lock in the purchase price of their harvest with a grain or rice buyer. The buyer would also lock in a purchase price for the harvest and at the same time have guaranteed delivery of the asset by the seller at a stipulated time.

The case for *salaam* can be illustrated using an example. A grain buyer wishes to purchase 100 tons of grain from a farmer, 90 days from today. Assuming the current price of grain is $30,000 per ton, the spot price for 100 tons is therefore $3,000,000. The buyer expects grain prices to increase as harvest season comes to a close and negotiates with a farmer for 100 tons of grain at a price of $29,000 per ton. The farmer agrees to this discount price as the farmer will use the sum of $2,900,000 to finance the production of 100 tons of grain. The $1,000 per ton less that the farmer is receiving for his produce is considered as cost of financing the crop.

At contract initiation, the buyer pays the farmer $2,900,000 and the farmer agrees to deliver 100 tons of grain in 90 days. The buyer can also demand certain collateral from the farmer to ensure that the farmer performs his side of the contract. This collateral can even be the farmer's land, machinery, or any other asset. If all goes well, and the farmer performs his side of the contract, the product will be delivered to the buyer in 90 days as scheduled. If the farmer fails to deliver the asset on time, this will be considered a default of the contract terms and the buyer may seize the collateral obtained to recover losses.

Assuming all goes well and the 100 tons of grain is delivered on schedule, the grain buyer can either hold onto the inventory or sell onward in the grain market. If prices of grain have indeed risen to say \$31,000 per ton, the grain merchant makes a tidy profit of \$2,000 per ton. If, however, grain prices have fallen to say \$28,000 per ton, the grain merchant will have a loss of \$1,000 per ton.

Accounting Treatment for *Salaam* Contract

To understand the accounting treatment for the *salaam* contract, we use the following illustration.

Parties to the contract are an Islamic Bank, Party A, and Party B. An Islamic Bank enters into a *parallel salaam* contract with Party B to sell 10,000 tons of rice to B for a price of \$980 per ton. Party B makes full payment in advance to the Islamic Bank for the commodity. As the Islamic Bank is not in the trade of producing rice, the Islamic bank contracts with Party A to purchase 10,000 tons of rice at a discount price of \$950 per ton. The Islamic Bank makes full payment to A in advance. A, on the other hand, contracts to deliver the rice in 90 days.

The spot market price of 10,000 tons of rice is \$10,000,000 at \$1,000 per ton. As mentioned before, *salaam* price is usually lower than the market price, hence let us assume that it is priced at \$9,500,000 and the *parallel salaam* price would be \$9,800,000. *Parallel salaam* is a contract where one party, ABC, receives a purchase orderer from another party, XYZ, for a good, the processing of which is then negotiated with yet a third party, DEF. Parties ABC and DEF are said to be in a *parallel salaam* contract, whereas ABC and XYZ are in a *salaam contract*.

To go back to our example, the Islamic Bank will make a profit of \$300,000 on this transaction. Party B takes performance risk on the Islamic bank, and the Islamic Bank takes performance risk on Party A.

The accounting entries are as shown in Table 7.1.

Can the Buyer Sell the Asset before Delivery to a Third Party?

An issue to address is whether the grain merchant can actually contract to sell the grain to a third party at a profitable price before actually receiving

TABLE 7.1 Accounting for *Salaam* Contract

	Debit		Credit	
Bank receives *salaam* price from B	Cash	9,800,000	*Salaam* liability	9,800,000
Bank enters into parallel *salaam* with A, pays parallel *salaam* price	//*Salaam* financing	9,500,000	Cash	9,500,000
Party A delivers 10000 tons of rice = commodity and retires obligation under parallel *salaam* contract with bank	Commodity	9,500,000	//*Salaam* financing	9,500,000
Bank sells commodity to B and retires its liability of *salaam* with B	*Salaam* liability	9,800,000	Commodity	9,500,000
Bank records income up front of 300,000			Income	300,000

delivery of the grain. This would be in effect selling an asset again without having ownership of it.[2]

An interesting approach to this contract is that of entering into a *salaam* first and then a parallel *salaam* contract. In essence, a grain merchant would first enter into a deferred delivery sale contract of *salaam* with a third party to deliver 100 tons of grain at $31 per ton in 90 days. After securing this contract the grain merchant would then enter into a *salaam* contract with a farmer to deliver 100 tons of grain at a purchase price of $29 per ton. The third party would pay the merchant in full and the merchant would pay the farmer in full. The third party would have exposure on the merchant and the merchant would have exposure on the farmer.

Default Scenarios

Either counterparty may default on their side of the contract, either willingly or unwillingly. If weather conditions are such that the farmer's crop is

[2]In *salaam*, selling the asset before delivery is generally not permissible under all *mazhabs*, with the base of ruling from a *hadith* where the Prophet (saw) stated, "Whoever buys foodstuff, he should not sell it until he has taken possession of them." —Sahih Muslim, *hadith* no. 2808.

destroyed partially or in full, the farmer will default on delivery of the grain. The merchant will in turn default on any other commitments entered into.

However, if market prices of grain increase to say $40 per ton, the farmer may be tempted to willingly default on delivery to the grain merchant and even pay the merchant back $2,900,000 and sell the 100 tons of grain in the market for $40 per ton for $4,000,000. In such a situation of rising market prices, the farmer or seller has an incentive to default on the contract in order to obtain a higher purchase price from the regular market.

Additionally, if market prices fall to $23 per ton, the grain merchant would have an incentive to not take the delivery from the farmer, but as the merchant has already paid the purchase price for the produce, there is little chance that the buyer would default on taking delivery of the asset. The modern futures exchanges circumvent such possibilities in forward sales by the mechanism of maintaining margin accounts from both parties to a contract.

The *salaam* contract possibly is the least explored contract in terms of its applications to the development of financial markets, but the author is quite certain that in the Islamic economy of the Ottoman Empire, it must have served as a common hedging tool for purchases of grain, rice, and wheat in the bazaars across the vast expanses of the Empire.

Payment of Partial Purchase Price

The current version of the contract requires the buyer to pay the purchase price in full to the seller. If this condition could be "waived" and the buyer could negotiate with the seller with only partial payment of the purchase price, the *salaam* contract would closely resemble a purchase on margin contract. In the context of the above, where a grain merchant contracts with a farmer to sell 100 tons of grain at the price of $29, the grain merchant may only pay say 10 percent of the purchase price, which would only be $290,000, thereby freeing up capital to invest in other endeavors. The buyer would then have to pay the balance of the purchase price of the asset on delivery. With payment of partial purchase price another variant of the product could be developed if the buyer would be able to sell the asset to a third party prior to taking delivery of the asset.

Types of Assets

The traditional models of *salaam* contracts were applied to agricultural products; however, the concept can also be applied to financial assets such as equities. In such a scenario, Party B would purchase, for instance, 10,000 shares of a company such as IBM at a discount if the seller contracts to deliver the actual stocks within 30 days. If the current market price for IBM stock is $100, a *salaam* buyer may negotiate a price of $99 with a seller, giving the seller 30 days to utilize the purchase price paid of $990,000 for 30 days. In those 30 days the seller may invest the money at the market risk free rate for a nominal return, and purchase stock options in IBM for 10,000 shares at a price equal to or lower than $99. The seller must be in a position to transfer title in 10,000 shares in IBM to the buyer within the stipulated time.

This application of the *salaam* contract could open up the door to new products within the Islamic capital markets. We refer the reader to a paper on "Reverse Salaam" authored by Professor Yusuf Saleem, Mohammad Ghaith Mahaini, and Hussain Kureshi, published in *International Shariah Research Academy Journal*, June 2014.

ISTISNA

The contract of *istisna* behaves similarly to the contract of *salaam* with two major differences: the contract of *istisna* is typically applied to made-to-order industrial goods,[3] and the purchase price need not be paid in full at the time of contract initiation. The contract of *istisna* is applied to such goods as airplanes, ships, made-to-order luxury goods like cars or yachts, and housing. We can best explain the contract flow by looking at an example.

We shall explain the contract using a simple example. XYZ Airlines wishes to purchase an aircraft from Airbus but does not want to take performance risk on the airline. XYZ Airlines wishes to engage a financial intermediary to take on the performance risk. ABC Islamic Bank agrees and contracts with Airbus to purchase an aircraft on deferred delivery basis with payments made in installments. The Islamic Bank then sells the aircraft to the airline at a profit. Thus, ABC enters into a *parallel istisna* with XYZ to sell an aircraft in two years for a price of $130,000,000. The purchase price is paid in 8 quarterly payments of $16,250,000 each. ABC contracts via an *istisna* contract to purchase the aircraft from Airbus for $100,000,000 paid in 8 quarterly payments of $12,500,000. The difference in the two prices is the bank's reward for taking on the performance risk of Airbus. If Airbus fails to deliver the said aircraft within two years or the stipulated time, ABC

[3]The classical *istisna*, which involves two parties: the buyer and the manufacturer. See International Shariah Research Academy (ISRA) (2012). "Islamic Financial System: Principles and Operations," 2012.

Islamic bank will have to compensate the airline by providing an alternative aircraft or by paying financial damages. It is crucial to understand that the airline is contracting with the bank for the delivery of the aircraft and not the aircraft manufacturer. Another variant of this product will involve a sale price of $130,000,000, which can be paid in installments that may continue even after the plane is delivered.

In our simple illustration, however, XYZ Airlines wishes to buy an A380 from Airbus. The cost price of one A380 is, for instance, $100,000,000. XYZ Airlines wishes to wholly finance the purchase of the aircraft with the help of an Islamic bank. ABC Islamic Bank offers to enter first into an *istisna* contract with XYZ to sell the aircraft for $130,000,000 with delivery promised in two years. ABC agrees to the terms and promises to pay $16,250,000 every three months to ABC Bank. ABC Bank will then enter into a parallel *istisna* contract with Airbus and contract to purchase one A380 for $100,000,000 from the aircraft manufacturer with the purchase price paid as different phases of the project are completed. ABC's payments to Airbus would match the payments received from XYZ. ABC will ensure that the construction of the aircraft will be completed in stages, where each stage will comprise a time span of three months. Airbus will provide proof of the same to the Islamic bank and the Islamic bank will furnish the same proof of partial completion to XYZ before receiving payment from XYZ. This would become a *phased payment plan*, based on the partial completion method.

If all goes well, Airbus will hand over the aircraft to ABC in two years, at which point it will receive its last installment of the $100,000,000 purchase price or parallel *istisna price* and ABC Bank will deliver the aircraft to XYZ Airlines and receive its last installment of the $130,000,000 owed to the bank. Any delays in delivery of the aircraft would create complications that may affect the terms and conditions of the final installment payment and any penalties.

What is important to understand here is that ABC Bank is not financing the purchase of the aircraft, but in fact is the first buyer of the aircraft and then the seller of the aircraft to XYZ Airlines for a profit. As in *murabahah* it is unlikely that the title of the aircraft is ever transferred to the ownership of ABC Bank, and in effect the partially completed aircraft never leaves its hanger until XYZ Airlines takes direct delivery itself. The transaction cost of actually taking ownership title of the bank would greatly affect the purchase price paid by XYZ Airlines.

The net arrangement of combining a parallel *istisna* with an *istisna* contract behaves like a *murabahah* contract where an asset is purchased from one party at cost and then sold to a third party at a profit.

However, ABC Bank has taken exposure on Airbus, and can demand some kind of collateral from the manufacturer to ensure it does not default on its delivery date. This could take the shape of a performance guarantee or *kafalah*.

The contract of *istisna* lends itself very easily to contracts of real estate development, manufacturing of luxury yachts, ships, and a host of other circumstances.

Accounting Treatment for *Istisna*

Let us see the following example to understand the accounting treatment for *istisna*. Assuming the spot market price of one airplane (available for delivery on spot) is $100,000,000, the *istisna* price negotiated between the Islamic bank and B Airline is $98,000,000 and parallel *istisna* between the Islamic bank and Airbus is priced at $95,000,000. The Islamic bank purchases an aircraft for $95,000,000 from Airbus and sells it to XYZ Airlines for $98,000,000. Payment is to be made in three years with the last installments paid upon delivery of the asset.

As we can see in the illustration, there are three phases involved in this *istisna* and parallel *istisna*. The first phase is on the initiation of the contracts where the bank books a receivable of $32,666,666.67 against Airline XYZ and pays cash of $31,666,666,667 to Airbus to begin construction of the airplane. At the end of the first period when the manufacturer retires one-third of the manufacturing project, the bank will bill Airline XYZ for Phase 1, and receive cash from Airline XYZ of $32,666,667. In this manner, the bank finances the construction of each phase of the aircraft (Table 7.2).

At the conclusion of this contract, Airline XYZ will receive the aircraft for a payment of $98,000,000, the bank will earn an income of $3,000,000 over three years, and Airbus will receive its price of $95,000,000.

In contracts of *istisna*, the bank can bill its client as each phase of production is concluded or defer the billing to a time even beyond the completion of the entire project, allowing Airline XYZ time to put the plane to work and begin earning revenues. The receivables against XYZ will therefore continue into financial periods beyond the manufacturing of the airplane.

In this manner the *istisna* contract incorporates performance risk and credit risk.

CONCLUSION

Both the contracts of *salaam* and *istisna* offer interesting opportunities in agricultural finance and in financing real estate developments and unique

TABLE 7.2 Accounting for *Istisna* Contract (1)

	Price of 1 Airplane	100,000,000		
	Parallel Istisna Price	98,000,000		
	Istisna Price	95,000,000		
	Profit	3,000,000		
	Debit		Credit	
PHASE I				
Bank ABC at beginning of contract, books receivable against XYZ	ISTISNA RECEIVABLE	32,666,666.67	ISTISNA LIABILITY	32,666,666.67
and contracts to deliver aircraft. ABC makes payment to Airbus				
and enters into // *salaam* with Airbus.	// ISTISNA FINANCING	31,666,666.67	CASH	31,666,666.67
Airbus delivers on Phase I of manufacturing project	PHASE I OF AIRPLANE	31,666,667	// ISTISNA FINANCING	31,666,667
and retires obligation under parallel *istisna* contract with Bank.				
Bank bills XYZ for the work done and receives payment in cash, thus records income as difference	CASH	32,666,667	ISTISNA RECEIVABLE	32,666,667
retiring the receivable against XYZ and records income.				
Bank bills B Airline for Phase I and retires Phase I liability.	ISTISNA LIABILITY	32,666,666.67	PHASE I OF AIRPLANE	31,666,667
Bank records income earned on Phase I of the project.			INCOME	1,000,000

(*continued*)

TABLE 7.2 (Continued)

	Debit		Credit	
PHASE II				
Bank ABC at beginning of contract, books receivable against XYZ	ISTISNA RECEIVABLE	32,666,666.67	ISTISNA LIABILITY	32,666,666.67
and contracts to deliver aircraft. ABC makes payment to Airbus				
and enters into // *salaam* with Airbus.	// ISTISNA FINANCING	31,666,666.67	CASH	31,666,666.67
Airbus delivers on Phase I of manufacturing project	PHASE II OF AIRPLANE	31,666,667	// ISTISNA FINANCING	31,666,667
and retires obligation under parallel istisna contract with Bank.				
Bank bills XYZ for the work done and receives payment in cash, thus records income as difference	CASH	32,666,667	ISTISNA RECEIVABLE	32,666,667
retiring the receivable against XYZ and records income.				
Bank bills B Airline for Phase I and retires Phase I liability.	ISTISNA LIABILITY	32,666,666.67	PHASE I OF AIRPLANE	31,666,667
Bank records income earned on Phase I of the project.			INCOME	1,000,000

PHASE III				
Bank ABC at beginning of contract, books receivable against XYZ	ISTISNA RECEIVABLE	32,666,666.67	ISTISNA LIABILITY	32,666,666.67
and contracts to deliver aircraft. ABC makes payment to Airbus				
and enters into // *salaam* with Airbus.	// ISTISNA FINANCING	31,666,666.67	CASH	31,666,666.67
Airbus delivers on Phase I of manufacturing project	PHASE III OF AIRPLANE	31,666,667	// ISTISNA FINANCING	31,666,667
and retires obligation under parallel istisna contract with Bank.				
Bank bills XYZ for the work done and receives payment in cash, thus records income as difference	CASH	32,666,667	ISTISNA RECEIVABLE	32,666,667
retiring the receivable against XYZ and records income.				
Bank bills B Airline for Phase I and retires Phase I liability.	ISTISNA LIABILITY	32,666,666.67	PHASE I OF AIRPLANE	31,666,667
Bank records income earned on Phase I of the project.			INCOME	1,000,000

industrial and consumer goods, but the contracts are rarely found on balance sheets. The concept of *salaam* in particular can be applied to capital markets products as a *salaam* contract can behave very much like a conventional discount bond if it is used to mobilize funds. Although *salaam* is theoretically envisioned to finance the production of goods, it can also be used to mobilize funds, the value of which is linked to a certain amount of commodity or asset to be delivered in the future. We would like to draw the attention of financial engineers to the possibilities offered by this product.

CHAPTER 8

Bai al Sarf

The contract of *bai al sarf* is to exchange a price for a price in the same or different currency, that is, an exchange in currency. A number of *shariah* scholars are of the opinion that *bai al sarf* can only be done between two of the same kind of medium of exchange such as gold with gold, but generally the majority of the *shariah* scholars in various jurisdictions feel the exchange could be between two different forms of mediums of exchange such as between gold and silver, and gold and dinar.

In the exchange of price for price in the form of currencies, Islam has put certain rules to limit the use of money strictly as a medium of exchange. The aim is to prevent the "pricing of money" and use of it as a form of commodity, as reflected in a *hadith* reported by Abu Sa'id al-Khudri, where the Prophet (saw) had said: "Gold for gold, silver for silver, wheat for wheat, barley for barley, dates for dates and salt for salt, should be exchanged like for like, equal for equal, and hand-to-hand. If the types of exchanged commodities are different then sell them as you wish, if they are exchanged on the basis of a hand-to-hand transaction."[1]

BASIC RULINGS ON *BAI AL SARF*

According to AAOIFI standards,[2] it is permissible to trade between currencies, provided that the following criteria are observed:

- Taking possession before leaving one another.

  It is prohibited that any parties leave without having the possession of the currency exchanged. This is due to the fact that should one or both parties leave each other before they possess the currency in question,

[1]Sahih Muslim, Book 10, *Hadith*, no. 3852.
[2]AAOIFI *Shariah* Standard no. 1, "Trading in Currencies."

this transaction becomes a form of a sale of debt. *Al kali bi al kali*, as one may put it, a sale of debt against debt, is strictly prohibited under *shariah* law.

- Equal for equal transaction.

  Quality of the currency is not taken into consideration. For example, the quality of the salt being exchanged does not matter. One kilogram of high-quality salt does not mean it can be exchanged directly into 2 kg of lower-quality salt. Should one wish to do so, they can go and sell the higher quality of salt for cash and then buy the lower quality of salt using the proceeds that he or she received from the first transaction. Quantity is the main consideration in *bai al sarf*.
- Freedom from conditions.

  Khiyar al shart is not to be placed into the contract of *bai al sarf*. No conditional option can be stipulated and imposed on any party to withdraw from the contract. *Khiyar al shart* also, in a way, prevents the complete transfer of ownership, hence it is prohibited.
- Nondeferment in the exchange of one of the currencies.

  Under *bai al sarf* the delivery of any of the currencies should not be done in deferment, else the contract is considered null and void. As mentioned in the previous ruling, both parties in the transactions have to take possession of the currency before leaving one another. This is related to the issue on the next ruling.
- Shall not be carried out on the forward or futures market.

  Bai al sarf has to be done on the spot. Transactions such as forwards, futures, options, and swaps has elements of deferments in the delivery and payment of the currency. This would lead to the emergence of *riba al nasi'ah*. This is the reason why, as enacted by the OIC (Organization of Islamic Countries) *fiqh* academy,[3] OIC *fiqh* academy prohibits conventional forward, options, and other kind of derivatives.

The application of *bai al sarf* concept is confined in a spot-based currency exchange, as seen in Figure 8.1. Spot forex transactions are generally permissible as even though the numbers may differ, both currencies have different intrinsic values and purchasing power.

Other uses of the concept of *bai al sarf* can be found in the contract of gold investment savings account. For instance, in Kuwait Finance House (KFH), the gold investment savings account would involve a process

[3]OIC Fiqh Academy, 7th session, 1992, www.fiqhacademy.org.

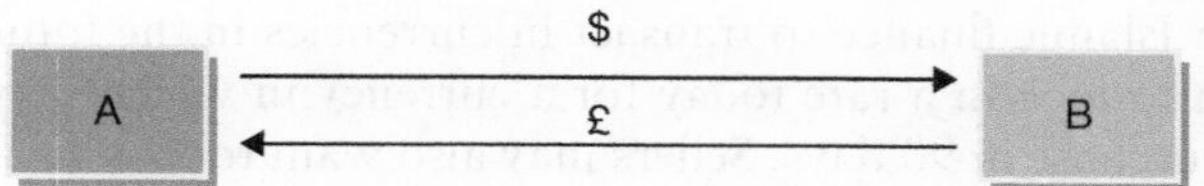

A sells USD 1000 in exchange for GBP 599 from B at spot exchange rate.

FIGURE 8.1 *Bai al Sarf*

whereby both parties, the institution and the client, would agree to a particular rate before the client is able to purchase gold and place the gold with KFH for safekeeping. Payment for the gold can be made by check, debit card, credit card, money transfer, or cash. All of these are considered as cash payment, even when the payment is made by using a credit card as the bank would receive the payment as a form of cash from the credit card issuing institution. Another example for the use of this concept is the *shariah*-compliant forex investment product.

What constitutes money nowadays? Can fiat/paper money be considered as well? For this issue, the OIC ruled that as long as the money is considered as a legal currency, then it comes under the rule of *bai al sarf*. Hence, even though in many cases it is used for hedging purposes that can benefit both parties involved in the transaction, it does not meet the ruling or the criteria for *bai al sarf*, especially in the use of forward contracts or other derivatives for hedging purposes, which means that there is a delay or deferment in any of the pillars of the contract. The solution that the market and *shariah* scholars come up with for this is the use of *wa'd* (unilateral promise) and *wa'dan* (two unilateral promises).

CONCLUSION

In the world of modern-day international trade, currency exchanges are an essential component of all transactions. The flow of goods from one part of the world to another has reached a scale never before seen in history. Today, goods can be manufactured in several countries with costs incurred in varying currencies and sold to buyers in a completely different set of countries with their own currencies. Each transaction requires an exchange of currency to accompany the exchange of goods. However, many buyers and sellers agree to the terms and conditions of their transactions in advance, with deliveries and payments being executed in the future. This requires the flexibility in Islamic finance to transact in currencies in the futures market. Buyers wish to lock in a rate today for a currency in which they may need to make a purchase in 90 days. Sellers may also want to lock in an exchange rate today to convert a payment received in 90 days into local currency. All of these needs require the industry to look at the possibilities of *wa'ad*-based transactions under which various currency hedging tools can be developed.

CHAPTER 9

Bai al Dayn

Bai al dayn is essentially a contract of the sale of debt. Being a contract of sale, there must be all the elements or pillars of a sales contract such as legitimacy of contracting parties, and offer and acceptance. Between the contracting parties there must be a subject matter of sale, a price, and delivery of the asset. The asset in this case, however, is a financial asset or a debt.

The Majelle defined *dayn* as a matter that is due, that is, the money owed by a certain debtor.[1] *Shariah* scholars have defined debt to include any moneys owed in a contract of *qard, murabahah, ijara, bai bithman ajil*, and many others.[2] Any basket of receivables owed by one party to another, whether they are generated by a deferred credit sale, a contract of rent, or a contract of loan, is considered to be debt.

Shariah allows the transfer of debt though what it is called the *assignment of debt* or *hawalah*. This trading of debt at par is allowed unanimously by all Islamic jurists as it does not give any benefit to the purchaser and is free of elements such as *riba, gharar*, and *maiser*.[3] It is considered that the *bai al dayn* purpose is genuine and it is in the benefit of the parties involved (*maslahah*).[4] The issue here is to sell the debt to a third party that is a nondebtor and on a discounted value. Depending on the underlying essence inside the debt, most *shariah* scholars are of the opinion that selling a money-based debt to a third party on a discounted basis is not accepted with the exception of Malaysia's *Shariah* Advisory Council.[5]

---

[1] *The Majelle*, Art no. 158.

[2] Al-Zuhaili, Wahbah, *Al-Fiqh al Islami wa Adillatuhu, Islamic Jurispudence and its Proof* (1989). *Dar al Wafa*.

[3] OIC Fiqh Academy, 16th meeting, 2002.

[4] Dr. Siddiq al-Dharir, *Al-Gharar wa Atharuhu fil Uqud* (Cairo: Thaqafa Press, 1967).

[5] The basis for this resolution can be observed in *Resolutions of the Securities Commission Shariah Advisory Council*, 2nd edition, by Securities Commission Malaysia, 2007.

In the contemporary practice, *bai al dayn* is used mainly for liquidity purposes and/or for the aim of capital gains resulting from the tradability of the debt certificates.

PURCHASE PRICE, RENTAL PAYMENTS, RECEIVABLES, AND DEBT

Such a pooling of all money payments as debt can be contentious as a credit price and a sequence of rental payments are part of two very different contracts that deal with the payment of money. Contracts of sale have different rights and obligations attached than contracts of lease. To illustrate our point we look carefully at a *mudharabah* sale contract where a total purchase price of $12,000 has to be paid on the first of every month. The timeline in Figure 9.1 illustrates the sequence of cash flows.

The purchase price installment is due on the first of every month, and not a day before that. If the payment becomes overdue on the first, the legal status of the payment is not that of the purchase price anymore but legally transforms from being a purchase price to that of a debt or a receivable.

The entire sequence of payments become due only on specific dates, even though ownership of the asset is transferred to the buyer. Upon contract initiation, is it fair to refer to the entire purchase price as legal debt? Is it still a purchase price, or can the same payment be a purchase price and a debt at the same time, or does it become debt when it is overdue? The issue to raise here is that the entire sequence of 12 payments are considered to be purchase price payments. Each becomes due on different dates. If the buyer is overdue on the first installment to be paid on January 1, all other 11 payments are not overdue as yet. The seller can only claim the first payment at this point. How can the seller distinguish the overdue payment on January 2 from all the subsequent payments due? Although all other 11 payments are due to the seller, they are not due at the same time and certainly not on January 2.

A test of this idea is that the seller can also in a court only rightfully claim the overdue payment on January 2 and not the other 11 payments.

$1,000	$1,000	$1,000	$1,000	$1,000	$1,000	$1,000	$1,000	$1,000	$1,000	$1,000	$1,000
1	2	3	4	5	6	7	8	9	10	11	12
1st Jan.	1st Feb	1st Mar	1st Apr	1st May	1st June	1st July	1st Aug	1st Sept	1st Oct	1st Nov	1st Dec

FIGURE 9.1 Purchase Price Payment Schedule

There is a legal distinction between the overdue payment and the other 11 payments due. We see the overdue payment only as debt and the remainder 11 payments as still purchase price and therefore contend that the rule on *bai al dayn* does not apply to selling the remaining portion of the purchase price.

RENTAL PAYMENTS DUE IN AN *IJARA* CONTRACT

Rental payments become due on a lessee on enjoying the usufruct of an asset. In a sale contract the ownership of the subject matter of the sale is transferred at contract initiation, and the entire purchase price becomes due on the seller. In a contract of rent, however, the lessee is not liable for the rental payments of the lease contract all at once; only on enjoyment of the usufruct of the leased asset does that particular interval's rental payment become due. We again propose that rent only becomes debt when it is overdue and that legally it should be treated differently.

We propose that purchase price and rental payments are not debt and therefore can be sold at a discount, at par, or at premium to a third party without violating any laws of the *shariah*.

FINANCIAL PRODUCTS

The sale of debt, or receivables, is an important concept in the world of conventional finance. Banks go through a meticulous process of developing portfolios of home mortgages, or car loans, and then sell them at a discount to another bank or entity. The bank or entity that purchases the debt is now entitled to all the installments to be paid by customers. Often customers are not even aware that their mortgages have been sold to another bank.

We can illustrate the concept of sale of debt with a simple example. Bank ABC develops a home mortgage portfolio of $500,000,000. What this means is that the bank disbursed an amount of say $250,000,000 to customers to finance the purchase of their houses, and the borrowers have to repay the bank $500,000,000 over a period of 25 years. In reality some part of the portfolio will be repaid early, other amounts will be due in 10 years, others in 15 years, and so on. The receivables of $500,000,000 will in fact also be packaged into smaller subsets. Each subset will be defined by the asset quality or the creditworthiness of the borrower.

Of the $500,000,000 outstanding receivables, $200M may be of AAA quality, $200M of BBB quality, and $100M of C quality. In any case Bank ABC will repackage its loan portfolio and sell it all to one bank or several banks for a discounted price of $450,000,000 and receive cash from the purchasing Bank DEF. Bank DEF will pay ABC $450,000,000 and will now be exposed to all the risks attached with the portfolio and all the returns. Bank DEF will therefore in fact recover $500M from all the home financiers as per their individual mortgage terms.

This process is seemingly harmless, but can prove to be epidemic, if Bank ABC is not meticulous in building up its portfolio and misrepresents the asset quality of the receivables to the purchasing bank. Bank ABC has an incentive to book bad loans, as it plans to sell them to a third party without giving them full disclosure of the borrowers' true creditworthiness. In fact, Bank ABC can repackage the loans in such a way that 10 loans of Class AAA are packaged with 5 loans of Class C to come up with 15 loans of Class BBB. By repackaging the bad loans with the good loans, Bank ABC can conceptually pass on an infected portfolio to another bank. If Bank ABC is a reputable, global bank, no one would question their motives. Such actions were the basis for causing the Global Financial Crises of 2008; a detailed discussion is beyond the scope of this work and the intelligence of the author.

SALE OF EQUITY

However, if Bank ABC developed a portfolio of home mortgages not under contracts of debt but under *musharakah mutanaqisah*, Bank ABC would actually have equity stake in all the houses purchased by their customers. Bank ABC could then in fact sell this same portfolio of $500M not as debt but as equity by transferring its equity claim to the houses in their portfolio to another bank. The sale of such a portfolio would also not stir the anguish of any *shariah* scholar as it would not be a sale of debt or *bai al dayn*.

OIC Fiqh academy allows the sale of debt on a discounted value and regarded this reduction of debt in light for the debtor to accelerate its repayment, *only* if this transaction occurs between the creditor and its debtor and as long as the creditor-debtor relationship remains bilateral.[6] AAOIFI also endorsed this practice, which is referred to as *da wa ta'ajjal.*[7] All in all, the question on the permissibility of debt exchange on a discount is on what type of transaction the debt was created. If it was created from a sale and purchase of commodity, which entails the debt to have a profit and principal portion, then it is allowed to be regarded as *mal* and traded at a discount. But if it is a debt that was created based purely on a money-to-money transaction, then it is regarded as a "currency," which means the trading of this kind of debt is only allowable at par, such as in an instance of *sukuk*, where

[6]OIC Fiqh Academy, 7th Session on installment sale, 1992.
[7]AAOIFI *Shariah Standard*, no. 16.

it is encouraged that the market should concentrate on issuing asset-backed *sukuk* where issues such as *ribawi* sale of monetary debt for cash money can be avoided[8] and the discounting practice would not be a problem as well.

CONCLUSION

The authors of this work disagree with the current interpretation of the concept of debt and subscribe to the meaning afforded by the *Mejelle*, where debt is defined as matter that is due. We feel that in a deferred payment sale contract, a sale price only becomes "due" on the date that the payment needs to be made. On any date prior, the purchase price is legally simply a purchase price, which can be sold at discount, par, or premium depending on market circumstances. Similarly, in the case of rental payments, rent becomes due only once usufruct of an asset is enjoyed, and the rent becomes due. On any date prior to the date on which rent is due, it is simply rent and can be sold at a discount, par, or premium. We realize that we are at odds with much of the industry on this topic.

[8]Ibrahim, U. (2002), "Securitization of debts: *Bay al Dayn,*" paper presented in Islamic Bonds Colloqium, June 24, 2004, Conference Hall 2, Securities Commission Malaysia, p. 13.

CHAPTER 10

Bai al Urbun

Urbun represents the very simple concept of a downpayment. *Ibnu qudamah* defined it as "a transaction whereby the buyer buys a commodity and pays a deposit of one dirham or more on the understanding that the deposit will be considered part of the purchase price if the buyer decides to continue with the contract. If the buyer decides to withdraw from the contract, the seller will forfeit the deposit."[1] It has been confused with options and other financial products found in the marketplace but in essence it is really just a downpayment.

As always, the best way to explain the concept is by using an example. Party A and B are parties to a sale contract, where Party B will sell an asset to Party A. Party B, however, does not own the asset that is to be the subject of sale. Party A promises Party B to purchase a particular asset from Party B if Party B can secure that asset from a vendor within a certain time frame. To show his or her keenness to purchase the asset, Party A offers Party B a deposit. If Party B secures the asset for Party A, this deposit will become part of the purchase price. If Party B secures the asset for Party A, but Party A decides not to purchase the asset, Party B is entitled to retain the deposit paid as *urbun*.

- **Scenario 1**
  Party A contracts with Party B to purchase an asset worth $100,000. Party B does not own the asset and obtains a deposit of $10,000 from Party A to secure Party A's interest in the transaction. Party B secures the asset within the time frame offered by Party A and the sale is executed. Party A only pays a balance of $90,000 and secures ownership of the asset.
- **Scenario 2**
  Party B fails to acquire the asset in the stipulated time frame and returns the deposit of $10,000 to Party A.

[1]International Centre for Education in Islamic Finance (INCEIF) (2006), *Applied Shariah in Financial Transaction*.

- **Scenario 3**
  Party B secures the asset in time, but Party A decides to withdraw from the promise to buy the asset. Party B retains the deposit of $10,000.

Urbun is therefore a partial payment of the price of an asset, which entitles the buyer to *the right to buy an asset* but does not obligate the buyer to do so. If the buyer does in fact purchase the asset, the *urbun* becomes part of the purchase price, and if the buyer does not purchase the asset, the seller retains the *urbun* as compensation for his or her trouble.

According to some of the Fiqh schools,[2] *urbun* contains *gharar* and injustice as it gives the right to the seller without anything in return. However, the proponents[3] for *urbun* put forth the argument that the seller, in the case whereby he or she received *urbun*, has to forgo the opportunity cost of selling the asset to another person during the waiting period. *Urbun* gives the right to purchase to the seller within a specified period of time, with the ownership still falling with the seller. There is no sales contract in this matter; instead it is more of a promise between the seller and the buyer on the asset.

In most cases, *urbun* is paid in the form of cash. However, we propose that financial asset can also be considered to be used for *urbun* as it is of value, tradable and transferable. The seller can take the value of the *urbun* on spot value and consequently, during the times where the full price has to be paid, the value of the financial asset can be adjusted. If the value of financial asset has gone down or up, then the amount that the buyer has to pay is the remaining price after adjusting the fall or increase in the value of the *urbun* on that point of time.

The payment of *urbun* gives the buyer a financial right to purchase an asset for a specific price in the future. Due to this feature, this contract has been compared to conventional options. However, conventional options are stand-alone contracts, and buyers of option contracts have to pay a separate consideration for buying an option price. This is not the case for an *urbun* contract, it is not a stand-alone sale contract nor does it carry its own separate consideration. In other words, Party A cannot sell his or her downpayment to Party C and transfer the right to future ownership to Party C.

Historically much of the Muslim world remained an agricultural economy and continues to be today. Contracts of *urbun* offer hedging opportunities that are usually necessary in sale and purchase of commodities that experience price volatility.

Let us work our way through an example (Figure 10.1). Party A is a grain merchant who wishes to purchase 10 tons of grain from Party B in the

---

[2]Ibnu Rusyd, *Bidayah al-Mujtahid*, vol. 2.

[3]Wahbah Al-Zuhaili, Rafiq Yunus al-Misri, Shaykh Abd Allah al-Bassam, and Ibn Qayyim al-Jawziyyah.

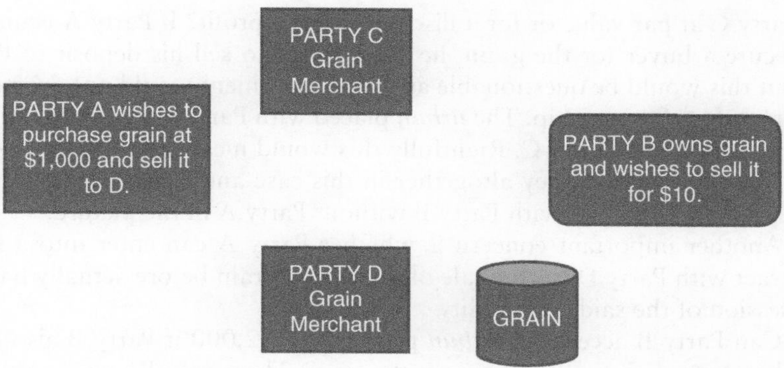

FIGURE 10.1 Grain Purchase (1)

future. The spot price of grain is $1,000 per ton. Party B offers to sell Party A 10 tons of grain at the market price, but Party A is hesitant to close the deal as he has yet to find a buyer for the commodity willing to offer a reasonable price. Party A offers to pay a deposit to Party B, requesting that Party B holds 10 tons of grain for Party A for 30 days, but does not guarantee that Party A will buy the grain in 30 days. The deposit amount is $2,000 or 20 percent of the total purchase price. If Party A buys the grain, this amount will be part of the total price of $10,000, and if Party A does not purchase the grain, Party B can hold onto the $2,000 as compensation for holding 10 tons of stock for Party A.

Several issues arise in this arrangement (Figure 10.2). Can Party A sell the *urbun* payment to Party C, thereby transferring the rights and obligation attached with the downpayment to Party C? Can A sell the *urbun* payment

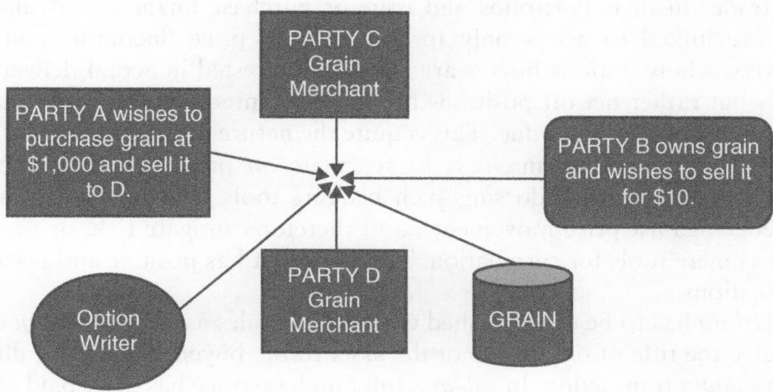

FIGURE 10.2 Grain Purchase (2)

to Party C at par value or for a discount or at a profit? If Party A is unable to secure a buyer for the grain, he may decide to sell his deposit to Party C, but this would be questionable as *urbun* placement would not constitute any transfer of ownership. The *urbun* placed with Party B is between Parties A and B, not with Party C. Rightfully this would mean that Party A would just lose the *urbun* money altogether in this case and Party C would enter into a new transaction with Party B without Party A in the picture.

Another important concern is whether Party A can enter into a sales contract with Party D for the sale of 10 tons of grain before actually having possession of the said commodity.

Can Party B accept the *urbun* payment of $2,000 if Party B also does not have possession of the grain at the time? These are all issues pertinent to the *shariah*, as the law does not permit the sale of assets not in one's possession.

A conventional options contract resembles *urbun* in that it grants the option buyer to purchase a certain asset from a seller at a particular price known as the exercise price. The option holder may choose to exercise the option or not. A conventional option, however, is sold by a party that writes the option to the party that buys the option. The option has its own price and the option may be written by a third party that may or may not own the asset at the time of issuing the option. In the case of a "naked option," the option writer does not own the asset before granting a third party the right to buy the asset at a future date. The option writer, however, is liable to be able to deliver the commodity mentioned in the option contract if the buyer chooses to exercise it. Failure to do so would be deemed a default on the part of the option writer or seller.

In conventional finance, options may be offered by parties that do not have ownership of the underlying asset. Such parties usually have speculative trades in their portfolios and issue or purchase financial instruments that are linked to assets only to benefit from price fluctuations in the markets. Many options buyers are also not interested in actual delivery of assets but rather net off positions by trying to enter into sale transactions before delivery becomes due. This is quite the nature of markets for options and as the underlying intent is to speculate on prices, *shariah* scholars have been averse to endorsing such hedging tools. Options can be used to hedge against price movements, and therefore mitigate risk, or may be used as mere tools for speculation. The tool itself has positive and negative applications.

Urbun has to be distinguished with margin sales as well, as *urbun* does not give the title of ownership of the asset to the buyer. *Urbun* also differs from *salaam* transaction. In *salaam*, full purchase price has to be paid at the beginning of the contract. It is one of the conditions in *salaam* and hence *urbun* is not applicable in this contract.[4] Many have been misled by associating *urbun* with such transactions above, namely options, *salaam*, and in the application of many other derivatives products, while by right *urbun* differs from these concepts. Moreover, even though *urbun* sale is currently endorsed by Malaysia's SAC and OIC Fiqh Academy, until this moment, there have not been any clear resolutions on some of the issues in *urbun*, such as the issue of reverse *urbun* on whether the seller should pay a compensation should the transaction not be executed due to the seller's inability to present the asset or subject matter in question. It is also not clear if by paying an *urbun* price, the buyer can resell the goods to a third party before actually taking full delivery of the goods or having paid a full purchase price for them.

CONCLUSION

The contract of *urbun* leaves many questions unanswered and we have alluded to these in this chapter. The rights of the buyer or the party that makes the payment are unclear as to whether the buyer can resell the asset to a third party before having made full payment. If this condition is permitted, then futures can be transacted in a manner that we are accustomed to seeing in the conventional space. As mentioned before, the concept has been confused with modern-day options and this is incorrect because the contract of *urbun* does not carry its own consideration, nor can it be traded.

[4]OIC Fiqh Academy approved of *urbun* sale under the condition that the time frame has to be predetermined, *urbun* is considered as part of price if the purchase is executed, and it is not applicable to sales, which stipulate the reception of either of the two elements of exchange in the contract setting or both.

CHAPTER 11

Ijarah and Its Variants

Ijarah is a contract of leasing. Bank Negara Malaysia refers to a contract involving "an exchange of usufruct or benefits of an asset or a service for rent or commission for an agreed period."[1] It involves two parties, a lessor and a lessee, and an asset that is to be leased. As a financial instrument, the contract of *ijarah* is rather straightforward. A lessor acquires an asset and leases it out to a lessee for a specific duration. The consideration paid by a lessee for enjoying the usufruct of the asset is referred to as *ujr* or rental payment.

The prerequisites for a contract of lease are similar to contracts of sale and we need not delve into them again. There are, however, some additional features in lease contracts. In conventional finance, there are two types of leases, an operational lease and a financial lease. The two are similar, except that in the latter, the lessee undertakes to purchase the asset leased after the lease duration expires at a pre-agreed price. In an operational lease, there is no such undertaking. The traditional scholars of Islamic finance do not recognize a financial lease as it implies two contracts combined into one.[2] One is a contract of lease, and the other is a contract of sale. We have mentioned before that the *shariah* does not recognize one contract being contingent on another.

Another salient distinguishing feature of an operating lease is that the asset remains in the ownership of the lessor. The lessee merely enjoys the usufruct of the asset, and cannot claim ownership of the asset. The lessor is also therefore responsible for maintaining the suitability of the asset such that the lessee is able to enjoy the usufruct of the same. Expenses associated

[1] Bank Negara Malaysia (BNM) (2010), *Shariah Resolutions in Islamic Finance: Second Edition,* http://www.bnm.gov.my/microsites/financial/pdf/resolutions/shariah_resolutions_2nd_edition_EN.pdf, accessed July 2014.

[2] It is reported in a *hadith* that Prophet Muhammad (saw) prohibited from making two contracts in one contract.—Sunan Al-Thirmizi, 2/514.

with normal usage of the asset are borne by the lessee, but any expenses related to maintaining the asset in such a condition that the asset is usable lie with the lessor. Another condition of the pure *ijarah* contract is that it can be terminated unilaterally. The lessee enjoys the legal right to terminate the contract prematurely if the lessee no longer requires to enjoy the usufruct of the asset. Even if a lessee agrees to lease an asset for five years from a lessor, and chooses after the third year to terminate the lease, the lessee can do so without being liable for the rent for the remaining two years.

However, the lessee may have to compensate the lessor for prematurely terminating the agreement.

These restrictions of the *shariah* present Islamic banks with certain issues. Islamic banks operating under Basel rules need to hold more capital for "Assets Held Till Maturity" on their balance sheets.[3] An Islamic bank may easily buy a new car, for instance, from a vendor and lease it to a customer for five years, but for the entire duration of the contract the asset will remain on the balance sheet of an Islamic bank and an Islamic bank would therefore have to hold additional capital until the Islamic bank actually sells or disposes of the asset. Again, the Islamic bank has to take ownership risk of the asset under consideration. The Islamic bank would also have to incur additional expenses on maintaining the suitability of the asset for the period of the lease and would not be able to pass on these costs to the customer. All rental income from an *ijarah* contract is treated as income in the income statement of an Islamic bank.

An Islamic bank would also have to bear the additional risk that the lessee may terminate the contract at any point during the lease agreement. This would make it difficult for an Islamic bank to anticipate future cash flows, and also in pricing the product.

Needless to say, enhancements have to be made to the original concept of *ijarah* to develop financial products. Currently, three enhancements of the *ijarah* contract that are in vogue are normal *ijarah*, *ijarah muntahiya bi tamleek*, and *al ijarah thumma al bai*.

NORMAL *IJARAH*

As the name implies this is a rather generic product, where an Islamic bank acquires an asset and then leases it out to a lessee for a specific period for a

[3]Bank of International Settlements (2006), *Basel II: International Convergence of Capital Measurement and Capital Standards: A Revised Framework*, http://www.bis.org/publ/bcbs128.htm, accessed July 2014.

specified rental payment. The asset remains in the ownership of the Islamic bank, until such time that the bank sells or disposes of the asset. The bank must maintain additional capital for this duration as well.

The lessee provides no undertaking to purchase the asset at the maturity of the lease agreement. It is not entirely clear, however, if Islamic banks maintain the suitability of the asset or not. However, if a lessee does in fact decide to prematurely terminate the contract, Islamic banks do reserve the right to charge a prepayment penalty to the lessee.

An Islamic bank that enters into a contract of *ijarah* treats the rental payments due to the bank as receivables on its balance sheet. As with other receivables in *murabahah*-based sales contracts, the bank is required to maintain capital as a buffer in case the lessee defaults on payments. The pure *ijarah* contract therefore burdens an Islamic bank with capital charges for owning the asset leased out, and for the receivables created by the rental agreement itself. This makes this product in its pure form an expensive financial product, and likely less competitive in comparison to an operating lease or a financial lease in the conventional space.

The asset must also be reported on the balance sheet as per the rules of the *shariah* at current market value.[4]

ACCOUNTING ENTRIES FOR *IJARAH* CONTRACT

In general, the accounting entries for an *ijarah* contract would be illustrated as in Table 11.1. Suppose that the asset value is $100,000 and would be leased throughout a whole year with monthly payments. The bank's required return is 20 percent, hence the total payment would amount to $120,000.

TABLE 11.1 *Ijarah* Contract

Asset Value	100,000
Ijarah Contract Tenor	1
Payments	Monthly
Total Payments	12
Banks Required Return	20%
Total UJR Payments	120,000
Monthly Payment	10,000

[4]See AAOIFI, "*Financial Accounting Standards (FAS)*"; International Financial Reporting Standards (IFRS).

As the bank acquires the asset, the bank would record it under the category of asset and as it enters the *ijarah* contract, the bank would take out the asset of $100,000 and create a new account of *ijarah receivable* of $120,000, which constitutes both the principal asset value and the unearned income of $20,000. Every *ijarah* payment of $10,000 made would be recorded as a deduction from the *ijarah* receivable account, and at this point in time, there is a decrease in unearned income and the bank recognizes an income of $1,667 from the *ijarah* contract. The same applies for every payment made to the bank until the end of the facility (Table 11.2).

TABLE 11.2 Accounting Treatment for *Ijarah* Contract

	Debit		Credit	
Bank acquires asset	Asset	100,000	Cash	100,000
Bank enters Ijarah contract	*Ijarah* Receivable	120,000	Asset	100,000
			Unearned Income	20,000
Payment 1	Cash	10,000	*Ijarah* Receivable	10,000
	Unearned Income	1,667	Income	1,667
Payment 2	Cash	10,000	*Ijarah* Receivable	10,000
	Unearned Income	1,667	Income	1,667
Payment 3	Cash	10,000	*Ijarah* Receivable	10,000
	Unearned Income	1,667	Income	1,667
Payment 4	Cash	10,000	*Ijarah* Receivable	10,000
	Unearned Income	1,667	Income	1,667
Payment 5	Cash	10,000	*Ijarah* Receivable	10,000
	Unearned Income	1,667	Income	1,667
Payment 6	Cash	10,000	*Ijarah* Receivable	10,000
	Unearned Income	1,667	Income	1,667
Payment 7	Cash	10,000	*Ijarah* Receivable	10,000
	Unearned Income	1,667	Income	1,667
Payment 8	Cash	10,000	*Ijarah* Receivable	10,000
	Unearned Income	1,667	Income	1,667
Payment 9	Cash	10,000	*Ijarah* Receivable	10,000
	Unearned Income	1,667	Income	1,667
Payment 10	Cash	10,000	*Ijarah* Receivable	10,000
	Unearned Income	1,667	Income	1,667
Payment 11	Cash	10,000	*Ijarah* Receivable	10,000
	Unearned Income	1,667	Income	1,667
Payment 12	Cash	10,000	*Ijarah* Receivable	10,000
	Unearned Income	1,667	Income	1,667
	Total Receipts	120,000		120,000
			Total Income	20,000

IJARAH MUNTAHIYA BI TAMLEEK

Ijarah muntahiya bi tamleek on paper is meant to be an operating lease.[5] However, the rental payments are tabulated in such a manner that if the lessee makes all rental payments within the term of the contract or before, the asset is transferred to the ownership of the lessee. This pricing mechanism hints at the fact that the lessee provides an undertaking that the lessee will purchase the asset at the end of the rental agreement, and a purchase price component is added to the rental payment that a customer pays every month.

If an Islamic bank leases out a $10,000 car to a customer for five years, the monthly installment would include a $166.67 charge, which would be a payment for the car, if the bank sells the car at its cost. In addition to this, the Islamic bank will charge a rental payment for five years. Typically, a monthly installment, or the monthly "rent" under such a contract, would be higher than the rent paid in a normal *ijarah* contract or operating lease.

All other conditions under this contract are similar to that of a normal *ijarah*.

AL IJARAH THUMMA AL BAI (AITAB)

This contract, as its name suggests, is a combination of two contracts, one a contract of lease and another a contract of sale. *AITAB* is merely a contract of lease that terminates with the lessee buying the underlying asset via a sale contract. The terms of the sale contract are agreed on at the time of entering into the sale contract, and this violates, in some scholars' opinions, that one contract cannot be conditional on another. Here, the contract of lease is contingent on the lessee agreeing to purchase the asset at the termination of the lease contract.

The asset is typically sold at its salvage value to the lessee on expiry of the lease agreement. The salvage value is a function of the asset's cost price, and the methodology used to calculate depreciation in the value of the asset. For instance, a customer approaches an Islamic bank for *AITAB* facility on a car that costs $69,000 for four years. After incorporating the profit rate, the bank agrees to give the facility that entails a monthly payment of $1,500.00 per month and a sale price of $15,000 at the end of the *AITAB* facility. The lessee pays a total sum of $72,000 in rent over four years and then purchases the car at the end of the fourth year for $15,000.

---

[5]Brian, Kettell, *Introduction to Islamic Banking and Finance* (West Sussex: Wiley Finance, 2011).

In the latter two variants of the *ijarah* contract, Islamic banks are albeit required to maintain ownership of the asset under question. This practice would incur additional capital charges for the bank, and if the opportunity cost of this capital is passed onto customers, this product would be more expensive than a conventional lease.

In practice, however, for instance in car leasing products, Islamic banks lease out a car under either *AITAB* or *ijarah muntahiya bi tamleek* to customers. The title of the car is actually transferred straight from the car dealer to the customer's name. The Islamic bank, however, hypothecates the car in the name of the bank under the contract of *rahn*, and records a receivable in its books for the amount of the rental payments due. When a customer makes full payments under *AITAB* and then a subsequent payment to purchase the car, or when a customer in a *ijarah muntahiya bi tamleek* contract makes all payments, the Islamic bank simply releases its hypothecation on the vehicle. In fact during the entire lease period, the car remains in the ownership of the customer.

Islamic banks also do not always ensure suitability of the asset or vehicle in question and all expenses related to maintaining the vehicle are borne by the customers. If the bank had to ensure the suitability of the asset, this would greatly increase its costs. Imagine if the said vehicle was recalled by the manufacturer; the Islamic bank would have to provide the customer with an alternative vehicle or surrender the claim to any rental payments while the car is recalled.

As one can see, this clause of maintaining the suitability of the asset is impractical for an Islamic bank to implement. Second, Islamic banks also cannot own assets on their balance sheet as per current banking laws and Basel requirements.

SALE AND LEASEBACK

In relation to this matter, one of the common contemporary uses of *ijarah* contract is through what is called *sale and leaseback*, that is, the execution of a *bai* contract followed by *ijarah* contract back to the original seller. This model is apparent in, for instance, *ijarah sukuk*, whereby the originator of the *sukuk* will sell the asset to the *sukuk* holders through a special-purpose vehicle, lease it back from the *sukuk* holders, and also promise to buy back the asset on maturity. The issue in this modern use of *ijarah* contract is that in most *ijarah*-based *sukuk*, the *sukuk* certificate held by the investors represents the right to claim on a certain amount of rent, through what is claimed to be as a result of the transfer of "beneficial ownership," but not the claim of shared ownership on the asset itself. More on this matter is discussed in later chapters.

CONCLUSION

The modern implementation of the concept of *ijarah* is also an imperfect modification of the classical concept of *ijarah*. As we have seen with sale-based contracts of *BBA* and *murabahah*, without making enhancements to traditional concepts, their application to the development of modern financial products is seriously constrained.

CHAPTER 12

Wadiah

Wadiah is a contract that is used on the liability side of the balance sheets of Islamic banks. Classically speaking *wadiah* is a contract by virtue of which one party keeps an asset with a counterparty for safekeeping purposes for a specific period of time (Figure 12.1).[1] The counterparty accepts the responsibility of looking after the asset voluntarily and typically does not charge a fee for this service.

Party A owns an asset and places the asset for safekeeping with Party B. Party B accepts the asset and the responsibility for safekeeping without charging any fee. Party A can ask for the asset back without any conditions at any time. The asset kept for safekeeping is referred to as *wadiah*. So far this contract seems simple enough; now let us complicate it. We do not get into the different interpretations of the contract of *wadiah* of the four traditional schools of legal thought. We examine the features of the contract using some common sense.

The classical usage of this contract had an element of trust in it. Party A trusted Party B with an asset; the latter accepted without consideration. As there is no element of consideration, it is difficult to understand the rationale behind this concept as a bilateral contract for commercial usage. Unfortunately the architects of Islamic finance adopted the closest practice they could find in Islamic traditions and modified it to fit a commercial scenario. *Wadiah* like *kafalah* in the traditional literature is not referred to as a commercial transaction and is in fact referred to in the context of a social contract of a benevolent nature. For example, a resident of Damascus may leave for Egypt for trading purposes and leave certain assets with a well-trusted citizen of the city to safeguard certain precious belongings like gold. Any costs

[1]The legality of *wadiah* can be observed from the following verses: 4:58: "Verily, Allah (sat) commands that you should render back the trusts to those, to whom they are due." 23:8: "Those who are faithfully true to their trusts (amanah) and to their covenants."

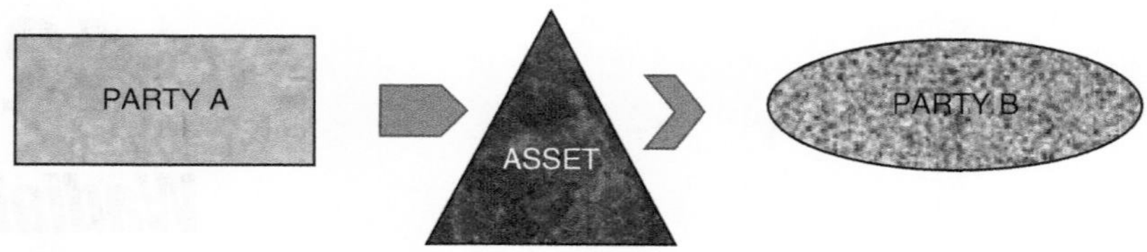

FIGURE 12.1 Party A Uses Party B as Counterparty

associated with maintaining the asset can be borne by the original party to not in-convene the trustee accepting the asset. As the trustee accepts the asset without any consideration, it was accepted that the trustee would not use the asset for any commercial gain and would return the asset to the original party on demand. This in its basic form is the contract of *wadiah*.

FORMS OF *WADIAH*

In fact, there are two forms of *wadiah*. The first is *wadiah yad al amanah* (safekeeping with trust) whereby the custodian doesn't have the right to utilize the *wadiah* but will be liable only in case of loss due to negligence.

The second is *wadiah yad al dhamanah* (safekeeping with guarantee) whereby the custodian can utilize the *wadiah* (i.e., the asset placed in safekeeping) but will be liable *dhamen* in case of any impairments incurred. Islamic bank offerings such as safety deposit boxes are contracted under *wadiah yad al amanah*. Under this contract the Islamic bank is not permitted to use the contents of the safety deposit boxes for any economic activity.

Islamic banks use the contract of *wadiah yad al dhamanah* (safekeeping with guarantee) to mobilize deposits. Assets in kind such as valuables and gold can be kept as a *wadiah yad al dhamanah*, or capital can be kept as a *wadiah yad al dhamanah*. In the event the asset being kept as *wadiah yad al dhamanah* is money, or capital, the trustee or Islamic bank is liable for any losses if the capital is utilized in any economic activity or to fund a financial asset. In this chapter we shall be referring to *wadiah yad al dhamanah*.

ENHANCEMENTS TO *WADIAH*

This basic concept of *wadiah* later evolved in Islamic finance into a contract. Deposits are mobilized by Islamic banks using the *wadiah* contract, where moneys are received from depositors under a contract of "safekeeping" and then further channeled into financing assets. If the original party allows the trustee to use the asset, the trustee may do so, but if the asset depreciates in value as in the case of banking where the trustee lends these funds out to a third party, the trustee must make good the losses. Thus, if funds mobilized from depositors using the contract of *wadiah* are lent onward to a third party, and the third-party borrowers default, the trustee must make good on the losses as the moneys lent belong to the depositor and not the custodian. This is a first modification to the concept of classical *wadiah*, of guaranteeing the asset. *Wadiah* in its original essence is an *amanah*-based contract or a trust-based contract, not a contract for commercial consideration.

In its modern application in Islamic banking the trustee, which in this case is an Islamic bank, may utilize funds mobilized under the contract of *wadiah*, provided the account holder permits this. The moneys received from customers can be channeled by Islamic banks into financing debt-based contracts or lease contracts to third parties unknown to the depositor providing the funds. The depositor hence becomes a capital provider. This is not the original intent behind the *wadiah* contract; placing an asset with a party for safekeeping is different than being a capital provider as the latter has various other consequences.

Islamic banks mobilize on demand deposits under the category of current accounts and savings accounts, which all bankers refer to as CASA. These are low-cost funds as there is no profit to be paid on these deposits. Typically a *mudi* or depositor is not expecting any profit from the *mustawada* or custodian as the original purpose of keeping the asset is only for safekeeping. If an asset is placed for safekeeping alone, then the deposited asset is referred to as a *wadiah*.

Another enhancement to the original concept of *wadiah* is to mix the assets or money placed with an Islamic bank by one depositor with assets placed for safekeeping of other depositors. This is illustrated in Figure 12.2.

Traditionally, the *mustawda* would not mix assets kept by one *mudi* with assets kept by another *mudi* or depositor. There is also no precedence of combining these assets and using them to finance credit-based contracts as is the practice of Islamic banks today.

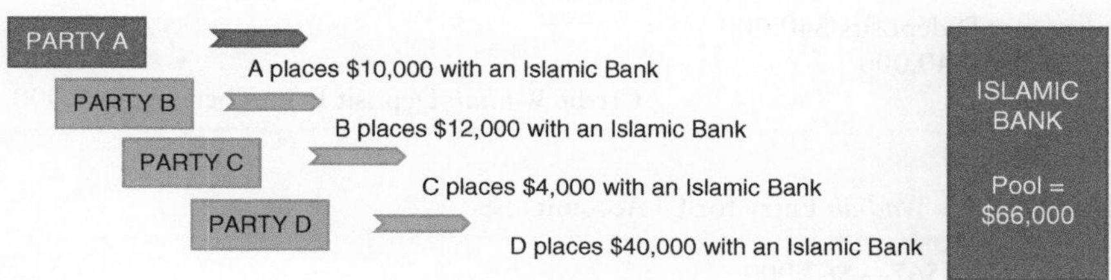

FIGURE 12.2 Deposits in an Islamic Bank

An Islamic bank would accept the deposits of the customers as illustrated earlier, record them as liabilities in its balance sheet and further use the combined moneys to extend financing to third parties. The financing amounts are treated as assets in the bank's balance sheet (as financing or receivables), as they will generate profit for the bank.

Islamic banks are certainly not permitted to comingle shareholders' funds (capital) with those of depositors to finance assets. The custodian (bank) is not to mix its own funds (capital or equity) with those of depositors and this is why Islamic banks (unlike conventional banks) maintain separate records for depositors' funds, investments financed by utilizing depositors' funds, and returns on investments financed by depositors' funds.

Let us examine how the above transactions are reflected in a balance sheet.

Banks maintain several ledgers in their accounting books. Other than the typical asset, liability, equity entries in a balance sheet, banks maintain internal ledgers of pools of funds. For each *wadiah* deposit below the Islamic bank will generate an account number, which the customer will use to transact his (or her) funds with. For illustrative purposes we have assigned Customers A, B, C, and D respective account numbers in Table 12.1.

However, the Islamic bank has received $62,000 of cash as well. These funds are pooled into an internal liability account of the bank that will have its own account numbers. See Table 12.2.

TABLE 12.1 *Wadiah* Entries for an Islamic Bank's Customers

Customer A Deposits $10,000 Debit cash $10,000	
	Credit *Wadiah* Account A number 123 $10,000
Customer B deposits $12,000 Debit cash $12,000	
	Credit *Wadiah* Account B number 121 $12,000
Customer C deposits $4,000 Debit cash $4,000	
	Credit *Wadiah* Account C number 112 $4,000
Customer D deposits $40,000 Debit cash $40,000	
	Credit *Wadiah* Deposit D number 122 $40,000

TABLE 12.2 *Wadiah* Entry for Gl Accounts

Cash—A114567—$62,000	
	Wadiah Liability L23433—$62,000

TABLE 12.3 Extending a *Murabahah* Facility

Credit Cash A114567 $20,000	
	Debit *Murabahah* Financing Asset $20,000

The custodian has pooled all of the customers deposit into a single internal cash general ledger asset account with the number A114567 and created a liability reflecting the fact that this money **does not belong to the bank (custodian) but to the depositor.**

Let us see what happens when the Islamic bank extends a *murabahah*-based financing of $20,000 to Customer E. The Islamic bank credits the account of E with $20,000, but where does this money come from? The bank also books an asset (its own asset, not that of the depositors) in its own books.

To the question, Whose money is the bank (custodian) using?, the answer is simply "yours," or that of customers A, B, C, and D combined. The Islamic bank will not divide the $20,000 between the balances maintained by the customers, because despite the fact that the bank has used its money, its balances in their accounts are **unaffected.** The balance of depositors in their account statements are still as shown in Table 12.4.

Were Customers A, B, C, and D to come to the Islamic bank the next day and find that their balances had been reduced by $4,000 each so that the IFI could extend a *murabahah* financing to Party E, the customers would raze the building to the ground. They would insist that they **only placed their balances with the Islamic Bank for safekeeping.**

Actually seeing numbers and accounting ledgers brings home how financial intermediation works.[2]

TABLE 12.4 Customer Balances

Customer Name	Account Number	Balance
Customer A	123	10,000
Customer B	121	12,000
Customer C	112	4,000
Customer D	122	40,000
Total Balance		**66,000**

[2]Thanks to Dr. Shahul Hameed of INCEIF for demonstrating this.

MONEY CREATION

> *A good banker knows that ultimately what he or she does rests on a benign white lie. The customer lends the bank money in the form of a deposit and the bank then lends it out multiple times. That is the basis of banking. It is a construct built on trust. It all rests on creating sufficient confidence in order that everyone does not get worried enough to ask for their money back at the same moment. Because if they do the bank is probably sunk.*[3]

Has the bank created money out of thin air? It has not used shareholders' funds to extend the financing; it has used depositors' funds for this purpose, but the balances of the depositors with the IFI are still unaffected. This is the art of banking and the essence of money creation. This is a *shariah* issue that has not been addressed in 14 modules and one year of lectures on Islamic banking. Money creation is not a consequence of a fractional reserve banking but is the result of the unique type of business a bank performs. In essence the business of banking is money creation.

I illustrate this point with several scenario analyses using our Customers A, B, C, D, and E and an Islamic bank.

Imagine our very same depositors who place their funds with an Islamic bank, and Customer E borrows $20,000 from the same bank, as shown in Table 12.5.

The IFI has several options to fund this loan to Customer E. It studies the patterns of withdrawals of all depositors and realizes that Customer D is a retired woman and withdraws on average only $10,000 at the end of each month. The IFI will then (in very simplistic terms) fund the loan for the first three weeks with Customer D's money.

TABLE 12.5 Loan to Customer E

Customer Name	Account Number	Balance
Customer A	123	10,000
Customer B	121	12,000
Customer C	112	4,000
Customer D	122	40,000
Total Balance		**66,000**

Customer Name	Loan
Customer E	20,000

[3]Iain Martin, *Making It Happen: Fred Goodwin, RBS and the Men Who Blew Up the British Economy* (New York: Simon & Schuster, 2013).

TABLE 12.6 Where Is the Loan Funded From?

Customer Name	Account Number	Balance	Customer Name	Loan
Customer A	123	10,000	Customer E	20,000
Customer B	121	12,000		
Customer C	112	4,000		
Customer D	122	20,000		
Total Balance		**46,000**		

The results on the customer's accounts should look like the example in Table 12.6.

However, if Customer D walks into the branch unexpectedly and finds $20,000 missing, she is likely to raze the roof to the ground. Technically, however, the bank has not done anything amiss provided the customer understands the terms of account opening.

Another option may be that the IFI realizes that Customers A to D use only 30 percent of their moneys during the month and the IFI takes $5,000 from each customer's account to fund the loan to Customer E. As Customer C only has a deposit of $4,000 in the account, the bank takes $10,000 from Customer D's account.

The bank statements of these customers will then look like Table 12.7.

However, if all the customers simply verified their balances on the Internet and found money missing from their accounts, they would be extremely unhappy. This is not, however, how a "banking business" operates. If it did, it would be considered a Ponzi scheme, where the bank would lend out money to borrowers and would repay depositors with other depositors' money. In essence, if the $20,000 loan was funded entirely by Customer D's deposit of $40,000 and she walks in to withdraw her full $40,000, then the bank would pay her off using Customers A, B, and C's money combined, in essence paying one customer off with another customer's money.

TABLE 12.7 Funding Loan from Other Customers

Customer Name	Account Number	Balance	Customer Name	Loan
Customer A	123	5,000	Customer E	20,000
Customer B	121	7,000		
Customer C	112	4,000		
Customer D	122	10,000		
Total Balance		**26,000**		

TABLE 12.8 How Should a Loan Be Funded?

Customer Name	Account Number	Balance
Customer A	123	10,000
Customer B	121	12,000
Customer C	112	4,000
Customer D	122	40,000
Total Balance		**66,000**

Customer Name	Loan

TABLE 12.9 Reduced Customers' Balances

Customer Name	Balance	30% of Balance	Balance
Customer A	10,000	3,000	7,000
Customer B	12,000	3,600	8,400
Customer C	4,000	1,200	2,800
Customer D	40,000	12,000	28,000
Total Balance		**19,800**	**46,200**

Customer Name	Loan
Investment Scheme	19,800

But then how exactly do banks operate? Imagine the same scenario but based on a different contract, say one of profit sharing or agency, where each customer places funds with a financial institution and requests the IFI to invest 30 percent of their funds in investment schemes. The customers will understand then that the balances in their accounts will be 30 percent less than the amount they deposited and their statements would be as reflected in Table 12.8.

When the customers authorize the FI to **deduct 30 percent of their respective balances** and invest the funds into some investment scheme that can include a *murabahah* loan to Customer E, the statements will look like Table 12.9.

The customers will place 30 percent of their money in an investment scheme and only the residual balance will be available on demand. The invested amounts will hopefully generate returns that will be distributed among the customers according to their contributions. The underlying contracts for such an arrangement or investment would be a combination of *wadiah* and *wakalah* or *wadiah* and *mudharbah*. If the Islamic bank shares in the returns generated from the investments of $19,000, this would be a *wadiah mudharabah* model, and if the IFI merely takes an upfront fee for managing the funds, this would be a *wadiah wakalah* model. In principle, the funds kept in residual balances will be available on demand and will be

TABLE 12.10 Who Takes the Hit?

Customer Name	Account Number	Balance	Customer Name	Loan
Customer A	123	10,000	Customer E	20,000
Customer B	121	12,000		
Customer C	11	4,000		
Customer D	122	40,000		
Total Balance		66,000		

under the *wadiah* contract and the funds invested in the investment account will be under either a *wakalah* contract or a *mudharabah* contract.

We have still not been able to solve the mystery as to how a bank is able to finance assets without recording any deduction in the value of deposits placed by depositors, as shown in Table 12.10.

At no point are customers' balances ever affected by the bank's financing activities. Unless all borrowers default on their financing contracts, then the IFI may see all the customers at the door looking for their money. Banks are the only financial institutions in the world that are able to treat for financing activities by not writing down the value of the deposits they use to fund the loans. They maintain a complex set of "book entries" to match their liability book with their asset book, which is a subject discussed in a separate chapter. Banks are allowed to take funds from depositors, use those very funds to make loans to other customers, and yet at no time do the depositors feel that their money has been channeled to borrowers. They have access to their moneys on demand. Banks match their liability book to their asset book, but this is an exercise to maintain accounting books, not necessarily real numbers.

The impact of a financing contract comes home when as a banker you witness the disbursal of a loan just using book entries. Cash is paid to a borrower but no depositor's account is debited. In fact, banks do not debit customers' accounts, they use the pool of funds they have developed from customers' accounts, which is typically referred to as a general ledger liability account. When banks transfer customers' balances into their own books as a liability, they are able to use the funds (literally the cash raised) to give loans from that general pool and not any specific account holder's account and thereby the liability then **funds the asset.**

To sum up, depositors place funds with a bank; the bank lends the funds to a borrower. Funds are credited into the borrower's account, yet there is no depletion in the values of depositor's balances. Nor has the bank used any other funds, either.

In fact, the situation described earlier where the bank has liabilities of $66,000 and financing assets of $20,000 is a circumstance of excess liquidity. The bank can easily lend another $46,000. In fact the bank can even lend out $50,000 more; all it would have to do is borrow the money from another bank to fund the gap. The only way to understand complex systems is to break them down into their simplest parts. The earlier mentioned model of financial intermediation is adopted by Islamic Banks, albeit using *shariah*-"compliant" contracts, yet this model is attributed to "creating money out of thin air." On a broader scale an economic system dependent on banks, or where all moneys in an economy are channeled through banks, will *create* bubble economies, not by excessive lending or low interest rates. The element of money creation is **built into the banking model.** Wealth is created by handing out loans to borrowers, yet the wealth of the capital provider is never depleted. Deposits are only at risk when borrowers begin to systemically default on their loans; only then can the ripple effects reach actual balances held by depositors.

In simple terms, if you place $100 with me, and I lend $100 to a third person, your balance of $100 with me should technically vanish. But as a bank, I am allowed to treat that deposit as a liability, and lend you $100 when you walk in the branch without having to call in my loan, either. So either I pay you using another depositor's money (which would not be too dissimilar to a Ponzi scheme) or I must liquidate my asset (which would be impractical) or I must borrow from some other party to pay you (again, it would be kind of like a Ponzi scheme). In the world of conventional banking, deposits are treated as loans from customers and conventional loans are treated as loans to borrowers. The difference between the rate on deposits and the rate on loans is a bank's income. In essence, managing the liability book is in some ways akin to a Ponzi scheme, not only because loans or finance contracts are long term in nature, whereas deposits are short term in nature, **but because a bank is allowed to maintain the value of a customer's deposit as a liability even when the moneys mobilized have been converted into an asset.**

CONCLUSION

The architects of Islamic banking have embraced this same model without reservation. To conclude, although *shariah* scholars focus on the permissibility of using the funds, beyond this permissibility is the mechanics of creating assets from these liabilities, and the permissibility of the accounting treatment for these transactions and entries, which the author feels is a more crucial debate. The issue to address is that the business of banking is the business of creating money, and *shariah* scholars need to add some commentary here.

If moneys are treated as deposits in banks, they create a web of complications as deposits are payable on demand, but the moneys have been lent out to third parties. If moneys are invested as funds, this issue does not arise as funds are not payable on demand but are payable either at the maturity of a specified time period, or at the maturity of the assets into which the funds are invested. We address these financial products when we discuss the contracts of *wakalah* and *mudharabah* and we look at the models of asset management businesses, investment banking, funds management, and finance companies.

CHAPTER **13**

Qard

The contract of *qard* is one of lending money. It is not a sale contract or a lease contract, but rather a contract where one party transfers ownership over a certain asset to a counterparty. The counterparty is permitted to utilize the asset, but is required to return the asset after a specific period of time. The counterparty may return an asset similar in quality and quantity to the one borrowed provided the lender agrees to the arrangement.[1]

The asset or subject matter lent may be an asset like an object, such as a machine, a tool, or it may be money. In either circumstance, the borrower is required to return the asset, and is liable if the asset suffers any damages, but the borrower is not required to return anything more than borrowed, so an interest payment would be out of the question if the subject matter borrowed is money.

In the context of Islamic finance, one party that has surplus money may lend the money to a counterparty that suffers from a deficit of money for a specific period of time. The borrower enjoys full ownership rights over the money borrowed, and may spend it, invest it, or even lend it to another party. However, the borrower is required to return the borrowed sums, but is not required to return any excess over and above the amount borrowed. The borrower may as a courtesy to the lender for lending money, pay the lender an excess amount at his or her discretion using the concept of *hibah* (Figure 13.1).

[1] "He who will give Allah qard al hasan, which Allah will double into his credit and multiply many times." [Al-Baqarah (2): 245] "If you give Allah qard al hasan, he will double it to your credit and he will grant you forgiveness." [Al-Tagabun (64):17] "And give Allah qard al hasan." [Al-Maidah (5): 12] "And give Allah qard al hasan, it will be increased manifold to their credit." [Al-Hadid (57): 18] "Who is he that will give Allah qard al hasan? For Allah will increase it manifold to his credit." [Al-Hadid (57):11] "Establish regular prayer and give regular charity and give Allah qard al hasan"---. [Al-Muzzammil (73): 20]

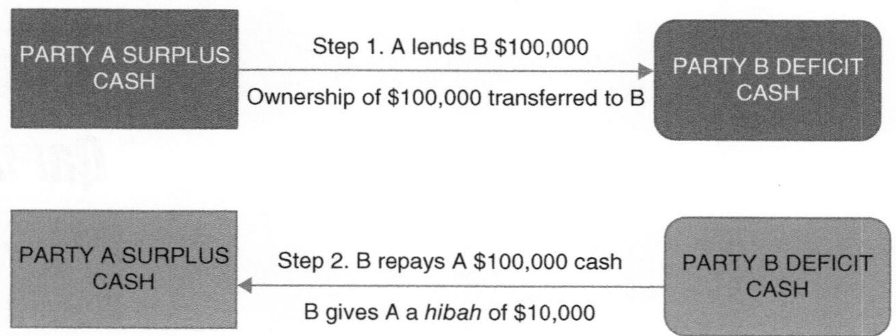

FIGURE 13.1 *Qard* Process Flow

The payment of *hibah* is at the discretion of Party B, and cannot be made a condition by Party A for extending the loan. Nor can the amount of the *hibah* be tabulated *ex-ante*. If the loan is made conditional on the giving of *hibah*, the loan becomes impermissible and the *hibah* becomes *ribah*.

APPLICATIONS OF THE CONTRACT OF *QARD*

The contract of *hibah* can be used by an Islamic bank on the liability side as well as on the asset side of the balance sheet.

If *qard* is employed on the liability side, the Islamic bank will mobilize funds by borrowing moneys from capital providers in the marketplace. Customers will lend the Islamic bank money under the contract of *qard*; the Islamic bank will guarantee repayment of the loan within a specified period of time. It will be at the discretion of the Islamic bank to return the loan with any additional gift of *hibah* or not.

The amount lent by the customer is then recorded as a deposit placed by the customer in the Islamic bank. This deposit is a demand deposit and here comes an enhancement to the contract of *qard*, where the depositor can withdraw, or "call in the *qard* loan" at any time, or can deposit money into the account or "enhance the loan amount" at any time. Strictly speaking every time the customer withdraws or deposits an amount with an Islamic bank, the customer enters into a new contract with the Islamic bank.

On the asset side, the application of the *qard* contract is straightforward. An Islamic bank may extend a loan to a customer for a specified period of time. The Islamic bank may obtain collateral from the borrower under the contract of *rahn*, or a guarantee from a third party as a credit enhancement. However, the Islamic bank cannot demand of the borrower to pay an amount in excess of the loan amount as this would be tantamount to charging interest on loans.

QARD AS A DEPOSIT INSTRUMENT

Islamic banks may mobilize deposits using the contracts of *wadiah* and *qard*. Both contracts require the Islamic bank to guarantee repayment of the money placed under *wadiah* or lent under *qard*. National Deposit Insurance Schemes cover funds mobilized under these contracts, as they are referred to as *deposits* and are payable on demand. The Islamic bank is not required to pay any amount in addition to the *wadiah* amount or *qard* amount, but may pay a *hibah* to depositors at its own discretion. This *hibah* as discussed earlier may be a percentage of the amounts placed with the Islamic bank. Islamic banks cannot advertise the feature of *hibah* when mobilizing funds and cannot commit to the payment of *hibah*, either.[2] The Islamic banks are also required to ensure that the payment of *hibah* does not become a customary practice.

RECORDING OF *QARD*

Any amounts placed with an Islamic bank will be recorded as a liability. When an Islamic bank receives a cash deposit from a customer of, say, $100,000, the following entries are made. The entries are very similar to the ones we observed in the chapter on *wadiah*.

Debit Cash	$100,000
Credit *Qard* Liability Customer A	$100,000

When a customer withdraws funds, the entries are as follows:

Credit Cash	$100,000
Debit *Qard* Liability Customer A	$100,000

The bank also accepts these deposits and pools them into a liability fund and utilizes the money to extend financing to other parties. This can be seen in Figure 13.2.

When customers withdraw funds from their accounts, they actually withdraw from a joint pool of funds. Islamic banks maintain records of individual customer's balances and also maintain internal ledgers of what percentage of funds mobilized under *qard* or *wadiah* for that matter are

[2] See Bank Negara Malaysia, "Hibah (Shariah Requirements and Optional Practices) Exposure Draft," December 2013.

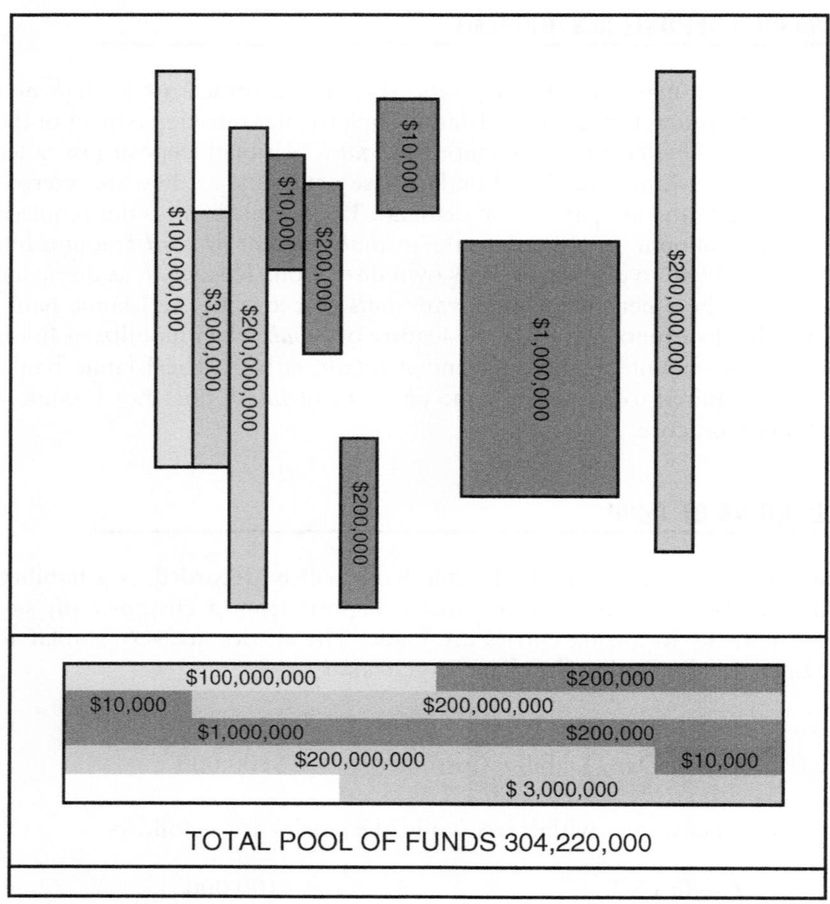

FIGURE 13.2 The Concept of Pooling Funds

used to finance assets. We see in the chapter on income distribution how depositors into the *qard* pool are rewarded via the contract of *hibah* from the returns generated by investment of these funds.

CONCLUSION

The contracts of *qard* and *wadiah* behave in a similar manner and are found typically on the liability side of Islamic banks.

CHAPTER 14

Mudharabah

The contract of *mudharabah* is considered to be one of the pillars of Islamic finance and yet it is a subject of intense controversy. The contract is basically one of partnership between two parties, where one party is a capital provider and the second party is an entrepreneur. The capital provider does not interfere in the management of the funds provided to the entrepreneur and is compensated by the latter with a share in the returns generated by economic activity or investments initiated by the entrepreneur.

The contract involves two parties, one a *rab ul maal* or capital provider and the other a *mudharib*, or entrepreneur. The capital provider transfers capital into the control (not the ownership) of a *mudharib*, and instructs the *mudharib* to engage the funds into commercial activity to generate returns. The *rab ul maal* may specify the kinds of commercial transactions the *mudharib* may engage in or may leave the contract open ended where the *mudharib* may engage in any commercial enterprise he or she may find suitable. At this stage, a *mudharib* behaves like an agent of a *rab ul mal*, or capital provider (Figure 14.1).

The *mudharib* can charge an upront fee for acting on behalf of the capital provider and managing the latter's funds or assets. The status of a *mudharib* evolves during the various stages of a contract as the status of a *mudharib* is much like a wakeel in the initial stages of the contract; as profits are generated with the efforts of the *mudharib*, the *mudharib's* status is upgraded to that of a partner. As a partner the *mudharib* enjoys certain rights over the profits according to a pre-agreed profit sharing ratio.

The *mudharib* employs the capital into various lines of business, for instance, including purchasing assets on spot basis and selling them to customers on a deferred payment basis. In this context, the *mudharib* is using the *rab ul mal*'s capital to enter into debt financing. If profits are generated from the commercial enterprises undertaken, the *mudharib* and the *rab ul mal* share the profits on a pre-agreed profit-sharing ratio (PSR). So if any commercial enterprise earns, say, \$100,000 in 90 days, and the PSR is 70 percent to the capital provider and 30 percent to the *mudharib*, then the

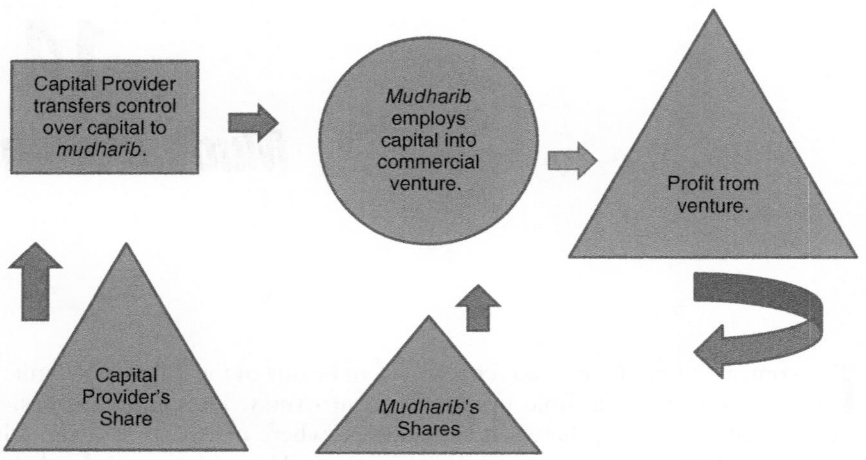

FIGURE 14.1 *Mudharabah* Process Flow

capital provider will earn $70,000 and the *mudharib* will earn $30,000. If the *mudharib* returns the capital provided back to the capital provider, the *mudharabah* contract is thereby terminated. If the capital is reinvested into another commercial enterprise, then the *mudharabah* contract is renewed. If the *rab ul mal* wishes to liquidate his or her position before the returns have matured, the *mudharib* can compensate the *rab ul mal* via executing a **constructive liquidation** of assets and calculating the *rab ul mal*'s share of the profits. The *mudharib* may pay off the *rab ul mal* with his or her own funds, or find another *rab ul mal* to replace the original capital provider.

So in essence, one capital provider may have contracts with different *mudharib*s, but each must be provided separate lots of capital. Similarly, a *mudharib* may be engaged by several capital providers, provided the capital provided by various capital providers is kept separately or maintained in distinctive records. The *mudharib* can combine the capital provided by various *rab ul mal*s and invest the funds thus raised collectively, but must maintain proper records of each *rab ul mal*'s share of capital and share of profits. When a commercial enterprise generates profit, the *mudharib* de facto becomes a partner of the capital provider and is entitled to a share of the profits.

A unique element here is that in case the commercial enterprise generates losses, the *mudharib* is not liable for losses, unless it can be demonstrated that the *mudharib* acted with negligence, or misappropriated the funds, or made investments contrary to the instructions provided by the *rab ul mal*.[1]

[1]Muhammad Yusuf, Saleem, *Islamic Commercial Law* (Singapore: Wiley Finance, 2013).

What is crucial to understand is that the *rab ul mal* cannot interfere in the management of the capital; the *rab ul mal* may provide guidelines or specify how capital is to be invested but cannot interfere with the workings of the *mudharib*. The *rab ul mal* has the right to know how the capital is deployed, however. The *mudharib* maintains all relevant records of profits and losses; all profits are to be distributed post-ante, that is, after they have been generated. The *mudharib* is also not able to guarantee any returns nor the principal capital employed.

If we replace capital providers with bank customers, and the *mudharib* with an Islamic bank, we have a profit-sharing account with no capital or profit guarantees.

SIMPLE APPLICATION OF *MUDHARABAH*

Imagine a *mudharib* that raises $800 from a *rab ul mal*, purchases an asset for $800, and sells it to a third party for $1,600 via a BBA contract over 16 equal payments of $100 each. Each payment has a principal repayment of $50 embedded in, whereby the *mudharib* will reduce his receivables with each payment of $50. Each installment will also have a $50 partial profit payment embedded in it. With each payment the *mudharib* will record a $50 profit from the sale.

On the payment of each installment, the *mudharib* will pay back the capital provider $50 of the $800 provided by the latter.

On the payment of each installment, the *mudharib* will share the profit of $50 as per a pre-agreed profit-sharing ratio of say 50:50. So the *mudharib* will record an income of $25, and the *rab ul mal* will record an income of $25.

After all installments have been paid, the *mudharib* would have recovered the $800 provided by the capital provider and returned the funds back to the capital provider. The *mudharib* would also have collected $800 in total profit, which would be shared on a 50:50 basis with the capital provider in 16 equal installments of $25 each.

The scenario is illustrated in Table 14.1.

At the inception of the *murabahah* sale contract, the *mudharib* is able to determine that the profit to be earned from the sale is $800 or 50 percent and then can at least offer (but not commit) to pay this return to the capital provider in easy installments. As this contract has a built-in profit rate determined ex-ante, it lends itself very easily to banking products. The extensive use of *mudharabah* contracts to mobilize funds from depositors and allocate the funds to fund *murabahah* contracts has become the addiction of Islamic banks, as it allows Islamic banks to communicate an indicative rate of return with fair accuracy to depositors. This indicative rate of return is closely linked to the profit rate applied in the *murabahah* sale contract.

TABLE 14.1 *Mudharabah*-Backed Cash Financing

	1	2	3	4	5	6	7	8	9	10	11	12	13	14	15	16	Total
Total Payment	100	100	100	100	100	100	100	100	100	100	100	100	100	100	100	100	1,600
Principal Payment—Capital Provider's Share	50	50	50	50	50	50	50	50	50	50	50	50	50	50	50	50	800
Profit Repayment	50	50	50	50	50	50	50	50	50	50	50	50	50	50	50	50	800
Capital Provider's Shares	25	25	25	25	25	25	25	25	25	25	25	25	25	25	25	25	
Mudharib's Shares	25	25	25	25	25	25	25	25	25	25	25	25	25	25	25	25	

PERPETUAL *MUDHARABAH*

Another deviation occurs if the capital provider is unwilling to go the long haul and pulls out of the contract after receiving three payments only (Table 14.2). As each capital provider liquidates his or her position the *mudharib* returns the capital provider his *full capital* along with the profit accrued up to that point, whether it is paid by the buyer or not. (For instance the purchaser may wish to pay the full sale price in installments but will pay the profit in one balloon payment at maturity.)

At every stage, the *mudharib* would require less funds to fund the asset as the outstanding amount is reduced with every payment. So if the first *rab ul mal* terminates the *mudharabah 1* contract, the *mudharib* would only need $1,300 from the second *rab ul mal* and so on.

RE-*MUDHARABAH*

Re-mudharabah is a circumstance where a *mudharib* becomes a *rab ul mal* in a subsequent transaction. In this arrangement a *mudharib* may receive for instance $1,000,000 from a capital provider, onward places the same $1,000,000 to a third party, and in turn then becomes the capital provider in the second transaction. The original *mudharib* entrusts the economic investments made by the second *mudharib* and enjoys a profit-sharing relationship with the second *mudharib* and the first *rab ul mal*.

RESTRICTED *MUDHARABAH* AND UNRESTRICTED *MUDHARABAH*

A capital provider in a *mudharabah* contract does not influence the *mudharib* on how invested capital may be employed, but certainly can choose different

TABLE 14.2 Financing Funded by *Mudharabah*

												MUDHARABAH 5			M 6	
									MUDHARABAH 4			4 payments pending			1 Payment	
						MUDHARABAH 3			7 payments pending							
			MUDHARABAH 2 $1300			10 payments pending										
MUDHARABAH 1 $ 1600			13 payments pending													
16 payments pending																
1	2	3	4	5	6	7	8	9	10	11	12	13	14	15	16	TOTAL
		300			300			300			300			300	100	1600
		150			150			150			150			150	50	800
		150			150			150			150			150	50	800

FINANCING FUNDED BY *MUDHARABAH* IN SIX STAGES

mudharibs on the basis of their expertise. The contract of *mudharabah* is more suited to asset management companies than banks where various fund managers disclose to investors their specific industrial sectors of investment, their risk profiles, their trading techniques, and the historical range of returns offered to investors. Fund managers, for instance, specialize in oil and gas sectors, in commodities, in commodity futures, in indexes, in stocks, in emerging markets stocks, in fixed income instruments, and in a wide array of other synthetic products. An investor chooses a fund manager for the sector he or she wishes, and discloses his or her risk appetite to the fund manager. By specifying the sector of investment that the investor seeks, and by specifying the risk profile of the investor, the investor offers the fund manager a *restricted mudharabah* contract. If the fund manager breaches the restrictions placed by the investor as *mudharib*, the latter will have to make good any losses.

However, if the investor chooses to leave all such investment decisions to the fund manager, this is an *unrestricted mudharabah* and the fund manager as *mudharib* enjoys more flexibility in making investment decisions. If a fund manager is employed under the contract of *mudharabah*, the manager enjoys a share in the profits generated by investment of the investor's funds. If the fund manager is engaged under a contract of *wakalah*, then the fund manager only receives a front-end fee for services irrespective of what returns are generated by the fund. Fund managers may also be rewarded on a performance basis under the contract of *juala*, where if the fund earns more than a certain percentage return, the fund manager can enjoy a share in the surplus earnings.

The application of *mudharabah* to mobilize funds from depositors that are used in credit financing and leasing is slightly misaligned to the principles of *mudharabah*. In a contract of *mudharabah* the investor, depositor, or capital provider must have some knowledge of the investments made by the *mudharib*. This information is disclosed by fund managers, but not by banks as their credit portfolios are typically kept secret to protect the privacy of their borrowers. *Mudharabah* account holders are left pretty much in the dark in exactly how their funds are channeled into acquiring assets and how these assets are performing. Fund managers offer investors an indication of how their fund is performing by offering a daily net unit value to investors that gives them an indication of what returns to expect. New rulings in Malaysia under IFSA 2013 now require Islamic banks to offer similar tools to investors to gauge the returns on their investments.

MUDHARABAH AS A DEPOSIT

Critics of Islamic banks feel that the contract of *mudharabah* has been misused to develop a fixed deposit product where an indicative rate of return is offered to customers up front. Classical scholars feel that if *mudharabah* is implemented in its true spirit, it cannot guarantee returns to capital providers nor guarantee their principals. Yet most Islamic banks do offer such guarantees on funds mobilized under *mudharabah* contracts. Furthermore, the bank as *mudharib* also makes good any losses by injecting funds from shareholders' capital as a *qard ul hassan* so as to not impact the returns promised to *mudharabah* account holders.

This practice is unique to Islamic banks. *Mudharibs* are not required to guarantee returns to their capital providers or investors, as the contract is one of partnership and implies risk sharing. However, if the *mudharib* is unable to secure additional funds by not guaranteeing investments, or is unable to compete with conventional banks, then Islamic banks end up guaranteeing any losses incurred on investments of *mudharabah* funds using their capital, in much the same manner as conventional banks do. This in turn discourages Islamic banks from funding risky assets with the money mobilized through *mudharabah* deposits. Islamic banks therefore much like their conventional counterparts are averse to financing start up projects, SMEs or such borrowers that are unable to provide any collateral as they pose considerable risk of default. This element of guaranteeing returns has reduced Islamic banks to the status of risk-averse conventional banks but this is not as much the doing of Islamic banks as it is the result of the mind-set of depositors and investors.

Banks do not lend, invest, or finance using their own money; it is the money of their depositors and investors that they use. But when banks are required to guarantee the funds mobilized by depositors, they must take steps to mitigate the risks of default posed by borrowers. The first such step of mitigating risks is to obtain adequate collateral from borrowers, and thus capital in the form of loans or financing is made available only to those with some financial or fixed assets accumulated in their portfolio. A consequence of such measures is that the rich get richer and the poor remain denied of capital and funding. Banks cannot be singled out and blamed for this, as it is investors or depositors who are equally to blame for creating this inequality in access of capital by being risk averse.

MUDHARABAH AS A FUND

Bank Negara Malaysia, through the Islamic Financial Services Act of 2013,[2] has requested all Islamic banks to segregate deposits and investment accounts, and requires Islamic banks to treat funds mobilized under the contract of *mudharabah* as investment funds.

[2]Islamic Financial Service Act 2013, Malaysia.

Previously *mudharabah* contracts were used to mobilize deposits. These deposits came under the countries national deposit insurance schemes, like deposits mobilized under *wadiah, qard*, and *commodity murabahah*. Assets funded by *mudharabah* deposits incurred capital charges for Islamic banks and losses were absorbed by shareholders.

As of 2013, however, Bank Negara Malaysia has instructed Islamic banks to phase in the new guidelines for *mudharabah* funds.[3] All funds mobilized under this contract now would not be guaranteed by the national deposit insurance scheme of PDIM.[4] To compensate for the increased risk thereby faced by investors, Islamic banks would have to offer high rates of return to their customers. This is a new product for Islamic banks and one that Malaysia is perfectly poised to launch as Malaysian Islamic banks offer a substitute fixed deposit product whereby customers can opt for *commodity murabahah*. Customers who wish to invest in a *mudharabah* fund and take the risk of losing their principal for higher returns can invest in *mudharabah* accounts. Assets funded by *mudharabah* funds do not incur capital charges for Islamic banks as any losses incurred on assets will be passed on directly to customers and would not be absorbed by banks.

INTERBANK *MUDHARABAH* PLACEMENTS

Islamic banks use the contract of *mudharabah* for interbank placements in the Islamic money market. Deficit banks that require funds from surplus banks invite them to place funds for various short-term maturities to fund assets held by the deficit bank. The deficit bank shares the returns generated from assets with the surplus bank on a pre-agreed profit-sharing ratio. This is illustrated in detail in the chapter on asset/liability management for Islamic banks.

INDICATIVE RATE OF RETURN

Islamic banks are unable to guarantee any returns on funds mobilized using *mudharabah* contracts. However, typically Islamic banks fund assets under contracts of *murabahah* and *ijara* on the asset side of their balance sheet, and are therefore confident that on their sale-based and lease-based contracts they will earn a specific rate of return. This rate is the fixed or floating profit

[3]Islamic Financial Service Act 2013, Malaysia.
[4]PIDM, www.pidm.gov.my, accessed June 29, 2014.

rate placed in sale contracts and the rental rates applied to *ijara* contracts. Deducting for operational costs, and the bank's share of returns, Islamic banks feel confident enough to offer depositors an indicative rate of return on *mudharabah* deposits. Depositors therefore treat funds placed in *mudharabah* accounts as fixed deposits, offering specific profit rates over a specific period of time.

PROFIT SHARING RATIO

The profit sharing ratio (PSR) is determined at the outset of a *mudharabah* contract. Before a *rab ul maal* transfers control over capital to the *mudharib*, both parties agree to the several terms and conditions. They must agree to the definition of *profit*, to how profit will be calculated, and how it will be shared between the *rab ul maal* and the *mudharib*. The contract of *mudharbah* is very interesting as the status of the *mudharib* evolves from being a sort of agent of the capital provider while undertaking economic activity, to becoming a partner of the *rab ul maal* when profits are actually declared. The onus of declaring profit is on the *mudharib* and not the right of the *rab ul maal*.

Thus, if the two parties agree on a PSR of 80:20, where capital provider earns 80 percent of declared profits and the *mudharib* earns 20 percent, for every $100 of profit, $80 will go to the capital provider and the balance to the *mudharib*. This ratio can change over the course of the arrangement between the two parties as well. If the *mudharib* is an Islamic bank, and the Islamic bank is facing an environment of increasing interest rates and needs to retain depositors, an Islamic bank can simply increase the PSR in favor of the capital provider or depositor. In this manner the depositor will effectively earn higher returns on funds placed with the bank.

Alternatively, if interest rates decrease, Islamic banks can alter the PSR in their favor, such that depositors earn less on their deposits. The same mechanism is applied in interbank placements where the capital provider is an Islamic bank with surplus funds and the *mudharib* is an Islamic bank with deficit funds.

IMPORTANCE OF DISCLOSURE AND ACCOUNTING TREATMENTS

Whether funds are mobilized as deposits or as funds, the most crucial factor is the accurate assessment of profit, and the full disclosure of earnings and losses accrued from the investment of *mudharabah* investors' funds. Islamic banks and fund managers may use funds to purchase financial assets such as Islamic bonds or *sukuk*, equities, or stocks in *shariah*-compliant firms, and government-issued commercial notes. Islamic banks use the funds to fund assets such as house financing, commercial financing under *murabahah* contracts, and the like. These assets are valued each year according to the market value of the assets on the balance sheet at the close of the financial year or quarter. For instance, in Table 14.3, a bank owns the following assets on its balance sheet.

The financial assets on the bank's balance sheet generate returns in two ways, one by virtue of coupon payments offered on fixed income instruments, and the other by appreciation in their prices. Equities offer dividends and capital gains as well. Receivables offer the bank a profit rate and compensate the bank with the payments made by the borrowers on their sale or lease contracts with the bank.

The problem lies in how profits may be calculated. In order to realize capital gains the bank must sell the financial assets at market value and share the profits with customers. However, banks report the capital gains as profits without selling the assets under special accounting treatments allowed by regulators, under the concept of *constructive liquidation*. This profit is shown as capital gains, but may or may not be realized in that the assets that appreciate in value may or may not have been sold. Although no cash has been paid on these capital gains, the assets are not sold, the bank still treats the difference in their market value and cost as profit, but this profit is not realized income. If the bank wishes to sell the asset in the future, the market value of the said assets may have declined and the bank may even record losses. If Islamic banks share such unrealized capital gains with *mudharabah* account holders, customers are compensated with profits that are not actually earned.

In the banking world, banks maintain reserves for profits paid out from unearned income; there is no mention of such reserves in the traditional literature.

MUDHARABAH AS AN ASSET PRODUCT

The contract of *mudharabah* can be used to develop an asset product based on equity financing. A bank can provide funds to a customer as a capital provider and share in returns generated by any economic activity undertaken by the latter. All profits would be shared as per a pre-agreed profit-sharing

TABLE 14.3 Actual Earnings versus Constructive Earnings

Assets	Amount	Expected Returns	Returns for the Month	Quantity Held	Buying Price	Market Value	Capital Gains
Short Term		Per Annum					
Central Bank Notes	100,000,000.00	3.00%	250,000.00	1,000,000.00	100.00	101.50	1,500,000
Sukuk	300,000,000.00	3.50%	875,000.00	300,000.00	1,000.00	1,003.00	900,000
Interbank Placements	200,000,000.00	5.00%	833,333.33				
Long Term							
Government Notes	350,000,000.00	6.00%	1,750,000.00	350,000.00	1,000.00	1,002.00	700,000
Equities	450,000,000.00	7.00%	2,625,000.00				
Muarabahah Financing	475,000,000.00	8.00%	3,166,666.67				
Ijara	150,000,000.00	8.50%	1,062,500.00				
Total	2,025,000,000.00		10,562,500.00				3,100,000.00
Total Returns							**Constructive Earnings**
Total Earnings							13,662,500
Customer's Share							10,930,000

ratio, but all losses would be borne by the bank. Such an arrangement is not very attractive to Islamic banks as it exposes them to considerable risk. Banks are not able to obtain any collateral from customers in such contracts nor can any capital or returns be guaranteed. Banks can, however, obtain third-party guarantees from those willing to provide them. In the event of default, the bank can claim losses from the third-party guarantor and not the immediate customer.

ACCOUNTING TREATMENT OF *MUDHARABAH* TRANSACTIONS

As a liability product, the accounting treatment for a *mudharabah* deposit is similar to that of *qard* or *wadiah* as Islamic banks have traditionally treated *mudharabah* as a liability account. However, certain critics feel that a *mudharabah* account should be treated not as a liability but as an off–balance sheet entry or as a fund. Any losses accrued by the fund depreciate the value of the fund and are recorded as losses in the income statement. The balance sheet entries are illustrated in Table 14.4 for a fund of $100,000 that experiences profits in Quarters 1 and 3 and losses in Quarters 2 and 4. Any profits generated by the fund are recorded as income and profits earned are credited into the fund's cash balances.

CONCLUSION

The new rulings on *mudharabah* in IFSA 2013[5] offer interesting opportunities for Islamic banking to evolve into an equity-based system as opposed to a debt-based system. Funds mobilized under *mudharabah* are not treated as deposits and guaranteed by the regulators or the banks themselves. These features may cause depositors to flee to conventional banks or to fixed deposit structures such as commodity *murabahah*. The product may also invite the interest of a new class of semi-depositors that have a risk appetite of investors. Such customers would be willing to take additional risks, provided that Islamic banks offer higher returns on these investments. It would be interesting to see how Islamic banks embrace the challenge of the new regulations and what new asset products are developed that satisfy the demand of riskier investments.

[5] Islamic Financial Service Act 2013, Malaysia.

TABLE 14.4 *Mudharabah* Fund Accounting Treatment

Event				Balance Sheet			Income Statement		Net Results	
	Profit	PSR	Bank Share		Debit	Credit	Debit	Credit	Balance in *Mudharabah* Financing	55,000
Beginning of Year				Cash		100,000			Starting Balance in Cash Account	100,000
				Mudharabah Financing	100,000				Ending Balance in Cash Account	(51,000)
Quarter 1	30,000	70:30	21,000	Cash	21,000			21,000	Total Gains	49,000
Quarter 2	(20,000)	70:30	(20,000)	*Mudharabah* Financing		−20,000	20,000		Total Losses	45,000
Quarter 3	40,000	70:30	28,000	Cash	28,000			28,000	Net Gains/Losses	4,000
Quarter 4	−25,000	70:30	(25,000)	*Mudharabah* Financing		−25,000	25,000			
Year-End Result			4,000							

CHAPTER 15

Musharakah

Musharakah is primarily a contract of partnership and mutual agency. Two or more legal entities may combine labor, expertise, capital, reputation, fixed assets, and other assets and create a legal commercial enterprise to undertake economic activity. Profits and losses are shared by the partners as is the management of the enterprise. The *shariah* dictates how profits and losses are to be shared. The Prophet ([saw] peace be upon him) specified in a *hadith* that profits may be shared on a pre-agreed ratio but losses are to be shared on the basis of the capital contributed by each participant.[1] This *hadith* is a precursor of the concept of limited liability the potential of which was not fully recognized by Muslim traders as much as it was by European merchants in the sixteenth century.

The concept of *mushrakah* allows numerous capital providers to contribute capital to commercial enterprises. The commercial enterprise created what is known as the *sharik* and it is a legal entity separate from partners that contributed capital to create it. This entity can undertake business in its own name, own assets, and incur debt. The most crucial point of the *sharik* is that in the event of default, partners in the *sharik* are only liable to lose the capital injected into the company and not their personal capital. Personal assets were segregated from assets of the *sharik* and the assets invested in the *sharik*. The *sharik* is therefore the forefather of the joint stock company, which itself later evolved into public listed companies.

The concept of *musharakah* and limited liability is the most important one that was contributed by the Prophet (saw) to the world of commercial trade and enterprise and is surprisingly an undertone in most texts on Islamic finance.

---

[1]It is narrated that the Prophet ([saw] pbuh) had said that the profit sharing from something that is not in a person's charge is not permissible, and that profit goes with liability.

MUSHARAKAH AND BANKING

The concept of *mushrakah* can be applied both to the liability side of a bank's balance sheet and to the asset side.

Customers or fund providers may offer funds to banks to invest in various economic ventures on a profit-and-loss-sharing basis; however, for each contract of *musharakah* the bank would have to create a separate legal entity on its books. A depositor would be a partner providing capital; shareholders would also provide capital to a separate legal enterprise. Both the depositor and the bank would have legal control over these funds and both could contribute to the management and investment of the funds pooled. Customers would then not be considered to be depositors as in the case of contracts of *wadiah* and *qard*, nor would they be investors in the *mudharabah*, but in effect would be partners. Both customer and the bank would have joint ownership and control of any assets controlled by the partnership. In such an arrangement, the bank and customer would pool funds to acquire specific assets in which ownership, risk, and returns would be shared. These assets could be financial assets such as receivables and these assets would in a sense be ring-fenced from the remaining assets on the bank's balance sheet.

The funds provided by the customer would not be a liability as under the contract of *musharakah*, returns and principal amounts are not guaranteed, nor can any one party obtain any collateral from the second party for performance as both parties have a relationship of joint ownership and not lender or borrower. The Islamic bank undertaking such a venture would report the funds contributed to the partnership, and the returns and losses generated in separate balance sheets as the arrangement would create separate legal entities. The Islamic bank could report the investment in the *mushrakah* arrangement as an equity investment in a subsidiary. The process flow is illustrated in Figure 15.1.

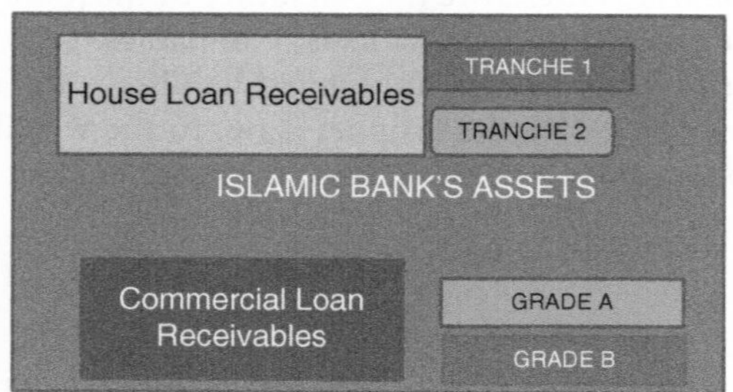

FIGURE 15.1 Bank Assets

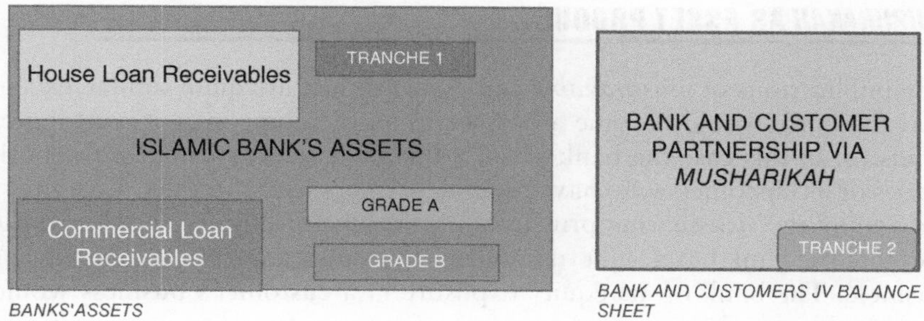

FIGURE 15.2 Bank and Customers as Joint Venture Partners

Imagine a bank with various assets on its balance sheet. In the example illustrated in Figure 15.2, the bank has house loan receivables and commercial loan receivables with each set having subsets based on quality and maturity. A customer wants to share the risks and returns on Tranche 2 of the house loan receivables and approaches the bank. We must recall that house loan receivables are typically long-term investments. If the customer is willing to provide funds that match the tenor of the various loans in Tranche 2, this arrangement would be possible. The appeal to the bank is that it no longer needs to fund this portfolio of Tranche 2 with deposits that incur expenses and capital charges.

The bank has spun off Tranche 2 into a separate entity in which it is a partner based on the capital provided by the customer and the bank itself. The risk of Tranche 2 receivables will be shared by the new customer and the bank. All returns on the portfolio will be shared by the two parties, with the bank bringing the income from Tranche 2 back into its own income statement.

The above arrangement is a viable alternative to securitizing mortgage portfolios and using them as assets to back issuances of *sukuk* or selling the housing loans portfolio at a discount to other parties. Both these practices and their misuse were contributors to the global financial crises of 2008.

Using this method banks can seek equity partners for certain risks and portfolios it holds on its balance sheets. The usage of derivatives such as interest rate swaps and currency swaps cannot mitigate credit risk. Credit default swaps, which are like insurance policies on loans, can cover for credit risk but these are risky instruments and are not accessible to small- and medium-size banks. Equity partners would undertake greater due diligence on such portfolios and not merely rely on ratings companies' opinions and risks would be shared by parties and not transferred from loan originators to other parties.

MUSHRAKAH AS ASSET PRODUCT

The implications of *mushrakah* as an asset product are quite similar, except that the bank would become a partner in all the companies it contributes funds to. In this case the bank is not a financier, but a partner in the businesses of its customers who have become partners with the bank. Customers may enjoy the risk-sharing principles of *mushrakah* but may not enjoy the fact that the bank has a right to influence the management of the customer's business. The bank on its equity exposure in a customer's business would not be able to obtain any guarantees of returns from its customers and therefore would not be able to guarantee returns to depositors who fund *mushrakah* assets. However, the bank would have actual ownership in the assets of the companies with which they do business. In the event that the investments generate no returns, the bank can liquidate the assets of the companies and recover its funds, avoiding the typical bank-initiated liquidation proceedings.

The contract of *mushrakah*, however, is never used for mobilizing funds by a bank other than in the context of issuing shares. It is not crafted into a financial product on the liability side of the balance sheet and due to the high-risk nature of the contract, Islamic banks are averse to using the contract on its asset side as well.

Basel places a higher risk weightage for assets under the *mushrakah* contract,[2] implying that the contract is not meant for debt-based financial intermediaries like banks and is more suitable for firms that operate as venture capitalists.

POOLING OF ASSETS IN *MUSHRAKAH*

One of the criticisms of equity is that two partners entering into a partnership with each other allows one to act on behalf of the other, allows each one control over capital of the other, and allows control over management of the assets acquired. Each partner may willingly surrender certain rights of management over the assets, but the rights of ownership are inherent in a *mushrakah* contract.

We use a simple example to illustrate this point. Party A owns \$100,000 worth of fixed assets. In Figure 15.3, Party A wishes to raise \$20,000 of capital for a new commercial opportunity.

Party A can borrow \$20,000 from creditors and incur a fixed expense of interest on the loan. The creditors would have no say in the management

[2]Bank of International Settlements, "Basel II: International Convergence of Capital Measurement and Capital Standards: A Revised Framework" (Basel, Switzerland: Bank of International Settlements, 2006).

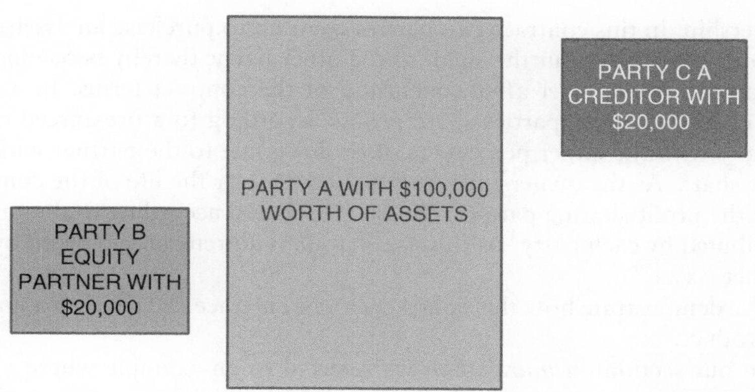

FIGURE 15.3 Pooling of Assets

of the company, nor would they have any ownership stake in the company's assets. Certain assets of the company may be kept as collateral with the creditors, but rights of creditors over collateral are only exercised in the event of default. Alternatively, Party A can raise funds from Party B who wishes to become a partner, not just in the assets that Party A will acquire with the additional capital provided by Party B, but in all the company's assets. Party A would be hesitant to take such an investor, exposing the entire company worth $100,000 to the equity partner for a 20 percent equity stake. This matter is resolved by issuing shares to Party B in exchange for the capital. Each share will entitle the shareholder to a share of profits generated by all the assets of the company and will entitle the shareholder to manage the company. If each share is worth $1, Party B has 20,000 shares, and Party A has 100,000 shares in the company. Party A still dominates the capital provided to the company, and thus enjoys the dominant share in profits, losses, and management.

However, when Party B or Party C contribute funds to Party A to acquire assets for new economic activity, they are entitled to dividends or interest payments not just from the economic activity their funds helped finance but from the assets of the entire company. There is no way of segregating the funds contributed by the creditors C or the equity partner B from the funds of Party A when their moneys are pooled together. This is a condition of a *mushrakah* contract.

MUSHRAKAH MUTANAQISAH

Mushrakah mutanaqisah offers a unique approach to financing the purchase of an asset. *Mushrakah mutanaqisah* (*MM*) is a concept of diminishing partnership. In this contract two parties contract to purchase an asset; over time one party buys out the share of the other party, thereby becoming the sole owner of the asset after conclusion of the contract terms. In a contract of *MM* the two parties share profits according to a pre-agreed ratio, typically with the larger percentage of profits going to the partner with the larger share. As the ownership pattern changes over the life of the contract so do the profit-sharing patterns. Losses are shared according to the capital contributed by each party[3] as this is a *shariah* requirement stipulated by the Prophet (saw).

We demonstrate how this contract can be enhanced to develop a financing product.

In our section on *murabahah* we referred to an example where a customer is looking to purchase a house worth $120,000. The customer makes a downpayment of $20,000 to the seller and approaches an Islamic bank to finance the balance of $100,000. The Islamic bank does so by "buying" the house from the seller for $100,000 and then selling it to the customer for $150,000 over 10 payment periods or years. The Islamic bank charges the customer a profit rate of 5 percent per annum and over 10 years earns a profit of $50,000 on the transaction. The purchase price for the Islamic bank is $100,000 and the selling price is $150,000. This can be seen in Table 15.1.

The *MM* structure offers an alternative. An Islamic bank and a customer co-own a house worth $120,000, with the Islamic bank's ownership being worth $100,000 and the customer's share $20,000. The two entities enter into an *MM* contract for 10 years, whereby the customer will gradually buy out the share of the Islamic bank, and for the period of 10 years as the customer will reside in the house, the customer will pay a rent to the Islamic bank under the contract of *ijara*. The important thing to note is that with each subsequent payment, the customer's share of ownership keeps increasing and subsequently the rental payment keeps decreasing as well. Table 15.2 illustrates how the above contract is executed.

At the outset, the Islamic bank owns 83 percent of the house with a $100,000 investment, and the customer has an ownership stake of 17 percent with a $20,000 equity stake. The Islamic bank charges a rental rate of 11.111 percent on the percentage of the asset that the Islamic bank owns. Each year the customer increases his or her equity stake by $10,000 and

[3]It is narrated that the Prophet ([saw] pbuh) had said that the profit sharing from something that is not in a person's charge is not permissible, and that profit goes with liability. This is also stated in one of the major Islamic legal maxims that, "Loss is burdened on those who have acquired profit (al-ghurm bil ghonm)." Any loss on the partnership should affect both partners, who each took a portion of the risk according to the amount invested/capital invested in the operations.

TABLE 15.1 *Mushrakah Mutanaqisah* Payments

			Profit	Principal		Profit Rate	Principal	Tenor	Profit	Sale Price
Initial cash outflow	CF0	−100,000				5%	100,000	10	50,000	150,000
Subsequent cash inflows	CF1	15,000	5,000	10,000						
	CF2	15,000	5,000	10,000						
	CF3	15,000	5,000	10,000						
	CF4	15,000	5,000	10,000						
	CF5	15,000	5,000	10,000						
	CF6	15,000	5,000	10,000						
	CF7	15,000	5,000	10,000						
	CF8	15,000	5,000	10,000						
	CF9	15,000	5,000	10,000						
	CF10	15,000	5,000	10,000						
	Total	150,000								
−100,000	15,000	15,000	15,000	15,000	15,000	15,000	15,000	15,000	15,000	15,000
0	1	2	3	4	5	6	7	8	9	10

TABLE 15.2 *Mushrakah Mutanaqisha* with *Ijara*

			Bank's Share	Customer's Share	Rent	11.1113%	Total Installment
	CF0	120,000	100,000	20,000	11,111		21,111.25
Initial cash outflow			83%	17%			
Subsequent cash inflows	CF1	10,000	90,000	30,000	10,000		20,000
			75%	25%			
	CF2	10,000	80,000	40,000	8,889		18,889
			67%	33%			
	CF3	10,000	70,000	50,000	7,778		17,778
			58%	42%			
	CF4	10,000	60,000	60,000	6,667		16,667
			50%	50%			
	CF5	10,000	50,000	70,000	5,556		15,556
			42%	58%			
	CF6	10,000	40,000	80,000	4,445		14,445
			33%	67%			
	CF7	10,000	30,000	90,000	3,333		13,333
			25%	75%			
	CF8	10,000	20,000	100,000	2,222		12,222
			17%	83%			
	CF9	10,000	10,000	110,000	1,111		11,111
			8%	92%			
	CF10	10,000	0				10,000
			0	100%			
	Total	100,000			50,001		150,001

−100,000	15,000	15,000	15,000	15,000	15,000	15,000	15,000	15,000	15,000	15,000
0	1	2	3	4	5	6	7	8	9	10

pays a rental payment to the bank. The rental payment decreases over the life of the contract as the customer's share in the house increases over time. The rental rate, however, remains constant for the period of the contract. The customer is exposed to higher rental payments in the initial years of the contract, which decline every year. At the end of 10 years, the Islamic bank earns a profit of $50,000, and recovers its investment of $100,000 in the house. The practical implications resemble a *murabahah* sale, but the contract is treated very differently from the perspective of risk and accounting treatments.

Capital Charge

This contract requires the Islamic bank to record the ownership of the house up to a value of $100,000 on its balance sheet. This amount decreases every year, but the Islamic bank must record this asset in assets held for sale and must provide a capital buffer for the life of the contract as per the formula

$$\text{Capital Adequacy Ratio} = \frac{\text{Economic Capital}}{\begin{array}{l}(\text{RW for Credit Risk} \times \text{Value of Asset})\\ +(\text{RW for Market Risk} \times \text{Value of Asset})\\ \times(\text{RW for Operational Risk} \times \text{Value of Asset})\end{array}}$$

As tenor is a contributing factor to the calculation of risk weightages, the long duration of the *MM* contract will attract a higher capital charge for an Islamic bank. If shareholders pass this requirement onto customers in the shape of a higher profit rate, an *MM* contract may be more expensive for a customer of an Islamic bank than a *murabahah* sale.

Collateral

The Islamic bank in this regard is a co-owner of the asset and if a customer defaults on his or her payments, the Islamic bank as co-owner can sell the asset to a third party to recover its investment. Whether the Islamic bank can recover all unpaid rental payments becomes a *shariah* issue[4] as the *MM* is not a standalone sale contract, but is a combination of a *mushrakah* contract, a sale contract, and an *ijara* contract.

---

[4]International Centre for Education in Islamic Finance (INCEIF), "Shariah Issues in Islamic Finance," 2011.

CONCLUSION

One would not be wrong to attribute the concept of *mushrakah* at the heart of risk taking, sharing, and equity financing. An underlying concept is also separating risk, as we saw that a capital provider's personal assets are separated from assets invested in a *sharik* in the case of default. The proponents of Islamic finance feel that Islamic banks have failed to embrace the spirit of Islamic banking by not sharing risks with their borrowers. Such critics fail to realize that banks are not investing their own funds, but those of depositors. The true face of a *mushrakah* is not a bank, but rather a venture capital firm, or an angel investor. The stock markets offer a good platform for risk sharing and ownership as well.

We predict that the future course of financial engineering in Islamic finance will lead to the creation of hybrids—financial products that share features of equity and debt like Islamic credit-linked notes. We refer our reader to our upcoming work on this topic, under Islamic derivatives and structured products.

CHAPTER 16

Hibah

Hibah is a unilateral contract, benevolent in nature, which does not require the same conditions of a bilateral contract, whereby one party to the contract transfers ownership of an asset to a counterparty without any consideration. The specific inherent nature of the *hibah* contract is the unilateral transfer of ownership of the *hibah* asset from the donor to the donee without any consideration or reward.[1] The transfer of ownership is not based on the performance of any act by the counterparty or payment of any price on spot or in the future. It is a voluntary act at the discretion of the party willing to surrender ownership of an asset to a counterparty. It is essentially a contract of giving a gift, nothing else. The party giving the gift must own the asset at the time of giving the gift, but can also commit to offering a gift to the counterparty in the future.

Once the asset has transferred ownership from the giver to the recipient, the asset cannot be repossessed by the original party.

Giving gifts is usually perceived as a personal act, not necessarily a commercial act, but just as an individual may offer a gift to another person, so may a company offer a gift to another company, individuals, or groups of individuals that are either stakeholders or customers.

Hibah allows one party to exchange assets with another. The giving of *hibah* cannot be contingent on any other contract, act, or consideration. It is given unilaterally at the discretion of a party to a commercial transaction.

FORMS OF *HIBAH*

Hibah can take the shape of goods and services and it can take the shape of money. In the latter context, the *hibah* can be a percentage of a nominal value of a separate contract, which the two parties are simultaneously involved in.

[1]Bank Negara Malaysia, "*Hibah (Shariah Requirements and Optional Practices): Exposure Draft*," 2013.

RESTRICTIONS ON *HIBAH*

A party cannot convince another party to enter into a contract of sale, debt, or exchange by promising a *hibah* as a gift if the two parties contract. The *hibah* cannot be used as an inducement to enter into another contract between the same parties or other related parties. *Hibah* therefore cannot be advertised as an inducement to enter into a contract.

The giving of *hibah* in a commercial transaction cannot take the form of customary practice or *urf*. Two parties to a contract cannot come to expect a *hibah* from the counterparty during the currency of a contract.

APPLICATIONS OF *HIBAH* IN BANKING

Hibah can be combined with any contract to allow one party to create benefit for another benefit. *Hibah* can be combined with *wakalah, juala, kafalah, hawalah*, or any of the sale-based contracts and lease-based contracts. What is essential, though, is that the payment of *hibah* cannot be a condition of contracting, and, therefore, the granting of *hibah* must remain at the discretion of the offering party, and the amount of its payment must not be predetermined, either. The mechanism by which *hibah* can be calculated may be predetermined, however.

Hibah Coupled with *Ijarah*

So let's have a brief look at how this contract can come into play. Imagine a contract of *ijarah*, whereby one party is a lessor and another party is a lessee. The lessor offers the lessee a gift as a reward for timely payments of *ujr* or rent for a financial period. This *hibah* can be a discount or *ibra* on the last rental payment of say 5 percent. So the lessor offers a 5 percent discount to the lessee as a *hibah* for good payment history.

The lessor, however, cannot convince the lessee to become a customer using this mechanism, nor can the lessee demand a *hibah* in the shape of a discount if the lessee makes all scheduled payments on time. The giving of *hibah* is at the discretion of the lessor (or even the lessee); its amount cannot be calculated in advance nor can it be a condition of the contract.

Hibah Coupled with *Wadiah*

We have covered the contract of *wadiah* in detail already, The contract is used by Islamic banks to mobilize deposits. The *wadiah* contract is revocable at any time and the party placing an asset with another party for safekeeping can withdraw the asset at any time. In the context of banking, if money is the asset placed with a counterparty, then the contract develops a product that resembles or behaves like a demand deposit. This demand deposit can be in the shape of a current account or a savings account.

Islamic banks that mobilize deposits using the *wadiah* contract reward their depositors with a monthly, quarterly, half yearly, or yearly *hibah* or gift, which is calculated as a percentage of the deposit placed with the Islamic Financial Institution (IFI). This practice certainly resembles the payment of interest on accounts in conventional banks. However, the unique difference here is that IFIs do not commit on the payment of any *hibah*, nor do they calculate any predetermined rate for the payment of *hibah*. In practice, however, *hibah* payouts have been closely linked to interest rates offered on various tiers of deposit placed in conventional banks. So interest rates have become benchmarks for *hibah* rates.

Hibah and *Bai al Wafa*

Bai al wafa is a contract whereby one party sells an asset to a counterparty with the *understanding* that if the seller pays the buyer the purchase price of the asset, the buyer will sell the asset back to the original seller.[2]

Step 1. Party A sells asset to Party B for nominal price x at time $t = 0$. Party B pays Party A cash for the asset.

Step 2. Party A pays back Party B original price of x, and Party B sells the asset back to Party A.

Party A buys back the asset from Party B in time $t + 1$, for the same price x. In essence, Party A has raised a collateralized loan by placing the asset with Party B for a time period and mobilizing moneys equivalent to the price x. However, the loan as such is interest free as Party A does not pay Party B any amount in excess of x as this would be *riba*. There is no reward to Party B for "buying" the asset for a limited time, as B is unable to use this asset. The ownership is a limited one, and we discuss this in detail on the chapter on *bai al wafa*. This transaction certainly resembles a repo in conventional finance, especially if the asset under question is a financial asset.

However, Party A can at his or her discretion reward Party B for entering the purchase and sale-back agreement (reverse repo from Party B's point

[2]*The Majelle*, section 118, defines *bai al wafa* as a sale with the condition that as price of the cost of goods sold is paid back by the seller, the buyer will return the particular goods back to the seller.

of view), by paying Party B an additional amount of z where z is *hibah* calculated as a percentage of x. Bear in mind that this is at the discretion of Party A and cannot be a condition of the contract as otherwise it becomes *riba*.

Hibah and Other Contracts of Sale and Exchange

At this stage the reader can assess that the contract of *hibah* can be coupled with a variety of contracts of sale and exchange as a reward for one party performing a certain covenant of an independent contract in a timely manner. *Hibah* is combined with the contract of *qard*, or lending to reward the lender for lending moneys to a borrower. However, again, the payment, the amount, and the condition to pay the *hibah* cannot be predetermined.

Companies can reward customers with giveaways for purchasing their goods, although in this case the *hibah* becomes conditional on the purchase and becomes a *shariah* issue.

ENHANCEMENTS TO *HIBAH*

The continuous payment of *hibah* as a reward paid by one party to a contract to incentivize the counterparty and making this payment into a financial product certainly is an enhancement of the original contract of *hibah*. The contract can be coupled with any bilateral or unilateral contract. A bank can offer a *hibah* to borrowers in the shape of discounts or *ibra* if the borrower makes all payments on time. *Hibah* can be offered to participants in a *takaful* scheme for making all payments as per schedule or for not filing any claims during a policy period. Usually, the shape of this gift is in the form of a discount or *ibra*. However, the payment of *hibah* cannot be made a covenant of a contract, nor can the amount of *hibah* be predetermined. For any gesture of reward to retain the essence of *hibah* it must have the element of being a discretionary reward.

Hibah and Cost of Fund

From a practical perspective, Islamic Banks are tempted to refer to the rate offered on CASA deposits as a cost of fund. *Shariah* departments in Islamic banks resist this temptation as it implies that Islamic banks have a predetermined rate of *hibah* in mind and any amount given as a gift cannot be referred to as a cost. Similar objections are made when an indicative rate of return on *mudharabah* deposits is referred to as a cost of deposit as the profit paid to *mudharabah* account holders is meant to be calculated *post-ante*, that is, when the profit is actualized. Profit sharing ratios are determined *ex-ante*.

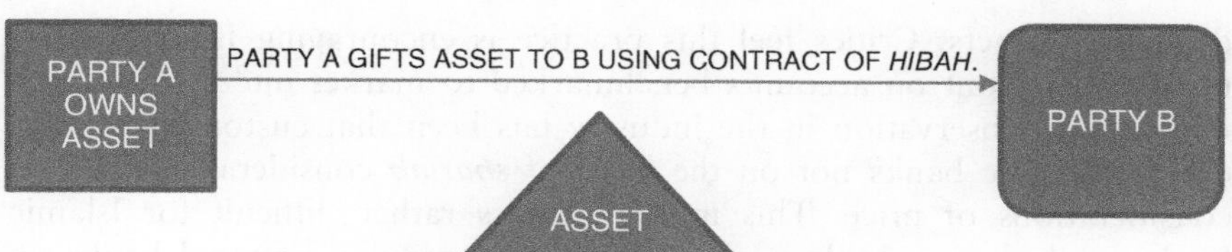

FIGURE 16.1 *Hibah* Process Flow

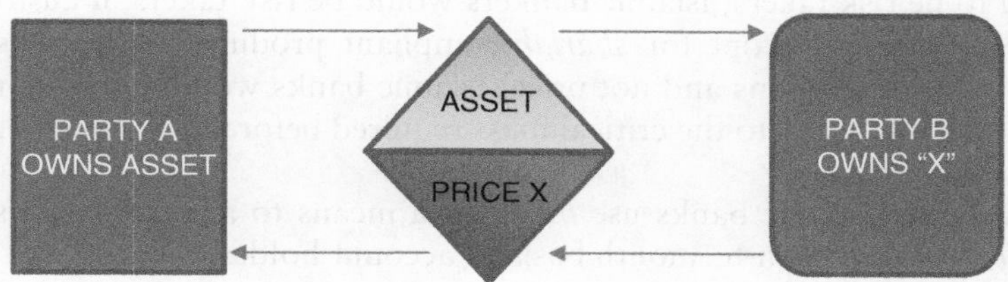

FIGURE 16.2 Step 1—*Hibah* and *Bai al Wafa*

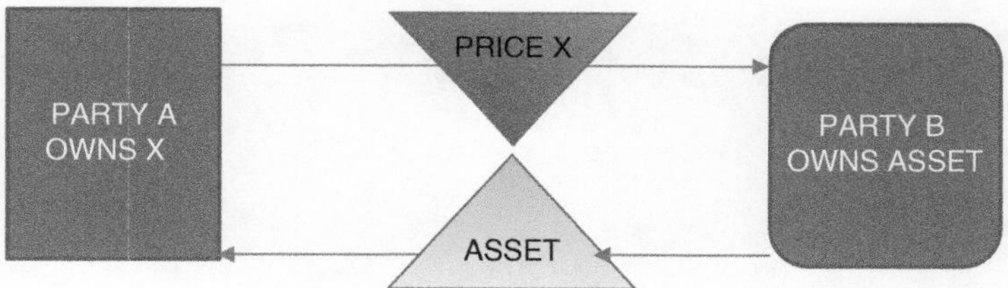

FIGURE 16.3 Step 2—*Hibah* and *Bai al Wafa*

Many Islamic banks, especially those that are window operations of conventional banks, have to follow the rules of their respective finance departments and treasury departments and must price asset products based on estimated cost of funds that are used to fund the asset. If any CASA deposits are used to fund the asset, this becomes problematic as a *hibah* rate, from the perspective of certain *shariah* specialists, cannot be treated as a cost of fund as this defeats the precepts of the contract of *hibah*.

CONCLUSION

The application of *hibah* has become a contentious issue in Islamic banking as it has begun to behave like *ribah*. Islamic banks have begun to advertise indicative rates or historical rates of *hibah* payouts on various deposit contracts. Critics feel this practice is encouraging Islamic banks to offer a payout on accounts benchmarked to market interest rates. An unfortunate observation in the industry has been that customers tend to opt for Islamic banks not on the basis of *shariah* considerations but on considerations of price. This makes matters rather difficult for Islamic banks as they are unable to compete with larger conventional banks on the basis of price. Critics need to focus on educating customers more than just pointing fingers at Islamic banks for their practices. If customers are willing to be risk takers, Islamic bankers would be risk takers; if customers would be willing to opt for *shariah*-compliant products on the basis of religious considerations and not price, Islamic banks would have the room to breathe, and grow to the critical mass required before they can enter into price competition.

Currently Islamic banks use *hibah* as a means to attract deposits and pay *hibah* on a month-to-month basis to account holders.

CHAPTER 17

Kafalah

Kafalah is a unilateral contract of guarantee where one party agrees to stand in the place of a debtor before his or her creditors. See Figure 17.1.

The concept can be explained by using a simple example involving three parties. Party A purchases an asset from Party B on a deferred payment basis. Party B requires some assurances that Party A will make the required payments. Party C provides Party B such assurances that in the event Party A defaults on payments to Party B, Party C will make good all losses.

This arrangement can also be modified to where Party A commits to deliver certain goods in the future to Party B, for which Party A has already taken the sale price, like in *salaam* and *istisna* contracts. Party C stands in on Party A's behalf that in the event Party A does not fulfill his or her obligations, Party C will do so by providing the required goods or making good the losses incurred by Party B.

Let's assume Party A owes Party B a deferred payment of $150,000, to be made in lump sum in 90 days. Party A arranges for Party C to be a guarantor for $150,000. Now Party B has recourse to Party C in the event that Party A defaults. Party A does default on the payments due to Party B in 90 days, and Party C makes good the payment of $150,000 owed to Party B.

A question arises now: Does Party C have recourse to Party A to recover losses? The answer is yes, Party C does have recourse to Party A. In fact, Party C can also obtain a *rahn* or collateral from Party A before agreeing to stand in as a guarantor. However, if Party A had a suitable asset to provide as *rahn* in the first place, this asset could have been placed as collateral with Party B.

There are certain circumstances that surround this issue. *Kafalah* in the traditional literature is covered as an act of brotherhood in a social context and not a commercial context. Muslims were encouraged to stand in place for another Muslim to vouch for one another's reputation, so

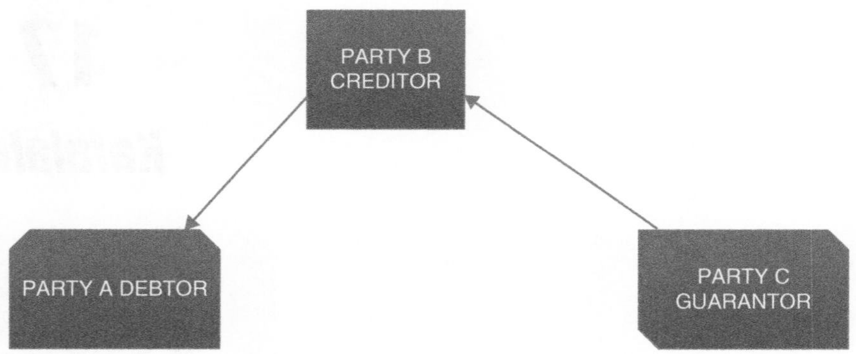

FIGURE 17.1 *Kafalah* Process Flow

to speak.[1] It was not considered as a commercial contract; however, its application to trade is easy to imagine.

One trader could guarantee the integrity of another trader in another city. However, if the guarantor offers to provide a guarantee on a voluntary basis, then the guarantor has no recourse to the debtor. If the debtor approaches the guarantor for a guarantee, then the guarantor has recourse to the debtor. The creditor's approval is not required for the debtor to make such arrangements, as in the event of default the creditor will approach the original debtor for payment and then will approach the guarantor. The latter serves as a credit enhancement, but the presence of a guarantor does not absolve the debtor from his or her obligations to the original creditor.

If Parties C and B settle for a payment of $130,000, can Party C have recourse to Party A for $150,000?

Kafalah seems to present itself as a contract of indemnity, where a guarantor agrees to indemnify a creditor for losses. It does not seem to behave as a contract of benefit. Theoretically, Party C should settle with Party A for $130,000 only, but can in fact have recourse to Party A for the full amount of $150,000.

Can Party C charge a fee for this service? If Party C charges say a $10,000 fee for this service provided to Party A, and Party A defaults on payments to Party C in 90 days. However, Party A is able to liquidate assets in 100 days at a profit and repays Party C the agreed $150,000. Party C now

[1]Based on the *hadith* of Prophet's (saw) saying: "It is unworthy of a Mu'min (a person with faith) to injure people's reputations; and it is unworthy to curse any one; and it is unworthy to abuse any one; and it is unworthy of a Mu'min to talk arrogantly."

paid Party A's creditors $150,000 and earned from Party A $160,000. This excess of $10,000 is seen by *shariah* scholars as an excess or *riba*.

The authors believe that Party C in a guarantee contract is not providing credit to Party A, as, in fact, Party B is doing so, but provides **credit cover** to Party A. This is a service and Party C can be compensated for providing this service as *ujr* for services.[2] *Riba* in definition is an excess over and above the principal debt. Party C in this case is not involved in a debt transaction. Party B does not benefit from any excess of money over the principal either. Party B only eliminates the fulfillment risk through asking party A to secure a guarantee from another trustworthy party. Therefore, the service fees paid to party C should not be considered as *riba*.

The application of *kafalah* in commercial contexts, however, is in itself an enhancement from the context in which it is mentioned in the traditional texts.

Applications of *kafalah* are obvious in the context of "Stand-By Letters of Credit," where an Islamic bank agrees to make payment to an exporter when goods are received at the docks. This service is provided by an Islamic bank on an importer's behalf to bridge the trust gap between two traders in two different countries.

Kafalah can also be used to guarantee performance of a particular act, or to indemnify a third party from losses if a contracting counterparty fails to perform its end of the deal. This application is utilized in letters of guarantees.

WHO CAN BE A GUARANTOR?

To answer this, anyone can be a guarantor, but in the context of our discussion on Islamic finance, governments can act as guarantors for capital markets debt instruments issued by different entities. Corporations can act as guarantors for each other in various credit-based transactions.

Regulators can act as guarantors for commercial financial institutions. Deposit insurance schemes offer depositors a guarantee for their deposits placed within all licensed financial instruments within a legal jurisdiction. *Takaful* has an implicit guarantee clause in it, where a *takaful* operator agrees to stand in and make good all losses suffered by a participant under a certain negative event or peril.

---

[2]The permissibility of *ujr* charge on *kafalah* services is supported by many contemporary *shariah* scholars and *shariah* councils. For more details, see *Shariah Resolution in Islamic Finance*, 2nd edition, by Bank Negara Malaysia and *Majallah Majma' al-Fiqh al-Islami* by OIC Fiqh Academy.

The applications of the *kafalah* contract are widespread in modern economic systems. However, according to *shariah* scholars the activity guaranteed must be *shariah*-compliant, but for many the issue is of charging a fee for this service.

In most Muslim countries, however, there is unanimity in accepting the element of charging this fee, and guarantee-based products are on the shelf of all Islamic banks in all major Muslim countries, including Malaysia, the Gulf Cooperation Council (GCC), Saudi Arabia, Pakistan, Indonesia, Turkey, and others.

PRODUCTS BASED ON *KAFALAH*

Islamic banks are able to offer letters of guarantee under the concept of *kafalah*. Performance guarantees are most often used in construction contracts where banks guarantee performance of certain acts by one party in favor of a counterparty. Letters of credit can also be devised using the same concept where banks offer guarantees that a debtor will pay a creditor when a certain obligation comes due. The letter can serve as a credit enhancement and can greatly reduce the cost of borrowing. Such guarantees can be offered by financial institutions in favor of their customers or can also be issued by governments in the case of issuances of sovereign *sukuk*.

Guarantees are nonfunded facilities and are off–balance sheet transactions. Islamic banks that have agreed to act as guarantor for the liabilities of their customers maintain reserves and collateral (from the customer) to secure their risks. Islamic banks are not exposed to any cash outlays unless their customer defaults on the performance of a certain act.

Guarantees can also be offered by customers to secure debt-based financing from Islamic banks. A buyer in a *murabahah* contract can offer personal guarantees or third-party guarantees to provide a cushion of comfort to the lending institution or the seller.

Guarantees may also be obtained from a seller in a *salaam* contract by a buyer. The seller who has promised to deliver certain goods in the future for a purchase price paid on the spot runs the risk of nonperformance. This risk can be mitigated by securing third-party guarantees issued by Islamic banks.

BACK-TO-BACK GUARANTEES

Back-to-back guarantees is a common concept in the conventional industry. Party A undertakes to guarantee Party B in favor of Party C. Party B has to perform a certain act for Party C by a certain time. Party C is referred to as the beneficiary of the guarantee. However, Party B can, on the back of Party A's guarantee, act as guarantor to another Party D as well if Party A allows this. To illustrate this point, imagine a Chinese IT firm based in Shanghai bids for contracts in another country, say Pakistan.

The company "Huaweis" has banking relationships with the Industrial and Commercial Bank of China (ICBC) in Beijing. Huaweis enjoys several banking facilities with the bank, which include an umbrella limit of \$100,000,000 as a guarantee. ICBC guarantees Huaweis for any contractual obligation it enters into up to a limit of \$100,000,000. Huaweis sets up a subsidiary in Pakistan and bids for a contract from a cellular service provider, called Ufone. Ufone is offering a tender to IT firms to revamp its systems and convert them all to 4G. All participants must submit bid guarantees for \$2,000,000 and, if awarded, the contract must submit performance guarantees issued by an A-rated bank for \$50,000,000.

Huwaeis Pakistan instructs a local bank in Pakistan to issue a guarantee in Pakistan in favor of Ufone backed by the guarantee issued by ICBC in favor of Huaweis in China. This would be a back-to-back guarantee. In the event of default, the local bank in Pakistan will pay Ufone and will recover the amount directly from ICBC China.

This product is still in its embryonic stage of development and can be called *re-kafalah*.

CONCLUSION

The contract of *kafalah* lends itself to develop nonfunded facilities within Islamic banks, to serve as a tool for credit enhancement in issuances of capital markets instruments, and is a fundamental concept of the *takaful* industry. It would be advisable for *shariah* scholars not to throw this rather simple contract into any controversy.

CHAPTER 18

Wakalah, Hawalah, Ibra, and *Rahn*

The contracts of *wakalah, hawlah, ibra,* and *rahn* play an essential role in Islamic finance as they support core contracts. *Wakalah* combined with *murabahah* results in a product called *murabahah by purchase orderer*. Similarly, *rahn* allows a creditor to obtain collateral from debtors and therefore plays a critical role in debt financing or debt-based sale contracts.

WAKALAH

Wakalah is one of the many supporting contracts that is used in the Islamic finance sphere. It comes from the root word *wakkala*, which means to perform a task on the behalf of another, that is, the delegation of duties or job to another person/entity. According to AAOIFI, *wakalah* is "the act of one party delegating the other to act on its behalf in what can be a subject matter of delegation."[1] It can be comparable to the concept of agency in general, whereby one party (*muwakkil*) would give authorization to another (*wakil*) to perform a task as an agent on behalf of the *muwakkil* in the matters that can be delegated. This is done either voluntarily or for a fee.

The legality of *wakalah* is derived from the main sources of *shariah* law. Apart from the Qur'an,[2] there is also a *hadith* that mentioned the Prophet ([saw] pbuh) had commended one of his companions when he had instructed his companion to buy a sheep for him, which in turn brought the Prophet (saw) an additional dinar as a profit from his business dealing.[3] *Wakalah* concept is also generally accepted by all classic and contemporary *shariah* scholars.

The concept is quite general and the practice of appointing an agent to perform or facilitate trading or a form of transaction is common.

[1]AAOIFI *Shari'ah Standard*, Standard No. 23, Clause 2/1.
[2]The Holy Qur'an, SUrah al-Kahf, verse 19.
[3]Sahih Al Bukhari, *hadith* 3370.

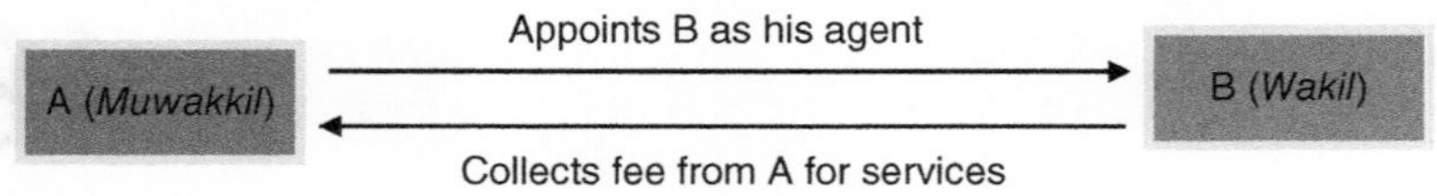

FIGURE 18.1 *Wakalah*

For instance, Party A would appoint Party B to buy a particular car on his behalf. Party B would approach the seller and buy the item on behalf of Party A. The delivery of the item can be done directly to Party A or to Party B. Also, in return of the services done by Party B, Party A can pay a form of fee to his *wakil*. This is illustrated in Figure 18.1.

A simple application of the concept of *wakalah* lies in *mudarabah*, where the *mudharib* acts as a *wakil* to the capital provider (*rabb-ul-mal*). It is to be noted, however, that *wakil* may not have the same freedom as a *mudharib* as they may only be appointed to execute a particular task accordingly. This is referred to as the *restricted wakalah* or *wakalah muqayyadah*. This is where the *wakalah* contract is confined within specific instructions, such as a particular condition and/or within a certain time constraint; therefore, the *wakil* cannot breach or violate the conditions that have been stipulated by the *muwakkil*.

There are other classifications of the *wakalah* contract, which are based on the time frame of the agency/principal relationship: *wakalah ghayr muaqqatah* (*wakalah* without time limit) and *wakalah muaqqatah* (temporary *wakalah* with a specified time constraint), stipulation of payment (with fee or nonfee *wakalah*), *wakalah bi tadaqhi al-dayn* (agency for receiving debt), *wakalah bi qabrh al-dayn* (agency for taking possession of debt), and many more. However, another one, which is generally applicable apart from *wakalah muqayyadah*, would be *general wakalah* or unrestricted *wakalah*. General *wakalah* or *wakalah mutlaqah* is where the *muwakkil* would let the *wakil* or agent act on his behalf for any matters in the interest of the *muwakkil* and within the customary practices in the jurisdiction.

Contemporary Application of *Wakalah*

To understand further the current use of the *wakalah* concept, we illustrate its application within a *commodity murabaha* contract. As the reader may already know, the mechanism of *commodity murabaha* contract is based on the *tawarruq* and involves a few parties: the customer, the bank, and the brokers for the commodity traders. A more detailed flowchart of the mechanism of this contract can be seen in the previous chapters. After the customer with the surplus funds deposits an amount of money in the bank, she or he subsequently appoints the bank to perform as an agent to buy the commodity from Broker A. For this transaction, the bank may choose to charge or not charge a fee on the service it performed. Then, after the bank had bought the commodities as specified in the *aqad*, the bank would also act again on behalf of the customer to receive the delivery of the asset and keep the asset based on *amanah* or trust.

Another example of the usage of the *wakalah* concept is in *murabahah* to purchase orderer (MPO) during the stage whereby the customer appoints the Islamic bank to buy the asset as identified on his or her behalf from the vendor. Apart from all these exchange-based contracts, the *wakalah* concept can also be applied to equity-based contracts, such as *musharakah*. Hereby all partners inside the *musharakah* act as agents to each other. One partner may become the *wakil* for the others in actions such as buying, selling, transacting, or leasing the portion or shares of the *musharakah* asset among themselves. *Wakalah* contract is also currently applied in *wakalah bil istithmar sukuk*, *wakalah* liquidity management, and as one of the many models of *takaful*.

One of the main issues in the usage of *wakalah* concept in contemporary Islamic financial transaction would be what it is known as *bai al-wakil linafsihi*, when the agent sells the asset to himself. An instance for this is when the bank as an agent sells the asset owned by the customer to itself in a *Bai Bithman Ajil* (*BBA*) contract. This is questionable as it would result in the issue of conflict of interest, that the bank may act against the interest of the customer as the principal.

HAWALAH

Hawalah is derived from the root word *'ahawwul*, which means *transfer* or *removal*. That is, *hawalah* is the act of removing or transferring from one place to another. The *Majelle* defines *hawalah* as "to make a transfer from one debtor account to the debtor account of another."[4] In *fiqh muamalat, hawalah* is where there is a shift of obligation from one debtor to another party, which would free the initial debtor from his or her transferred liability.

The mechanism of a simple *hawalah* can be seen in Figure 18.2.

Let's say that Party A has a debt obligation toward Party B, while at the same time, Party C has a debt obligation toward Party A. Therefore, through *hawalah*, all three would agree that instead of Party A fulfilling his dues to Party B, and Party C to Party A, Party B can collect whatever is due to him or her by Party A from Party C. This practice is done as an alternative method in paying debts, as endorsed by the Prophet ([saw] pbuh) in the *hadith* whereby

[4]*The Malelle*, art 673.

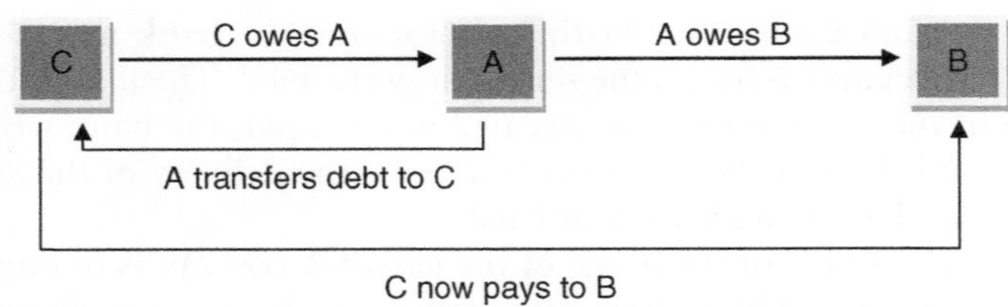

FIGURE 18.2 *Hawalah*

he said, "The deferment (of paying debt) by the richer is injustice, so if one of you get the offer from another to transfer your debt to another person, just accept it."

Types of *Hawalah*

The transfer can be unrestricted or restricted. *Unrestricted hawalah* refers to when the transfer is done without the reference to the debt on the transferee. That is, referring to the previous scenario, unrestricted *hawalah* would mean that Party C may not have a debt he has to fulfil toward Party A. A majority of scholars argue that this can be referred to as *kafalah*; however, in a sense it differs from *kafalah* (guarantee) whereby under *hawalah*, the principal debtor would be released completely from the obligation that is transferred to the other debtor. In *kafalah* the principal debtor is still the one under the obligation to fulfill its due to the creditor.

Another form of transfer that is more commonly referred to as *hawalah* is *restricted hawalah*, which requires a relationship between Parties C and A, apart from the initial relationship between Parties A and B, for Party A to shift his obligation to the other party. *Hawalah al-dayn* and *hawalah al-haq* both come under this category. *Hawalah al-dayn* is the transfer of debt just like the scenario of Parties A, B, and C, earlier. AAOIFI defines this type of *hawalah* as a transfer of debt from the transferor (A) to the payer (C).[5] On the other hand, *hawalah al haq* would refer to the transfer of right for debt from one creditor to another, in which from the previous scenario would be transfer of right for debt from Creditor A to Creditor B. It is a form of replacement of one creditor with another creditor.[6] When this *hawalah* is constructed, the debt is not paid to the initial creditor (A) because the right for C's debt is now assumed by B.

---

[5]AAOIFI *Shariah Standard* No. 7, clause 2.
[6]Ibid.

In certain conditions, the transferee can even ask for compensation from the transferor, particularly when the transfer is initiated by the transferor. Should the transfer be initiated by another party, say, the creditor, the transferee is not eligible to claim for compensation from the transferor unless in the form of *hibah* or charity.

Modern Use of the Contract of *Hawalah*

One of the modern uses of *hawalah* concept is in bills of exchange (*suftajah*), which is commonly used for settling accounts, collection of taxes, and disbursement of government dues. For instance, the debtor wants to make payment in another place through a second person. Hence, the debtor passes the responsibility of payment of his debt to the creditor to the second person that owes him a debt. The original debtor gives a portion of his property to a merchant, and the merchant will use his money to pay to another person in the other place.

Other use is for the issuance of checks by a current account holder in a bank, whereby the issuer would be the transferor, the bank would be the transferee of the obligation to the merchant/creditor. Banker's checks are also based on the concept of *hawalah* under the same structure as check issuance. Traveler's checks, bank drafts, remittances, and negotiable instruments all fall into the same category.

Issues in *Hawalah*

Generally the debt has to be established prior to the contract of *hawalah* or else the transfer of obligation would amount to the contract of agency (*wakalah*). This debt should be binding as well, as it would affect the obligation of the transferee and it would eliminate the element of *gharar* in the form of contingent liability. However, the *Shafi* school of thought allows the transfer of debt that would ultimately bring about obligation and liability, for example, the liability of price that would take place if an option is exercised.

It is generally accepted that the consent of principal debtor will affect the validity of the *hawalah* contract. However, some classical and contemporary jurists are of the notion that the *hawalah* process may not require a full consent from all parties, for example, the transferor, the creditor, or the transferee. Especially in the case of the creditor's consent for the transfer of debt, it is argued whether this would affect merely the enforceability of the contract as well as the conclusiveness of the contract. However, looking at the application, practically *hawalah* needs the consent of the transferor to effect a valid, enforceable, and smooth functioning of the operation of *hawalah*. Issues such as the difference in creditworthiness of the transferor and the transferee can ensue; for example, when the transferor transfers his debt to the transferee, the creditor may not agree with the creditworthiness of the transferee. This may have implications for the risk that the creditor would agree to assume.

Hawalah and *Bai al Dayn*

It is to be noted that *hawalah* differs from *bai al dayn,* though both contracts are concerned with the transfer of debt from one party to another. While *hawalah* is permissible and accepted in all *shariah* jurisdictions, *bai al dayn* is still subject to dispute by the Muslim jurists. *Hawalah* involves the transfer of debt at par from the principal debtor to another party while *bai al dayn* is the sale of debt in exchange for liquid asset or cash at a discount done by the creditor. Therefore, in specific cases within *hawalah* the creditor can even recourse back to the principal debtor in the event that the transferee cannot fulfill his dues. On the other hand, once the principal creditor in *bai al dayn* sells the debt to another party, this party cannot recourse back to the principal creditor in the event of default by the debtor.

IBRA

Ibra by definition is to waive or drop the right of claim of a creditor to his debtor. It is to release an amount of obligation that is due to a party from another person. According to Bank Negara Malaysia, *ibra* represents the waiver on right of claim accorded by a person to another person that has an obligation (*zimmah*) that is due to him.[7]

Within the Islamic finance world, *ibra* is commonly applied and given by the bank to its customers as a form of rebate when the customers settled their debt prior to the settlement period in the contract agreed by both parties, for instance. *Ibra* is also given for other reasons, such as default, financing restructuring, in the event of cancellation of contract of financing before maturity, and is also used in the variable-rate financing products. This is one of the tools for Islamic banks to stay competitive with the conventional banks as under the conventional system the customers are only required to pay the amount of accrued interest up to the date of the early settlement

[7]Bank Negara Malaysia (BNM) (2013), *Guidelines on Ibra' (Rebate) for Sale-Based Financing*, http://www.bnm.gov.my/guidelines/01_banking/04_prudential_stds/Updated_GL_on_Ibra_Final_Sept2013.pdf, accessed July 2014.

or termination of the contract. It is also a form of risk management where the bank would attempt to minimize the risk mismatch between asset and liability sides of the bank's books.

Generally, in a sale-based financing agreement between an Islamic bank and a customer, there will be a selling price that would be computed based on a fixed profit margin at the initiation of the contract. This would be the total amount due to the bank should the customer repay the installment in normal due course in a fixed-rate financing contract. Therefore, the selling price would incorporate the principal sum and the profit margin throughout the term of the contract. *Ibra* granted to the customer would be up to the total amount of the *deferred profit* at the point of early settlement, for instance, as the bank would be expected to recover all the outstanding principal sum from the customer, as can be seen in Figure 18.3.

Let's say that on the *n*th month of installment, a customer decided to approach the bank to settle his financing facility early. At that point of time, the balance of deferred profit is \$20,000, with outstanding selling price \$100,000, and due to settling within a lock-in period, there is an early settlement charge of \$300. Therefore the *ibras* given would be:

$$\begin{aligned} \text{Ibra} &= \text{Deferred Profit} - \text{Early Settlement Charges} \\ &= \$20{,}000 - \$300 \\ &= \$19{,}700 \end{aligned}$$

Hence the total settlement amount that has to be paid is:

$$\begin{aligned} \text{Settlement Amount} &= \text{Outstanding Selling Price} + \text{Installments Due} \\ &\quad + \text{Late Payment Charges} - \textit{Ibra} \\ &= \$100{,}000 + \$0 + \$0 - \$19{,}700 \\ &= \$80{,}300 \end{aligned}$$

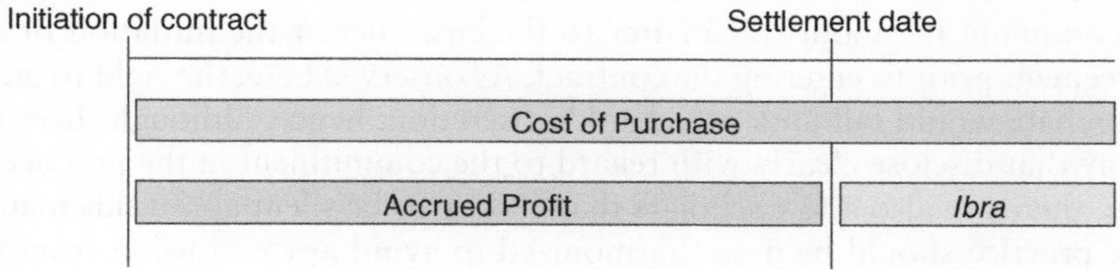

FIGURE 18.3 *Ibra* on Early Settlement

Under the floating rate financing product, there are two profit rates that are disclosed: contracted profit rate and the effective profit rate. Contracted profit rate would be fixed and determined at the beginning of the agreement and is used as the margin rate for the bank to arrive at the selling price. This price would also function as the ceiling cap comprising the principal sum and the profit margin and is at a higher rate as compared to the profit rate for the fixed-rate financing product. That is, the contractual selling price and the periodic installments would be relatively higher than the fixed-rate financing facility. This is where the *ibra* comes in.

For example, a financing agreement is made between an Islamic bank and a customer for the purchase of a house using *BBA* concept with a ceiling rate of 15 percent per annum, and the agreed monthly installment to be made would be $1,000 per month over an agreed term. Supposing that the effective profit rate is derived from BFR (base financing rate) plus 2 percent and the current BFR is 8 percent, the effective profit rate would be 10 percent. Hence the amount of *ibra* in that month would be the difference between the ceiling rate of 15 percent per annum and the effective profit rate or 10 percent per annum. The effective monthly installment would be $800, for instance, after deducting the *ibra*. The following month, the BFR rises to 9 percent, which means the effective profit rate would be 11 percent. The amount of *ibra* would be less as compared to the month before and the effective monthly installment would be $900 (amount is for illustrative purposes only). *Ibra* would be granted at every point of installment such that the amount of payment would be reduced to match the current market level. It is noted, however, that in the event of rising market rates, the facility's profit rate would be capped at the ceiling rate of 15 percent per annum, regardless of how far the market rate has gone up.

Disclosure of *Ibra*

It is required in Malaysia that the bank has to disclose its commitment in granting *ibra* as a clause in its offer letter to the customers. The minimum disclosure would be specifying the situations in which *ibra* would be granted, and the *ibra* calculation formula for such situations. The bank is to communicate about this matter to the customer at the initiation of the agreement prior to entering the contract. As observed here, the right to grant the rebate would fall under the bank's discretion; hence, although there are many that disclose clearly with regard to the commitment in the practice of *ibra*, there are also a few scholars that choose to be silent about this matter. The practice should be more harmonized to avoid any confusion from the customers in the market.

RAHN

An asset or collateral is commonly charged as a form of security for a loan. In Islamic finance, the concept that is defined by this is called *rahn*, which literally means *to detain an object*. According to the *Majelle*, *rahn* is "to make a property a security in respect of a right of claim, the payment in full of which from that property is permitted."[8] This pledge serves as a security until the repayment of the debt is done and at the same time functions as a moral push to ensure that the borrower would repay the debt. This practice has been done since the time of the Prophet ([saw] pbuh) where he once purchased food grains from a merchant on credit and then pledged his armor to this person.[9]

The mechanism of *rahn* can be seen in Figure 18.4.

Rahn allows Islamic banks to mitigate credit by securing collateral from the borrower. The risk-weightage, for instance, assigned for a *BBA* financing facility secured with collateral is lower than an unsecured facility. The lower risk is contributed by the fact that in the event of default or inability to repay by the debtor or borrower, the liability may be recovered from the pledged asset's value. The main features of *rahn* are as follows:[10]

- The asset being used as the pledge are only those that have a sale value.
- The contract of *rahn* and the acceptance of the pledged asset does not mean that the debt is canceled. The demand for repayment by the creditor still exists regardless of whether there is an asset charged against the debt.

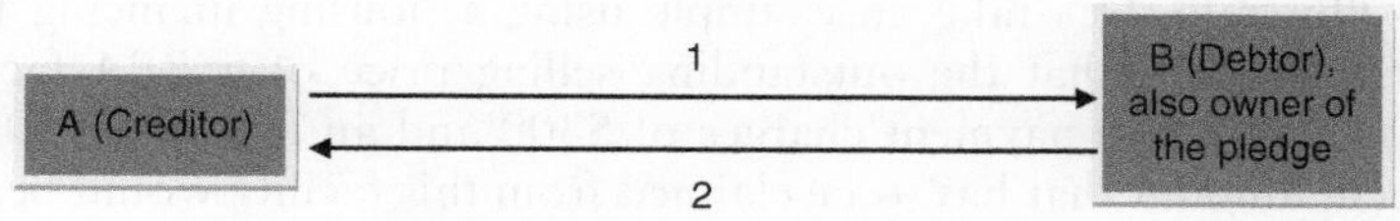

1. A sells something to B on credit, or gives B a loan
2. B pledges his asset to A until he pays his due

FIGURE 18.4 *Rahn*

[8] *The Majelle*, art 701.
[9] Sahih Al Bukhari, vol. 5.
[10] Zamir Iqbal and Abbas Mirakhor, *An Introduction to Islamic Finance Theory and Practice*, 2nd ed. (Singapore: John Wiley & Sons, 2007).

- Should the borrower refuse to make the payment at the end of the debt term, the creditor can approach the court to induce or force the debtor to sell the asset pledged under *rahn* to recover the debt. Moreover, if necessary, the court would have the authority to sell the charged asset should the debtor still refuse to do so.
- A pledged asset can be used as a charge for more than two debts from different creditors. The issue would be on how much value could be charged for the respective debts. The majority of the schools of thought are of the opinion that in the event where the value of the charged asset has been used to partially secure a loan, then the remaining part of the asset can be subsequently charged to another loan.[11]

Unlike the contract of *bai al wafa*, the pledgee is not allowed to use or utilize the asset pledged for the loan. There is no transfer of ownership in *rahn* and the legal position of the creditor is only as a trustee of the asset. He cannot sell it out during the term of the loan and any damage inflicted on the asset due to his negligence would be his liability. Maintenance, safekeeping expenses, and *takaful* cost would be borne by the owner of the asset.

In the case of default, a creditor can act as an agent to sell off the *rahn* item on behalf of the debtor. After the asset is sold and it so happens that there is an extra balance over and above the loan amount, then the balance should go back to the debtor, after deducting the transaction costs. This is supported by a *hadith* from Abu Hurairah, narrating that the Prophet ([saw] pbuh) had said, "A charged asset will not diminish from its owner. Any profit of the charged asset belongs to its owner and any liability must be borne by him."[12]

To illustrate, let's take an example using a housing financing facility default. Supposed that the outstanding selling price of a *BBA* facility is \$150,000, with late payment charges of \$300 and an *ibra* of \$3,000. The settlement amount that has to be claimed from this facility would be:

$$\begin{aligned}\text{Settlement Amount} &= \text{Outstanding Selling Price} + \text{Installments Due}\\ &\quad + \text{Late Payment Charges} - \textit{Ibra}\\ &= \$150{,}000 + \$0 + \$300 - \$3{,}000\\ &= \$147{,}300\end{aligned}$$

[11]l-Sawi, *Hasyiyah Al-Sawi 'ala Syarh al-Saghir*, Dar al-Ma 'arif, 1982, vol. 3, 307.
[12]Ibnu Hajar al-'Asqalani, *Bulugh al-Maram min Adillah al-Ahkam*, Matba'ah al-Salafiyyah, 1928, 176.

The house, then, is auctioned and the proceeds received from it amounted to $150,000. As the proceeds from the auction of the house are more than the settlement amount to be payable by the customer, the customer is entitled to the difference of $2,700 from the transaction.

Can Financial Assets Be Used as a Pledge Item as Well?

As mentioned previously, the items being used for *rahn* are only those that have a market value, that is, they have to be of value and deliverable.[13] It would be preferable that the asset used for *rahn* is a tangible asset. According to some *shariah* scholars,[14] financial assets such as receivables, cash, or the like are also permissible to be used as a *rahn* item as long as it is acceptable from both parties. *Sukuk* can also be placed as an asset for *rahn*, as can *shariah*-compliant securities. It is of value, tradable, and transferable, moreover its trading is highly regulated by an external form of authority, which requires integrity and a certain market standards.

CONCLUSION

The contracts discussed in this chapter provide the necessary support to sale-based and lease-based contracts to develop financial products. The contract of *wakalah* is essential to the industry on its own as it plays a vital role in Islamic banking, *takaful*, and asset management. The contract of *hawalah* plays a vital role in the development of many retail banking products and services. *Ibra* has helped develop a pricing mechanism for any deferred payment–based contracts.

[13]Al-Samarqandi, *Tuhfat al-Fuqaha'*, Dar al-Kutub al-'Ilmiyah, 1983, vol. 3, 40.
[14]Shariah Advisory Council, Bank Negara, Malaysia.

CHAPTER 19

Shariah: Sources, Interpretation, and Implementation

For a Muslim reader this section is quite a simple read and many things sound familiar. Within the framework of Islamic law, the Quran serves as the central text from which the law is extracted. It is considered to be the primary source of law without question. The second source of law is the *hadith*, which is a compilation of the sayings and doings of the Prophet ([saw] peace be upon him). The first person to interpret the verses of the Quran was the Prophet Muhammad [saw] himself, but his interpretations were based on divine inspiration; he left no methodology for interpreting the Quran. He also left no process or guidelines for developing a methodology for interpretation.

After the Prophet ([saw] peace be upon him) passed away, the companions of the Prophet (saw) were referred to for interpretations of verses; the most revered companions were such illustrious personalities as Hadrat Abu Bakr, Hadrat Umar, Hadrat Uthman, Hadrat Ali, and the wives of the Prophet ([saw] peace be upon him). As the companions of the Prophet also passed away, the successors became the next layer of authority on religious edicts.

Individuals who knew verses of the Quran and recollected *hadiths* began to gain importance in Muslim society and they became the revered scholars of society. The first criterion for scholarship was therefore recollection of the Quran and the *hadith*. The second criterion for scholarship, which was based on how to interpret the data provided in these two texts, evolved much later in time.[1]

[1] *Middle East Insurance Review* (2012), Shariah Column: "Ask Your Scholar: What Makes a Shariah Scholar?" http://www.meinsurancereview.com/Magazine/ReadMagazineArticle/aid/10443/Shariah-Column-ndash-Ask-Your-Scholar-What-makes-a-Shariah-scholar, accessed July 2014.

In the development of Islamic scholarship, the process of data compilation actually came after the process of development of legal schools of thought. After the demise of the Prophet (saw), and his closest companions, the leaders of the Muslim world began to interpret the laws to suit their own needs. As a reaction to this, figures such as Imam Abu Hanifa, Imam Shafi, Imam Maliki, and Imam Hanbali emerged on the scene 200 years after the demise of the Prophet (saw) and developed a systematic approach to extracting laws from the verses of the Quran and the *hadith* literature. The end product of this systematic approach came to be known as "Usul ul Fiqh," or the principles of developing law.

Professor Yusuf Saleem writes, "The scholars of the first and second centuries after the demise of the Prophet, concerned themselves with laying down the rules of interpretation and introducing methods that govern reason."[2] Laws were now extracted from what came to be known as "Secondary Sources of Law" and included the following:

- *Qiyas* (or analogy)
- *Ijtihad* (consensus of scholars)
- *Urf* (customary practices)
- *Istihsan* (juristic preference)
- *Maslahah al murasala* (common good)
- Practices of the People of Madina
- *Saad ul dhariah* (preventing legal means to achieve illegal ends)

The four individuals mentioned earlier did not adopt all seven sources of law, and as they differed in methodologies they also differed in conclusions. Reason was employed in reaching conclusions, but reason was left subordinate to revelation. Diversity of opinion became a natural consequence but was treated with respect and tolerance.

A framework for law was developed to govern acts of worship, and to govern the actions of humankind in the domain of commerce, trade, politics, warfare, family life, inheritance, and so on. In fact no aspect of human existence was left outside the domain of the law.

Actions were placed into five general categories, *wajib* (obligatory), *mandub* (recommended), *haram* (forbidden), *makruh* (abominable), and *mubah* (optional). Legal consequences were spelled out for the performance of such actions or the omission of such acts; legal courts were set up to pass judgments on rulings. Certain actions were left to the personal domain of individuals to be judged in the Afterlife; others became the domain of

---

[2]Muhammad Yusuf Saleem, "*An Introduction to the Theoretical Foundations of Islamic Transactions*" (Selangor, Malaysia: Ilmiah Publishers, 2012).

the legal system and a system of developing jurists developed to pass legal rulings. The legal schools developed the rulings and the jurists passed the rulings and the state executed the rulings.

After this legal framework was developed, another six individuals surfaced on the pages of history, Imam Bukhari, Muslim, Tirmidhi, Abu Dawud, Al-Nasa'i, and Ibn Majah, who compiled a vast corpus of *hadith* to filter the genuine *hadith* from those with poor chains of transmission or questionable content and meaning. Within 400 years after the Prophet (saw) passed away, the legal framework and the secondary literature of the religious system was fully developed. This legal framework was adopted by the various communities within the Muslim world and various empires that saw the light of day during the course of Muslim history. The process of interpreting the law and developing rules to govern new circumstances remained vibrant and didactic right until the time of the colonial invasions of the Muslim world. The last compilation of commercial laws is found in the Ottoman *Mejelle*.

All throughout this period, however, the process of development of intellectual thought was both organic and institutionalized. Yet, no formal standard was developed to determine what qualifications were required to be a scholar. Bear in mind that contrary to popular opinion, many scholars of the Quran and *hadith* were also learned in other sciences, such as astronomy, biology, medicine, physics, mathematics, chemistry, history, anthropology, and linguistics. No domain of knowledge was deemed "secular" as the study of nature revealed the Signs of God.

The recent development of scholarship, void of any knowledge of any other aspect of human existence, is actually an aberration in the history of Islamic scholarship and certainly not the norm. Therefore, for a *shariah* scholar to have any influence on, say, banking transactions, it would be considered normal for the said individual to have a detailed understanding of banking, financial mathematics, regulations, processes, and commercial realities. In countries such as Pakistan, anyone from a village cleric is considered a scholar who issues legal opinions without any formal qualification aside from being versed in the Quran and Arabic. Mass popularity has never been a criterion in Islamic history for scholarship. Despite readily accessible public education systems, it seems hard to understand why scholars have not dedicated themselves to learning all aspects of the various sciences.

MODERN-DAY *IJTIHAD*

Resolutions passed by *shariah* councils of commercial organizations and regulators are a somewhat recent development. Currently, there is no professional endorsement of who is a *shariah* scholar and who is not. The traditional requirements of a working knowledge of Arabic or memorization of the Quran are now obsolete with the existence of readily available software that provide English translations and easy searches for relevant verses on a digital platform. All the books of *hadith* are readily available *en masse* in a manner never seen before in history.

The result of such readily available data is that we are all in our minds mini-scholars and have a judgment on everything under the sun.

However, the *shariah* councils of the commercial Islamic banks and their regulators are handpicked by the board of the banks or the regulators, and their compensation is also derived from the revenues of the commercial entity or the regulator. Institutions are tempted to employ those scholars who "agree" with their perspectives, as much as commercial banks are tempted to employ scholars who "toe their line." This latter concept is referred to rather shamefully as *shariah shopping*, where Islamic banks only employ those scholars who are either very pragmatic in their approach or very "easy to work with."

However, what can be questioned is whether a resolution passed by a handful of scholars (typically five) at the *shariah* advisory council of any entity be considered *ijtihad*. A real *ijtihad* should include representatives from all over the Muslim world, but each Muslim country has its own system (or lack thereof) for developing scholars. The OIC Fiqh Academy may offer the only platform that brings together scholars from all over the Muslim world, but each country passes its own legal opinions on various matters related to Islamic banking, and their Parliaments then endorse those opinions and give them the backing of law, or not.

Consequently, an imperfect *ijtihad* is supported by an Act of Parliament before an opinion becomes law. I say imperfect *ijtihad* because an *ijtihad* of Malaysian scholars cannot be seen as an *ijtihad* in the complete sense, any more than the *ijtihad* of Pakistani scholars in a board room or the *ijithad* of Arab scholars in Jeddah, not to say anything of an *ijtihad* of *shia* scholars in Iran.

Currently, the Muslim world is rife with conflict and differences of opinion. Two large sects dominate the Muslim landscape and divide the Muslim world: Sunnis and Shias. Iran is the intellectual thought leader in the domain of Shia thought, whereas the Sunni world sees Saudi Arabia as a thought leader. Muslim countries like Pakistan and Iraq have large *shia* and *sunni* populations. Differences of opinion are not so rife as both these countries limit the application of Islamic law to personal matters such as sex, alcohol, and gambling. If legal rulings were applied from the *shariah* to commercial transactions, there may be cause for conflict as *shia* tradesmen may not wish to follow *sunni* rulings or vice versa.

This is not the only problem. Although many Muslim countries have credible business schools, medical colleges, and engineering universities, there are a handful of institutions that impart knowledge of *shariah*. We should avoid the phrases "religious schools," or "centers of learning of religion," as the study of *shariah* is a process similar to the study of common law for which candidates attend such famed institutions as Harvard, Yale, or Kings College in London. The study of *shariah* is above all the study of a specific system of law, and is open to Muslims and non-Muslims alike.

It is quite possible to imagine an Islamic bank employing a professional banking lawyer with a detailed knowledge of the *shariah* to advise on matters of relevance to Islamic banks. Being a Muslim is not a criterion to being proficient in Islamic law. Instead of waiting for Muslim countries to develop their institutions it might be relevant to attach departments of Islamic studies and *shariah* to institutions like Harvard, Yale, Columbia University, Cornell University, and London School of Economics. Governments of the Muslim world should develop their own accredited institutions for learning their own laws. Hadrat Ali in Nahjul Balagha once said, "Man can live without religion for a while, but cannot live without laws."

WHOSE *SHARIAH* IS IT, ANYWAY?

This can be a loaded discussion and we thought of developing an understanding of the *shariah* using standard discussions on *muamlat, fiqh, usul ul fiqh*, and matters relating to *ibadat*. The discussion can be extended to primary and secondary sources of the *shariah*, but this work has been comprehensively dealt with by Professor Yusuf Saleem (2012) in his book, *An Introduction to the Theoretical Foundations of Islamic Transactions*. Another comprehensive work is *Principles of Islamic Jurisprudence* by Professor Mohammad Hashim Kamali (2003). Both professors are lecturing in different institutions in Malaysia at the time of writing this work.

At this juncture we comment on those entities, bodies, and scholars that have contributed to the literature on Islamic finance and have implemented certain Acts of Parliament or royal decree in various legal jurisdictions and countries.

In the context of modern democracies, the parliament of every country is the only legislative body that can make a certain act into a law. Therefore, legislative power lies with the parliament. In monarchies, law is a product of royal decree issued by the ruler or king, and some Muslim countries operate with a dual political system that involves a monarchy and a parliament. Interpreting this law and passing judgments in the light of the law is the job of courts.

Many Muslim countries have been former colonies of European powers, and have thereby inherited the system of English common law, or Dutch law, or Portugese law, or French legal systems depending on their various histories. Post-independence, many of these countries made attempts to either fully replace their inherited legal system (and its institutions) based on secular values with the codes of the *shariah* or Islamic law with varying degrees of success; others made an attempt to integrate the secular legal system with that of the Islamic legal system. To our understanding, aside from countries like Iran, Sudan, and Saudi Arabia, most other countries have semblances of a partial dual legal system, but the conventional legal system dominates the *shariah* legal system as the law of the land.

If this is not cause for enough confusion, the traditional centers of learning of *shariah* across the Muslim world are no longer unanimously accepted by Muslims across the world. With differing sectarian views, or differences in *madhabs*, currently asking for unanimity on *shariah* rulings is quite a demanding request. Therefore, there is also no standardized qualification for a *shariah* scholar.

It is generally accepted that a medical doctor must pass certain examinations set by the medical board of regulators of a country before he or she is allowed to treat patients. A lawyer is required to also pass certain examinations and enter into the tutelage of a practicing lawyer before embarking on a legal career. Needless to say, all countries of the world have not only developed or adopted standards for these professions but have also developed institutions that impart the necessary training and accreditations. These institutions are either recognized in a specific country or are recognized globally depending on their standards and quality.

Such institutions are lacking in the domain of learning Islamic law. There is also no standard in vogue in the domain of qualifying to be a *shariah* scholar. Certain "scholars" believe that knowledge of the Quran, the *hadith*, the Arabic language, Muslim history, *fiqh, usul ul fiqh* is adequate to be a *shariah* scholar. Others feel that along with this knowledge a *shariah* scholar should also "specialize" in a specific domain such as finance, medicine, economics, physics, or chemistry to provide rulings on matters relevant to that specific field. Therefore, for instance, a *shariah* scholar who provides a legal opinion on matters relevant to Islamic banking and finance should also have a detailed knowledge of banking and finance as well as the *shariah*. Sadly, this is not always the case and this is a leading contributor to the diversity and misunderstanding on rulings regarding matters that pertain to Islamic finance.

Thus, each country has its own set of qualified *shariah* scholars. Some of them are appointed as consultants to the government or become members of a *shariah* council and provide rulings, or opinions, or *fatwas* on various matters. These may be relevant to matters of worship, ideology, dissemination of religious teachings, academic curriculums, overseeing operations of mosques, *zakat* funds, *waqfs*, and may also involve matters of commerce, trade, finance, and banking.

Some countries have a central *shariah* advisory board of scholars that advise on all these matters, with representatives working with relevant arms of the government, or they have specialized boards such as the *Shariah* Advisory Council (SAC) of Bank Negara Malaysia. The SAC in Malaysia consists of various scholars and not only advises the central bank on matters related to *shariah* but also has a broad range of functions overseeing the operations of Islamic financial institutions.[3] The SAC in Malaysia is probably the most organized such body to date.

Various Islamic financial institutions may also have their own internal *shariah* boards that advise on products, processes, governance frameworks, and operations. These independent boards must refer to the central *shariah* advisory board of the government or the respective central bank for any enhancements to product lines, procedures, processes, and so on. In the case of Malaysia, for instance, the SAC of the Bank Negara Malaysia is a body authorized to issue *fatwas* or recommendations, which are classified as either "Standards," which Islamic financial institutions must follow, or "Guidelines," which are recommendations. Some of these standards can be passed into law by an act of Parliament and the most relevant example of this is the recently issued law by the Parliament of Malaysia known as the Islamic Financial Services Act (IFSA) of 2013. IFSA 2013 is the most comprehensive piece of legislation developed for the Islamic financial intermediation industry, and the country has been generous enough to offer this legislation for free to other countries by posting the entire text on the website of Bank Negara Malaysia.

Any serious student of Islamic finance should refer to the websites of Bank Negara Malaysia for a wide menu of exposure drafts, standards, guidelines, resolutions, and other material of practical importance.

So back to our question: Who makes the laws? Certain groups of scholars placed in certain government divisions or bodies set up with government funding are currently involved in this process. Certain entities provide recommendations, research, discourse, and discussion on various issues; others have the force of law behind them. Standard-setting bodies include the Islamic Financial Services Board (IFSB) in Malaysia, the Accounting and Auditing of Islamic Financial Institutions (AAOIFI), the Organization of Islamic Countries Fiqh Academy, the Islamic Development Bank, International Shariah Research Academy for Islamic Finance (ISRA), *shariah* boards of various prominent institutions like Kuwait Finance House, Dubai Islamic Bank, and ultimately *shariah* advisory boards of central banks and other regulatory bodies across the Muslim world. It is these entities that decide what the *shariah* says on a particular issue, and they decide on how to interpret certain verses, sayings, legal maxims, rules, and so on.

---

[3]Bank Negara Malaysia, "Learn about the Bank," www.bnm.gov.my/index.php?ch=7&pg=715&ac=802, accessed July 2014.

Extracts from a document developed by the Bank Negara Malaysia, referred to as an exposure draft on *bai al inah*, are included here. It contains in it references to the Quran and the *hadith*, which establish the permissibility of *bai al inah*. We leave it to the reader to determine whether the interpretations are relevant.

BNM/RH/CP 028–2 ISLAMIC BANKING AND *TAKAFUL* DEPARTMENT

Bai' 'Inah (*Shariah* Requirements and Optional Practices) Exposure Draft—Page 17/20

Appendices

18. Appendix 1 Legitimacy of *bai' 'inah*.

18.1. The legitimacy of the *bai' 'inah* arrangement is derived from the Quran and founded on the Sunnah of Prophet Muhammad ([saw] peace be upon him).

The Quran

18.2. The following Quran verse implies the general permissibility of *bai' 'inah*.

"... whereas Allah [sat] SWT has permitted trading and forbidden usury ... " (Surah al-Baqarah, verse 275)

18.3. Two sales contracts executed separately and independently, with no interrelation with one another are the important elements in the *bai' 'inah* arrangement and, therefore, it is a valid contract in the *shariah*.

"O believers! When you contract a debt from one another for a fixed period, put it (its amount and period of payment) in writing ... " (Surah al-Baqarah verse 282)

The Sunnah of the Prophet Muhammad ([saw] peace be upon him)

18.4. There is no direct juristic authority from the Sunnah of the Prophet ([saw] peace be upon him) on the legitimacy of the *bai' 'inah* arrangement. It is deemed permissible based on the general permissibility of sales in Islamic law.

BNM/RH/CP 028–2 ISLAMIC BANKING AND TAKAFUL DEPARTMENT

Bai' 'Inah (*Shariah* Requirements and Optional Practices) Exposure Draft—Page 18/20

18.5. The following *hadiths* imply the general permissibility of *bai‘ ‘inah* arrangement.

لكسب ا i. أيسئل: ـــسلموالله عليه اى صلـبيلنا أنـــالله عنهاضي رــــفعرافاعة بن رعن "
أطيب؟ لقا: ا لمعـ ,و ربركل بيع مولرجل بيده."

The Prophet Muhammad ([saw] peace be upon him) was reported to have said: "The best earning is what man earns with his own hands and from a permissible trade" (Narrated by Hakim, Al-Mustadrak, Hadith no. 2160)

برجلا ii. على خيرستعمل اسلم والله عليه الله صلى ا لسور أنالله عنه اضي ر ةهرير بيأعن "
لسورالله يا وا لا :لقا ؟ اهكذ برخيتمركل أ:سلموالله عليه الله صلى ا لسور له بتمر جنيب فقاءفجا
لا تفعل :سلموالله عليه الله صلى ا لسور لفقا ،لجمعابع ينبالصاء امن هذ علصاانا لنأخذ إنالله ا
"هم جنيبا.رابتع بالداثمهم رابالثلاثة بالبينلصاعءوا

The Prophet ([saw] peace be upon him) appointed a person as governor of Khaybar, who [later] presented him with an excellent type of dates. The Prophet (saw) asked, "Are all the dates of Khaybar like this?"

He replied, "[No, but] we barter one *sa‘* of this (excellent type) for two *sa‘* of ours, or two *sa‘* of it for three of ours." Allah's apostle said, "Do not do that (as it is a kind of usury), but sell the mixed dates (of inferior quality) for money, and then buy the excellent dates with that money" (Sahih Bukhari, Hadith no. 2201).

CONCLUSION

We hope the reader has had enough opportunity to make a judgment for himself or herself if the contracts behind Islamic finance fulfill any broader Islamic purpose. We requested the reader at the beginning of this work to investigate the expectations with which this subject has been approached.

How would a book based on a Buddhist philosophy fulfill a practitioner's aspirations? For Muslim readers this is a valid concern. For non-Muslim readers the spiritual element may or may not have any relevance.

The architects of Islamic finance are fully aware of the limitations of their model, but unless Islamic banks and depositors together do not make a fundamental switch in their approach to capital, nothing much can change.

We as authors do not promote any interpretation or advocate any perspective. We feel our approach to the content has been to call a spade a spade.

CHAPTER 20

Islamic Asset Management and *Shariah* Screening

This chapter is concerned with financial assets and products that are traded on capital markets that the *shariah* deems permissible, and the functioning of capital markets themselves. A methodology of *shariah* screening has been developed by scholars that determines if a certain asset is *shariah*-compliant or not. As we discuss financial markets, the screening is applied by and large to equities. Shares reflect ownership in a company, whereby shareholders share in the profits of a company through the payments of dividends. Shareholders also earn profits from capital gains due to the appreciation in the value of the underlying shares.

The *shariah* permits having an equity stake in a company via the mechanism of owning shares in it under the concept of *musharakah*. Although certain scholars opine that classical *musharakah* was between individuals themselves, modern shareholding is not a partnership between individuals as much as it is between individuals and a corporate legal entity. However, much of the Muslim world is open to the idea of shareholding and in fact would prefer to have much more of it.

The *shariah* does not permit ownership of all kinds of businesses, though. The *shariah* does not permit an equity stake in pig farms, alcohol breweries, wineries, or in businesses that earn interest, such as banks and insurance companies. Given the modern scale of business divided between permissible and nonpermissible activities, with a group of companies, having certain subsidiaries involved in permissible activities and other businesses involved in impermissible activities, *shariah* scholars decided to develop a methodology for screening.

For the time being, there is no internationally recognized standardized approach to *shariah* stock screening. Many *shariah* boards adopt different methodologies in their *shariah* screening process, such as by Malaysia's Securities Commission (SC), Dow Jones, FTSE, Standard & Poor's (S&P), and MSCI, to name a few. A small example is the level of tolerance thresholds for interest-based debt, which are set to 30, 33, or 33.33 percent by Malaysia's SC, Dow Jones, FTSE, and S&P, and MSCI, respectively. Differences in threshold, emphasis on either the financial ratios or qualification with regard to business activities, or the use of market capitalization versus the total asset value as the denominator[1] would result in differences in the *shariah*-compliance outcome for a particular stock. A given stock may be listed as *shariah*-compliant by Malaysia's SC, but not under Dow Jones Islamic market indexes.

Despite the variation in methodologies adopted by different jurisdictions, the process of *shariah* stock screening can be generally classified into sector screening, financial screening, and dividend purification.[2]

Sector screening is a qualitative process whereby stocks are screened based on whether the core business or primary activities of the underlying company are deemed to be *halaal* or non-*halal*. This is usually the first stage in any *shariah*-screening process before proceeding to the financial screening stage. Table 20.1 shows samples from DJIMI and S&P *shariah* index criteria for sector screening.[3]

In certain jurisdictions, such as Malaysia, sector screening is more lenient in the sense that there is a certain level for which the companies can

TABLE 20.1 List of Nonpermissible Activities in Sector Screening for DJIMI and S&P *Shariah* Index

Dow Jones Islamic Market Index	S&P *Shariah* Index
Alcohol	Advertising and media (with certain exceptions)
Pork-related products	Alcohol
Conventional financial services	Cloning
Entertainment	Financials (with certain exceptions)
Tobacco	Gambling
Weapons and defense	Pork
	Pornography
	Tobacco
	Trading of gold and silver as cash on deferred basis

[1] W. C. Pok, "Analysis of Shariah Quantitative Screening Norms among Malaysian Shariah Compliant Stock," *Investment Management and Financial Innovations* 9, no. 2 (2012): 69–80.

[2] ISRA, "Islamic Financial System: Principles and Operations," 2012.

[3] S&P Dow Jones Indices, "Dow Jones Islamic Market Indices," www.djindexes.com/islamicmarket/?go=shariah-compliance.

TABLE 20.2 Activity-Based Benchmarks (Effective November 2013)

5%	To access the level of mixed contributions from activities that are clearly prohibited such as *riba*-based activities, gambling, liquor and pork; interest income from conventional accounts and instruments and tobacco-related activities.
20%	To assess the level of contribution of mixed rentals from *shariah*-noncompliant activities; to assess the level of mixed contributions from activities that are generally permissible according to *shariah* and have an element of *maslahah* (public interest), but there are other elements that may accept the *shariah* status of these activities, for example, hotel and resort occasions.

Source: Malaysia: World's Islamic Finance Marketplace, www.mifc.com.

have minor income from nonpermissible activities. These so-called mixed companies are then assessed according to the benchmarks applicable for each type of impermissible activity. An extract of the most recent criteria[4] is shown in Table 20.2.

Consequently, those that passed the first filter would be assessed under the financial screening process. Generally the financial screening stage is when these stocks are evaluated to the extent that the interest-based financing and/or the interest-based income dominates the figures in the balance sheet. Using preset ratios, the companies' interest-based debts are compared to either the market capitalization or the total asset. Commonly, as mentioned earlier, the figures for these ratios cannot exceed 30 percent, 33 percent, or 33.33 percent. Examples of financial ratios that are being adopted by DJIMI are given here.

DJIMI FINANCIAL SCREENING CRITERIA

- Debt to Market Cap

Exclude companies for which Total Debt divided by Trailing Twelve Month Average Market. Capitalization (TTMAMC) is greater than or equal to 33 percent. (Note: Total Debt = Short-Term Debt + Current Portion of Long-Term Debt + Long-Term Debt.)

(*Continued*)

[4]MIFC, "Shariah Screening Methodology: Adopting a Two-Tier Quantitative Approach," 2013.

- Liquid Assets to Market Cap

  Exclude companies for which the sum of Cash and Interest-Bearing Securities divided by TTMAMC is greater than or equal to 33 percent.

- Receivables to Market Cap

  Exclude companies if Accounts Receivables divided by TTMAMC is greater than or equal to 33 percent. (Note: Accounts Receivables = Current Receivables + Long-Term Receivables.) Companies passing the above screens are qualified to be included as components of the Dow Jones Islamic Market Index.

There is also another step in the *shariah* screening process, whose adoption brings about controversies and issues. *Dividend purification* is where the noncompliant fraction of the revenue received is to be purified or cleansed. The issues in its adoption are whether the cleansing should be done at the income-distribution stage by the company or should be left at the discretion of the shareholders or the unit trust managers. If the apportionment to charity is done by the company, what of the non-Muslim investors? What about the capital gains that occur during the year? Would that fall under the revenue that has to be cleansed as well?

Currently, there are many debates regarding the matter on purification and not all *shariah* jurisdictions adopt this method, including Malaysia. What Malaysia does that is unique is something they call *qualitative analysis*, apart from the quantitative analysis that involves sector and financial screening. Hereby, the decision on the listing of the company would also be derived from the assessment on the image factor, *maslahah*, *umum balwa*, and so on. The two additional criteria given for the mixed companies are as follows:

1. The public perception or image of the company must be good.
2. The core activities of the company are important and considered *maslahah* (benefit in general) to the Muslim *ummah* (nation) and the country, and the nonpermissible element is very small and involves matters such as *umum balwa* (common plight and difficult to avoid), *urf* (custom), and the rights of the non-Muslim community, which are accepted by Islam.[5]

[5]Suruhanjaya Sekuriti, Securities Commission Malaysia, "Information Required for the Syariah Compliance Review at Pre-IPO Stage," www.sc.com.my/wp-content/uploads/eng/html/icm/Pre-IPO_Infotemplatel1.pdf, accessed August 2014.

All in all, companies that fulfill the screening of these criteria would be listed in the perspective indexes. However, if we look closer, the screening criteria, regardless of which *shariah* jurisdiction it falls into, are relatively insufficient and might be unfair in certain circumstances, such as the times when there is economic downturn that can affect the cash level in a company, or a highly competitive market, which will influence the amount of accounts receivable during the period. More filters and factors should be taken into account in the screening criteria. On another note, apart from all these qualitative and quantitative assessments, *shariah* scholars should come up with screening methodologies that are also in line with *maqasid shariah*, such as to incorporate the ethical aspects and corporate social responsibility of the company. There is still much room for these indexes to be improved and developed, preferably in a more harmonized and/or standardized manner throughout the world.

CAPITAL MARKETS

Capital markets are best described as markets where financial instruments are bought and sold, or where deficit units issue financial instruments to attract capital from surplus units. A stock exchange, for instance, is a platform where companies issue shares to raise capital and where investors go to invest capital. This is the primary function of a stock exchange and the market for initial public offerings (IPO) is known as *primary markets*. Another important feature of a stock exchange is that it allows investors to sell shares they have purchased in a company to a third party if they wish to exit a position or a holding in the secondary market.

The only time a company actually receives money into its accounts is at the stage of an IPO. All subsequent buy-and-sell arrangements in the shares are settled between investors and the issuing company is not a direct beneficiary of any cash flows. The secondary market, however, has critical importance to the primary market as the demand and supply of a company's shares after they have been issued determine the price of the company's stock.

IPO STAGE

To illustrate with a simplistic example, imagine if XYZ Company involved in cement manufacturing wishes to raise $300,000,000 in capital, it will first go through regulatory requirements to become a publicly listed company (PLC). As a PLC the company can raise capital from the general public.

Regulators therefore require XYZ to make full disclosures of its audited financial records, and to make a commitment that it would continue to do so at periodical intervals so that investors have all the necessary information they need to make an investment in the company. XYZ having done so, it is also required to prepare a full prospectus for its equity issue, as a sales pitch to invite investors. The company has to convince potential shareholders and investors to invest in XYZ.

XYZ is a cement company, so it may not have access to institutional investors like mutual funds, asset management companies, insurance companies, and high-net-worth individuals. XYZ approaches an investment bank to facilitate the issue for a *wakalah* fee. If investment bankers have done their job well, the share issue will be fully subscribed.

Finally XYZ is permitted to issue 30M shares at $10 each and on a specific date the IPO is announced. XYZ Company offers 30,000,000 shares to the investing public, but also maintains 20,000,000 shares in the names of the directors in the existing XYZ Company. In this way the company has a total of 50,000,000 shares, of which 20,000,000 are held by the directors of the existing firm (which may be all members of one family), and 30,000,000 are offered to the public. In this manner the original directors also negotiate control over the newly formed company.

Institutional investors are able to purchase shares through electronic applications and retail investors also throw in their orders. An institutional investor may buy $20M worth of shares whereas a retail investor may buy just $2,000. In today's world of electronic trading the entire process of the IPO can be concluded in a matter of just a few hours. Let us illustrate an order book for an IPO. Imagine the IPO is announced for Monday morning at 9 on June 7, 2012. The company is well received by the market and orders for the shares keep flooding in, as in Table 20.3.

As one can see from the example, all shares are sold by the eight trades, and XYZ Cement Company receives its $300,000,000. In reality, investors that own 2 or 3 percent of a company's shares are consider to be large shareholders.

Witnessing the success, the IPO late-movers get in the game and AB Insurance wants to buy shares in XYZ. The exchange informs AB Insurance that the IPO is fully subscribed and that AB must now buy from any one of the investors that picked up the shares in the first round. All AB has to do is place an order for 1,000,000 shares on the electronic platform of the exchange and offer its price. Obviously, anyone who bought shares for $10 will sell at a profit. AB Insurance offers a price of $10.50 for the shares, and no one is willing to sell. AB then offers $11 for the shares, and A Insurance Company offloads 1,000,000 shares and sells to AB for a tidy profit of $1,000,000, all in a day's work. The proceeds of this sale do not go to XYX Cement but to A Insurance Company. This trade and all subsequent trades happen in the secondary market. Trading volume in the IPO market

TABLE 20.3 IPO Stage

Trades	Customer Name	Order Size Shares	%	IPO Price	Order Value
	Total IPO issue	30,000,000		10	300,000,000
		Primary Trades			
1	A Insurance Company	3,000,000	10	10	30,000,000
2	B Insurance Company	4,000,000	13	10	40,000,000
3	C Asset Management	3,600,000	12	10	36,000,000
4	D Asset Management	5,400,000	18	10	54,000,000
5	E Mutual Fund	6,500,000	22	10	65,000,000
6	F Mutual Fund	5,000,000	17	10	50,000,000
7	G Municipal Fund	2,000,000	7	10	20,000,000
8	Retail Orders	500,000	2	10	5,000,000
	Total Shares Held	30,000,000			300,000,000

TABLE 20.4 Day 1 Closing Trade

Secondary Trades					
Trades	**Customer Name**	**Order Size Shares**	**%**	**IPO Price**	**Order Value**
1	Buy order AB INS	1,000,000		11	11,000,000
	Sell order A INS	1,000,000			—

is obviously 30,000,000 shares, as XYZ Cement offers 30M shares for sale, and various buyers buy 30M shares. So far in the secondary market, trading volume for XYZ Cement shares is 1,000,000 shares (Table 20.4).

The shareholding pattern at the end of Day I is reflected in Table 20.5. Note that all holdings are now valued at the closing price in the secondary market and no longer the IPO price.

On the next trading day, June 8, the market witnesses additional deals of just 2,000,000 but at markedly increased prices. The last lot of shares is traded at $13 a share (Table 20.6).

As per market convention, all shares held by shareholders will be valued at $13 per share. Let us examine the impact of these trades on the value of each investor's shareholdings in Table 20.7.

The last trade on June 8 of 2,000,000 shares sets the final price or the last price of the shares at $13 per share, which has a considerable impact in the value of the shareholdings of all investors.

A Insurance Company, which bought 3,000,000 shares at $10 per share, ends up selling 1,000,000 shares for $11 for $1 profit. A Insurance Company

TABLE 20.5 Closing Day Positions

Trades	Customer Name	Order Size Shares	%	Closing Price	Market Cap.
	Total IPO issue	30,000,000		11	330,000,000
		Day I Closing Positions			
1	A Insurance Company	2,000,000	7	11	22,000,000
2	AB Insurance Company	1,000,000	3	11	11,000,000
3	B Insurance Company	4,000,000	15	11	44,000,000
4	C Asset Management	3,600,000	13	11	39,600,000
5	D Asset Management	5,400,000	20	11	59,400,000
6	E Mutual Fund	6,500,000	24	11	71,500,000
7	F Mutual Fund	5,000,000	18	11	55,000,000
8	G Municipal Fund	2,000,000	7	11	22,000,000
9	Retail Orders	500,000	2	11	5,500,000
	Total Shares Held	**30,000,000**		**Total Market Cap.**	**330,000,000**

TABLE 20.6 Day 2 Trades

		Secondary Trades Day 2I			
Trades	Customer Name	Order Size Shares	%	Closing Price	Order Value
2	Buy order FF Mutual	2,000,000		13	26,000,000
	Sell order F Mutual	2,000,000			

on Trading Day 2 has 2,000,000 shares valued at $13 per share. A Insurance Company would earn a profit of $3,000,000 if it chose to sell all its shares at the price of $13 per share, thus earning a total profit of ($1M on day 1 and $6M on day 2) $7M, making an ROI of 23.33 percent in just two days!

MARKET INTEGRITY

Is it possible to imagine that the last trade of Day 2 for 2,000,000 shares between FF Mutual and F Mutual is a fictitious sale to merely escalate the price, referred to as a "wash sale" in the industry? The market on June 8 takes the starting price or opening price as the closing price on June 7. If F Mutual and FF Mutual colluded to artificially inflate the prices of the shares, the main beneficiaries would be the existing shareholders, including

TABLE 20.7 Day 2 Closing Positions

Trades	Customer Name	Shares Held	IPO Price	Valued at IPO Price	Market Price	Valued at Last Closing Price
	Total IPO Issue	30,000,000	10	300,000,000	13	390,000,000
1	A Insurance Company	2,000,000	10	20,000,000	13	26,000,000
2	B Insurance Company	4,000,000	10	40,000,000	13	52,000,000
3	C Asset Management	3,600,000	10	36,000,000	13	46,800,000
4	D Asset Management	5,400,000	10	54,000,000	13	70,200,000
5	E Mutual Fund	4,500,000	10	45,000,000	13	58,500,000
6	F Mutual Fund	3,000,000	10	30,000,000	13	39,000,000
7	G Municipal Fund	1,000,000	10	10,000,000	13	13,000,000
8	Retail Orders	500,000	10	5,000,000	13	6,500,000
	IPO Buyers Holdings:	**24,000,000**		**240,000,000**		**312,000,000**
9	AB Insurance	1,000,000			13	13,000,000
10	EE Mutual	1,000,000			13	13,000,000
11	WR Insurance	2,000,000			13	26,000,000
12	FF Mutual	2,000,000			13	26,000,000
	Secondary Buyers Holdings:	6,000,000				78,000,000
Market Capitalization		**30,000,000**	**10**	**300,000,000**	**13**	**390,000,000**

TABLE 20.8 FF Mutual Trade

2	Buy order FF Mutual	2,000,000	13	26,000,000
	Sell order F Mutual	2,000,000		

the directors of XYZ, as this would reflect a $3 increase in their share price in just two days, an increase in the value of their holdings of 30 percent (Table 20.8).

Certainly such practices do happen, although the efficient market hypothesis tends to refute this argument. When the share price is increased to $13, some investors that did not enter the IPO may feel left out and may be happy to start buying the shares at even $13.50, $13.75, $14 per share, expecting to sell the shares to other investors at even higher prices at some point in the future.

In this manner the initial buyer of the IPO may actually exit from all holdings within a week and, assuming that all investors in the IPO sold their shares at an average price for $14, they would make returns of 40 percent in seven days.

Is it also possible for shareholders to start dumping their shares to bring prices down to even below $10 and then to mop up all the shares again at

TABLE 20.9 Reduced Prices

	Secondary Trades Day 2			
1	Buy order WR Ins.	1,000,000	9.5	9,500,000
	Sell order G Fund	1,000,000		—
2	Buy order FF Mutual	2,000,000	8	16,000,000
	Sell order F Mutual	2,000,000		

TABLE 20.10 Valuations at $8

Trades	Customer Name	Shares Held	IPO Price	Valued at IPO Price	Market Price	Valued at Market Price
	Total IPO	30,000,000	10	300,000,000	8	240,000,000
1	A Insurance Company	2,000,000	10	20,000,000	8	16,000,000
2	B Insurance Company	4,000,000	10	40,000,000	8	32,000,000
3	C Asset Management	3,600,000	10	36,000,000	8	28,800,000
4	D Asset Management	5,400,000	10	54,000,000	8	43,200,000
5	E Mutual Fund	4,500,000	10	45,000,000	8	36,000,000
6	F Mutual Fund	3,000,000	10	30,000,000	8	24,000,000
7	G Municipal Fund	1,000,000	10	10,000,000	8	8,000,000
8	Retail Orders	500,000	10	5,000,000	8	4,000,000
	IPO Buyers Holdings:	**24,000,000**		**240,000,000**		**192,000,000**
9	AB Insurance	1,000,000			8	8,000,000
10	EE Mutual	1,000,000			8	8,000,000
11	WR Insurance	2,000,000			8	16,000,000
12	FF Mutual	2,000,000			8	16,000,000
	Secondary Buyers Holdings:	6,000,000			8	48,000,000
Market Capitalization		30,000,000	10	300,000,000	8	240,000,000

$8 per share and still sell them again at $10 a share, making a 20 percent return? All that one would have to do is make the last two trades on Day 2 to be at $9.50 or $8 (Table 20.9).

This would make all shareholders' valuations to be priced at $8. If this event can trigger off a panic sale, some shareholders will be selling their shares at $9, $8, $7.75 to minimize their losses. But its important to consider that when somebody is selling shares, there may be someone buying shares (Table 20.10).

Buyers will feel that existing shareholders are overreacting, and buy up all available shares for sale; or maybe someone knows something other investors do not, that the prices are being deliberately manipulated. If, at the end of the day, EE Mutual and G Mutual end up with 15 million shares valued at $8 a share, one could suspect them of having manipulated the markets. This suspicion would grow into certainty if these two companies slowly began offloading their shares for $8.45, $8.50, $9, and $10.50 and making huge profits. The trail of such manipulation is even further disguised if EE Mutual and G Mutual execute this manipulation using subsidiaries and associated companies or in collusion with other fund managers, especially if these funds managers are also offshore companies.

Artificially increasing prices and artificially decreasing prices is considered a crime by the ethical standards of all markets, be they commodities markets, markets for cloth, or markets for stocks. The sheer volume, however, of these transactions in capital markets makes the task of monitoring such movements in prices an impossible task for regulators.

Small-capitalization stocks are more vulnerable to such manipulation as the numbers of shares floated in a market are small. It is far more difficult to manipulate stocks with a market capitalization of say $100 billion where possibly share buying of $10 billion is required to manipulate share prices by 1 or 2 percent. Penny stocks are the most vulnerable to such manipulation.

MARKET REGULATION

Regulators exist for every market, whether markets for capital or for food stuff or even real estate. The Muslim world developed the institution of the *hisbah* to regulate market activities such as hoarding, price manipulations, and artificially created price increases. The first *muhtasib* in Islamic history was the Prophet (saw) himself. Despite the misconception of the role of women in Islamic society, the first formally placed *muhtasib* was, in fact, a woman by the name of Samra' bint Nuhaik al-Asadiyyah. The lady was appointed by none other than Hadrat Umar (ra) himself.

Price manipulation is not only a violation of the markets but also a violation of the *shariah*. The regulator for capital markets is usually referred to as the *securities commission*, and as we have mentioned before, a *shariah* board is now in place in many securities commissions offices in the Muslim world; their role is currently just limited to vetting the *shariah*-compliance of the companies listed on the *shariah* index. *Shariah* advisors, however, should be further trained in the mechanics of stocks trading so that they may be able to identify price manipulations as well. Their role should be enhanced to such areas as well.

Trading volumes have grown over the past 100 years. As the New York Stock Exchange states, five instruments were traded on the NYSE in

2001 **Volume tops 2 billion**
January 04
Volume of trading on the NYSE exceeded 2 billion shares for the first time on this day, when 2.129 billion shares changed hands. This record-volume day followed the previous day's 1/2-percentage-point interest ratecut by the Fed Reserve, which lowered the fed funds rate to 6 percent. NYSE.com

FIGURE 20.1 NYSE Trading Volume on January 4, 2001

1792;[6] by the year 2001, 2.129 billion shares were traded on the NYSE (Figure 20.1).

The volume was triggered off by a .50 percent decrease in the Fed's rates, giving the reader an idea of how much money invested in the exchange is borrowed money.

The New York Stock Exchange is the largest capital market in the world; the numbers below illustrate that in dollar amounts more than the GDP of an average country is traded on the NYSE in one month, with 76,436,100,000 shares traded in January alone or almost 3 billion shares per day (Table 20.11).

Table 20.12 shows the statistics for 2013, and reveals that close to $27 trillion of money was employed in executing buy-and-sale transactions on the NYSE. The question we wish to raise is simple: What is the value to the real economy of these transactions? How many jobs did this trading create? How much value did these trades create? Was all this trading directed toward speculative goals only, with funds managers hoping to just benefit from slight

TABLE 20.11 NYSE 2014 Trading Volumes

Consolidated Volume in NYSE Listed Issues, 2014				
	Trading Days	Consolidated Share Volume (millions)	Consolidated Trades (thousands)	Consolidated Dollar Volume (billions)
January	21	76,436.10	378,767.80	2,761.40
February	19	70,309.60	358,601.20	2,634.40
March	21	72,845.00	363,716.90	2,671.00
April	21	72,200.30	381,613.80	2,712.90
May	21	64,202.30	339,004.80	2,350.60

Source: www.NYSEdata.com (June 22, 2014, 4:27 P.M.).

[6]NYSE, www.NYSE.com, accessed June 22, 2014.

TABLE 20.12 NYSE 2013 Trading Volumes

Consolidated Volume in NYSE Listed Issues, 2013				
	Trading Days	Consolidated Share Volume (millions)	Consolidated Trades (thousands)	Consolidated Dollar Volume (billions)
January	21	76,056.10	302,205.00	2,274.10
February	19	69,724.80	286,428.40	2,205.40
March	20	69,330.30	282,205.70	2,148.70
April	22	77,640.70	324,396.50	2,420.20
May	22	77,081.10	313,772.60	2,502.80
June	20	76,618.20	303,140.60	2,404.40
July	22	68,574.40	281,304.70	2,223.70
August	22	65,352.90	276,894.80	2,095.70
September	20	67,212.10	266,633.80	2,134.30
October	23	77,524.00	322,319.60	2,589.60
November	20	64,208.30	267,734.90	2,201.70
December	21	66,223.10	307,180.10	2,317.20
Total	252	855,546.00	3,534,216.70	27,517.80

Source: www.NYSEdata.com (June 22, 2014, 4:27 P.M.).

price changes? Would the economy at large be better off if speculative funds were invested in real economic activity?

What is also important for the Muslim world is to not merely accept the financial institutions of the developed world with blind faith. Certainly Islamic capital markets should not be a platform to drain the real economy of capital. Capital markets were envisioned by its founders as a mechanism of collecting surplus moneys from millions of individuals' hands and injecting them into the economy to spur growth, create jobs, and improve the well-being of the citizens of the country.

With the evolution of speculative trade practices, approved by regulators, traders invested with borrowed moneys at low interest rates, and invested in the secondary market (remember the money does not go to the issuing company in this case) and just waited to sell the shares when their prices moved by even the slightest percentage.

Table 20.13 shows how different levels of changes in prices generate returns for a fund manager. For instance, a fund manager managing \$100,000,000 will generate \$1,000,000 in returns if all the stocks in his or her portfolio appreciate by 1 percent. It is rare for such an event to happen. Similarly if market movements in stock values are .01 percent *per hour*,

TABLE 20.13 Percentage Changes in Market Values

$ Amount Invested	Percentage Change in Market Values of Underlying Asset									
	0.001%	0.01%	0.1%	.5%	1%	2%	3%	5%	7%	10%
1,000,000,000	10,000	100,000	1,000,000	5,000,000	10,000,000	20,000,000	30,000,000	50,000,000	70,000,000	100,000,000
750,000,000	7,500	75,000	750,000	3,750,000	7,500,000	15,000,000	22,500,000	37,500,000	52,500,000	75,000,000
500,000,000	5,000	50,000	500,000	2,500,000	5,000,000	10,000,000	15,000,000	25,000,000	35,000,000	50,000,000
250,000,000	2,500	25,000	250,000	1,250,000	2,500,000	5,000,000	7,500,000	12,500,000	17,500,000	25,000,000
100,000,000	1,000	10,000	100,000	500,000	1,000,000	2,000,000	3,000,000	5,000,000	7,000,000	10,000,000
50,000,000	500	5,000	50,000	250,000	500,000	1,000,000	1,500,000	2,500,000	3,500,000	5,000,000
25,000,000	250	2,500	25,000	125,000	250,000	500,000	750,000	1,250,000	1,750,000	2,500,000
10,000,000	100	1,000	10,000	50,000	100,000	200,000	300,000	500,000	700,000	1,000,000
5,000,000	50	500	5,000	25,000	50,000	100,000	150,000	250,000	350,000	500,000
1,000,000	10	100	1,000	5,000	10,000	20,000	30,000	50,000	70,000	100,000
500,000	5	50	500	2,500	5,000	10,000	15,000	25,000	35,000	50,000
250,000	3	25	250	1,250	2,500	5,000	7,500	12,500	17,500	25,000
100,000	1.00	10	100	500	1,000	2,000	3,000	5,000	7,000	10,000

for instance, the fund manager would earn $100,000 if all stocks in the portfolio appreciated in value by .01 percent in that interval. The fund manager would in essence then be glued to his screens, looking for the slightest movement in prices in the secondary markets to generate returns. Mathematical models would be developed to anticipate changes, identify trends, and all in all make a quick buck. Not a penny of the fund managers' portfolio is invested in any real commercial activity of any real meaning. The markets have become legitimate casinos where trillions are invested in hoping that the better number comes up.

Islam forbids speculative trading.[7] This should be an axiom of Islamic capital markets, despite the fact that speculators defend their position as providing liquidity to the market, providing price discovery, working as market makers, and so on. If so, speculative trading should be limited to less than 33 percent of all trading so that the flow of capital is not redirected from companies, and companies' stock prices are not inflated or deflated merely by the actions of speculative traders.

At least in this way one can ensure that $18 trillion is allocated to real assets, or actual business enterprises, or on long-term positions in companies that add value to an economy and provide returns. Speculative traders are right 50 percent of the time at best; often returns made in one year are wiped out manifold in subsequent years.[8]

VALUATIONS

Speculative traders also look at the concept of value in different ways. They do not look at a stock price as a function of future earnings over an extended period:

Price = Present Value of Future Earnings

= Present Value of Dividends + Capital Gain

Or Price = f(perceived value)

Or Price = f(cost of borrowing)

Price = f(how soon I can sell it for a profit)

Or where price is a function of any intrinsic value, price is just a function of expected value and perceived values. Manipulating perceptions is not a

[7]Kitab Al-Buyu, *Sahih Muslim Book*, 10.

[8]Nicholas Nassim Taleb, *Fooled by Randomness: The Hidden Role of Chance in Life and in the Markets* (New York: Random House, 2008).

crime; manipulating prices is. Investors armed with an explosive media network can influence perceptions of what is valuable and what is not. Further, the time horizons of speculative traders are much shorter than those who seek to take long-term positions in companies. A traditional investor (known as a "fundamentalist") looks at a company's balance sheet, its core business, its prospects, the prospects for the industry it is in, and then makes a decision to invest in a company, hoping to share in the earnings the company will generate over a 3-year, 5-year, or 10-year span.

The modern trader may not hold onto 30 percent of his portfolio for longer than a half hour. Portfolios are divided into long-term, medium-term and short-term segments. Long-term investments are made by keeping fundamentals in mind, medium-term investments are a hybrid portfolio, and short-term portfolios may experience hundreds of buy-and-sale trades in a single day. It is the sheer impact of these short-term trades that influences prices that literally blur the actual value of a company as reflected in its share price. To conclude, therefore, the share price may or may not truly reflect the real value of a company's assets and prospects, and if price fails to reflect this, then it is no longer a true price. According to the *shariah*, if any component of a contract is not truly reflective of the reality, such that the description of the goods does not actually reflect the good, or its price is not a reflection of its true price, the sale and purchase transaction should in principle be made null and void.

ZERO SUM GAME

Islamic capital markets should not be a zero sum game. In a sale purchase transaction of shares a buyer benefits if the value of the shares increases after purchase and the seller loses out on what could have been earned. It is the ability of the buyer and/or the seller to anticipate market conditions. However at a macro level, capital markets are no longer benefiting the economy; they are failing to channel funds into real economic activity. The growing listing of derivatives contracts and options contracts offers a more baffling figure with total "Over-the-Counter Derivative" contracts having a nominal value of $18.6858 trillion as of December 31, 2013.[9] Exchange-traded derivatives had a turnover of $364.7 trillion on futures contracts of $27.757 trillion and a turnover of $123 trillion on options contracts of $44.951 trillion.[10] I did not even know the world had that kind of money.

[9]Bank of International Settlements.

[10]Ibid.

Although derivatives instruments can function as hedging tools and offer mechanisms of sharing risk, they have themselves become objectives of speculative transactions. The subject of derivatives will be discussed is subsequent publications.

THE ROLE OF CAPITAL MARKETS IN THE SPHERE OF ISLAMIC FINANCE

Capital markets have been guilty of only being able to raise capital or debt for large corporations and governments. They do not cater to the needs of small businesses that in fact employ usually more than 50 percent of a country's workforce. The agricultural sector is also left out of this market, unless banks dedicated to agricultural financing are able to access funds from the stock markets or through bond issuances. Farmers and small business owners simply cannot access the capital markets for funds directly. In fact, listing requirements for companies and their instruments require that companies maintain a minimum turnover or revenue for a certain time before seeking public funds. This minimum turnover is usually in millions.

The economies of the Islamic world are heavily skewed toward agriculture, and small- and medium-size businesses. Only large state-owned oil and gas companies, or private banks, or cement companies, and so on, are able to tap into capital markets for funds. The ironic thing is that many of the investors are insurance companies, fund managers, and pension fund managers who invest savings of everyday people, but never invest in businesses set up by those same kinds of everyday people.

The role of venture capitalists is to identify entrepreneurs with good ideas or products and fund them through private investments of capital. Venture capitalists or angel investors are real risk takers and the domain of Islamic finance is much in need of such risk appetite. Companies like Microsoft, Apple, LinkedIn, Tesla, would never have become the mammoths they are today if certain investors had not backed these companies at various stages of their evolution.

FARMER *SUKUK* OR EQUITY NOTES

A critical component of society that have throughout history had difficulties to raise funds are farmers due to the high risks associated with the nature of their work. Farmers always require funds before planting season to purchase fertilizer, hire labor, purchase seeds and crop medicines, to rent machinery, and so on. Many farmers also lock in the sale price of their harvest using a variant of the concept behind a *salaam* contract, but buyers do not always pay the purchase price in full at the time of contract initiation. Independent farmers could organize themselves and discount their receivables to be obtained from commodity merchants and use the funds to build better storage facilities, purchase transportation units to transfer goods to markets that offer better prices, and so on.

The instrument, a farmer's *sukuk*, could in fact be a short-term *sukuk*, for instance, based on the contract of *bai al dayn* and could be listed on a country's exchange. The maturity of the instrument could be linked to the cycles of the seeding and harvesting season and could be structured like a short-term discount bond with no coupon payments.

If this idea seems too benign, refer to the following statement regarding Charles Mitchell, one of the founding fathers of Citibank, who made himself noticeable with the following deal.

> *Mitchell's first major deal with his firm Mitchell and Company had been selling a block of 430,000 of equipment notes secured by New York harbor scows.*[11]

Capital markets can serve private interests of investors and national investors. In fact, some of the most successful floatations of bonds was during World War I, when the United States floated Liberty Bonds to raise funds to finance the United States' reluctant involvement in Europe's mess.

> *The US wound up selling nearly $17 billion in Liberty bonds. McAdoo wanted to reach the broadest population of bond buyers possible—from small farmers to businessmen to workers. By doing so, he inadvertently created a new generation of American investors who would later participate in the 1920s stock bubble.*[12]

CONCLUSION

Capital markets yet need to show their true potential in the world of Islamic finance. With the Muslim world having a population of 1.3 billion, a culture of saving, and a vibrant middle class, the possibilities for funding projects of development and commercial enterprises are endless.

---

[11]Nomi Prins, *All the Presidents' Bankers: The Hidden Alliances that Drive American Power* (New York: Nation Books, 2014), 50.
[12]Ibid., 49.

CHAPTER 21

Pricing, Income Distribution, and Risk Sharing in Islamic Banks

Pricing of *shariah*-compliant financial products has followed a similar track to pricing conventional products. The readers at this stage should not be surprised at the similarities by now. However, the legitimacy of a *shariah*-compliant product does not lie in its pricing but in the rights extended to parties to a contract and the obligations arising from the same. If these rights and obligations are *shariah*-compliant, the contract and hence the product is compliant. Price is not a litmus test. Income sharing is another crucial aspect of Islamic banking and we explore this concept along with risk sharing in this chapter.

PRICING OF ISLAMIC FINANCIAL PRODUCTS

The price of any product is primarily a function of its cost. Other factors, such as demand, greatly impact the price of a product as well. A company that manufactures shoes, for instance, would incorporate into the price of one shoe the following five elements:

1. A portion of the fixed costs associated with the plant, property, and equipment that is dedicated to the manufacturing of shoes.
2. The variable costs of raw materials, utilities, wages, salaries, distribution costs, advertising costs, and packaging costs that are directly or indirectly related to the manufacturing of shoes.
3. The expected rate of inflation.
4. The costs of financing (if any).
5. A required rate of return on capital invested.

The sum of the above factors would resemble a *murabahah* pricing formula of cost plus profit. An Islamic bank like a conventional bank does not have any "Costs of Goods Sold" on its income statement, but rather incurs a cost of fund. This cost of fund is the average return that needs to be paid to depositors to mobilize their funds. If we recall, Islamic banks like other banks do not finance borrowers using shareholders' funds, but instead use depositors' funds. Depositors require a return on their funds placed in Islamic banks; this return constitutes an Islamic bank's cost of fund.

Islamic banks bear the costs associated with identifying customers, mobilizing sales teams to collect deposits from customers, administrative costs, salaries, IT costs, and costs associated with acquiring office spaces. These costs can be lumped into overheads and include fixed and variable costs. Islamic banks also factor the rate of inflation into their pricing models so that the value of money received in future does not depreciate.

Islamic banks are also required to maintain statutory reserves with their central banks and these reserves earn no returns. Islamic banks pass on the opportunity cost of placing these funds in reserves at the risk-free rate to borrowers as well.

Like conventional banks, Islamic banks are faced with the problem of borrowing short and lending long. Islamic banks rely on short-term deposits of 1 month, 3 months, or 6 months to finance assets with tenors of 1 year, 3 years, 5 years, 25 years, and so on. Constantly faced with this asset/liability mismatch, all Islamic banks must rely on the interbank money markets to borrow funds from other banks in case they experience a surge in assets or an attrition in their deposits. These funds are lent from one bank to another for varying tenors depending on the maturity of the market. In the Islamic banking industry these funds are not lent but funding is done between Islamic banks on a *mudharabah* basis. The rate applied to these *mudharabah* contracts between Islamic banks is a function of the market's interbank overnight rate (IBOR).[1]

Islamic banks may also as a last resort obtain funds from the central bank's window, where the central bank acts as a lender of last resort. This is usually a high rate, and is also referred to as the *central bank's policy rate*, as the central bank controls market liquidity by increasing or decreasing these rates.

To recap, all the components mentioned earlier, which include overhead costs, opportunity costs of funds kept in reserves, inflation, interbank borrowing costs, and cost of borrowing from the lender of last resort, contribute to a bank's pricing mechanism.

Banks' pricing mechanisms can be divided into two broad categories. One is the return paid to depositors, which is a function of interest rates

[1]Islamic Interbank Money Market, "Statistics: Islamic Interbank Rates," http://iimm.bnm.gov.my/index.php?ch=7, accessed July 2014.

disclosed by central banks to the public. Deposits that are not rewarded by any returns offer the lowest cost of funds as is the case in current accounts. Second in line are savings account holders followed by depositors in fixed deposit schemes under *mudharabah* or commodity *murabahah*. Within these categories, retail depositors are usually offered lower rates of return than are institutional depositors. Next in line, interbank *mudharabah* funding is expensive, as a surplus bank takes a share of the profits of the deficit bank. Finally, the policy rate of the central bank would be the highest rate in the market.

The second category of pricing is linked to what banks charge borrowers in terms of a profit rate, or *ijara* rate. This price is a function of the direct cost of fund, coupled with all the additional costs mentioned earlier. To top it off, shareholders demand a rate of return on their investment of capital, but although it is not their funds that are actually utilized in financing borrowers, shareholders' funds are utilized in setting up the Islamic bank's infrastructure to enable mobilization of funds.

As the main function of Islamic banks is financing borrowers who purchase or lease goods on deferred payment bases, Islamic banks face credit risk, and pass on credit risk premiums to borrowers as well. The well-known principle of the higher the risk the higher the return applies to Islamic banking. The profit rate charged to a low-risk customer like a sovereign government for instance may be 1 percent, whereas the rate built into a *murabahah* contract with a B-rated corporation may well be 4 percent. In this case, the credit risk premium faced by the Islamic bank in financing the corporation is passed back onto the customer.

Islamic banks faced with the situation of borrowing short and lending long are faced with market risk. The profit rate at which assets are booked depends a great deal on the cost of funds at which funds can be mobilized. Funds are mobilized on a continuous basis, and if market interest rates increase, depositors would demand higher returns on their deposits, shrinking the margins or spreads enjoyed by banks. Such movements in interest rates affect banks' income and are referred to as *market risk*. Islamic banks can add a factor of this risk into the profit rate applied in pricing their products to counter any unpredictable movements in price changes.

$$\begin{aligned}\text{Profit Rate} = f\,[&(\text{cost of fund}) + (\text{operational costs}) + (\text{SRR costs})\\ &+ (\text{expected inflation rate}) + (\text{central bank policy rate})\\ &+ (\text{interbank rates}) + (\text{credit risk premium})\\ &+ (\text{factor for market risk}) + (\text{required rate of return})]\end{aligned}$$

One can see that the profit rate imputed into a financial product is a function of several variables. Each variable can be assigned a different weightage or sensitivity factor.

PRICE VERSUS *SHARIAH*

One can, however, argue that this is quite similar to a pricing model of a conventional bank. One can further argue that Islamic banks should not face the same issue with cost of funds as *hibah* is paid at the discretion of IFIs and profits are paid to depositors in *mudharabah* accounts on a *post-ante* basis. This means that only when profits are actualized every month-end, are profits shared with depositors, so in essence Islamic banks do not commit to depositors any rate of return on their deposits and as such have no committed cost of funds.

Herein lies an element in the mind-set of depositors who require Islamic banks to communicate an indicative rate of return on *mudharabah* deposits and an indicative rate of *hibah* as well. It is the market expectations of the customers that draws Islamic banking into a system that mirrors conventional banking. Islamic banks would be quite delighted if they could mobilize funds without guaranteeing principal amounts in *mudharabah* accounts or guaranteeing returns or *hibah*, either. It is customers themselves who have rejected this model and not the IFIs.

In order to compete with conventional banks, Islamic banks have been forced to offer deposit products by announcing an indicative rate of return. If Islamic banks fail to deliver on this commitment, they have in the past lost deposits to conventional banks. Customers who opt for Islamic banking are still comparing *shariah*-compliant financial products with conventional products on the basis of price and not on the basis of the legitimacy of the underlying contract.

Critics of Islamic banking, especially users of Islamic banking products, have criticized Islamic banking products as being more expensive than conventional products and have thus referred to them as *nonshariah*-compliant. Price is not a benchmark for determining the legitimacy of the underlying contracts that structure Islamic financial products and such criticism is not well founded. Islamic banking is a new industry, and in fact the architects of financial products in IFIs are forced to comply with the *shariah* the best they can, but customers still base their choice on price. Muslims at the very least should migrate from conventional banking to *shariah*-compliant banking to help Islamic financial institutions reach the critical mass they need to enhance the financial system and make it more equity-based.

A legitimate criticism of Islamic banking would be if depositors bear credit risk and market risk as we see in the next section, they should be rewarded with higher returns. Second, if credit risk premium is also passed onto borrowers, then what risk are Islamic banks incurring, only market risk and liquidity risk. The profits they earn are considerably disproportionately higher than what depositors earn despite the fact that banks use depositors' capital to extend financing contracts and make investments. So if the major source of funding is provided by depositors, they should be earning a greater proportion of the returns. We examine this point in greater detail in the next section.

BENCHMARK FOR PRICING

Certain capital markets instruments, like *sukuk*, use LIBOR as a pricing benchmark for international issuances of *sukuk* to attract international investors.[2] For domestic retail and corporate products the function highlighted earlier serves as a basic formula. A legitimate criticism of this model would be that if Islamic banks are not "lenders" in spirit but in effect are partners to businesses, then for commercial facilities, the natural profit rate of businesses with which Islamic banks partner should be the benchmark for pricing. Alternative benchmark rates of return can be the rate for *zakat* of 2.5 percent or the GDP growth rate in an economy. This issue is being addressed in upcoming papers in various academic journals.

For instance, if an Islamic bank finances the purchase of construction equipment to a construction company, the Islamic bank should use the profit rate of the construction industry as its benchmark as in essence the Islamic bank will earn a share in the profits earned by the company. This approach would be applicable to contracts of *musharakah* and *mudharabah*, where in form and essence an Islamic bank is a partner in the business of its clients and not a financier. These facilities cannot obtain any collateral from their clients, but become joint owners in the assets of their businesses.

With such an approach, Islamic banks would have a diversified exposure to various sectors of the industry, each with its own risk-and-return profile, and would earn an average rate of profit from the various businesses the bank is partnered in.

CRITICISM ON PRICING MODELS

Mainstream critics of Islamic banking also criticize how Islamic banks charge a predetermined profit rate in their *murabahah*-based contracts and

---

[2]Rodney Wilson, "Innovation in the Structuring of Islamic Sukuk Securities," *Humanomics* 24, no. 3 (2008: 170–181).

ijara-based contracts. Let us just examine the stream of returns to two fictitious clients (Table 21.1), one that has obtained a *murabahah*-based working capital facility, and the other, an *ijara*-based facility.

The two clients experience the earlier cited sequence of returns in their respective business for a period of 12 months. In turn, if an Islamic bank were to be a true partner in their client's business they, too, would earn different rates of return in their income statements. The annual average on the *murabahah* facility is 2.33 percent and on the *ijara* facility is 1.50 percent. As an Islamic bank is essentially an intermediary, it could pass on these return streams to depositors and investment account holders as per the following pattern assuming that the profit-sharing ration is 70:30, with 70 percent profits being routed to depositors.

If customers were willing to accept varying rates of returns every month and at times even negative returns, where they lose a little principal amount, Islamic banking could function without any hurdles. As an intermediary, the Islamic bank would share the fate of the clients with its depositors, the essence of risk sharing in my opinion. However, customers or depositors do not behave in this fashion. Even customers of Islamic banks demand an explicit guarantee on their principals, and an implicit guarantee on an indicative rate of return. It is this consumer behavior that has set the tone for Islamic banks and not vice versa. In essence, an Islamic bank can then just offer an indicative rate of return of either 1.63 percent per annum or 1.05 percent per annum, depending on the structure of their asset portfolios, whether it is skewed in favor of *murabahah* contracts or *ijara* contracts (Table 21.2).

If customers are willing to share risks with the Islamic banks in terms of accepting variable returns, then we can speak of risk sharing.

PROFIT EQUALIZATION RESERVE

The profit equalization reserve (PER) is simply a reserve fund created to smooth returns over a period of time generated by some business activity. It represents a fraction of the gross income set aside for this purpose.[3] In the earlier example, the client that is enjoying the *murabahah* facility experiences varying returns over a 12-month period. At times,

[3]Bank Negara Malaysia (BNM) (2011), *Guidelines on the Recognition and Measurement of Profit Sharing Investment Account (PSIA) as Risk Absorbent*, Guideline number BNM/RH/GL 007-11, Islamic Banking and Takaful Department, http://www.bnm.gov.my/guidelines/01_banking/01_capital_adequacy/06_psia.pdf, accessed July 2014.

TABLE 21.1 Income Stream from Assets

Asset Side												
Murabahah facility returns for 12 months												Average
−3.00%	2.00%	4.00%	3.00%	5.00%	3.00%	2.00%	−2.00%	3.00%	4.00%	3.00%	4.00%	2.33%
1	2	3	4	5	6	7	8	9	10	11	12	
Ijara facility returns for 12 months												
−2.00%	3.00%	−2.00%	−4.00%	4.00%	5.00%	4.00%	3.00%	4.00%	3.00%	−3.00%	3.00%	1.50%
1	2	3	4	5	6	7	8	9	10	11	12	

TABLE 21.2 Payments on Liabilities

Liability Side												
Indicative returns from investment in *murabahah* facility with PSR of 70:30												
0.00%	0.00%	0.00%	0.00%	0.00%	0.00%	0.00%	0.00%	0.00%	0.00%	0.00%	0.00%	0.00%
1	2	3	4	5	6	7	8	9	10	11	12	
Indicative returns from investment in *ijarah* facility with PSR of 70:30												
0.00%	0.00%	0.00%	0.00%	0.00%	0.00%	0.00%	0.00%	0.00%	0.00%	0.00%	0.00%	0.00%
1	2	3	4	5	6	7	8	9	10	11	12	

the returns are even negative. If the *murabahah* facility is funded by a *mudharabah* fund, and the Islamic bank offers an indicative rate of return of 1.63 percent to the depositor, the Islamic bank would then maintain a reserve that will be funded in months when the bank earns more than 1.63 percent. A certain percentage of this excess will be maintained in the reserve fund to cover shortfalls in returns below 1.63 percent, which in the case of the *murabahah* facility occurs twice in a 12-month period. At year-end, any unpaid reserves remain in the PER account and are rolled over to the next financial year.

The PER has caused certain controversy in Malaysia over whether any unpaid balances in the reserve belong to depositors or to shareholders, and in fact in the Islamic Financial Services Act of 2013[4] the reserve has been done away with.

As we see in the coming section, PER is deducted from returns generated from investment of depositors' funds, and therefore it is depositors who end up bearing market risk. In this section we can clearly see the impacts of the concept of risk sharing. If depositors and shareholders alike share the returns experienced by businesses and households to whom banks extend financing arrangements, all parties sink and swim together. However, in the current scenarios, where depositors demand fixed returns on their deposits and shareholders pass on the risk of credit financing to borrowers and depositors, Islamic finance has actually created a model of risk sharing that even conventional banks have not been able to. We examine this in detail in the next section.

INCOME DISTRIBUTION

A typical income statement of an Islamic bank may look something like Table 21.3.

The income statement is that of an undisclosed Islamic bank. Islamic banks are meant to maintain separate ledgers for depositors' funds, investment of depositors' funds, returns generated from investment of depositors' funds and shareholders' funds, investment of shareholders' funds, and returns generated from investment of shareholders' funds.

Looking at the figures for 2011, we see that income generated from the investment of depositors' funds is $831 million, and income generated from investment of shareholders' funds is $5.52 million. The combined income is $832.164 million. However, unlike in conventional banks where the first expense is simply interest expense, which is paid out to depositors, in this

[4]Laws of Malaysia, Islamic Financial Services Act 2013, www.bnm.gov.my/documents/act/en_ifsa.pdf, accessed July 2014.

TABLE 21.3 Income Statement of an Islamic Bank

	Year 2	Year 1
Income derived from investment of depositors' funds and others	831,218	716,265
Income derived from investment of shareholders' funds	5,520	70,543
Total income derived	**836,738**	**786,808**
Allowance for impairment losses	−2,277	(3,208)
Profit equalization reserve	(2,297)	−3,000
Total distributable income	**832,164**	**780,600**
Income attributable to the depositors	−479,498	−419,957
Total net income	**352,666**	**360,643**
Personnel expenses	−26,480	−27,171
Other overheads and expenditures	−161,879	−109,130
Profit before *zakat* and taxation	**164,307**	**224,342**
Zakat	−200	−211
Profit after *zakat* before taxation	**164,107**	**224,131**
Taxation	−73,785	−41,854
Net profit for the financial year	**90,322**	**182,277**
Earnings per share—basic (sen)	32.38	20.40

case credit risk is passed onto depositors in the shape of a charge for impairment losses of $2.2 million. In effect this Islamic bank is passing credit risk onto depositors, which even conventional banks are not able to do. Second, another charge referred to as the profit equalization reserve is also charged to depositors.

The PER is deducted from income and serves as a reserve in the event that assets perform lower than expected in any given month, or to counter any adverse movements in changes in cost of funds. The reserve is utilized by the Islamic bank when assets do not generate enough funds to pay a promised indicative rate of return to depositors. This fund serves as a buffer for market risk, and, in effect, Islamic banks pass on market risk to depositors as well.

After these deductions, total distributable income is in fact reduced to $832 million. But actual income paid to depositors is only $479 million. We began with $831 million and we shaved off $352 million (42 percent) to pay depositors only $479 million (58 percent). The Islamic bank claims this residual $352 million for itself, which includes the bank's share from income derived from investment of current account deposits, the bank's share from income derived from savings account deposits, and the bank's share from investment of *mudharabah* funds (Table 21.4). The Islamic bank pays all expenses from this residual, taxes, and *zakat* and earns a net profit of $90 million.

TABLE 21.4 Balance Sheet

Liabilities	Year 2	Year 1
Deposits from customers	17,249,648	16,300,706
Deposits of Fis	2,177,647	3,150,399
Bills and acceptances payables	143,788	51,311
Islamic derivatives financial instruments	19,647	16,386
Other liabilities	484,928	903,979
Provision for taxation	24,554	10,365
Capital financing	*275,593*	275,597
Total Liabilities	20,375,805	20,708,743
Equity	**Year 2**	**Year 1**
Share capital	700,000	700,000
Reserves	652,741	468,803
Total Equity	1,352,741	1,168,803
Assets	**Year 2**	**Year 1**
Cash and short-term funds	1,118,151	2,228,830
Deposits with other banks	—	138,985
Financial assets held for trading	3,887,786	4,711,127
Financial investments held for sale	1,736,274	1,407,486
Financial investments held to maturity	983,091	701,667
Financing and advances	13,351,032	12,012,071
Islamic derivatives financial instruments	14,355	—
Other assets	123,035	208,891
Statutory deposits	504,061	451,187
Property and equipment	5,577	5,807
Intangible assets	4,336	5,927
Deferred tax assets	848	2,568
Total Assets	21,728,546	21,874,546

To illustrate our point we refer to another fictitious balance sheet and income statement in Table 21.5. ABC Bank has total deposits of $1.2 billion, of which $300 million are current accounts, $400 million are savings accounts, and $500 million are *mudharabah* deposits. The bank has total financing of only $760 million; 40 percent of total current account balances are used to fund assets, as are 60 percent of savings accounts and 80 percent of *mudharabah* deposits. Total financing of $760 million is funded by $120 million of funds sourced through current accounts, which constitutes 15.79 percent of total funds; $240 million are sourced from savings

TABLE 21.5 ABC Bank

	Balance	% Utilized in Financing	Amount Utilized in Financing	% of Total
Current account	300,000,000	40	120,000,000	15.79
Savings accounts	400,000,000	60	240,000,000	31.58
Mudharabah accounts	500,000,000	80	400,000,000	52.63
Total Deposits	**1,200,000,000**		**760,000,000**	

TABLE 21.6 Income from CA, SA, IA

Total income generated from investment of CA, SA, and IA	45,600,000

TABLE 21.7 Income from CA

Share of CA	%	Amount
From total income	15.79%	7,200,000
Return on deposit	2.40%	
Actual *hibah* rate	1.00%	
Actual *hibah* paid on CA		3,000,000
Shareholders' share from CA		***4,200,000***

accounts, which are 31.58 percent of total funds, and $400 million come from *mudharabah* accounts or 52.63 percent of total funds.

As per Table 21.5, 15.79 percent of total income earned should go to current account holders, 31.58 percent should go to savings accounts holders, and 52.63 percent should go to *mudharabah* account holders. Total income generated is $45.60 million from investment of depositors' funds (Table 21.6).

In effect, $7.20 million should be paid out to current account holders as 15.79 percent of total income of $45.60 million. This would mean a 2.40 percent (7.2M divided by 300M) payout of *hibah* to current account holders. ABC Bank, however, decides to only pay 1.00 percent *hibah* to current account holders and retains $4.20 million for shareholders. This is illustrated in Table 21.7.

As can be seen in Table 21.8, savings account holders are given similar treatment.

TABLE 21.8 Income from SA

Share of SA	%	Amount*
From total income	31.58%	14,400,000
Return on deposit	3.60%	
Actual *hibah* rate	2.50%	
Actual *hibah* paid on SA		10,000,000
Shareholders' share from SA		*4,400,000*

*Numbers are rounded.

TABLE 21.9 Income from IA

Share of IA	%	Amount
From total income	52.63%	24,000,000
Profit equalization reserve	3.00%	−720,000
Residual income for IA		23,280,000
Profit-sharing ratio	70:30	
Customers' share	70.00%	16,296,000
Shareholders' share	30.00%	*6,984,000*
Return on Deposit for IA	**3.26%**	

*Numbers are rounded.

Savings account holders contributed 31.58 percent to the total fund pool that was used to finance assets, and therefore are entitled to $14.40 million of returns on their funds. This would make the rate of *hibah* on savings accounts 3.60 percent (14.4M divided by 400M), but instead ABC Bank pays out only $10.0 million in *hibah*, which is effectively only 2.50 percent of return for savings account holders. The balance of $4.40 million is retained by shareholders as their income.

Mudharabah account holders contribute 52.63 percent of the total pool of funds used to finance assets and have a profit-sharing ratio with the bank of 70:30 (Table 21.9). This entitles *mudharabah* account holders to an income of $16.80 (=70%*52.63%*45.60M), which would reflect a return on deposits of 3.63 percent. However, ABC Bank deducts $720,000 in profit equalization reserves and credits *mudharabah* account holders with just $16.296 million in income; 30 percent income is retained by ABC Bank as its share of the profits under the contract of *mudharabah*. This 3 percent PER is deducted keeping in mind that an indicative rate of return of 3.26 percent has been communicated to investment account holders.

Table 21.10 compares what the depositors are entitled to and what they actually receive in terms of returns. Bear in mind though that as per

TABLE 21.10 Depositors' Returns

Depositors' Returns	**Entitled to**		**Actual**		**Passed onto Shareholders**
Return on CA	2.40%	7,200,000	1.00%	3,000,000	4,200,000
Return on SA	3.60%	14,400,000	2.50%	10,000,000	4,400,000
Return on IA	3.36%	16,800,000	3.26%	16,296,000	0
Total return for depositors		38,400,000		29,296,000	8,600,000

TABLE 21.11 Returns on Funds

Total Shareholders' Returns		
From investment of CA		4,200,000
From investment of SA		4,400,000
From investment of IA		6,984,000
Total Returns from Deposits		**15,584,000**
Total Equity		200,000,000
SRR with 0% returns at 4% of deposit		–48,000,000
SH capital invested in IN S/T assets at 3%	3.00%	152,000,000
Returns from investments of shareholders' fund		4,560,000
Total Shareholder Returns		20,144,000
Return on Equity		**10.07%**

their contracts current account holders are not entitled to any returns on their deposits as these are on demand deposit accounts although the current account holders are still paid 1 percent as *hibah*' $504,000 is retained from the returns paid to investment account holders as a *mudharib fee,* which is communicated to investment account holders at the beginning of the contract.

Table 21.11 shows in a very simplistic manner how ABC Bank earns returns from investment of current account funds, investment of savings account funds, investment of *mudharabah* account funds, and from investment of its own capital.

ABC Bank earns $15.584 million from investment of depositors' funds, and $4.560 million from investment of its own funds in short-term liquid assets, making a combined income of $20.144 million. The return on equity for ABC Bank is 10.07 percent, whereas the average return to depositors who contribute 100 percent of the funds used to finance the bank's business is a mere 2.16 percent on average basis.

We have not taken into consideration any deductions for impairment charges. Assume ABC Bank estimates expected losses to be a mere 1 percent of total outstanding financing; this amount will be deducted from the income attributable to depositors. Let us examine the impact of this entry on the income earned by depositors.

Table 21.12 looks at returns before impairment charges are levied to account holders.

Table 21.13 looks at the impact of just 1 percent of assets of $760,000,000 of impairment charges.

Net returns drop significantly in dollar terms for current account holders that end up paying $1.2 million in impairment charges, savings account holders pay $2.40 million from their returns, and *mudharabah* account holders pay $4.0 million in impairment charges. These numbers

TABLE 21.12 Return to Depositors before Impairments

Depositors' returns	In %	In $ Terms
Return on CA	1.00	3,000,000
Return on SA	2.50	10,000,000
Return on IA	3.00	16,296,000
Total Return for Depositors		29,296,000

TABLE 21.13 Returns with 1 Percent Impairment Charges

Impairment Charges on Financing of					760,000,000
Total impairments	1.00%	7,600,000			Return on account.
Deducted from income due to CA holders	0.16%	1,200,000	Net return on CA	1,800,000	0.60%
Deducted from income due to SA holders	0.32%	2,400,000	Net return on SA	7,600,000	1.90%
Deducted from income due to IAH holders	0.53%	4,000,000	Net return on IAH	12,296,000	2.46%
Total impairments		7,600,000	Net return for depositors	21,696,000	

*Numbers are rounded to the thousands.

TABLE 21.14 Returns with 2 Percent Impairment Charges

Impairment Charges of Financing of					760,000,000
Total impairments	2.00%	15,200,000			
Deducted from CA	0.32%	2,400,000	Net return on CA	600,000	0.20%
Deducted from SA	0.63%	4,800,000	Net return on SA	5,200,000	1.30%
Deducted from IAH	1.05%	8,000,000	Net return on IAH	8,296,000	1.66%
Total impairments		15,200,000	Net return for depositors	14,096,000	

reflect 40, 24, and 24.54 percent of pre-impairment revenues for each pool. After impairments, depositors are left with $21.696 million or 1.12 percent returns on their funds.

If impairment charges increase to 2 percent, let us examine the impact on depositors' returns in Table 21.14.

The reader can easily observe the impact of 2 percent charge for provisioning for expected losses. Current account holders earn a mere .20 percent on the funds they provide to the bank. Savings account holders earn 1.30 percent and *mudharabah* deposit holders earn a mere 1.66 percent for providing more than 50 percent of the funds to the pool.

It is meaningful to mention that a 3 percent rate of expected losses would actually create negative returns as can be seen in Table 21.15.

The impact of impairments is significant as the expected losses rate is multiplied by the total financing amount, which is a considerably high number. Conventional banks deduct provisioning reserves not from the income attributable to depositors but from their own income.

On a final note we demonstrate how the income to be paid to *mudharabah* account holders is divided among various *mudharabah* account holders as each account holder has fixed his or her deposit for varying periods.

For illustration purposes, we pool the $500 million worth of *mudharabah* funds into pools of one-month contracts, two months, three months, and six months. Each pool is assigned a weightage factor with pools of deposits with longer maturity terms assigned a higher factor as they contribute to financing assets for longer periods of time. The resultant exercise reveals that *mudharabah* account holders that place their funds for six months receive 5.70 percent return on their deposits, whereas

TABLE 21.15 Returns with 3 Percent Impairment Charges

Impairment Charges on Financing of					760,000,000
Total impairments	3.00%	22,800,000			
Deducted from CA	0.47%	3,600,000	Net return on CA	(600,000)	−0.20%
Deducted from SA	0.95%	7,200,000	Net return on SA	2,800,000	0.70%
Deducted from IAH	1.58%	12,000,000	Net return on IAH	4,296,000	0.86%
Total impairments		22,800,000	Net return for depositors	6,496,000	
			Average return for depositors		0.54%
			Weighted average return for depositors		0.34%

TABLE 21.16 Distribution of *Mudharabah* Income

Distribution of *Mudharabah* Income					*Mudharabah* Income	16,296,000	Return on Deposit (%)
		%	Factor	Factored Total	Factored %		
One month	100,000,000	20	0.6	60,000,000	11	1,844,830	1.84
Two months	150,000,000	30	0.9	135,000,000	25	4,150,868	2.77
Three months	100,000,000	20	1.1	110,000,000	21	3,382,189	3.38
Six months	150,000,000	30	1.5	225,000,000	42	6,918,113	4.61
Total	500,000,000	1		530,000,000	1	16,296,000	

one-month, two-month, and three-month contract holders earn 2.28, 3.42, and 4.18 percent, respectively (Table 21.16).

For a detailed exposition on the subject the reader may refer to *Financial Accounting Standards 5—Disclosure of Bases for Profit Allocation Between Owner's Equity and Investment Account Holders*, issued by Accounting and Auditing Organization for Islamic Financial Institutions and to the text for the course *IE 1002 Reporting of Islamic Financial Transactions* at International Centre for Education in Islamic Finance 2012/1433 AH CIFP Program.

RISK SHARING IN ISLAMIC BANKS

The unique proposition of a financial system built on Islamic principles is the idea of risk sharing. However, we observe that in actual practice Islamic banks in certain jurisdictions are passing on credit risk to borrowers and depositors. Borrowers absorb credit risk by paying a credit risk premium, and depositors share in credit risk by paying a portion of impairment charges from the income generated by investment of depositors' funds. Profit equalization reserve is also deducted from the income generated by investment of depositors' funds and therefore market risk is also passed onto depositors by Islamic banks. A conventional bank, on the other hand, would first recognize interest income without segregating whether it was generated by investment of shareholder funds or depositors' funds. In fact, no such segregation is reported by conventional banks. However, the first expense deducted in an income statement of an Islamic bank is interest expense. Thus, depositors are given their due before any other stakeholders, nor are they asked to pay any share of impairment charges or absorb any market risk. This is done entirely by shareholders from their share of residual income.

Such practices tend to defeat the essence of Islamic banking. If credit risk is passed onto borrowers and depositors, and market risk is also passed onto depositors, then one may well ask what is the basis for risk sharing, and what entitles shareholders of Islamic banks to residual profits other than the profits generated by investing shareholder capital, and the *mudharib* fee for managing *mudharabah* funds. In fact, depositors of Islamic banks should enjoy higher returns than depositors in conventional banks as they absorb credit risk and market risk. Sadly, this, too, is not the case.

CONCLUSION

We have examined in this chapter how income sharing is a critical component of Islamic banking. Islamic banks must segregate depositors' funds from shareholders' funds and maintain records of profits and losses generated by investing these funds. Profits must be shared as per the terms and conditions of the contracts. This is all contingent on accurate and full disclosures on the part of the financial institution.

We have also examined how it is possible for Islamic banks to pass on credit risk to borrowers and depositors and how this practice defeats the essence of Islamic banking principles. Even market risk is passed onto depositors in the shape of PER. At this stage income distribution is not being supervised by *shariah* advisors in many institutions. We feel that this aspect of the Islamic bank should be brought to the attention of the *shariah* committees to ensure a more equitable distribution of income and sharing of risk.

CHAPTER 22

Sukuk and Rights of *Sukuk* Holders

Many works on Islamic finance begin with references to existing material, books, and publications on the topic and then attempt to provide their own critique or just toe the line of their predecessors. I have made every effort to avoid this pitfall, simply because I believe as a writer it hinders my ability to express my own ideas on a subject. In fact new publications or PhDs are meant to offer new insight into existing phenomenon or provide a platform for observing new phenomenon altogether.

I provide the reader with an exhaustive list of what has been said about *sukuk* by other authors. I take my own unique stance on this subject, as this is the most eye-catching topic in Islamic finance and grabs the most headlines.

Before I do touch on the topic I first examine briefly other capital markets instruments that exist in conventional and Islamic finance.

Financial markets exist to primarily help fund deficit individuals, corporations, or governments. We initially focus on corporations for the discussion on *sukuk*. Corporations are also of various size and complexity and have access to various sources of funding. A company may start as a sole proprietorship, relying initially on the funding capacity of the founding owner. This company may evolve into a partnership to raise capital from an additional partner or managerial expertise, shared business skills, networks, and so on. Sole proprietorships and partnerships are not required to disclose their financial statements to the general public as no funding is sourced from them. A growing company may then register itself as a private limited firm and issue shares that are sold privately to various shareholders or investors. These shareholders become directors in the firm and either are involved in the management of the company or are just sleeping partners.

Sole-proprietorship firms, partnerships, and private limited firms have access to the individual capital of the owners, retained earnings or excess profits of the companies, or financing provided by commercial banks through various financial instruments. Financial instruments help companies raise money. Companies are able to access funds based on their size, revenues, profitability, capital, and business prospects. Mature companies with sufficiently large revenues are able to negotiate more favorable terms with banks, whereas start-ups, or companies in the initial years of growth, may either not be able to source funds from banks or do so at very high costs.

Banks that finance business operations do so for a consideration, which in simple terms is interest. They also secure their exposure on companies by taking the companies' assets as collateral. In some cases even the assets of the company directors are also taken as collateral by the bank. Assets such as property are mortgaged to banks, assets like vehicles are hypothecated, inventory can be pledged, and financial assets can be lien marked in favor of the bank. These are just different ways of giving the bank the right to liquidate assets of a company or its owners in case the company defaults on any loan.

Islamic banks are also able to secure such rights under the contract of *rahn*. In the case of more complex companies, which include private limited firms and publicly listed companies, banks create what is known as a charge on the assets of a company. This charge can be on the current assets of a company, on its fixed assets, and it can be on future assets as well. Current assets of a company include among other things cash, inventory, and accounts receivable of a company, whereas fixed assets refers to such things as plant, property and equipment, and other assets. The concept of a "charge" allows banks to seize control over specific assets of a company and liquidate them to recover the bank's total exposure in case of default.

To understand the implications of this concept, let us examine the balance sheet of XYZ Company in Table 22.1 and the implications of debt financing via bank borrowing, equity financing, and debt financing by issuing bonds. Finally, we examine financing raised by issuing *sukuk*.

RIGHTS OF LENDERS IN DEBT FINANCING

From Table 22.1 we can see that XYZ Company has total assets worth \$128 million, which are funded by liabilities of \$8 million and equity of \$120 million. The company is well funded by internal sources, but for various reasons has secured bank financings worth \$7 million and agreed to allow the bank to create a charge on its current assets (of inventory) worth \$25 million. However, if for some reason XYZ Company does not have the cash flows to make the monthly or quarterly payments on the debt, the bank has the right to liquidate \$25 million of assets to recover its

TABLE 22.1 Balance Sheet of XYZ Company

Balance Sheet of XYZ Company			
Current Assets			
Cash	2,000,000	Debt/Equity	5.83%
Accounts Receivable	1,000,000	Debt/Total Assets	5.47%
Inventory	25,000,000		
Fixed Assets			
Property	40,000,000		
Plant and Equipment	60,000,000		
TOTAL ASSETS	128,000,000		
Liabilities			
Accounts Payable	1,000,000		
Short-Term Debt Outstanding	3,000,000		
Long-Term Debt Outstanding	4,000,000		
Equity			
Share Capital	100,000,000		
Retained Earnings	20,000,000		
TOTAL EQUITY	120,000,000		
TOTAL LIABILITIES + EQUITY	128,000,000		

money. This point hits home if one were to see a revised balance sheet of the company. Imagine the shareholders of XYZ take all retained earnings out of the company as dividends. The company has two years of poor sales and losses are buffered by capital and capital is reduced to $70 million (Table 22.2).

The company now has equity of only $70 million and is essentially funding its operations with account payable and debt. Total debt is $25 million, and the banks have obtained a charge on current assets of $25 million. If XYZ fails to make three payments on its borrowings, the bank has the right to seize its current assets, liquidate them, and recover their outstanding dues. Although total debt is just 19.53 percent of total assets, failure to make any installment payments would compromise the assets worth $128 million. Thus companies must realize that debt is a double-edged sword.

Islamic debt is no different. If this short-term and long-term debt were obtained through contracts of *murabahah*, it still would have to be repaid.

A crucial point to understand from the bank's point of view is that the bank can exit its relationship with XYZ Company under two scenarios. Either XYZ Company pays the debts owed to the bank in full with all interest payments or the bank sells the debt to a third party either at a discount or at par value. As per the balance sheet of the company, the bank has $15

TABLE 22.2 Changes in XYZ

Balance Sheet of XYZ Company			
Current Assets			
Cash	2,000,000	Debt/Equity	35.71%
Accounts Receivable	1,000,000	Debt/Total Assets	19.53%
Inventory	25,000,000	Payables/Equity	47.14%
Fixed Assets			
Property	40,000,000		
Plant and Equipment	60,000,000		
TOTAL ASSETS	128,000,000		
Liabilities			
Accounts Payable	33,000,000		
Short-Term Debt Outstanding	15,000,000		
Long-Term Debt Outstanding	10,000,000		
Equity			
Share Capital	70,000,000		
Retained Earnings			
TOTAL EQUITY	70,000,000		
TOTAL LIABILITIES + EQUITY	128,000,000		

million exposure in short-term debt and $10 million exposure in long-term debt on XYZ. If the bank that has lent this money charges 4 percent interest on short-term debt, the bank can conceivably sell this debt to a third party at 3 percent interest, and the third-party bank will assume the credit risk or recovery from XYZ. Similarly the long-term debt can be sold after reaching a present value of future cash payments.

Selling of debt depends on the banking rules of a country, and may not be a viable option in all circumstances. From the perspective of Islamic finance, this opens the door of the contract of *bay ul dayn*, which is a controversial issue.

RIGHTS OF EQUITY HOLDERS

Now that we have in simple terms demonstrated the rights and powers of lenders let us look at the same of equity holders. Let us assume that this same company decides to raise capital now from private investors worth $25 million to pay off its short-term and long-term debts to stop the bank manager from making unwelcome visits to the company (Table 22.3).

TABLE 22.3 Equity Injection

Balance Sheet of XYZ Company			
Current Assets			%
Cash	2,000,000	Debt/Equity	0.00
Accounts Receivable	1,000,000	Debt/Total Assets	0.00
Inventory	25,000,000	Payables/Equity	34.74
Fixed Assets		Share Capital I/Equity	73.68
Property	40,000,000	Share Capital II/Equity	26.32
Plant and Equipment	60,000,000	Capital I/Capital II	280.00
TOTAL ASSETS	128,000,000	Capital II/Capital I	35.71
Liabilities			
Accounts Payable	33,000,000		
Short-Term Debt Outstanding			
Long-Term Debt Outstanding			
Equity			
Share Capital I	70,000,000		
Retained Earnings			
Share Capital II	25,000,000		
TOTAL EQUITY	95,000,000		
TOTAL LIABILITIES + EQUITY	128,000,000		

Let us refer to these private investors as Company ABC. Now ABC has a 26.32 percent shareholding in XYZ Company, and therefore has an ownership stake in *all* the assets of the Company XYZ worth $128 million. This is the uncomfortable aspect of joint ownership or partnership. Partners with a limited injection of capital enjoy ownership rights over the assets of the entire company, which may well exceed the size of their investment.[1]

From XYZ's perspective, however, ABC is a better alternative to the bank, which after being paid off has released all claims to the current assets of the company. The bank had a claim of only $25 million of XYZ's assets, but ABC now has a claim on $128 million worth of XYZ's assets. The distinguishing feature between ABC and the bank is that ABC *does not have to be paid back*. XYZ Company is not obligated to repay the $25 million injected into the company by ABC. Unlike the case of the bank, where XYZ had to repay the debt owed to the bank and all interest payments levied on the

[1]Further reading can be obtained from Rafaul La Porta, Florencio Lopez-Desilanes, and Andrei Shleifer, "Corporate Ownership Around the World," *Journal of Finance* 54, no. 2 (1999): 471–527.

debt, XYZ does not have to pay back ABC. ABC, however, has a right to be involved in the management of the company, and has a right to future profits of the company until perpetuity. If ABC is unable to generate revenues from the investment in XYZ, ABC can sell its investment in XYZ to other parties either through selling its shares on an exchange (if the company is listed) or through a private sale. ABC may sell its stake in XYZ at a profit, at a loss, or at par depending on how other companies value ABC's investment in XYZ. This valuation would be based upon the future earning power of XYZ.[2]

Equity in a company is valued based on the expectation of future earnings of any company as equity instruments entitle its holders to future revenues. Increased earnings in the joint venture between XYZ and ABC can be retained by the company as retained earnings to finance future expansion, buffer for losses, or be shared between the two in the shape of dividends. Increased earnings will also increase the value of ABC's stake in the company. *Shariah*-compliant equity behaves in exactly the same manner; the only difference is that the business operations of the company in which the equity stake is made are *shariah*-compliant. We have already covered the concept of *shariah screening* in previous chapters.

RIGHTS OF BONDHOLDERS

Alternatively, XYZ Company can borrow $25 million from investors by selling bonds worth $25 million (Table 22.4). A commercial bank would help XYZ develop a prospectus, which is a complex proposal for borrowing funds, or in essence a feasibility report. The bank would also help float the bond that will help XYZ Company find suitable investors. The bonds could be listed on a stock exchange where investors would buy them, or they could be placed privately through a private placement.

The bonds would carry a specific maturity date and offer investors a specific coupon payment at regular intervals. On maturity, the bonds would be redeemed by XYZ returning to bondholders the amount lent to XYZ Company.

The bondholders would, however, also have an implicit charge on the assets of the company to secure their investment. Bondholders are in effect lenders and they must secure their interests by seeking collateral from the issuing company.

The reader must appreciate that if XYZ Company is unable to pay its utility bills, for instance, the utility company will disconnect power supplies

[2]Geoffrey Poitras, *Valuation of Equity Securities: History, Theory and Application* (Singapore: World Scientific, 2010).

and telephone lines to XYZ. If XYZ cannot pay its bills subsequently, the utility company can file a lawsuit in a court to recover its dues.

If XYZ Company experiences financial distress and is unable to pay employees' salaries for three months, then the employees can also just file legal cases against the company; they **cannot seize the assets of the company, liquidate them, and recover their dues.** Lenders enjoy such powers, be they banks or bondholders. Bondholders therefore have an implicit charge on all current and fixed assets of a company and can in effect seize control of the company's assets if it fails to make scheduled payments.

This power of lenders makes companies vulnerable to banks and the capital markets for debt. Companies need capital to grow and at times retained earnings are not sufficient to expand in the markets that companies operate in. Companies could learn from Islamic principles of living within one's means, as the Prophet (saw) discouraged followers from falling into debt.[3]

TABLE 22.4 Bond Issue

Balance Sheet of XYZ Company			
Current Assets			
Cash	2,000,000	Debt/Equity	35.71%
Accounts Receivable	1,000,000	Debt/Total Assets	19.53%
Inventory	25,000,000	Payables/Equity	47.14%
Fixed Assets			
Property	40,000,000		
Plant and Equipment	60,000,000		
TOTAL ASSETS	128,000,000		
Liabilities			
Accounts Payable	33,000,000		
Long-Term Bonds Issued	25,000,000		
Equity			
Share Capital	70,000,000		
Retained Earnings			
TOTAL EQUITY	70,000,000		
TOTAL LIABILITIES + EQUITY	128,000,000		

[3]The Prophet once said, "Allah will forgive the martyr all his sins except for his debts" (Muslim). In another *hadith* narrated by Jaabir, the Prophet (saw) would not pray on a debtor when he died.

Companies can raise capital by issuing equity notes, but this dilutes the shareholding of existing shareholders, and new shareholders may demand a right to interfere in the management of the company. It is rather difficult to do business with other people's money and yet do it your own way; in other words, you cannot have your cake and eat it, too.

USE OF SUBSIDIARY COMPANIES AND SPECIAL-PURPOSE VEHICLES

Companies evolved various strategies to protect themselves from the power of lenders. One such strategy was not to borrow directly in the company's name but to set up a subsidiary and borrow funds from either banks or capital markets in the name of the subsidiary. This is known as a special-purpose vehicle (SPV).

To illustrate this point we refer back to XYZ Company. XYZ Company takes $1,000,000 from its capital and sets up a subsidiary known as XYZ II (Table 22.5).

XYZ Company with $70 million of capital spins off into XYZ I and XYZ II with the former having $69 million of capital and the latter having

TABLE 22.5 Using an SPV

Balance Sheet of XYZ Company			
Current Assets			
Cash	2,000,000	Debt/Equity	35.71%
Accounts Receivable	1,000,000	Debt/Total Assets	19.53%
Inventory	25,000,000	Payables/Equity	47.14%
Fixed Assets			
Property	40,000,000		
Plant and Equipment	60,000,000		
TOTAL ASSETS	128,000,000		
Liabilities			
Accounts Payable	33,000,000		
Short-Term Debt Outstanding	15,000,000		
Long-Term Debt Outstanding	10,000,000		
Equity			
Share Capital	70,000,000		
Retained Earnings			
TOTAL EQUITY	70,000,000		
TOTAL LIABILITIES + EQUITY	128,000,000		

TABLE 22.5 (Continued)

Balance Sheet of XYZ I Company			
Current Assets			
Cash	2,000,000	Debt/Equity	35.71%
Accounts Receivable	1,000,000	Debt/Total Assets	19.53%
Inventory	25,000,000	Payables/Equity	47.14%
Fixed Assets			
Property	40,000,000		
Plant and Equipment	60,000,000		
TOTAL ASSETS	128,000,000		
Liabilities			
Accounts Payable	33,000,000		
Short-Term Debt Outstanding	15,000,000		
Long-Term Debt Outstanding	10,000,000		
Equity			
Share Capital	70,000,000		
Retained Earnings			
TOTAL EQUITY	70,000,000		
TOTAL LIABILITIES + EQUITY	128,000,000		

Balance Sheet of XYZ II Company			
Current Assets			
Cash	300,000	Debt/Equity	0.00%
Accounts Receivable		Debt/Total Assets	0.00%
Inventory		Payables/Equity	0.00%
Fixed Assets			
Property	300,000		
Plant and Equipment	400,000		
TOTAL ASSETS	1,000,000		
Liabilities			
Accounts Payable			
Short-Term Debt Outstanding			
Long-Term Debt Outstanding			
Equity			
Share Capital	1,000,000		
Retained Earnings			
TOTAL EQUITY	1,000,000		
TOTAL LIABILITIES + EQUITY	1,000,000		

$1 million of capital. XYZ II floats a bond in the market seeking $26 million of funding from investors to retire the short-term and long-term debt of XYZ I. In certain jurisdictions this may be allowed. Alternatively, XYZ II may use the $26 million of funds to buy assets from XYZ. In the latter case XYZ II may buy some plant and equipment from XYZ I, and the ownership of this asset is transferred from the books of XYZ I to XYZ II. In fact XYZ II can in its bond prospectus disclose that the purpose for raising funds from the bond market is in effect to purchase these assets from XYZ I Company.

XYZ Company sells some of its fixed assets to its subsidiary and receives $26 million in cash (Table 22.6).

The impact of the bond sale and subsequent purchase of assets from XYZ I is reflected in balance sheet above. Now XYZ I Company has $28 million of cash on its balance sheet as well as $26 million of debt. XYZ II has $26M of liabilities and new assets of $26 million on its balance sheet.

In the next step XYZ I uses its newly raised cash and pays off its debts. In essence, XYZ I Company retires its debts using moneys raised by XYZ II. The liability is now on XYZ II's books, as can be seen in Table 22.7.

XYZ II is not a functioning entity but just a subsidiary on paper. The assets sold to XYZ II are likely never to have moved from one place to another. XYZ II's offices may just be on another floor in the same building. The original assets sold to XYZ II may still be functioning in the same manner, producing the same goods that are sold in XYZ I's name to consumers. Nothing substantial may have changed.

Now in effect, what happens if XYZ I goes bankrupt? Can the bondholders of the bonds issued by XYZ II have recourse to the assets of XYZ I or to the assets of XYZ II, or to the assets of both entities? XYZ I has $102 million of assets, whereas XYZ II only has $26.40 million worth of assets. Bondholders in this case would only have recourse to the assets of XYZ II and ***not*** XYZ I. Through this mechanism of an SPV, XYZ I is able to protect its assets in the event it defaults on a bond or loan.

Only assets worth the amount of money borrowed are in effect encumbered and liquidated and the company remains safe from lenders and bondholders alike. Bankruptcy proceedings are filed against XYZ II. Bondholders seize the assets of XYZ II and sell the assets for whatever value they can get from the markets and recover their moneys. If the assets sell for more than $26 million, such that bondholders recover their principal and interest, then so be it. If the assets sell for less than $26 million, bondholders *cannot* claim the difference from XYZ I.

Now that XYZ II Company is burdened with bond payments of $26 million plus interest, these need to be recovered by the economic cash flows generated by the cash flows generated from the assets purchased from XYZ I. XYZ II can employ these assets purchased and retire the bonds from the

TABLE 22.6 Asset Sale Through SPV

Balance Sheet of XYZ I Company			
Current Assets			
Cash	28,000,000	Debt/Equity	37.68%
Accounts Receivable	1,000,000	Debt/Total Assets	20.31%
Inventory	25,000,000	Payables/Equity	47.83%
Fixed Assets			
Property	40,000,000		
Plant and Equipment	34,000,000		
TOTAL ASSETS	128,000,000		
Liabilities			
Accounts Payable	33,000,000		
Short-Term Debt Outstanding	15,000,000		
Long-Term Debt Outstanding	11,000,000		
Equity			
Share Capital	69,000,000		
Retained Earnings			
TOTAL EQUITY	69,000,000		
TOTAL LIABILITIES + EQUITY	128,000,000		

Balance Sheet of XYZ II Company			
Current Assets			
Cash	300,000	Debt/Equity	0.00%
Accounts Receivable		Debt/Total Assets	0.00%
Inventory		Payables/Equity	2,600.00%
Fixed Assets			
Property	300,000		
Plant and Equipment	26,400,000		
TOTAL ASSETS	27,000,000		
Liabilities			
Long-Term Bonds	26,000,000		
Equity			
Share Capital	1,000,000		
Retained Earnings			
TOTAL EQUITY	1,000,000		
TOTAL LIABILITIES + EQUITY	27,000,000		

TABLE 22.7 SPV'S Liabilities

Balance Sheet of XYZ I Company			
Current Assets			
Cash	2,000,000	Debt/Equity	0.00%
Accounts Receivable	1,000,000	Debt/Total Assets	0.00%
Inventory	25,000,000	Payables/Equity	47.83%
Fixed Assets			
Property	40,000,000		
Plant and Equipment	34,000,000		
TOTAL ASSETS	102,000,000		
Liabilities			
Accounts Payable	33,000,000		
Short-Term Debt Outstanding			
Long-Term Debt Outstanding			
Equity			
Share Capital	69,000,000		
Retained Earnings			
TOTAL EQUITY	69,000,000		
TOTAL LIABILITIES + EQUITY	102,000,000		

Balance Sheet of XYZ II Company			
Current Assets			
Cash	300,000	Debt/Equity	0.00%
Accounts Receivable		Debt/Total Assets	0.00%
Inventory		Payables/Equity	2,600.00%
Fixed Assets			
Property	300,000		
Plant and Equipment	26,400,000		
TOTAL ASSETS	27,000,000		
Liabilities			
Long-Term Bonds	26,000,000		
Equity			
Share Capital	1,000,000		
Retained Earnings			
TOTAL EQUITY	1,000,000		
TOTAL LIABILITIES + EQUITY	27,000,000		

sales generated *or* XYZ I Company can agree to *buy back* the same assets on a deferred basis, in installments whose frequency and size match the principal and coupon payments on the bond. In this event, when all payments to bondholders are retired, XYZ I Company can transfer the capital injected into XYZ II back to XYZ I and close XYZ II altogether.

HOW *SUKUK* FINANCING COULD WORK?

Special-purpose vehicles (SPVs) are an essential component of the *sukuk* industry. We go back to our company XYZ and call it now i-XYZ (Table 22.8). We shall first demonstrate a sale-and-buyback *sukuk* structure.

XYZ Company has had a transformation and now calls itself i-XYZ. It spins off into i-XYZ I and i-XYZ II much like in our discussion earlier. i-XYZ I has short-term and long-term financing under *murabaha* contracts worth $26 million, and wishes to refinance these debts by issuing *sukuk* in the marketplace.

i-XYZ II develops a prospectus for a *sukuk* issuance and aims to raise $26 million from the capital markets to buy $26 million worth of assets from

TABLE 22.8 Sukuk Financing

Balance Sheet of of i-XYZ Company			
Current Assets			
Cash	2,000,000	Debt/Equity	35.71%
Accounts Receivable	1,000,000	Debt/Total Assets	19.53%
Inventory	25,000,000	Payables/Equity	47.14%
Fixed Assets			
Property	40,000,000		
Plant and Equipment	60,000,000		
TOTAL ASSETS	128,000,000		
Liabilities			
Accounts Payable	33,000,000		
Short-Term Debt Outstanding	15,000,000		
Long-Term Debt Outstanding	10,000,000		
Equity			
Share Capital	70,000,000		
Retained Earnings			
TOTAL EQUITY	70,000,000		
TOTAL LIABILITIES + EQUITY	128,000,000		

(*continued*)

TABLE 22.8 (Continued)

Balance Sheet of i-XYZ I Company			
Current Assets			
Cash	2,000,000	Debt/Equity	37.68%
Accounts Receivable	1,000,000	Debt/Total Assets	25.49%
Inventory	25,000,000	Payables/Equity	47.83%
Fixed Assets			
Property	40,000,000		
Plant and Equipment	60,000,000		
TOTAL ASSETS	128,000,000		
Liabilities			
Accounts Payable	33,000,000		
Short-Term Debt Outstanding	15,000,000		
Long-Term *Murabaha* Financing	11,000,000		
Equity			
Share Capital	69,000,000		
Retained Earnings			
TOTAL EQUITY	69,000,000		
TOTAL LIABILITIES + EQUITY	128,000,000		

Balance Sheet of i-XYZ II Company			
Current Assets			
Cash	300,000	Debt/Equity	0.00%
Accounts Receivable	—	Debt/Total Assets	0.00%
Inventory	—	Payables/Equity	0.00%
Fixed Assets			
Property	300,000		
Plant and Equipment	400,000		
TOTAL ASSETS	1,000,000		
Liabilities			
Accounts Payable			
Short-Term Debt Outstanding			
Long-Term Debt Outstanding			
Equity			
Share Capital	1,000,000		
Retained Earnings			
TOTAL EQUITY	1,000,000		
TOTAL LIABILITIES + EQUITY	1,000,000		

i-XYZ I. The prospectus offers in essence a feasibility report of what cash flows i-XYZ II will be able to generate if it purchases these assets and how the *sukuk* holders would benefit from the investment.

i-XYZ II issues *sukuk* certificates that are not equity shares, **but temporary ownership certificates in the assets that i-XYZ II will purchase from i-XYZ I.** The *sukuk* certificates are not ownership certificates in the Company i-XYZ II as this would make them shares, nor are they ownership certificates in *any other asset* of i-XYZ II.

i-XYZII issues *sukuk* to purchase the assets of i-XYZ I much as in the same manner we looked at in terms of bond issuances (Table 22.9).

i-XYZI Company receives $26 million in cash and settles its short-term and long-term *murabahah* facilities (Table 22.10).

In the final leg of the process i-XYZ I contracts to *buy back* the same assets sold to i-XYZ II on a deferred basis with a payment schedule that matches the payments to be made to *sukuk* holders.

i-XYZ I will buy the assets back on a cost-plus-profit basis at, for example, $28 million. The additional $2 million will be the return offered to *sukuk* investors over the span of time that i-XYZ I takes to pay i-XYZ II. On the books, i-XYZ I would have recovered ownership of the said assets and booked a liability of $28 million, and i-XYZ II would have sold the assets back to i-XYZ I and booked a receivable for $28 million.

To keep the entries simple, we assume that i-XYZ I buys back the assets for only $26 million (Table 22.11).

In this sale-and-buyback arrangement, what happens if i-XYZ is not able to make its payments on the *sukuk* certificates? To what assets would *sukuk* holders have recourse? One may well question whether i-XYZ II has the right to sell the assets back to i-XYZ I, because the assets are technically owned by the *sukuk* holders. Second, if these assets are transferred back to i-XYZ I, what assets do *sukuk* holders have recourse to if the company fails to pay on time? The only assets left on the balance sheet of i-XYZ II were the receivables of $26 million owed by i-XYZ I. In this scenario the *sukuk* holders are actually left out in the cold and have no recourse to assets. Of all the scenarios discussed, it seems *sukuk* holders have the least rights in comparison to equity holders and bondholders.

SALE AND LEASEBACK

Another, safer variant of the buyback arrangement is the sale-and-leaseback variant. Company i-XYZ I sells assets to i-XYZ II for $26 million and then i-XYZ II leases the asset back to i-XYZ I. In this way the asset remains in the ownership of i-XYZ II and the lease payments match the payouts made to *sukuk* holders.

TABLE 22.9 Asset Buybacks

Balance Sheet of i-XYZ I Company

Current Assets			
Cash	28,000,000	Debt/Equity	37.68%
Accounts Receivable	1,000,000	Debt/Total Assets	20.31%
Inventory	25,000,000	Payables/Equity	47.83%
Fixed Assets			
Property	40,000,000		
Plant and Equipment	34,000,000		
TOTAL ASSETS	128,000,000		
Liabilities			
Accounts Payable	33,000,000		
Short-Term Debt Outstanding	15,000,000		
Long-Term *Murabahah* Financing	11,000,000		
Equity			
Share Capital	69,000,000		
Retained Earnings			
TOTAL EQUITY	69,000,000		
TOTAL LIABILITIES + EQUITY	128,000,000		

Balance Sheet of i-XYZ II Company

Current Assets			
Cash	300,000	Debt/Equity	0.00%
Accounts Receivable		Debt/Total Assets	0.00%
Inventory		Payables/Equity	2,600.00%
Fixed Assets			
Property	300,000		
Plant and Equipment	26,400,000		
TOTAL ASSETS	27,000,000		
Liabilities			
Long-Term *Sukuk*	26,000,000		
Equity			
Share Capital	1,000,000		
Retained Earnings			
TOTAL EQUITY	1,000,000		
TOTAL LIABILITIES + EQUITY	27,000,000		

TABLE 22.10 Cash Raised

Balance Sheet of i-XYZ I Company			
Current Assets			
Cash	2,000,000	Debt/Equity	0.00%
Accounts Receivable	1,000,000	Debt/Total Assets	0.00%
Inventory	25,000,000	Payables/Equity	47.83%
Fixed Assets			
Property	40,000,000		
Plant and Equipment	34,000,000		
TOTAL ASSETS	102,000,000		
Liabilities			
Accounts Payable	33,000,000		
Short-Term Debt Outstanding			
Long-Term *Murabahah* Financing			
Equity			
Share Capital	69,000,000		
Retained Earnings			
TOTAL EQUITY	69,000,000		
TOTAL LIABILITIES + EQUITY	**128,000,000**		

Balance Sheet of i-XYZ II Company			
Current Assets			
Cash	300,000	Debt/Equity	0.00%
Accounts Receivable		Debt/Total Assets	0.00%
Inventory		Payables/Equity	2,600.00%
Fixed Assets			
Property	300,000		
Plant and Equipment	26,400,000		
TOTAL ASSETS	27,000,000		
Liabilities			
Long-Term *Sukuk*	26,000,000		
Equity			
Share Capital	1,000,000		
Retained Earnings			
TOTAL EQUITY	1,000,000		
TOTAL LIABILITIES + EQUITY	**27,000,000**		

TABLE 22.11 Where Is the Asset?

Balance Sheet of i-XYZ I Company			
Current Assets			
Cash	2,000,000	Debt/Equity	37.68%
Accounts Receivable	1,000,000	Debt/Total Assets	25.49%
Inventory	25,000,000	Payables/Equity	47.83%
Fixed Assets			
Property	40,000,000		
Plant and Equipment	34,000,000		
TOTAL ASSETS	102,000,000		
Liabilities			
Accounts Payable	33,000,000		
Short-Term Debt Outstanding	26,000,000		
Long-Term *Murabahah* Financing			
Equity			
Share Capital	69,000,000		
Retained Earnings			
TOTAL EQUITY	69,000,000		
TOTAL LIABILITIES + EQUITY	128,000,000		

Balance Sheet of i-XYZ II Company			
Current Assets			
Cash	300,000	Debt/Equity	0.00%
Accounts Receivable	26,000,000	Debt/Total Assets	0.00%
Inventory		Payables/Equity	2,600.00%
Fixed Assets			
Property	300,000		
Plant and Equipment	26,400,000		
TOTAL ASSETS	27,000,000		
Liabilities			
Long-Term *Sukuk*	26,000,000		
Equity			
Share Capital	1,000,000		
Retained Earnings			
TOTAL EQUITY	1,000,000		
TOTAL LIABILITIES + EQUITY	27,000,000		

In this contract the originator sells the asset to the SPV. The SPV issues the *sukuk* to purchase the asset and then leases the asset to the originator. The asset remains on the balance sheet of the lessee (i.e., the SPV). The rental payments mirror coupon payments to the *sukuk* holders. At the conclusion of the lease contract the originator buys back the asset. The SPV uses these proceeds to redeem the principal amount. This is a much safer alternative to sale and buyback.

As per the terms of the lease contracts under *ijara*, we know that the lessee ultimately buys back the asset from the lessor at the conclusion of the lease agreement. This falls nicely into a redemption plan for a *sukuk* as the last payment made by i-XYZ I to i-XYZ II would be the purchase price of the asset, and the final payment to the latter, which will be used to redeem the outstanding balances owed to *sukuk* holders.

In this arrangement, if i-XYZ I does have difficulty in making payments to i-XYZ II, *sukuk* holders can liquidate the assets on the balance sheet of i-XYZ II to recover their investments. In no case would *sukuk* holders have recourse to the assets of the parent company or i-XYZ I.

In the terminology of Islamic finance, i-XYZ I may be referred to as the *originator* and i-XYZ II would be the *issuer*.

THE ROLE OF THE SPV

The special-purpose vehicle is a wholly owned subsidiary of the parent company seeking to raise funds from a *sukuk* issue. The parent company would likely be a publicly listed company whereas the SPV would be a private company. The *sukuk* itself would probably be traded on an exchange. The SPV would issue the *sukuk* on the basis of the creditworthiness of the parent listed company, but the liabilities will be parked on the balance sheets of the SPV and not the parent company. It is also important to note that the financial statements of the SPV would be reported in the consolidated financial statements of the parent company as the SPV would not need to disclose or publish its own financial statements separately. As the SPV is a wholly owned subsidiary of the parent company, the parent company runs and manages the SPV by placing its own director and management in the SPV.

In effect the parent company can park its loans, or financing contracts, or bad assets in the books of the SPV and hide certain assets and liabilities from its own balance sheet. The SPV also serves as a bankruptcy remote vehicle, whereby the assets of the parent company are protected from liquidation if the SPV defaults on any debt obligations to lenders.

OTHER *SUKUK* STRUCTURES

Sukuk can be structured using any of the sale or lease contracts that we discussed earlier. Whether the underlying contract is of a sale and buyback, or sale and leaseback, the contracts of *murabahah, bai bithman bai al inah, bai al wafa*, and the variants of *ijara* can be applied. The reader can just interchange Party A with the originator, and Party B with the SPV. The SPV will issue *sukuk* to buy assets from the originator on a spot purchase price. The originator will then buy back or lease back the asset from the SPV for a deferred credit price or a lease arrangement. The cash flows from the originator to the SPV will match the cash payouts that would be made to investors in the *sukuk* and will reflect investors' principal payments and their returns.

ISTISNA SUKUK

The contract of *istisna* is typically used for contracts that involve deferred delivery of the subject matter. We can refer back to our XYZ Company as an airline that requires funds to purchase an aircraft from Airbus. XYZ Company creates an SPV called XYZ. The latter develops a prospectus identifying the business prospects of owning an A3180 Airbus and how that would generate revenues for the company and investors alike. The prospectus is floated among investors and funds are raised by XYZ to purchase an Airbus A3180.

Recall that the purchase price in an *istisna* contract need not be paid up front. XYZ now makes an order to Airbus for a single A3180 aircraft in which *sukuk* holders enjoy ownership interest and risk. A question to raise is that if the asset is owned by the *sukuk* holders, why is it reported in the balance sheet of the SPV at all? *Sukuk* holders enjoy temporary ownership rights over the asset till such time the *sukuk* holders choose to sell the asset to a third party.

To proceed with our example, Airbus is commissioned to manufacture the plane for XYZ. XYZ makes partial payments to Airbus as each stage of manufacturing is completed, yet continues to make "profit" payments to *sukuk* holders for their investment. These payments are made from the existing revenues from the sale of tickets of the Parent Company XYZ.

The point we wish to highlight is that in theory a *sukuk* is a unique financial instrument. It behaves like both equity and bonds. Although the contract represents asset ownership, and *sukuk* holders literally own the asset they invest in, they have to be paid back as if they were bondholders. In the earlier scenario, *sukuk* holders could become partners with XYZ and actually enjoy the returns generated by the asset over a long term. XYZ would then compensate *sukuk* holders with dividends as when profits were to be earned. Yet, *sukuk* holders' ownership would be temporary and not perpetual. At some stage XYZ would redeem the *sukuk* certificates by buying back their ownership certificates at a pre-agreed price. The returns for the *sukuk* holders would be a combination of the dividends they receive and the profit they make on the sale of the asset to the originator.

The dividends can be calculated *post-ante* depending on the terms of the contract, but as the investment of *sukuk* holders is for a limited time only, typically, investors prefer a fixed payment every quarter that resembles coupon payments on bonds as they are determined *ex-ante*.

In the example above, XYZ Airline can promise 5 percent coupon rates over a period of 10 years and contract to buy the aircraft in 10 years at a predetermined rate so that the yield on the investment is 7 percent over 10 years. Alternatively, XYZ would just commit to pay dividends once the aircraft is in service with unpredictable cash flows. XYZ could still commit to buy back the aircraft from investors in 10 years for a predetermined price, but investors would be unsure of their yield as no coupon or dividend rate is settled upfront. Typically, the *sukuk* market and investors' demands have pushed the *sukuk* to behave more like a bond offering a fixed yield to investors upfront.[4]

To drive a previous point home, in the event that XYZ is unable to make scheduled payments on the *sukuk*, investors would again only have recourse to the assets of XYZ, which is the one aircraft purchased from Airbus. If XYZ defaults on payments before the aircraft is completed, investors would have to either sell the unbuilt aircraft or wait for the aircraft to be completed before they can sell it to another airline to recover their moneys.

SIMPLE *SUKUK*

Sukuk offered a new financial product to the financial markets but has become transformed into a fixed income instrument. If we refer to a *sukuk* as just a certificate, two parties can negotiate a broad range of rights, obligations, and powers between the certificate owner and the certificate issuer.

[4]A. Lahsasna, and L. S. Lin, "Issues in Islamic Capital Markets: Islamic Bond/*Sukuk*," *in 3rd International Conference on Business and Economic Research Proceedings* (2012), pp. 12–13.

Vanilla *Sukuk*

The certificate issuer could extend temporary ownership rights to the bearer for a specific duration, to enjoy any profits earned by the issuer's business in that time period. For instance, the issuer issues a certificate to a prospective investor for $100,000,000, which entitles the investor to ownership rights over specific assets in the issuer's company. The issuer agrees to share any future profits generated from that specific asset, or from the operations of the issuer as a whole on a 50–50 basis. An important feature of this *sukuk* would be that the issuer does not need to return the $100,000,000 to the investors on maturity.

XYZ Company issues *sukuk* worth $100,000,000 to ABC. ABC enjoys ownership rights in specific assets of XYZ, and not all the assets of the company. ABC also cannot be involved in the running of XYZ's business and is unable to place a director on the board of XYZ and influence management decisions. ABC can share the profits of XYZ on a 50–50 basis for the next 10 years. XYZ is not bound to commit on the profit rate up front, nor is XYZ bound to repay ABC the $100,000,000 invested in the business. This sounds like quite a good deal for XYZ and possibly a deal of limited worth to the investor. However, at this stage, the vanilla *sukuk* is behaving as equity, as XYZ is not obligated to pay back the moneys invested to ABC, nor does ABC have to commit to a specific rate of return (Figure 22.1).

At this point, the *sukuk* certificate is behaving by and large as equity; however, *sukuk* holders do not enjoy any rights in the management of the company, nor is their ownership stake in perpetuity. There are no features as yet of a debt instrument.

If ABC is not happy with the returns provided by XYZ, ABC could withdraw its investment by selling the specific assets it has acquired of the company. If ABC's investment in XYZ was on the basis of purchasing shares in XYZ, then ABC could simply sell these shares to a third party. Shares, however, represent ownership in perpetuity and not for a limited time frame.

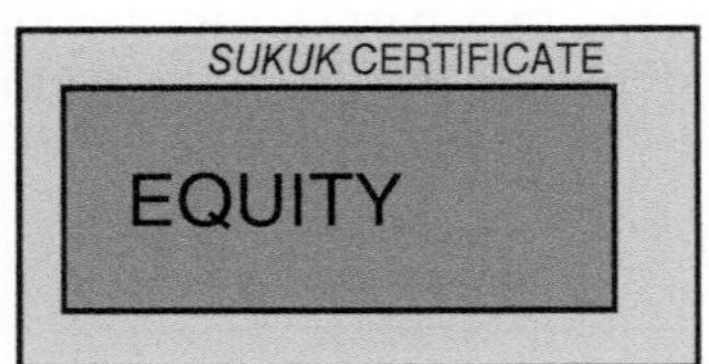

FIGURE 22.1 *Sukuk* Behaving as Equity

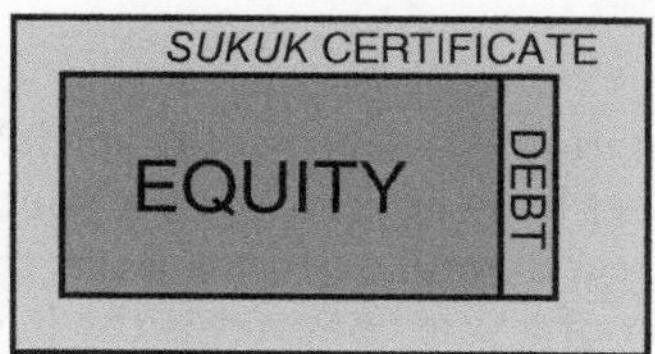

FIGURE 22.2 *Sukuk* Security with Debt

Alternatively, ABC could also demand the right to contribute to the running of the company so as to steer the business into profit-making ventures.

Vanilla *Sukuk* with Toppings

The earlier arrangement could be enhanced if XYZ commits a specific rate of return to ABC. This feature starts the journey of the vanilla *sukuk* to becoming a debt instrument. To illustrate, XYZ commits to offer ABC 5 percent per annum for their investment, but no arrangement is made to redeem ABC by paying back the monies invested in XYZ (Figure 22.2).

Vanilla *Sukuk* with Extra Toppings

In this product, XYZ commits a specific rate of return to the investors and contracts to redeem their investment at the maturity of the contract terms by paying the investors their principal investment back. At this stage, the vanilla *sukuk* has become a debt instrument that offers coupon payments, and is redeemed after a specific duration.

At this stage, an equity-like instrument has undergone a metamorphosis and has become a debt-like instrument (Figure 22.3). In any regard, investors in *sukuk* instruments should take care in reading the prospectus in detail to determine their rights and obligations.

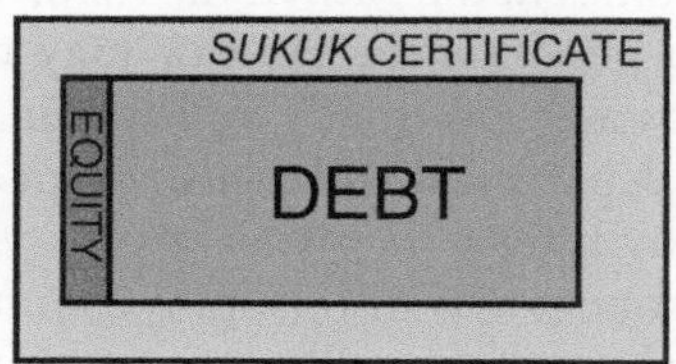

FIGURE 22.3 *Sukuk* Certificate as a Debt Instrument

Sovereign *Sukuk*

Can a government sell national assets even to itself? We have clearly established that *sukuk* issuances have underlying sale contracts between the issuer and the investor to create a dynamic of cash flows that resemble investment and returns. A condition of a sale contract is the legal capacity of the seller to sell the underlying asset, the existence of the asset, and the permissibility of the asset from a *shariah* point of view.

The foremost question that arises is: Does a government have the legal capacity to sell national assets? A government body, like a corporation, is a nexus of agency contracts. A government consists of democratically elected representatives that manage the executive wing of a government. The executive has a full-functioning body of civil servants and government employees to carry out the tasks of the executive. The government, in a democratic society, represents the interests of the citizens of the country and has certain responsibilities to carry out to provide public goods and infrastructure, preserve law and order, preserve national security, levy taxes on citizens, and even borrow money from lenders to finance different projects. Governments own vast amounts of assets, including public land, dams, railway tracks, the land on which railways are built, highways, and the land highways are built on and the tolls collected from these highways as well. However, can governments set up SPVs in which they are the only shareholder and then sell these national assets to these SPVs?

Governments are allowed to sell national assets when it comes to a process of privatization, where governments sell national assets like state-owned companies, or natural resources reserves to private parties to enhance productivity. Governments can also lease assets to private parties. These actions are, however, usually endorsed by an Act of Parliament.

The government can further segregate assets, such as highways, the land highways are built on, and the tolls collected from the highways. Let us consider a project taken up by the highway department of a fictitious country.

When building a highway the highway department would initially purchase all the land that comes in the path of the road. The federal government may borrow money to purchase the land or may use tax revenues to do the same. The proceeds will be transferred to the highway department's accounts. The highway department will then appoint a company to construct the highway and will pay it from its own sources.

The highway department may also employ a company to collect tolls on its behalf for a fee or a share of the toll revenues. However, can the highway department segregate these classes of assets? If the highway department were to make a fictitious balance sheet for a highway project, the land on which the highway is built and the materials gone into making the highway would come under fixed assets. Toll revenues would be part of sales, which would be further categorized into receivables or cash. If the highway department were to borrow money from banks to fund the project, how would the bank secure its loan?

Any bank that lends money to the highway department would *not* be able to effectively place a charge on the fixed assets of the highway department, as banks cannot seize public property and liquidate it. Nor would the bank be able to place a charge on the current assets of the highway department and assign all receivables to itself because this is government revenue.

A question can thus be posed: Could the highway department sell the fixed assets on its balance sheet to an SPV? Can the SPV then issue temporary ownership certificates in the underlying assets, which belong to the citizens of the country? Even if the highway department intended to buy back these very same assets for a credit price, the fundamental question that arises is: Is the highway department authorized to sell them at all?

This becomes a critical issue if the highway department defaults on the bank loan or the *sukuk*. To what assets would the *sukuk* holders have recourse?

CONCLUSION

We have examined how *sukuk* are issued using either sale-based or lease-based contracts. *Sukuk* issued with underlying contracts of *murabaha, bai bithman ajil, bai ul wafa,* and *tawarruq* involve sale of assets at a spot price and a buyback on a deferred price. Any *sukuk* issued with the earlier-mentioned contracts would certainly behave as debt instruments, whereas investors pay a purchase price on spot for a company's assets, which are redeemed by the company buying back these assets on a deferred basis at a credit price. *Sukuk* issued using *ijara* contracts that conclude with the sale of the leased asset are also seen as debt-based contracts. Investors purchase an asset from the company they are investing in and lease the asset back to the same. At the expiry of the lease contract the company in question purchases the asset back from the investor or *sukuk* holders.

Sukuk contracts using *istisna* or *salaam*, however, are combined with sale contracts and are also treated as debt-based *sukuk* structures.

What is common to all these structures is that the *sukuk* certificate is issued entitling holders to certain rights for a limited time only. *Sukuk* are not instruments of perpetual ownership. *Sukuk* instruments offer coupon payments and repayment of the principal amount, which is matched to a repurchase of assets initially bought by the *sukuk* holders. As such, *sukuk* in the capital markets of today behaves as a debt-based instrument. All of the previous structures require the sale of an asset from a company to *sukuk* holders. The seller or the company must therefore have clear ownership rights over the assets sold and bear the legal capacity to sell those assets.

CHAPTER 23

Risk Management for Islamic Banks

Risk is an inherent force on all marketplaces. Each industry offers its own unique risks and its own unique ways of managing these risks. The art of risk management consists of identifying risks, measuring risks, and mitigating risks. This is a classroom definition of risk management. Risk simply refers to the probability of events occurring that adversely impact future expected outcomes. Risk addresses the probability of such events occurring and the impact they have on any given system. Manufacturing companies face the risks that by the time products come to the marketplace they are obsolete, unwanted, or are selling at prices lower than the cost of production. Banks confront a host of different risks that are unique to the business model of banks.

Financial intermediaries mobilize deposits from households, companies, and governments and lend these deposits back to other households, companies, and governments. At one stage banks are borrowers of funds and at another stage they are lenders of funds. The risks that impact a bank's ability to mobilize funds at a certain cost are different from the risks they face in being able to recover moneys lent out to third parties. Islamic banks face many of the same risks that are faced by conventional banks. These risks are categorized into credit risk, market risk, and liquidity risk. Islamic banks also face *shariah* risk, which is unique to Islamic Financial Institutions (IFIs); however, that topic is discussed in other works.

CREDIT RISK

Credit risk is merely the risk of loss faced by a bank due to the inability of borrowers to make all the payments owed to the bank. This is risk of default, pure and simple, and can arise from changing financial circumstances of borrowers that affects their ability and willingness to return loans taken from banks. Banks therefore have in place a risk management process by virtue of which risk is identified, measured, and mitigated. Credit risk is identified as the risk of default.

It is measured by certain methods, which we discuss in detail, but what is an obvious measure of this risk is the impact on the bank's assets, liabilities, and income if a borrower fails to make payments on the bank's receivables.

Islamic banks experience credit risk in the same manner as conventional banks as they, too, have adopted credit financing models through credit-based sales and lease contracts. The discussion on credit risk to conventional banks is therefore applicable to Islamic banks as well.

Credit risk is mitigated at source by carefully screening borrowers for their creditworthiness and ability to repay any loan over a long period of time. The methods of credit analysis that are found in many conventional banks apply to Islamic banks as well, and by and large no matter how complex such analyses may be in their attempt to forecast a borrower's cash flow, they remain at best educated predictions.

A variant of the credit analysis technology is simply to focus on the assets pledged as collateral to secure a loan or financing contract and to measure the ease with which that asset can be liquidated for cash. A combination of assessing a borrower's creditworthiness and the quality of assets pledged make up the major portion of credit analysis. It is a little more complex for large corporations with various sources of revenue streams. The process becomes more complex if such companies have revenue streams in various currencies and have bank borrowings in various countries and in various currencies, where the companies' operations face political risk, currency risk, business risk, risk of nationalization, risk of competitor's manipulating currencies, prices, and so on. In essence, a lender/financier faces all the risks its client does. The higher the risk faced by the borrower in paying off installments on a loan facility, the higher the credit risk premium charged to that borrower. In the context of loan, however, a borrower must treat an interest payment or principal repayment as a fixed cost, in that these expenses need to be incurred whether the company can afford to pay them or not.

An Islamic bank that has facilitated a credit-based sale also stands in much the same way in respect to the client as a lender. An Islamic bank requires the borrower to make timely payments on financing contracts lest the bank liquidate collateral to recover its dues. An Islamic bank is not eager to sink or swim with the borrower, but rather seeks to swim in any circumstance.

The conventional finance universe developed mathematical models to measure and mitigate risk. Many of these models rely heavily on statistical analyses and probabilities. The Islamic banking universe has borrowed from this technology as well and also seeks recognition from International

Standard-Setting bodies such as Basel for the manner in which they conduct financial intermediation. There is an inherent contradiction here as Basel guidelines help to strengthen a bank's ability to lend, to develop systems of recognizing credit risk, and to have sufficient reserves and capital to cushion losses. Basel does not advise conventional banks to share business risk with their borrowers, or become co-owners in their businesses or assets. In fact the Basel framework discourages asset ownership for banks as we shall see in our discussion on risk weightages.[1]

The core business of banks is lending money, and the core risk they face is the risk of default of borrowers. Islamic banks experience risk in exactly the same manner. Therefore, banks maintain reserves in their balance sheets in case borrowers default on their payments. These reserves are of two kinds, one that is funded by setting aside a percentage of interest income, or in the case of Islamic banks, profit, and the other source of reserves comes from the capital of shareholders. The former builds up reserves for what is known as expected losses, and the latter for unexpected losses.

The conventional banking model and the Islamic banking model are similar in that shareholders put a small percentage of the total funds used to finance assets. In fact this capital is sufficient to set up the infrastructure of a bank and to maintain liquid reserves to buffer unexpected losses. As we have seen time and again in our discussions, the major source of funds is depositors.

Before beginning a detailed discussion on credit risk, we need to define some basic concepts such as capital adequacy, capital adequacy ratio, risk weightages, probability of default, and other related concepts.

Capital Adequacy

Capital adequacy is a rather self-explanatory term, and simply means the availability of adequate capital to conduct a certain business. Banks are required to maintain adequate capital to acquire the fixed assets of the bank and to maintain liquid reserves to buffer any losses that might be incurred if their financial assets begin to lose value.[2] For many banks, credit-based loans constitute the major portion of their portfolio and investments in various financial instruments make up the rest of their portfolio. Capital exists therefore to act as a buffer on any losses experienced by owning these assets. Such losses need to be made good, because these assets are not purchased with shareholders' money, but with depositors' money, which must be guaranteed at all times.

---

[1]See "Basel III Framework" by Bank of International Settlements.

[2]J. Hugonnier and E. Morellec, *Bank Capital, Liquid Reserves, and Insolvency Risk* (Tech. report, Swiss Finance Institute and EPFL, 2014).

Capital Adequacy Ratio

Capital adequacy ratio (CAR) is merely the ratio of capital to total risk-weighted assets. A capital adequacy ratio of 8 percent means that for every $1 of losses experienced by a bank, only 8 cents will be absorbed by the bank's capital and 92 cents will be absorbed by the depositors. To put into context, if a bank has $300 million in loans extended to homebuyers, and 10 percent of the borrowers default on their loans, thereby $30 million of loans becoming nonperforming, the bank will only absorb $2.4 million of the losses and $27.60 million will be absorbed by depositors in terms of reduced interest income or even reduced principal.

Implications of CAR

CAR is linked to the economic capital a bank must maintain and to the risk-weighted assets it holds on its balance sheet. Risk weighting is a rather simple methodology of assigning a risk factor to assets. A *Bai Bithman Ajil* (*BBA*) facility of $100,000 extended without collateral may be assigned a risk weightage of 150 percent. Thus the bank treats the exposure on the contract not as just $100,000 but in fact as $150,000. The same facility may be extended to a customer by obtaining collateral worth say $110,000. This would reduce the risk weightage assigned to the asset, for example, to 40 percent. The bank would then report its exposure on this contract not at $100,000, but only at $40,000.

As each of the two contracts exposes the bank to varying levels of risk, and likelihood of default, the amount of capital required to act as a buffer to cover losses will also vary. The riskier the financing, the more capital required. So CAR is a function of economic capital and the risk weightages assigned to total financing.

$$\text{CAR} = \frac{\text{Economic Capital}}{\text{Credit Risk Weighted Assets} + \text{Market Risk Weighted Assets} + \text{Operations Risk Weighted Assets}}$$

Credit risk contributes to more than 80 percent of all risk associated with financing contracts[3] and we can for our discussion ignore market risk and operational risk.

$$\text{CAR} = \text{Economic Capital (k)/Credit Risk Weighted Asset}$$

[3]Hennie Van Greuning and Zamir Iqbal, *Risk Analysis for Islamic Banks* (Washington, DC: World Bank, 2008).

If CAR stands at 8 percent, and the bank has $100,000 of financing with a risk weightage of 150 percent, the bank would have to maintain $12,000 of capital, whereas if the bank opted to finance with collateral, the asset would have a risk weightage of only 40 percent and the bank would only be required to maintain capital of $3,200.

Another way of looking at the relationship between CAR and risk weightage is that with limited or fixed economic capital, the bank would be limited to the maximum financing it could extend depending on the risk weightage of its aggregate portfolio.

If our Islamic bank has capital of $12,000, it can either extend one financing of $100,000 with risk weightage of 150 percent or it can extend $375,000 ($12,000/(0.08 × 0.40) worth of financing with 40 percent risk weightage. From the above equation we realize that the bank can do business up to a certain maximum amount, depending on the kinds of risks it is willing to take. These risks will be reflected in the risk weightages assigned to various kinds of assets it holds and the various forms of financing it is willing to extend.

The requirement for capital, or the limit on the amount that can be financed given a certain amount of capital, is valid as long as the asset is funded by guaranteed deposits. If the asset is funded by a nonguaranteed deposits like a pure *mudharabah* fund, that financing would be exempt from similar treatment, as all losses experienced on the asset will be passed on to the *mudharabah* fund participants and not the shareholders.

Risk Weightages

Risk weightage is a mathematical way of assigning a risk factor to a set of receivables or a financial asset. For illustration purposes, imagine a house loan to a doctor with a table income of $100,000 and another house loan to a first-time book writer (on Islamic finance) for the same $100,000. Certainly, the loan extended to the doctor is less risky than to the book author. The banking system devised a mechanism to attach a risk factor to the loan amount. To reflect the low level of risk attached to lending to a doctor, we can assign a risk factor of 0.5. From a risk point of view, the bank feels its exposure to the borrower is only $50,000. The book author may be assigned a risk factor of 1.2; thereby from a risk point of view the loan to the book author is actually $120,000. Although the nominal loan amounts are $100,000 in both cases, when adjusted for risk they become drastically different and are known as *risk-weighted assets*.

The capital needed by a bank to extend two loans of $100,000 each without risk adjustments would be $16,000. The capital needed to fund two loans now, one of $100,000 with risk weightage of 50 percent and one for $100,000 with risk weightage of 120 percent, is $13,600.

Components of Risk Weightage Calculations

The mathematical formula for calculating the credit risk weightage of a receivable, loan, or credit payment is as follows:

$$\text{Risk Weightage} = \text{Probability of Default} \times \text{Exposure at Given Default} \\ \times \text{Loss Rate Given Default} \times \text{Tenor}$$

We examine each variable in brief detail.

Probability of Default Probability of default is simply just the probability that a certain customer or borrower may default on a particular facility. It may be calculated for a single borrower or for a pool of borrowers that together constitute a portfolio for a bank. The simplest way to calculate such a probability is to examine previous data.

Imagine an Islamic bank that divides its CAR *ijara* customers into five categories. Category 1 poses the least risk of default and consists of doctors, lawyers, dentists, pharmacists, and bankers as well. This category presents a flawless repayment history and secure cash flows for the future. Category 2 consists of professionals with slightly less stable sources of income such as researchers and book writers. They are assigned Category 2. Each borrower is assigned such a code in a rather cold and quantitative manner. The Islamic bank that conducts this exercise looks at its portfolio over a five-year span and discovers that of the 30,000 loans extended to Category 1 borrowers, only 1,000 have defaulted, therefore creating a probability of default of 3.33 percent. Similarly Category 2 borrowers reveal a 6 percent probability of default, and so on. Looking at Table 23.1, it is quite easy to gauge that borrowers with high probabilities of default pose a greater risk to the bank, and therefore the bank is also entitled to charge a higher *ijara rate* on their lease agreements.

TABLE 23.1 Probability of Default in 2005

Risk Category of Lessee	Number of *Ijara* Financing Contracts Extended in 2005	Number of *Ijara* Financing Defaults	Probability of Default (%)
1	30,000	1,000	3.33
2	20,000	1,200	6.00
3	15,000	1,300	8.67
4	10,000	900	9.00
5	5,000	450	9.00

Actual probabilities are calculated in far more complex ways, but the reader should get the simple gist of the matter. However, probabilities are generated from observing past behavior and from anticipating future behavior of future borrowers. Assigning the city of Detroit a probability of default of 100 percent in 1970 must have been unthinkable, but yet it happened. "For instance, according to S&P, the estimated default rate for U.S. mortgage loans increased from 20 basis points prior to 2008 to 200 basis points after the crisis had been observed."[4]

Exposure at Given Default (EAGD) EAGD is a simple concept, and identifies the bank exposure at a certain stage in the life cycle of a receivable. Assume that a bank issues a home mortgage to a customer for $200,000. The customer is required to pay the bank $400,000 over 25 years. After 15 years the customer has paid the bank $300,000, leaving an outstanding amount of $100,000. At the beginning of the 16th year the bank's exposure at given default would be $100,000.

We extend this concept to our portfolio of auto-*ijara* contracts where we assume each lessee has reduced a certain percentage of his lease obligations. The residual balance is therefore the current outstanding amount or the exposure at given default (Table 23.2).

Loss Rate Given Default (LRGD) LRGD takes into account the value of collateral held by the bank. Assuming that the bank in our *ijara* case has a charge on the CARs leased to clients, the market values of these vehicles would be

TABLE 23.2 Probability of Default and EAGD

Risk Category of Lessees	Number of *Ijara* Contracts Extended in 2005	Number of *Ijara* Contracts Under Default	Probability of Default (%)	Average Facility Size	Original Facility Disbursed	Current Outstanding (EAGD)
1	30,000	1,000	3.33	40,000	1,200,000,000	720,000,000
2	20,000	1,200	6.00	35,000	700,000,000	420,000,000
3	15,000	1,300	8.67	30,000	450,000,000	270,000,000
4	10,000	900	9.00	15,000	150,000,000	90,000,000
5	5,000	450	9.00	10,000	50,000,000	30,000,000

[4]Vanessa Le Leslé and Sofiya Avramova, "Revisiting Risk-Weighted Assets: Why Do RWAs Differ Across Countries and What Can Be Done About It?" (IMF Working Paper, WP/12/90, 2012).

TABLE 23.3 Probability of Default and LRGD

Risk Category of Lessees	Number of *Ijara* Contracts Extended in 2005	Number of *Ijara* Contracts Under Default	Probability of Default (%)	Average Facility Size	Original Facility Disbursed	Current Outstanding (EAGD)	Current Market Value of Collateral/ CARs	Loss Rate Given Default (%)
1	30,000	1,000	3.33	40,000	1,200,000,000	720,000,000	960,000,000	−33
2	20,000	1,200	6.00	35,000	700,000,000	420,000,000	350,000,000	17
3	15,000	1,300	8.67	30,000	450,000,000	270,000,000	315,000,000	−17
4	10,000	900	9.00	15,000	150,000,000	90,000,000	45,000,000	50
5	5,000	450	9.00	10,000	50,000,000	30,000,000	20,000,000	33

treated as collateral for the receivables due to the bank. If the reader would note in Categories 2, 4, and 5 of Table 23.3 the current market values of the CARs are lower than the amounts owed to the bank. If these customers defaulted, the bank would not recover their receivables in full and would have to make good their losses from another source.

The mathematical computation of LRGD is *(EAGD − Collateral)/ EAGD*. This number reflects the percentage of the EAGD that cannot be recovered if collateral is liquidated. In Categories 1 and 3, the current market values of the collateral are in excess of the exposure of the bank; therefore, were the bank to liquidate all these vehicles, the bank would recover in excess of their outstanding dues on clients. The bank therefore does not need to maintain any excess reserves in this case.

Expected Loss (EL) Expected loss is precisely the amount that a bank would not be able to recover from a particular facility were it to default and were the bank to liquidate all collateral. The mathematical computation of EL is as follows:

$$EL = PD * EAGD * LRGD$$

Category 1 facilities have an EL of −$8,000,000, which means that even if all the lessees defaulted in the Category 1 portfolio, the bank would have sufficient collateral to recover any outstanding dues. Category 2 lease agreements do not offer the same comfort, and in fact if the portfolio were to default, the bank would experience losses of $4,200,000. It would be prudent therefore to build up a reserve of $4,200,000 to cushion losses in case Category 2 facilities do in fact default (Table 23.4). We assume in this illustration that the value of collateral for each and every lessee in each risk class is either more or less than the value of the outstanding EAGD. This assumption is just for illustrating the intuition behind the concept and is not practically valid.

TABLE 23.4 PD and Expected Losses

Risk Category of Lessees	Number of *Ijara* Contracts Extended in 2005	Number of *Ijara* Contracts Under Default	Probability of Default (%)	Average Facility Size	Original Facility Disbursed	Current Outstanding (EAGD)	Current Market Value of Collateral/ CARs	Loss Rate Given Default (%)	Number of Years Until Maturity	Expected Loss
1	30,000	1,000	3.33	40,000	1,200,000,000	720,000,000	960,000,000	−33	6	(8,000,000)
2	20,000	1,200	6.00	35,000	700,000,000	420,000,000	350,000,000	17	4	4,200,000
3	15,000	1,300	8.67	30,000	450,000,000	270,000,000	315,000,000	−17	5	(3,900,000)
4	10,000	900	9.00	15,000	150,000,000	90,000,000	45,000,000	50	3	4,050,000
5	5,000	450	9.00	10,000	50,000,000	30,000,000	20,000,000	33	2	900,000

The entire *ijara* portfolio presents the bank with an expected loss of \$2,750,000. The Islamic bank would therefore be wise to maintain a buffer of \$2,750,000 to cover expected losses that could arise from the risk of default on its *ijara* portfolio.

Unexpected Losses (UL) Unexpected losses are losses that are not accounted for by normal circumstances of credit default. These are losses that may arise from unexpected circumstances that affect the asset values on a bank's balance sheet. These may be caused by changes in the political environment, or adverse fluctuation in foreign currencies and interest rates caused by events outside the normal circumstances of doing business. Banks provision for such unexpected losses. The mathematical computation of UL is as follows:

$$UL = \sqrt{(PD)(1 - PD)} * EAGD * LRGD$$

The total unexpected losses from the *ijara* portfolio in Table 23.5 is (\$2,750,000), which means the Islamic bank with this portfolio does not need to make any provisions for unexpected losses.

Calculation of Risk Weightage

Before we examine the balance sheet of an Islamic bank we dwell for a moment on risk weightage once again. For illustration purposes we look at an Islamic bank with \$100,000,000 *murabahah* portfolio and we see how changes in PD, EAGD, LRDG, and tenor impact risk weightages and therefore economic capital.

$$RW = \text{Probability of Default (PD)} * \text{Exposure at Given Default (EAGD)}$$
$$* \text{Loss Rate at Given Default (LRGD)} * \text{Tenor}$$

Scenario 1 In this scenario, we work with a *murabahah* facility with an EAGD of \$100,000,000. We see the impact of increasing PD from 10 percent to 50 percent and how this impacts risk weightage (RW) and capital requirements in Table 23.6.

In Scenario 1, we see that the higher the probability of default, the higher the risk weightage of the asset, and the higher the amount of required capital. We also observe that when risk weightages are higher than 100 percent, the impact of risk amplifies the value of the risk-weighted asset. Such assets therefore require higher capital when their nominal values are adjusted for risk. Assets that score less than 100 percent risk weightage have a reduced impact on the risk-adjusted value of an asset and therefore require lower capital. Risk weightage is proportionately related to the value of probability

TABLE 23.5 PD and Unexpected Losses

Risk Category of Lessees	Number of *Ijara* Contracts Extended in 2005	Number of *Ijara* Contracts Under Defaulted	Probability of Default (%)	Average Facility Size	Original Facility Disbursed	Current Outstanding (EAGD)	Current Market Value of Collateral/ CARs	Loss Rate Given Default (%)	Number of Years Until Maturity	Expected Loss	Unexpected Loss
1	30,000	1,000	3.33	40,000	1,200,000,000	720,000,000	960,000,000	−33	6	(8,000,000)	(42,357,211)
2	20,000	1,200	6.00	35,000	700,000,000	420,000,000	350,000,000	17	4	4,200,000	16,117,643
3	15,000	1,300	8.67	30,000	450,000,000	270,000,000	315,000,000	−17	5	(3,900,000)	(12,099,512)
4	10,000	900	9.00	15,000	150,000,000	90,000,000	45,000,000	50	3	4,050,000	12,285,000
5	5,000	450	9.00	10,000	50,000,000	30,000,000	20,000,000	33	2	900,000	2,730,000

TABLE 23.6 Probability Scenario 1

Probability of Default (%)	Asset	Exposure at Given Default	Collateral	Loss Rate Given Default (%)	Tenor	Expected Loss	Risk Weightage (%)	Risk-Weighted Asset	Capital Needed
10	100,000,000	100,000,000	50,000,000	50	5	5,000,000	25	25,000,000	2,000,000
20	100,000,000	100,000,000	50,000,000	50	5	10,000,000	50	50,000,000	4,000,000
30	100,000,000	100,000,000	50,000,000	50	5	15,000,000	75	75,000,000	6,000,000
40	100,000,000	100,000,000	50,000,000	50	5	20,000,000	100	100,000,000	8,000,000
50	100,000,000	100,000,000	50,000,000	50	5	25,000,000	125	125,000,000	10,000,000

of default (PD). The higher the PD, the higher the risk weightage of the asset.

Scenario 2 Scenario 2 looks at the same facility, but with changes made to the amount of collateral offered (Table 23.7).

We can see that with 0 collateral, the risk weightage of the asset is at 50 percent, and this asset requires the highest amount of capital. With increasing amounts of collateral, the risk weightage is reduced as is the amount of capital required. Collateral remains therefore an essential component of credit-based financing.

Scenario 3 Scenario 3 analyzes the impact of tenor on risk weightages; therefore assets on a bank's balance sheet for longer tenors incur higher capital charges than short-term assets (Table 23.8).

Scenario 4 Scenario 4 in Table 23.9 also reveals the proportionate relationship between asset size and risk weightages.

Balance Sheet Analysis

We take our understanding of the concepts described and apply them to understand credit risk, market risk, and liquidity risk to an Islamic bank. We use for an example an Islamic bank with $102,000,000 in paid-up capital and see how the liabilities fund various assets on the balance sheet (Table 23.10).

Islamic Bank XYZ has $102 million worth of capital: $2 million is used to acquire fixed assets and set up the infrastructure of the bank; $100 million is placed in assets held for sale. This is the investment of shareholders' funds. The Islamic bank has total CASA deposits of $107.350 million, which fund $107.350 million worth of short-term assets and $687.750 million worth of long-term liabilities under commodity *murabahah* and *mudharabah* deposits, along with Interbank *mudharabah* fund $690.650 million worth of long-term assets. The balance sheet is perfectly matched with short-term funds funding short-term assets and long-term funds funding long-term assets.

We now add the earnings derived from these assets and the expenses incurred on liabilities as well in Table 23.11.

XYZ Islamic Bank earns returns on short-term assets of $1,256,000, which are funded by short-term liabilities that cost the bank $1,294,000. The bank is making a loss on the short end of the book. However, the bank earns $48,004,500 on long-term assets that include investments and financing assets, and these assets are funded by long-term deposits that cost

TABLE 23.7 Probability Scenario 2

Probability of Default (%)	Asset	Exposure at Given Default	Collateral	Loss Rate Given Default (%)	Tenor	Expected Loss	Risk Weightage (%)	Risk-Weighted Asset	Capital Needed
10	100,000,000	100,000,000	—	100	5	10,000,000	50	50,000,000	4,000,000
10	100,000,000	100,000,000	25,000,000	75	5	7,500,000	38	37,500,000	3,000,000
10	100,000,000	100,000,000	50,000,000	50	5	5,000,000	25	25,000,000	2,000,000
10	100,000,000	100,000,000	60,000,000	40	5	4,000,000	20	20,000,000	1,600,000

TABLE 23.8 Probability Scenario 3

Probability of Default (%)	Asset	Exposure at Given Default	Collateral	Loss Rate Given Default (%)	Tenor	Expected Loss	Risk Weightage (%)	Risk-Weighted Asset	Capital Needed
10	100,000,000	100,000,000	50,000,000	50	5	5,000,000	25	25,000,000	2,000,000
10	100,000,000	100,000,000	50,000,000	50	10	5,000,000	50	50,000,000	4,000,000
10	100,000,000	100,000,000	50,000,000	50	22	5,000,000	110	110,000,000	8,800,000
10	100,000,000	100,000,000	50,000,000	50	25	5,000,000	125	125,000,000	10,000,000

TABLE 23.9 Probability Scenario 4

Probability of Default (%)	Asset	Exposure at Given Default	Collateral	Loss Rate Given Default (%)	Tenor	Expected Loss	Risk Weightage (%)	Risk-Weighted Asset	Capital Needed
10	100,000,000	100,000,000	50,000,000	50	5	5,000,000	25	25,000,000	2,000,000
10	500,000,000	500,000,000	50,000,000	90	5	45,000,000	45	225,000,000	18,000,000
10	1,500,000,000	1,500,000,000	50,000,000	97	5	145,000,000	48	725,000,000	58,000,000
10	5,000,000,000	5,000,000,000	50,000,000	99	5	495,000,000	50	2,475,000,000	198,000,000

TABLE 23.10 Balance Sheet of Islamic Bank XYZ

Balance Sheet			
Assets		Liabilities	
Cash	25,000,000	*Wadiah* Current Accounts	32,350,000
Statutory Reserves	27,510,000	*Wadiah* Savings Accounts	75,000,000
Short-Term Notes	25,590,000		
Short-Term Assets	29,250,000		
Total S/T Assets Funded by S/T Deposits	107,350,000	Total S/T Deposits	107,350,000
Assets Held for Sale	**100,000,000**		
Total Short-Term Assets	**207,350,000**	**Total Short-Term Liabilities**	**107,350,000**
Assets Held Until Maturity	100,000,000	Commodity *Murabahah*	150,000,000
Long-Term *Sukuk*			
Financing	590,650,000	*Mudharabah* Deposit I	200,000,000
BBA Fixed Rate	164,750,000	*Mudharabah* Deposit II	200,000,000
BBA Floating Rate	150,000,000	*Mudharabah* Deposit III	137,750,000
AITAB	175,000,000	Total Deposits	687,750,000
Musharakah Mutanaqisah	85,900,000	Interbank *Mudharabah*	2,900,000
Mushjarikah	15,000,000		
Total Long-Term Assets	**690,650,000**	**Total Long-Term Liabilities**	**690,650,000**
Total Financial Assets	**898,000,000**	**Total Liabilities**	**798,000,000**
Fixed Assets	2,000,000	Equity	102,000,000
Building			
Computers			
Furniture			
Total Assets	**900,000,000**	**Total Liabilities + Equity**	**900,000,000**

the bank only $32,602,000. The bank enjoys a spread of $15,401,875 on long-term assets. The bank also earns an additional $2 million income from advisory services and therefore enjoys a net spread of $16.8 million after deducting operating expenses and impairment charges.

TABLE 23.11 Balance Sheet and Income Statement

Income Statement		Balance Sheet				Income Statement	
Income	Profit Rate	Assets		Liabilities		Profit Rate	Expense
12,500	0.05%	Cash	25,000,000	*Wadiah* Current Accounts	32,350,000	2%	647,000
—	0.00%	Statutory Reserves	27,510,000	*Wadiah* Savings Accounts	75,000,000	2%	647,000
511,800	2.00%	Short-Term Notes	25,590,000				
731,250	2.50%	Short-Term Assets	29,250,000				
1,255,550	S/T Profit	Total S/T Assets Funded by S/T Deposits	107,350,000	Total S/T Deposits	107,350,000	S/T Costs	1,294,000
3,000,000	3.00%	**Assets Held for Sale**	**100,000,000**				
		Total Short-Term Assets	**207,350,000**	Total Short-Term Liabilities	107,350,000		
6,000,000	6.00%	Assets Held Till Maturity	100,000,000	Commodity *Murabahah*	150,000,000	4%	6,000,000
42,004,500	7.11%	Long-Term *Sukuk* Financing	590,650,000	*Mudharabah* Deposit I	200,000,000	5%	10,000,000
11,532,500	7.00%	*BBA* Fixed Rate	164,750,000	*Mudharabah* Deposit II	200,000,000	4.95%	9,900,000

10,875,000	7.25%	*BBA* Floating Rate	150,000,000	*Mudharabah* Deposit III	137,750,000	4.75%	6,543,125
11,375,000	6.50%	*AITAB*	175,000,000	Total Deposits	687,750,000		
6,872,000	8.00%	*Musharakah Mutanaqisah*	85,900,000	Interbank *Mudharabah*	2,900,000	5.50%	159,500
1,350,000	9.00%	*Mushjarikah*	15,000,000				
48,004,500	L/T Profit					L/T Costs	32,602,625
	5.82%	**Total Long-Term Assets**	690,650,000	**Total Long-Term Liabilities**	690,650,000		4.23%
52,260,050	**Tot Profit Income**	**Total Financial Assets**	**898,000,000**	**Total Liabilities**	**798,000,000**	**Tot Proft Exp**	**33,737,125**
2,000,000	Fee Income	Fixed Assets	2,000,000	Equity	102,000,000	Operating Exp	3,000,000
		Building				Impairment Exp	721,950
		Computers					
		Furniture					
54,260,050	Total Income	**Total Assets**	**900,000,000**	**Total Liabilities + Equity**	**900,000,000**	Total Expense	37,459,075
						Spread	16,800,975

TABLE 23.12 Income Distribution

Income from Investment of Depositors' Funds	49,260,050
Income from Investment of Shareholders' Funds	3,000,000
Fee Income	2,000,000
Gross Income	**54,260,050**
Profit Paid to Depositors	33,737,125
Operating Expenses	3,000,000
Impairment Reserve	721,950
Total Expenses and Reserve	37,459,075
Net Income	**16,800,975**
Risk-Free Rate	2.00%
Assets	898,000,000
Return on Assets	1.8709%
Risk-Weighted Assets	519,413,000
Capital	100,000,000
Risk-Free Return on Capital	2,000,000
Return on Risk-Weighted Assets	18.8010%
Return on Equity	16.8010%

The assets are priced in such a manner as to pay all cost of funds expenses, operating expenses, and impairment charges, and they provide a decent return on capital to shareholders. This analysis is provided in Table 23.12.

We also provide the reader with a comprehensive analysis of the assets by assigning various risk weightages to all the asset classes. After assigning risk weightages based on arbitrarily assigned values for PD, EAGD, LRGD, and tenor we proceed with calculations of expected loss, unexpected loss, and required capital given a CAR of 8 percent (Tables 23.13 through 23.16).

Subsequently, we perform a capital requirement exercise to see if the bank is well capitalized using the formula $CAR = k/RWA$ for each category of asset and discover that our Islamic bank is well capitalized. The current portfolio of assets requires a capital of only $41.553 million, whereas it has a capital of $100 million. The bank can either take on riskier business, or more volume of business. For the latter option the bank will have to raise more funds in deposits from the markets. This can be done from the retail channel, or from the interbank market; however, the latter is a more expensive source of funds.

Credit Risk Mitigation

The credit risk the bank is exposed to is provisioned for by maintaining a reserve for expected losses from the income the bank earns from financing assets. Unexpected losses are provisioned for and shareholders' capital is used to buffer unexpected losses.

TABLE 23.13 Asset Classes

Asset Class	Asset	EAGD	PD (%)	Collateral	LRGD (%)	EL	Tenor	RW (%)
Cash	25,000,000	25,000,000	0.00	25,000,000	0	—	0.08	0
Statutory Reserves	31,000,000	31,000,000	0.00	31,000,000	0	—	0.08	0
Short-Term Notes	25,000,000	25,000,000	0.000024	20,000,000	20	1	0.16	20
Short-Term Assets	29,250,000	29,250,000	0.000029	25,000,000	15	1.2325	0.25	30
Assets Held for Maturity	100,000,000	100,000,000	0.000012	90,000,000	10	1.2000	0.25	30
Sukuk	300,000,000	300,000,000	0.00000066	275,000,000	8	0.16500	3.00	50
BBA Fixed Asset	164,750,000	164,750,000	0.00000054	150,000,000	9	0	10.00	80
BBA Floating	50,000,000	50,000,000	0.000007	49,000,000	2	0	10.00	70
AITAB	75,000,000	75,000,000	0.000000799	70,000,000	7	0	15.00	60
MM	60,000,000	60,000,000	0.0000006400	55,000,000	8	0	25.00	80
Musharakah	15,000,000	15,000,000	0.0000013300	—	100	0	5.00	100

TABLE 23.14 Asset Class by Risk Weightage

Asset Class	Amount	Risk Weightage (%)	RWA	Rationale	CAR (%)	k
Cash	25,000,000	0	0	Placed in commercial banks with A rating	8.00	—
Statutory Resrves	27,510,000	0	—	Placed with central bank	8.00	—
Short-Term Notes	25,590,000	20	5,118,000	Issued by central bank	8.00	409,440
Short-Term Assets	29,250,000	30	8,775,000	Issued by A-rated corporations	8.00	702,000
Assets Held for Sale	**100,000,000**	30	30,000,000	Issued by sovereign	8.00	2,400,000
Assets Held Until Maturity	100,000,000	50	50,000,000		8.00	4,000,000
Long-Term *Sukuk*				Issued by government-listed company		
Financing	590,650,000		425,520,000			
BBA Fixed Rate	164,750,000	80	131,800,000	Consumer	8.00	10,544,000
BBA Floating Rate	150,000,000	70	105,000,000	Commercial	8.00	8,400,000
AITAB	175,000,000	60	105,000,000	Commercial	8.00	8,400,000
Musharakah Mutanaqisah	85,900,000	80	68,720,000	Consumer	8.00	5,497,600
Mushjarikah	15,000,000	100	15,000,000	Commercial	8.00	1,200,000
	898,000,000		**519,413,000**	**Total Capital Needed**		**41,553,040**

TABLE 23.15 Expected Loss Calculations

Expected Loss							
Financing	**RW (%)**	**PD (%)**	**EAGD**	**Collateral**	**LGD**	**LRGD (%)**	**EL**
BBA Fixed Rate	80	0.30	164,750,000	100,000,000	64,750,000	39.30	194,250
BBA Floating Rate	70	0.20	150,000,000	40,000,000	110,000,000	73.33	220,000
AITAB	60	0.10	175,000,000	50,000,000	125,000,000	71.43	125,000
Musharakah Mutanaqisah	80	0.30	85,900,000	50,000,000	35,900,000	41.79	107,700
Mushjarikah	100	0.50	15,000,000		15,000,000	100.00	75,000
			Total Expected Loss				721,950

However, if 11 percent of the bank's assets lose all value, the bank's capital will be wiped out. It is unlikely for this to happen when banks engage in credit finance; however, when banks take increasingly leveraged positions on financial assets and positions on movements of oil prices, currency exchange rates, commodities prices, or any such asset that can be speculated in, banks can incur such huge losses that they can wipe out their capital and thus their ability to do business.

XYZ Islamic Bank is already highly leveraged; with capital of just $102 million it owns assets worth $900 million, a leverage ratio of 9:1. Leverage ratios of 22:1 are far more common in the banking industry today. XYZ Bank still has $58.447 million of unencumbered capital, and can actually finance assets worth close to $2 billion if its risk profile is the same as the assets on the balance sheet already. That would be a leverage ratio of 22:1.

Having understood how credit risk is measured and mitigated we turn our attention to the market risk. We invite the reader to view the guidelines offered by Bank Negara Malaysia on the subject. These have been listed for reference and further reading at the end of the chapter.

MARKET RISK

Market risk is the risk of losses being incurred by an Islamic bank when it experiences an increase in the costs of funds it mobilizes in order to fund short-term and long-term assets. The deposits or liabilities raised must fund assets that generate more returns than the costs of those liabilities, otherwise the bank will be doing negative business. Simply put, if banks raise expensive deposits of $100,000,000 at 5 percent and can only book assets worth $100,000,000 at 3 percent, the bank will be making a loss of 2 percent on the portfolio.

We examine the impact on XYZ Islamic Bank of a change in interest rates on its cost of funds and its revenues.

TABLE 23.16 Unexpected Loss Calculations

Unexpected Loss									
Financing	RW	EAGD	PD	Collateral	LRGD	1-PD	(PD)*(1-PD)	Sqrt (PD)*(1-PD)	UL
BBA Fixed Rate	80%	164,750,000	0.30%	100,000,000	39.30%	99.70%	0.30%	0.0547	3,541,002
BBA Floating Rate	70%	150,000,000	0.20%	40,000,000	20.00%	99.80%	0.20%	0.0447	1,340,298
AITAB	60%	175,000,000	0.10%	50,000,000	33.33%	99.90%	0.10%	0.0316	1,843,555
Musharakah Mutanaqisah	80%	85,900,000	0.30%	50,000,000	16.67%	99.70%	0.30%	0.0547	783,136
Mushjarikah	100%	15,000,000	0.50%		100.00%	99.50%	0.50%	0.0705	1,058,005
						Total Unexpected Loss			8,565,996

Scenario 1

The scenario in Table 23.17 looks at the income and expenses of XYZ Bank as a reference point.

Scenario 2

Scenario 2 in Table 23.18 examines the changes in the bank's income, if interest and subsequently imputed profit and rental rates increase by 1 percent.

Given an increase in interest rates in the market, we assume Islamic banking customers also demand higher profit rates on their deposits even in terms of *hibah*. However, the profit rates on all deposits cannot be changed immediately; within 90 days it is likely that profit rates would be increased by 1 percent.

Within that time frame, XYZ would be able to acquire new short-term notes from the market and increase the returns by 1 percent on its short-term assets. XYZ Bank, however, cannot change the profit rate built into *BBA* fixed rate contracts nor *musharakah mutanaqisah* contracts unless they have a floating rate mechanism in the contract structure.

The fixed rate contracts are like fixed rate loans on a bank's balance sheet and the pricing of such loans cannot be changed to accommodate movements in interest rates in the market. The bank is, however, paying 1 percent more on all deposits and therefore has an increased cost of fund of $41.261 million. Earnings on assets have also increased but only to $56.183 million. The impact of this increase is actually to reduce the net income of the bank to $13.199 million from $16.80 million.

However, if XYZ could alter the pricing on all its assets, the picture would look somewhat different and the Islamic bank would enjoy increased revenues of $17.731 million. The impact of interest rate changes will depend on how many liabilities on the bank's balance sheet are variable rate liabilities (VRL) and how many assets are variable rate assets (VRA). If a bank has more VRL than VRA, any increase in interest rates would increase cost of funds by a greater proportion than the bank could pass onto its borrowers by revising profit rates on contracts. Banks with rate-sensitive liabilities in excess of rate-sensitive assets lose spreads when interest rates are on the rise (Table 23.19).

Scenario 3

XYZ will experience a different fate when interest rates decline. XYZ in fact will earn higher spreads because of its balance of fixed rate assets and fixed rate liabilities as in Table 23.20.

TABLE 23.17 Islamic Bank Balance Sheet

Income Statement		Balance Sheet				Income Statement	
Income	Profit Rate	Assets		Liabilities		Profit Rate	Expense
12,500	0.05%	Cash	25,000,000	*Wadiah* Current Accounts	32,350,000	2%	647,000
—	0.00%	Statutory Reserves	27,510,000	*Wadiah* Savings Accounts	75,000,000	2%	647,000
511,800	2.00%	Short-Term Notes	25,590,000				
731,250	2.50%	Short-Term Assets	29,250,000				
1,255,550	S/T Profit	Total S/T Assets Funded by S/T Deposits	107,350,000	Total S/T Deposits	107,350,000	S/T Costs	1,294,000
3,000,000	3.00%	Assets Held for Sale	100,000,000				
		Total Short-Term Assets	207,350,000	Total Short-Term Liabilities	107,350,000		
6,000,000	6.00%	Assets Held Till Maturity	100,000,000	Commodity *Murabahah*	150,000,000	4%	6,000,000
		Long-Term *Sukuk*					
42,004,500	7.11%	Financing	590,650,000	*Mudharabah* Deposit I	200,000,000	5%	10,000,000
11,532,500	7.00%	*BBA* Fixed Rate	164,750,000	*Mudharabah* Deposit II	200,000,000	4.95%	9,900,000
10,875,000	7.25%	*BBA* Floating Rate	150,000,000	*Mudharabah* Deposit III	137,750,000	4.75%	6,543,125
11,375,000	6.50%	*AITAB*	175,000,000	Total Deposits	687,750,000		
6,872,000	8.00%	*Musharakah Mutanaqisah*	85,900,000	Interbank *Mudharabah*	2,900,000	5.50%	159,500
1,350,000	9.00%	*Mushjarakah*	15,000,000				

48,004,500	L/T Profit					L/T Costs	32,602,625
	5.82%	Total Long-Term Assets	690,650,000	Total Long-Term Liabilities	690,650,000		4.23%
52,260,050	Tot Profit Income	Total Financial Assets	898,000,000	Total Liabilities	798,000,000	Tot Proft Exp	33,737,125
2,000,000	Fee Income	Fixed Assets	2,000,000	Equity	102,000,000	Operating Exp	3,000,000
		Building				Impairment Exp	721,950
		Computers					
		Furniture					
54,260,050	Total Income	Total Assets	900,000,000	Total Liabilities + Equity	900,000,000	Total Expense	37,459,075
Spread							16,800,975

TABLE 23.18 Increasing Interest Rates

Income Statement		Balance Sheet				Income Statement	
Income	Profit Rate	Assets		Liabilities		Profit Rate	Expense
12,500	0.05%	Cash	25,000,000	*Wadiah* Current Accounts	32,350,000	3%	970,500
—	0.00%	Statutory Reserves	27,510,000	*Wadiah* Savings Accounts	75,000,000	3%	970,500
767,700	3.00%	Short-Term Notes	25,590,000				
1,023,750	3.50%	Short-Term Assets	29,250,000				
1,803,950	S/T Profit	Total S/T Assets Funded by S/T Deposits	107,350,000	Total S/T Deposits	107,350,000	S/T Costs	1,941,000
4,000,000	4.00%	Assets Held for Sale	100,000,000				
		Total Short-Term Assets	207,350,000	Total Short-Term Liabilities	107,350,000		
6,000,000	6.00%	Assets Held Till Maturity	100,000,000	Commodity *Murabahah*	150,000,000	5%	7,500,000
44,379,500	7.51%	Long-Term *Sukuk* Financing	590,650,000	*Mudharabah* Deposit I	200,000,000	6%	12,000,000
11,532,500	7.00%	*BBA* Fixed Rate	164,750,000	*Mudharabah* Deposit II	200,000,000	5.95%	11,900,000
12,375,000	8.25%	*BBA* Floating Rate	150,000,000	*Mudharabah* Deposit III	137,750,000	5.75%	7,920,625
12,250,000	7.00%	*AITAB* Floating	175,000,000	Total Deposits	687,750,000		
6,872,000	8.00%	*Musharakah Mutanaqisah*	85,900,000	Interbank *Mudharabah*	2,900,000	6.50%	188,500
1,350,000	9.00%	*Mushjarikah*	15,000,000				

50,379,500	L/T Profit					L/T Costs	39,509,125
	6.26%	Total Long-Term Assets	690,650,000	Total Long-Term Liabilities	690,650,000		5.17%
56,183,450	Tot Profit Income	Total Financial Assets	898,000,000	Total Liabilities	798,000,000	Tot Proft Exp	41,261,625
2,000,000	Fee Income	Fixed Assets	2,000,000	Equity	102,000,000	Operating Exp	3,000,000
		Building				Impairment Exp	721,950
		Computers					
		Furniture					
58,183,450	Total Income	Total Assets	900,000,000	Total Liabilities + Equity	900,000,000	Total Expense	44,983,575
						Spread	13,199,875

TABLE 23.19 Increased Interest Rates Again

Income Statement		Balance Sheet				Income Statement	
Income	Profit Rate	Assets		Liabilities		Profit Rate	Expense
12,500	0.05%	Cash	25,000,000	*Wadiah* Current Accounts	32,350,000	3%	970,500
—	0.00%	Statutory Reserves	27,510,000	*Wadiah* Savings Accounts	75,000,000	3%	970,500
767,700	3.00%	Short-Term Notes	25,590,000				
1,023,750	3.50%	Short-Term Assets	29,250,000				
1,803,950	S/T Profit	Total S/T Assets Funded by S/T Deposits	107,350,000	Total S/T Deposits	107,350,000	S/T Costs	1,941,000
4,000,000	4.00%	Assets Held for Sale	100,000,000				
		Total Short-Term Assets	207,350,000	Total Short-Term Liabilities	107,350,000		
7,000,000	7.00%	Assets Held Till Maturity	100,000,000	Commodity *Murabahah*	150,000,000	5%	7,500,000
47,911,000	8.11%	Long-Term *Sukuk* Financing	590,650,000	*Mudharabah* Deposit I	200,000,000	6%	12,000,000
13,180,000	8.00%	*BBA* Fixed Rate	164,750,000	*Mudharabah* Deposit II	200,000,000	5.95%	11,900,000
12,375,000	8.25%	*BBA* Floating Rate	150,000,000	*Mudharabah* Deposit III	137,750,000	5.75%	7,920,625
13,125,000	7.50%	*AITAB* Floating	175,000,000	Total Deposits	687,750,000		
7,731,000	9.00%	*Musharakah Mutanaqisah*	85,900,000	Interbank *Mudharabah*	2,900,000	6.50%	188,500
1,500,000	10.00%	*Mushjarikah*	15,000,000				

54,911,000	L/T Profit					L/T Costs	39,509,125
	6.76%	Total Long-Term Assets	690,650,000	Total Long-Term Liabilities	690,650,000		5.17%
60,714,950	Tot Profit Income	Total Financial Assets	898,000,000	Total Liabilities	798,000,000	Tot Proft Exp	41,261,625
2,000,000	Fee Income	Fixed Assets	2,000,000	Equity	102,000,000	Operating Exp	3,000,000
		Building				Impairment Exp	721,950
		Computers					
		Furniture					
62,714,950	Total Income	Total Assets	900,000,000	Total Liabilities + Equity	900,000,000	Total Expense	44,983,575
						Spread	17,731,375

TABLE 23.20 Decreasing Rates

Income Statement		Balance Sheet				Income Statement	
Income	Profit Rate	Assets		Liabilities		Profit Rate	Expense
12,500	0.05%	Cash	25,000,000	*Wadiah* Current Accounts	32,350,000	1%	323,500
—	0.00%	Statutory Reserves	27,510,000	*Wadiah* Savings Accounts	75,000,000	1%	323,500
255,900	1.00%	Short-Term Notes	25,590,000				
438,750	1.50%	Short-Term Assets	29,250,000				
707,150	S/T Profit	Total S/T Assets Funded by S/T Deposits	107,350,000	Total S/T Deposits	107,350,000	S/T Costs	647,000
3,000,000	3.00%	Assets Held for Sale	100,000,000				
		Total Short-Term Assets	207,350,000	Total Short-Term Liabilities	107,350,000		
6,000,000	6.00%	Assets Held Till Maturity	100,000,000	Commodity *Murabahah*	150,000,000	3%	4,500,000
38,754,500	6.56%	Long-Term *Sukuk* Financing	590,650,000	*Mudharabah* Deposit I	200,000,000	4%	8,000,000
11,532,500	7.00%	*BBA* Fixed Rate	164,750,000	*Mudharabah* Deposit II	200,000,000	3.95%	7,900,000
9,375,000	6.25%	*BBA* Floating Rate	150,000,000	*Mudharabah* Deposit III	137,750,000	3.75%	5,165,625
9,625,000	5.50%	*AITAB* Floating	175,000,000	Total Deposits	687,750,000		
6,872,000	8.00%	*Musharakah Mutanaqisah*	85,900,000	Interbank *Mudharabah*	2,900,000	4.50%	130,500
1,350,000	9.00%	*Mushjarikah*	15,000,000				

44,754,500	L/T Profit 5.40%	Total Long-Term Assets	690,650,000	Total Long-Term Liabilities	690,650,000	L/T Costs	25,696,125 3.28%
48,461,650	Tot Profit Income	Total Financial Assets	898,000,000	Total Liabilities	798,000,000	Tot Proft Exp	26,212,625
2,000,000	Fee Income	Fixed Assets Building Computers Furniture	2,000,000	Equity	102,000,000	Operating Exp Impairment Exp	3,000,000 721,950
50,461,650	Total Income	Total Assets	900,000,000	Total Liabilities + Equity	900,000,000	Total Expense	29,934,575
						Spread	20,527,075

With its negative income gap created by a surplus of VRL over VRA, the decrease in interest rates in the market lowers the bank's cost of funds to $26.212 million, whereas the bank does not revise downward expected returns on its *sukuk* or its *BBA* fixed portfolio or its *musharakah mutanaqisah* portfolio, either. Revenues fall to $48.461 million, against a drop in costs to $26.212 million, giving the bank an increased spread of $20.527 million.

Changes in interest rates affect Islamic banks more than conventional banks as many Islamic financing contracts do not allow for changes in the profit rate imputed in contracts. In such a case a regime of increasing rates adversely affects Islamic banks and a regime of decreasing rates positively affects Islamic banks. The way to mitigate market risk is to have a balance between rate-sensitive assets and rate-sensitive liabilities.

Islamic banks are faced with market risk on the basis of the changes in the values of the assets they hold on their balance sheet. Changes in interest rates not only affect the yields on receivables and the cost of funds used to fund these receivables but also impact the market value of assets such as equities and fixed income instruments. An increase in interest rates may see a flight of capital from equities markets into fixed income instruments, thus affecting the values of any stocks an Islamic bank may hold on its balance sheets. The increase in interest rates may also affect the value of the *sukuk* held by the bank on its balance sheet. The change in the value of these instruments would affect the earnings generated by the sale of these instruments.

Islamic banks are also exposed to the risks associated with changing values in the currencies they hold. Islamic banks typically hold various international currencies in their portfolios. The exchange rates on these currencies fluctuate on the basis of interest rates, changes in exports and imports, changes in political situations, and a host of other factors. Conventional banks typically are able to hedge these risks using various instruments such as options, but *shariah* scholars are averse to these instruments, which are typically known as *derivatives*.[5] Such instruments exist to hedge against adverse price movements in equities and fixed income instruments; however, Islamic banks are yet to develop a product menu acceptable to *shariah* scholars to adequately address the exposures undertaken.

Conventional banks have devised models to evaluate their exposure to risks using the concept of *value at risk*, which is beyond the scope of this book and may be the subject of subsequent editions.

[5]O. I. Bacha (1999), "Derivative Instruments and Islamic Finance: Some Thoughts for a Reconsideration," *Journal of Islamic Financial Services*, Vol. 1(1), pp. 9–25.

LIQUIDITY RISK

Balance sheet imbalances occur when there is a mismatch in short-term assets and short-term liabilities and between long-term assets and long-term liabilities. Islamic banks are required to maintain a "healthy" amount of assets in short-term investments, to provide a liquidity cushion in case debt-based assets default, and investment-based assets need to be converted into cash on a short notice. XYZ Bank in Table 23.21 has $210.550 million in short-term assets, of which $100 million are funded by capital and $110.55 million by depositors; $210.5 million of short-term assets is equivalent 23 percent of total assets. These assets also do not generate very high returns for the bank because they are short-term liquid assets. Banks would require that these assets be funded by either capital or very low-cost funds. This creates a dependency of all banks on what the industry calls *CASA* (Current Account and Savings Accounts). Although these funds are payable on demand, they are the cheapest source of funds for banks.

The example earlier indicates the impact on XYZ's balance sheet of not being able to source enough CASA funds and thereby having to rely on expensive funds in commodity *murabahah* and *mudharabah* deposits to fund even short-term assets. The impact of this change in the composition of funds is referred to as *liquidity risk*, and it is very visible in reduced net earnings for the bank of $14.30 million. In countries where private savings are channeled through insurance plans or centrally managed provident fund programs, retail customers, which are the backbone of CASA depositors, are scarce. Personal savings are pooled into institutional savings plans and these funds are then invested in fixed deposit schemes that demand high profit rates. In such situations banks are constantly struggling to raise CASA low-cost deposits.

PROFIT-SHARING INVESTMENT ACCOUNT

Related to the bank's exposure to credit risk, market risk, and liquidity risk, we discuss another method apart from the *al-bai* concept, which involves a one-off sale price with either spot or deferred payments. This is done through a profit-sharing investment account (PSIA), which is based on, for instance, the contract of *musharakah*. Introduced by the Islamic Financial Services Board, PSIA can be considered an equity deposit behaving like a mutual fund,[6] with no guarantee on either the principal amount or the profit.

[6]International Centre for Education in Islamic Finance (INCEIF), *Risk Management of Islamic Financial Institutions* Module Book, IB2002.

TABLE 23.21 Liquidity Risk

Income Statement		Balance Sheet				Income Statement	
Income	Profit Rate	Assets		Liabilities		Profit Rate	Expense
12,500	0.05%	Cash	25,000,000	*Wadiah* Current Accounts	2,350,000	2%	47,000
—	0.00%	Statutory Reserves	30,710,000	*Wadiah* Savings Accounts	25,000,000	2%	47,000
511,800	2.00%	Short-Term Notes	25,590,000				
731,250	2.50%	Short-Term Assets	29,250,000				
1,255,550	S/T Profit	Total S/T Assets Funded by S/T Deposits	110,550,000	Total S/T Deposits	27,350,000	S/T Costs	94,000
3,000,000	3.00%	Assets Held for Sale	100,000,000	Deficit	83,200,000		
		Total Short-Term Assets	210,550,000	Total Short-Term Liabilities	27,350,000		
6,000,000	6.00%	Assets Held Till Maturity	100,000,000	Commodity *Murabahah*	180,000,000	4%	7,200,000
42,004,500	7.11%	Long-Term *Sukuk* Financing	590,650,000	*Mudharabah* Deposit I	250,000,000	5%	12,500,000
11,532,500	7.00%	*BBA* Fixed Rate	164,750,000	*Mudharabah* Deposit II	200,000,000	4.95%	9,900,000
10,875,000	7.25%	*BBA* Floating Rate	150,000,000	*Mudharabah* Deposit III	137,750,000	4.75%	6,543,125
11,375,000	6.50%	*AITAB* Floating	175,000,000	Total Deposits	767,750,000		
6,872,000	8.00%	*Musharakah Mutanaqisah*	85,900,000	Interbank *Mudharabah*	2,900,000	5.50%	159,500
1,350,000	9.00%	*Mushjarikah*	15,000,000				

48,004,500	L/T Profit 5.80%	Total Long-Term Assets	690,650,000	Total Long-Term Liabilities	770,650,000	L/T Costs	36,302,625 4.54%
52,260,050	Tot Profit Income	Total Financial Assets	901,200,000	Total Liabilities	798,000,000	Tot Proft Exp	36,237,125
2,000,000	Fee Income	Fixed Assets	2,000,000	Equity	102,000,000	Operating Exp	3,000,000
		Building				Impairment Exp	721,950
		Computers					
		Furniture					
54,260,050	Total Income	Total Assets	903,200,000	Total Liabilities + Equity	900,000,000	Total Expense	39,959,075
						Spread	14,300,975

By sharing the risk exposure between *sharik A* (Party A—the bank) and *sharik B* (Party B—the customers) the use of PSIA can result in a lower capital charge as compared to the normal *al-bai* trading model. We see the implications of utilizing PSIA in the illustration below.

To find how much regulatory capital is needed with regard to the PSIA financing, the following formula is used:

$$\text{CAR} = \frac{\text{Regulated Capital}}{\begin{array}{r}(\text{RWA} - (1-\alpha)\text{RWA Funded by PSIA}\\ -(\alpha)\text{RWA Funded by PSIA as PER})\end{array}}$$

The risk absorbent alpha (α) defines the risk inherent and carried by the bank (this includes business risk as well). An α of 1 would mean that the bank is the one solely carrying the whole risk and an α of 0 would mean that the risk would be borne solely by the account holder. Suppose XYZ Islamic Bank has the assets in Table 23.22; assuming the PER amount is \$5 million and the α is 30 percent or 0.3, the capital needed would be:

$$0.08 = \frac{\text{Regulated Capital}}{(\$1025 \text{ million} - (1-0.3)\$500 \text{ million} - (0.3)\$5 \text{ million})}$$

$$\text{Regulated Capital} = 0.08\,(\$1025 \text{ million} - (1-0.3)\$500 \text{ million} - (0.3)\$5 \text{ million})$$

$$\text{Regulated Capital} = 0.08\,(\$1025 \text{ million} - \$350 \text{ million} - \$1.5 \text{ million})$$

$$\text{Regulated Capital} = \$53.88 \text{ million}$$

Now, we compare this with a situation in which the α is 1 and gives us a required capital buffer of 0.08*\$1,025 million = \$82 million. Hence XYZ Islamic Bank can enjoy a form of saving on the regulatory capital buffer of around \$28 million and use this amount for other financing facilities or investments.

TABLE 23.22 Asset Structure XYZ Islamic Bank

Asset	Amount (\$)	Risk Weight (%)	RWA (\$)
Murabahah	600 million	50	300 million
Ijarah	450 million	50	225 million
Musharaka	200 million	250	500 million
Total	1,250 million		1,025 million

In the case of PSIA depositors, the risk that is supposed to be borne completely by the bank is shared with the depositors. This would have an implication for the profit rate expectations by the depositors, which should be higher than those deposits under the contract of *wadiah* or general *mudarabah*. This topic, however, is beyond the scope of this chapter and is discussed later.

CONCLUSION

We have addressed the issues of credit risk, market risk, and liquidity risk. Islamic banks are exposed to much the same risks as conventional banks. In fact, until the development of a floating rate mechanism, Islamic banks were exceedingly vulnerable to market risk. The one subject we have not addressed is *shariah risk*, which is aptly covered in *Shari'ah Non-compliance Risk Management and Legal Documentations in Islamic Finance* (John Wiley & Sons) by Ahcene Lahsasna. The subject of risk deserves a book of its own and we hope to indulge the reader's interest in that area with subsequent publications.

REFERENCES

Risk-Weighted Capital Adequacy Framework (Basel 1—Risk-Weighted Assets Computation) **updated 10/23/2009.

Capital Adequacy Framework for Islamic Banks (Risk-Weighted Assets) ** effective January 1, 2013; i. Attachment 1—Reporting Manual; ii. Attachment 2—Reporting Templates.

Capital Adequacy Framework (Basel II—Risk-Weighted Assets) ** effective January 1, 2013; i. Attachment 1—Credit Risk Reporting Templates, Manual and Implementation Guidance; ii. Attachment 2—Operational Risk Reporting Templates and Manual; iii. Attachment 3—Market Risk Reporting Templates and Manual.

Risk Weighted Capital Adequacy Framework (Basel II)—Disclosure Requirements ** updated 08/13/2010.

Guidelines on Recognition and Measurement of Profit Sharing Investment Account as Risk Absorbent **updated 07/26/2011.

Capital Adequacy Framework (Capital Components) ** effective January 1, 2013.

CHAPTER 24

Asset/Liability Management for Islamic Banks

We could refer to this chapter as vanilla asset/liability management as Islamic banks still rely on traditional modes of funding, which is deposits. Conventional banks also rely on interbank borrowing, repos, reverse repos, swaps, and a host of other products to fund their assets. Islamic banks have yet to develop products that offer alternative sources of funding.[1]

We look at the basic problem faced by banks in general while funding their asset book. As always we illustrate our point by using an example. For illustrative purposes we refer to our familiar ABC Bank, which has the following assets and liabilities. In reality, a bank's balance sheets are far more complex, but the most complex of problems can be broken down to simple steps to develop one's comprehension.

ABC Bank has (for simplicity's sake) pooled its assets into three brackets as shown in Table 24.1. One bracket is of 30 days and contains $980 worth of assets, the other bracket is for 60 days and has $850 worth of assets. The last bracket is for 90 days and has $1,260 worth of assets. These assets generate returns, but need to be funded by liabilities. We shall assume that ABC Bank sources funds from deposits only and these are also mobilized as fixed deposits with three varying tenors. These tenors are 30 days, 60 days, and 90 days. The 30-day tenor has $380 in deposits, the 60-day tenor has $430 in deposits, and the 90-day tenor has $1,120 in deposits.

To summarize, the bank has three basic brackets for assets and liabilities. These are 30-day, 60-day, and 90-day brackets. However, the amount

---

[1]Hands down the primary source book for this discussion for conventional banks is Moorad Choudhry's *Bank Asset and Liability Management: Strategy, Trading and Analysis* (Singapore: John Wiley & Sons, 2007). Moorad is an authority on this subject and writes with clarity and simplicity on the most complex of topics.

TABLE 24.1 ABC Bank Funding Book

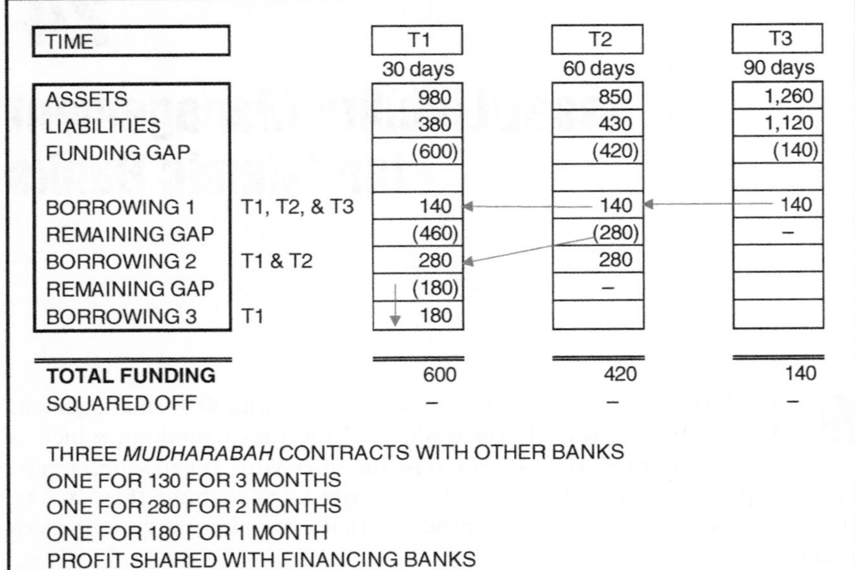

TIME		T1 30 days	T2 60 days	T3 90 days
ASSETS		980	850	1,260
LIABILITIES		380	430	1,120
FUNDING GAP		(600)	(420)	(140)
BORROWING 1	T1, T2, & T3	140	140	140
REMAINING GAP		(460)	(280)	–
BORROWING 2	T1 & T2	280	280	
REMAINING GAP		(180)	–	
BORROWING 3	T1	180		
TOTAL FUNDING		600	420	140
SQUARED OFF		–	–	–

THREE *MUDHARABAH* CONTRACTS WITH OTHER BANKS
ONE FOR 130 FOR 3 MONTHS
ONE FOR 280 FOR 2 MONTHS
ONE FOR 180 FOR 1 MONTH
PROFIT SHARED WITH FINANCING BANKS

of assets in each bracket varies from the amount of deposits available in that respective bracket. The difference between assets and liabilities within a specific bracket is known as a *funding gap*. The funding gap is the difference between the assets in a particular bracket and the liabilities in that bracket. The 30-day funding gap is $600, the 60-day funding gap is $420, and the 90-day funding gap is $140.

To fund these gaps, ABC Bank funds are raised under the contract of *mudharabah* from other Islamic banks that offer funds for various tenors at various rates. The market for these interbank fundings is referred to as the Islamic Interbank Money Market (IIMM).[2] ABC Bank funds its deficit with the surplus funds of other Islamic banks and shares the returns on the assets funded through a profit-sharing ratio.

The bank will receive funding for $140 for 90 days to cover the funding gap to finance assets with a maturity of 90 days. This amount will also cover part of the funding gap for 30 days and 60 days.

With the $140 day funds, the bank now has covered its 90-day funding gap; the 60-day funding gap is subsequently reduced by $140 to

[2]For more information on IIMM, visit http://iimm.bnm.gov.my.

($420–$140) and remains at $280. The 30-day funding gap is also reduced from $600 by $140 and falls to $460. ABC Bank then takes an additional $280 from the Interbank Money Market for 60 days. The impact of this second borrowing is to eliminate the 60-day funding gap altogether and to lower the 30-day funding gap to $180. Finally, ABC Bank takes $180 from the money markets under *mudharabah* contracts for 30 days and eliminates the 30-day gap as well.

What is important to understand here is that funds raised for 90 days also partially cover the bank's position for shorter tenors such as 60 days or 30 days. Funds borrowed for a 60-day period also cover the bank's position for 30 days.

In this manner ABC bank enters into three separate contracts for three separate tenors. It mobilizes $140 for 90 days from an Islamic bank under a *mudharabah* contract, which has its own terms and conditions such as profit-sharing ratio and expected return or indicative return. It is obvious that the returns committed to the advancing bank will be a function of the returns ABC Bank will earn on its own assets, which have maturities of 90 days.

The returns offered to another Islamic bank for advancing ABC Bank money for 90 days will be higher than the returns offered to ABC Bank's customers as the advancing bank will share a percentage of the returns earned from entering into such *mudharabah* arrangements with its own customers.

We elaborate this final point by looking at the 90-day contract closely. For illustrative purposes, we assume ABC Bank receives funds from XYZ Bank, which has a surplus of $140 as in Table 24.2.

ABC Bank enters into a *mudharabah* contract with XYZ Bank for $140 for 90 days with a profit-sharing ratio of 80:20. In essence, ABC Bank will pass on 80 percent of its earnings from assets worth $140 to XYZ as XYZ is funding these assets from its balance sheet. XYZ Bank will earn $1.60 ($140 × 5.80 percent × 365/90 × 80 percent) in 90 days as its share of the income of ABC Bank. This reflects a return of 1.143 percent (on a quarterly basis). If ABC Bank were to source $140 not from another Islamic bank but from its own depositors, it would pay 2.90 percent on an annual basis or 0.71 percent on a quarterly basis for these funds. Sourcing funds from

TABLE 24.2 ABC Bank and XYZ Bank Comparisons

	XYZ Bank			ABC Bank	
	90 Days	Returns		90 Days	
Assets	900	6.00%	Assets	1,260	5.80%
Liabilities	1,040	3.00%	Liabilities	1,120	2.90%
Surplus	140		Deficit	140	

depositors would only incur an expense of $.994. As one can see, sourcing funds from other Islamic banks is more expensive than sourcing from one's own depositors. The reason for this is quite simple. XYZ Bank has to share its income of $1.60 with its depositors as, after all, it is their funds that are placed with ABC Bank. So if XYZ Bank has an 80:20 profit-sharing ratio with its depositors, then $1.28 will be credited to XYZ's *mudharabah* account holders and $.32 will be recorded in the income of XYZ Bank.

Just to put this transaction into practical context, the reader can multiply the numbers by $100,000,000 as that is a number that better reflects the scale of single interbank transactions.

The same rationale can be applied to explaining 60-day and 30-day funding as well as to understand why taking funds from another bank is more expensive than from one's own customers

Table 24.3 examines another funding gap issue[3] and provides a slightly more complicated scenario.

The funding gap for 30 days is only $280, for 60 days it is $650, and for 90 days it is $50 only. The bank now raises $50 for 90 days, which squares off its books for 90 days, but leaves a residual funding gap of $600 for 60 days, and of $230 for 30 days. If the bank raised $600 for 60 days, it will be in a surplus for 30 days, so instead the bank raises $230 for 60 days. This covers the 30-day position and leaves a residual gap of $370 for 60-day

TABLE 24.3 Funding the Funding Gap

TIME		T1	T2	T3
ASSETS		1,000	850	1,250
LIABILITIES		720	200	1,200
FUNDING GAP		(280)	(650)	(50)
BORROWING 1	T1, T2, & T3	50	50	50
REMAINING GAP		(230)	(600)	–
BORROWING 2	T1 & T2	230	230	
REMAINING GAP		–	(370)	
BORROWING 3	T2		370	
TOTAL FUNDING		280	650	50
SQUARED OFF		–	–	–
THREE *MUDHARABAH* CONTRACTS WITH OTHER BANKS				
ONE FOR 50 FOR 3 MONTHS				
ONE FOR 200 FOR 2 MONTHS				
ONE FOR 390 FOR 1 MONTH IN T2				
PROFIT SHARED WITH FINANCING BANKS				

[3]Choudhry, *Bank Asset and Liability Management Strategy*.

assets. **The bank now raises $370 for 30 days, 30 days from today, to cover this gap** and squares its position for 60 days as well in this manner.

Essentially the treasury of the bank will have three unique transactions. It will raise $50 for 90 days today at the spot rate applicable for 90 days. The bank will raise $230 today for 60 days at the 60-day spot rate. However, the bank will raise funds for 30 days one month from now to cover the funding gap in the 60-day bracket; these funds will be raised at the 30-day futures rate, one month from now. Three different rates will apply here, two spot rates and one forward rate.

GAP LIMIT

To revert back to our discussion on funding gaps, banks, including Islamic banks, have limits on the gap that can be tolerated for each tenor bracket. This limit is expressed as a percentage of total liabilities, and for the bank in the example in Table 24.4 it is tabulated as 20 percent. This means the funding gap in any bracket cannot be more than 20 percent of total liabilities. As per the bank's data in Figure 24.1, it is well within its limits for all tenors.

SPOT RATES AND FORWARD RATES

Spot rates are interest rates for various tenors offered today; forward rates are interest rates offered or exchanged or traded on contracts that are for specific tenors but will be initiated in the future. A spot rate on a 30-day deposit

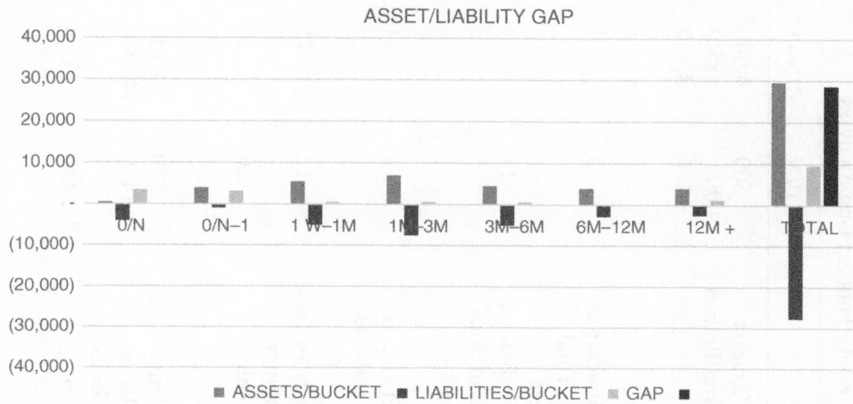

FIGURE 24.1 Illustration of Funding Gap

TABLE 24.4 Funding Gap Analyses

	0/N	0/N–1	1 W–1M	1M–3M	3M–6M	6M–12M	12M +	Total
Assets/Bracket	500	4,000	5,500	7,000	4,500	4,000	4,000	29,500
Liabilities/Bracket	(4,000)	(850)	(5,000)	(7,500)	(5,000)	(2,800)	(2,500)	(27,650)
Gap	3,466	3,150	500	*625*	*575*	*46*	*1,142*	9,504 28,650
Asset Bracket as % of Total Assets	2	14	19	24	15	14	14	100
Liability Bracket as % of Total Liabilities	14	3	18	27	18	10	9	100
Bracket Gap as % of Total Gap	36	33	5	7	6	0	12	100
Gap as % of Total Liabilities	12	11	2	2	2	0	4	
Gap Limit (%)	20	20	20	20	20	20	20	
Cumulative Assets	500	4,500	10,000	17,000	21,500	25,500	29,500	
Cumulative Liabilities	(4,000)	(4,850)	(9,850)	(17,350)	(22,350)	(25,150)	(27,650)	
Net Gap	(3,500)	(350)	150	(350)	(850)	350	1,850	

may be 4 percent on January 1, 2014. However, a spot rate for 30 days on February 1, 2014, may be either 4.1 percent if profit rates are expected to rise or 3.9 percent if profit rates are expected to decline. Forward rates reflect future expectations, and today's forward rates should be tomorrow's spot rates. It is crucial for banks to correctly estimate future rates. If profit rates are expected to increase, it is better for banks to fund future gaps by entering into contracts at today's rates. If, however, rates are expected to increase, banks should wait until the markets offer new rates before funding gaps.

As Islamic banks use the contract of *mudharabah* for funding their assets, the profit-sharing ratio (PSR) is altered for every contract term. For instance, the PSR maybe 80:20 for 30-day *mudharabah*, for 60 days it may be 85:15, and for 90 days it may be 90:20.

Given that billions of dollars are traded daily in money markets, such correct forecast of future rates can earn banks a tidy sum of money.

FUNDING SCENARIOS

In order to fund an asset of $100,000,000 for 90 days, an Islamic bank has four options to enter into *mudharabah* contracts. The bank can either enter into three contracts of 30 days each (Option A), or one contract for 30 days and one contract for 60 days using the *mudharabah* rate of 60-day contracts, 30 days from now (Option B). Option C allows the Islamic bank to enter in to one 60-day *mudharabah* contract at 60-day spot rates and one 30-day contract 60 days from now at a future *mudharabah* rate. Option D allows the bank to enter into one 90-day contract at today's 90-day spot rates. The illustration of this in Table 24.5 assumes that rates are increasing. Option A seems to be the lowest-cost option for the bank to fund the 90-day asset.

Table 24.6 demonstrates a similar funding problem albeit with decreasing rates. Despite the decreasing rates, the most effective option is for the bank to enter into three contracts for 30 days each. The two illustrations aim at illustrating the importance of spot rates and forward rates.

SHORT-TERM AND LONG-TERM RATES

No discussion on banking is complete without an understanding of short-term and long-term profit rates. I request that the reader indulge the author and allow the author to use conventional terms as they help present the argument more elegantly. The relationships between short-term and long-term rates are crucial to banks as they essentially borrow short and lend long. Funds are sourced for 1 day to 180 days and then lent out

TABLE 24.5 Increasing Rates

	INCREASING RATES						100,000,000					TOTAL
NOW	PSR		A	5.00%	5.10%	5.20%						
30 DAY RATE	80:20	5.00%		30	30	30		416,667	425,000	433,333		1,275,000
60 DAY RATE	85:15	5.50%										
90 DAY RATE	90:10	6.00%	B	5.00%	5.60%							
				30	60			416,667		933,333		1,350,000
IN 30 DAYS			C	5.50%		5.20%						
30 DAY RATE	81:19	5.10%		60		30			916,667	433,333		1,350,000
60 DAY RATE	86:14	5.60%										
90 DAY RATE	91:09	6.10%										
			D		6.00%					1,500,000		1,500,000
					90							
IN 60 DAYS												
30 DAY RATE	82:18	5.20%										
60 DAY RATE	87:13	5.70%										
90 DAY RATE	92:08	6.20%										

TABLE 24.6 Decreasing Rates

	DECREASING RATES	
NOW	PSR	
30 DAY RATE	80:20	5.30%
60 DAY RATE	85:15	5.50%
90 DAY RATE	90:10	5.60%
IN 30 DAYS		
30 DAY RATE	81:19	4.90%
60 DAY RATE	86:14	5.00%
90 DAY RATE	91:09	5.90%
IN 60 DAYS		
30 DAY RATE	82:18	4.30%
60 DAY RATE	87:13	4.80%
90 DAY RATE	92:08	5.30%

100,000,000	Rates	Periods (days)				TOTAL
A	5.30% / 4.90% / 4.30%	30 / 30 / 30	441,667	408,333	358,333	1,208,333
B	5.30% / 5.00%	30 / 60	441,667	833,333		1,275,000
C	5.50% / 4.30%	60 / 30	916,667	358,333		1,275,000
D	5.60%	90	1,400,000			1,400,000

for 1 year to 30 years. Long-term profit rates are typically higher than short-term rates for a very simple reason: opportunity costs.

Social behavioral theory would argue that for an individual to defer consumption of one unit of a good today, the incentive offered for deferring consumption today and saving resources would be to enjoy consumption of two units in the future.[4] If the same individual were to defer consumption today of one unit for only one unit tomorrow, there would be no incentive to do so.

So if a bank asks a customer to place money for one month or three months, it must offer higher rates on the three months' product to compensate the customer for deferring their consumption, and for allowing the bank to generate more returns in the longer term of 90 days.

There is also a mathematical logic to why long-term rates are higher than short-term rates. We illustrate this point by using a simple example.

An investor wishes to place $100,000 for one year with a bank. The bank offers the investor 3 percent for one year or T1, as in Table 24.7. At the end of the year the customer earns 3 percent profit of $3,000, and adds this back to the principal investment of $100,000, making the new total

TABLE 24.7 Rollover of Investments

1 YEAR INVESTMENTS	100,000	103,000	106,090	109,273
		3.00%	3.00%	3.00%
		T1	T2	T3
2 YEAR INVESTMENTS AT 6%	100,000		106,000	
		6.00%		
		T1	T2	
2 YEAR INVESTMENTS AT 6.09%	100,000		106,090	
		6.09%		
		T1	T2	
3 YEAR INVESTMENTS AT 9%	100,000			109,000
			9.00%	
		T1	T2	T3
3 YEAR INVESTMENTS AT 9.27%	100,000			109,273
			9.27%	
		T1	T2	T3

[4] Boris Heinrich, *Institutions, Behaviour and Economic Theory: A Contribution to Classical-Keynesian Political Economy* (Melbourne: Cambridge University Press, 1997).

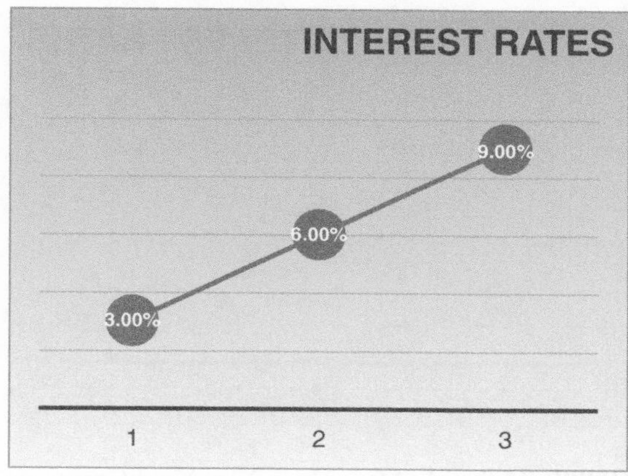

FIGURE 24.2 Simple Three-Year Yield Curve

$103,000, and invests this money for another year. At the end of the second year the investor earns $106,090 and repeats the same process and earns $109,273 at the end of the third year.

Alternatively, the bank can offer the investor a one-year product with a return of 3 percent, or a two-year product with a return of 6.09 percent, or a third-year return of 9.27 percent. Although it seems the bank is offering higher returns, it is in fact only offering 3 percent return for each one-year investment but is taking into account that at each year, earned profit will be added to the principal amount and reinvested. In effect, the bank is still offering 3 percent on investments for one year. The three-year yield curve would look something like Figure 24.2.

If the bank mobilized a deposit for one year, it would pay 3 percent for that deposit, using the short end of the yield curve to price its product. However, if the bank were to lend the money out for three years, it would use the long end of the yield curve and price the three-year loan at 9.27 percent at least. At this rate the bank would actually be making 0 spreads as it will in effect pay 9.27 percent for the deposit over a three-year period if the same depositor rolls over funds every year. If each year the bank mobilized funds at 3 percent per year, the bank would pay 9 percent for funds over three years and enjoy a spread of just 0.27 percent.

The slope of a yield curve reflects the added profit a bank must pay to convince an investor to place funds for each additional unit of time. Our earlier example illustrates that for every one-year interval the customer is willing to earn a 3 percent return; however, the customer may feel that after the first year, if the bank wishes to retain funds for another year, the bank must offer 7 percent return for two years to reward the investor for deferring consumption or utilization of funds for two years. Recall that even paying

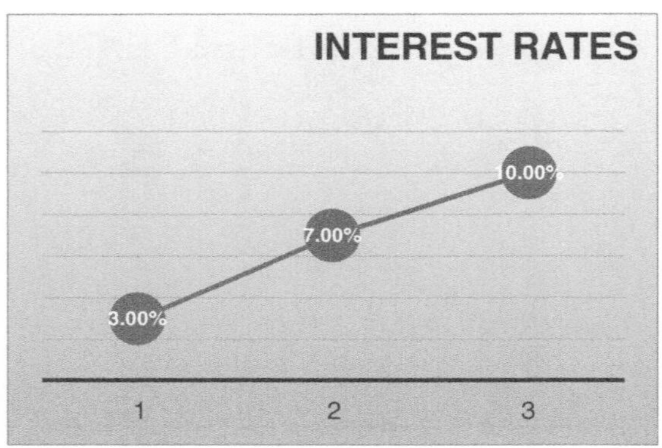

FIGURE 24.3 Modified Three-Year Yield Curve

6.09 percent for two years is the same as paying 3 percent for each year if the investor reinvests all principal and interest each subsequent year. Similarly, the investor may demand 10 percent for a three-year investment.

Figure 24.3 shows what the yield curve would look like in this case.

Consumers and investors may demand higher returns for equal periods of time that are combined into single long tenors. For instance, a customer may accept 3 percent per annum for a fixed deposit of three years and may settle for 3 percent per annum for the first three years of a five-year fixed deposit, but would likely demand 4 percent for the additional two years. This would make the five-year deposit pay a return of 3.4 percent per annum.

The yield curve in Figure 24.4 reflects a steady increase in demand for returns of $0.02 for every $1 investment per day.

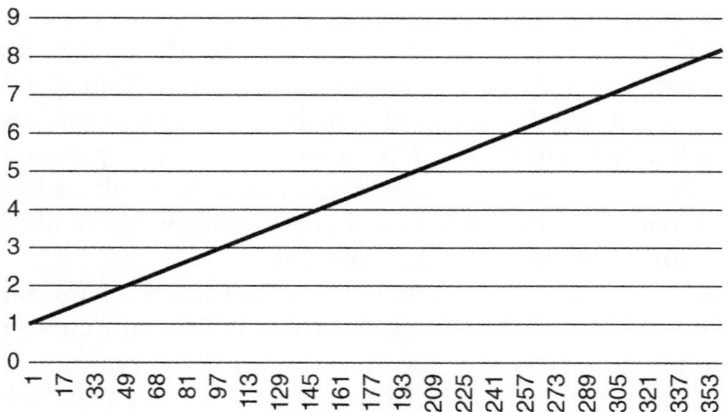

FIGURE 24.4 Constant Increase of $0.02 per Day

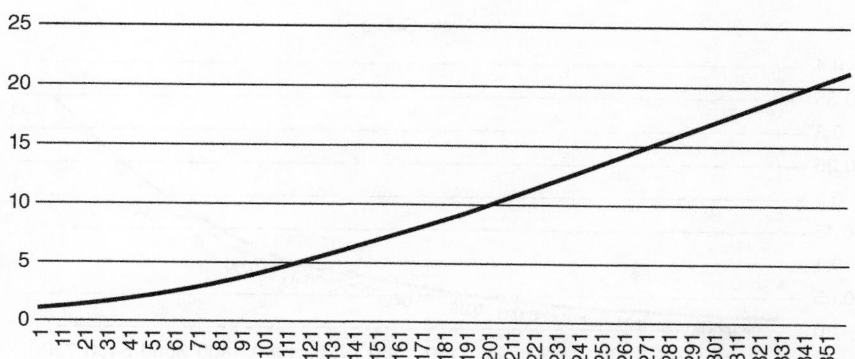

FIGURE 24.5 Increase at Regular Intervals

TABLE 24.8 Interest Rate Table

	1			0.25%		Elasticity	1.750%
	7	6	600%	0.50	0.25%	0.000417	2.000
	15	8	114	0.60	0.10	0.000875	2.100
	30	15	100	0.75	0.15	0.0015	2.250
	60	30	100	1.00	0.25	0.0025	2.500
	90	30	50	1.50	0.50	0.01	3.000
	180	90	100	1.75	0.25	0.0025	3.250
1	360	180	100	2.00	0.25	0.0025	3.500
2	720	360	100	3.00	1.00	0.01	4.500
3	1080	360	50	3.50	0.50	0.01	5.000
5	1800	720	67	5.00	1.50	0.0225	6.500
10	3600	1800	100	9.00	4.00	0.04	10.500
15	5400	1800	50	13.00	4.00	0.08	14.500
20	7200	1800	33	15.00	2.00	0.06	16.500

The yield curve in Figure 24.5 reflects varying demands in returns over a 365-day period, with the required return increasing with tenor.

Table 24.8 illustrates a fictitious case of how returns on deposits increase with tenor ranging from overnight deposits to 20-year investments. The column of elasticity measures the sensitivity of rates to increases in spans of tenor, or how sensitive are interest rates as tenors get longer. This is also a measure of the slope of the yield curve in Figure 24.6, and we can see this number increase dramatically as tenors begin to increase.

The workings in Table 24.9 simply consolidate some of the concepts we have studied already. Our Islamic bank in this case has total assets worth

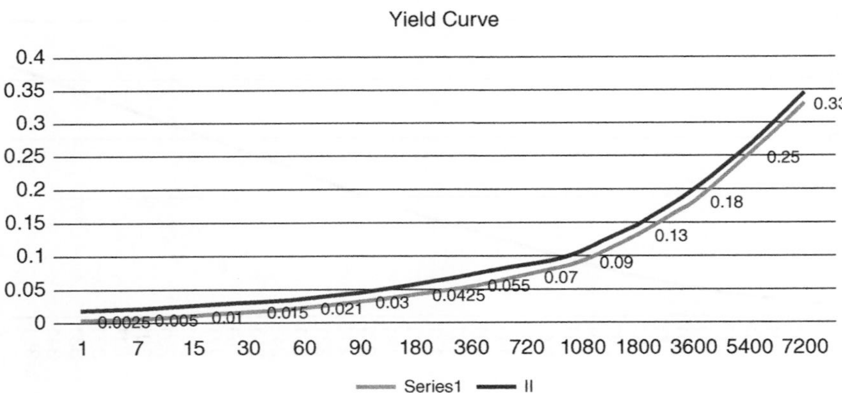

FIGURE 24.6 Yield Curve

$640 million with varying maturities. The bank has surplus liabilities of $646.5 million in deposits, also in different brackets of tenor. The bank has no funding gap and therefore does not require *mudharabah* funds from another Islamic bank. The bank earns a net income of $1.521 million with spreads of just 25 BPS. The capital required to fund this asset book is calculated as $42.293 million.

TIME VALUE OF MONEY

We wish to close this section on the concept of time value of money. *Shariah* scholars and academics alike do not recognize the time value of money.[5] This basically means that scholars are unable to recognize that $100,000 today is worth $120,000 tomorrow because they do not recognize any interest rates in an economy. As a student of Islamic finance, I have never understood this concept: $100,000 today may be worth $130,000 in one year or may be worth $60,000 in one year depending on the rate of inflation, and money's purchasing power. What is evident is that human behavior requires people to be compensated for deferring consumption or the satisfaction of wants. After all, much of economic theory is based on some very simple theories of human behavior, the first one being that humans consume goods and services to satisfy wants. The concept of deferred satisfaction simply underlines that

[5]This is based on the *hadith* on the exchange of *ribawi* items, which has to be of the same type and amount (*hadith*: Muslim).

TABLE 24.9 Asset/Liability Management

Tenor	15	30	60	90	180	360		Totals		
Asset Buckets	10,000,000	30,000,000	50,000,000	100,000,000	300,000,000	150,000,000		640,000,000		
%Age of Total	1.56%	4.69%	7.81%	15.63%	46.88%	23.44%			WAROA	1.65%
Return on Asset	0.60%	0.75%	1.00%	1.50%	1.75%	2.00%			WAROA	1.65%
Interest Income	*60,000*	*225,000*	*500,000*	*1,500,000*	*5,250,000*	*3,000,000*	*10,535,000*			
RW	20%	30%	50%	75%	80%	100%		RWA		
RWA	2,000,000	9,000,000	25,000,000	75,000,000	240,000,000	150,000,000		501,000,000	WARORWA	2.10%
%Age of Total	0.40%	1.80%	4.99%	14.97%	47.90%	29.94%			RW of Portfolio	83%
Liability Buckets	11,000,000	30,500,000	51,000,000	100,000,000	302,000,000	152,000,000		646,500,000		(6,500,000)
%Age of Total	1.70%	4.72%	7.89%	15.47%	46.71%	23.51%			WAVGCOF	1.39%
Cost of Liability	0.35%	0.50%	0.75%	1.25%	1.50%	1.75%			WAVCOF	1.39%
25 BPS Spread	*38,500*	*152,500*	*382,500*	*1,250,000*	*4,530,000*	*2,660,000*	*9,013,500*			
Interest Expense										
Funding Gap	(1,000,000)	(500,000)	(1,000,000)	—	(2,000,000)	(2,000,000)		(6,500,000)	−1.02%	Exc Liab
NII	*21,500*	*72,500*	*117,500*	*250,000*	*720,000*	*340,000*	1,521,500		Spread	0.25%
								NII	ROE	ROA
	Car	F	RW	L/D		25 BPS Spread		1,521,500	3.60%	0.24%
CAR = K/RWA	0.08	640,000,000	83%	1;1		50 BPS Spread		3,043,000	7.19%	0.48%
Equity	K=	42,293,653				100 BPS Spread NII		6,086,000	14.39%	0.95%
						125 BPS Spread		7,607,500	17.99%	1.19%
						150 BPS Spread		9,129,000	21.58%	1.43%

if a consumer is asked to defer consumption of a good or service today, he or she must be incentivized to do so. One such incentive is to offer two units of a good or service in the future.

In a fiat money economic system, what this means is that by taking from an individual $1,000 today for one year, which could purchase 10 apples, and 5 pounds of meat, assuming 0 percent inflation, we must compensate the individual with $1,040 so that he or she may acquire more apples and meat as a reward for deferring his or her wants at the beginning of the year. Otherwise, what would be the incentive to defer consumption?

There is definitely a time value of wants in human nature, and if money facilitates the satisfaction of wants, then, by default, money has a value associated with time, and it is inherent in the nature of things.

CONCLUSION

Islamic banks finance deficits in their asset/liability books using the contract of *mudharabah*. Islamic banks, like conventional banks, borrow short and lend long and utilize the Islamic Interbank Money Market to cover their positions. The IIMM is not a physical location, but merely a network of treasury dealers that trade over telephone lines.

Islamic banks have yet to evolve instruments that offer an alternative to deposits. It is likely we will witness a boom in financial products when either the traditional sources of funding dry up or Islamic banks look for smarter ways of mobilizing funds. Until then, Islamic banks rely on very basic notions of funding gaps, and the success of any Islamic bank's treasury lies in its ability to assess changes in market rates.

The authors have borrowed heavily from *Bank Asset and Liability Management Strategy, Trading and Analysis* by Moorad Choudhry, as currently there is no better rendition available to explain asset/liability management.

CHAPTER 25

Takaful

Takaful offers an exceedingly interesting subject of study for Islamic finance. It somehow brings to surface underlying currents in the whole problem of financial intermediation. Banking, asset management, fund management, wealth management, and even *takaful* (not insurance) reveals a set of agency contracts between those who supply funds and those who manage them. This underlying agency contract is not so visible in Islamic banking as it is in *takaful* and asset management. From one point of view *takaful* is a form of asset management,[1] where investors are replaced with participants whose funds or contributions are pooled together to cover participants for a negative event.

In Islamic banking, depositors' funds are pooled together and used to finance various credit- and equity-based contracts and purchase financial assets. Bankers do not earn an agency fee; rather they earn a spread between the funds they employ and the funds they deploy. They also share in the returns earned from investment in assets. Shareholder funds are, however, segregated from depositors' funds, a unique contribution of Islamic finance, and typically shareholders are not meant to earn returns from credit financing as then shareholders would be competing with depositors for business.

CONTRACT OF AGENCY

Takaful is a different beast altogether. It is a scheme by virtue of which individuals can protect themselves from the financial losses incurred by specific events. Figure 25.1 shows some of the risks individuals face that can lead to financial losses. These financial losses may be incurred directly, where damage is done to property owned by an individual or damage is done to the person thereby impairing his or her ability to earn a living.

[1]Sohail Jaffer, *Islamic Asset Management: Forming the Future for Shari'a Compliant Investment Strategies* (London: Euromoney Books, 2004).

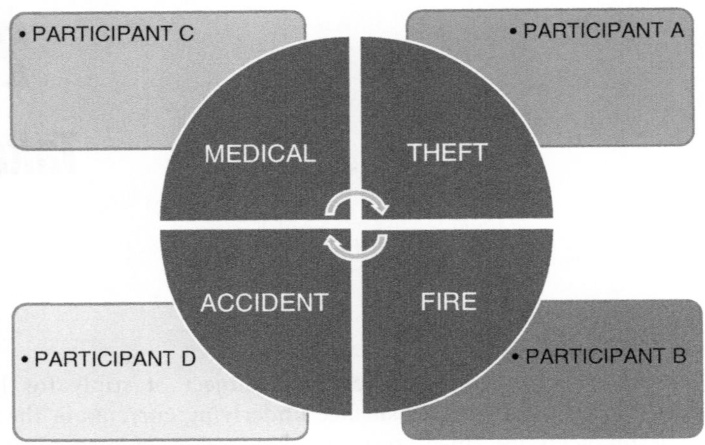

FIGURE 25.1 Total Risk in System

Certain schemes offer protection against negative events, and if that negative event does not occur, the participant is not entitled to any refund or benefit as such. Other schemes offer a benefit to a participant whether a negative event occurs or not.

The underlying principle behind *takaful* is a benevolent one, not a commercial one. Participants pool in funds to protect themselves, and appoint a professional manager to perform the necessary tasks. This is very close in concept to one of the first insurance companies in Europe. Even the modern insurance industry can be traced to Edinburgh and the establishment in the 1740s of the "Fund for a Provision for the Widows and Children of the Ministers of the Church Scotland."[2]

SHARIAH ISSUES WITH INSURANCE

Let us look at some underlying *shariah* issues with *takaful*. As a financial product within the conventional financial space, an insurance company offers to sell a policy to a potential customer, which will protect him or her from some specific negative event caused by some specific circumstances. A purchase price is paid for the policy by the buyer, and the seller sells coverage for a specific period of time, up to a maximum limit to the buyer. However, there is uncertainty in this contract in the minds of *shariah* scholars as to what exactly the buyer has purchased as it cannot be quantified at the time

[2]Iain Martin, *Making It Happen: Fred Goodwin, RBS and the Men Who Blew Up the British Economy* (New York: Simon & Schuster, 2013).

of contracting. This element of uncertainty or *gharar*, as it is known by Islamic scholars, makes the contract of buying an insurance policy invalid.

CONTRACT OF *TABARRU*

This does not mean that Muslims cannot seek alternatives. Participants in a *takaful* scheme contract with each other, not the *takaful* (or insurance company) to contribute to a fund (on a voluntary basis) using the unilateral contract of *tabarru*.[3] Participants contribute to a specific pool of funds that will be used to compensate participants for losses caused by specific events. Participants can contribute to various different funds at any given time. One may be a fund that protects a farmer from drought, and an other may protect a member from losses caused by fire, theft, or floods. Other funds may provide protection to family members against loss of life or limb for the earning member of a household.

The protection sought by a participant is linked to the size of the contribution, much like in an insurance policy. If a participant wishes to protect a valuable car from theft, the *takaful* operator will determine the amount of the contribution (to the fund) required for the fund to provide the necessary coverage. This contribution can be compared to an insurance premium, and is calculated using actuarial mathematics and probability numbers. In simple terms the contribution is a function of the probability of the event happening and the financial payout that is triggered by the event (i.e., the severity of the incident). This contribution is paid not as a purchase price for a policy but under the contract of *tabarru* as a donation.

Each participant will then be entitled to seek benefit or indemnity coverage from the fund if the participant suffers financial losses due to the occurrence of specific events. In essence, the participants agree to compensate each other, the participants also require each other to manage their affairs in such a manner as to not put an undue risk or burden on the contributed fund, and the participants employ a *takaful* operator to calculate appropriate contribution amounts based on the risk being covered, to collect said contributions, to manage claims, and to invest the fund in appropriate asset classes and therefore to ensure the fund is sustainable and sufficient to pay required claims.

For instance, participants may seek to cover themselves for risk of damage done to their motor vehicle in the event of an accident, fire, or theft.

[3]*Tabarru* simply means a transfer of ownership from one party to another without any required consideration from the receiving party. It falls under the contracts that allow and/or tolerate the presence of *gharar* to a certain extent, as stated in a legal maxim, "uncertainties are tolerable in the gratuitous contract."

A *takaful* operator will calculate a contribution amount based on actuarial mathematics to cover the risks involved to indemnify the customer in the event of losses. A contract of indemnity returns customers to their financial position prior to any negative event. Therefore, a customer cannot financially benefit from a *takaful* contract as such. The *takaful* operator will pool the contributions of all participants seeking coverage for their vehicles into a particular fund. These funds will be invested in short-term liquid assets, and when any participant suffers any losses due to some event, the *takaful* operator will compensate the participant from the fund after investigation of the circumstances and nature of the losses incurred.

The *takaful* operator will earn a *wakalah* fee for this service. This is an illustration of a role of a *takaful* operator and it certainly resembles the role of an insurance company but there are subtle and crucial differences. The *takaful* operator is acting as the agent of the participants, in the interest of the participants, and the fund is being compensated by a fixed upfront agency fee (*wakalah* model) and therefore a *takaful* operator does not have a vested interest in denying customers' claims, hoping to earn the difference between contributions and claims as income. The *takaful* model's main role is to protect the *takaful* fund and the participants. Participants, on the other hand, may seek compensation for any damages caused to their assets, under any circumstances, with no expectation for them to act in a responsible manner.

A participant may not accept any sense of responsibility for actions, and therefore may, for instance, drive at excessive speeds, or speak on a cell phone while driving, or not maintain the car brakes, knowing full well that that he or she will be covered for losses from a *takaful* fund, of which they are a member. The *takaful* operator will therefore attempt to protect the funds from such misuse of membership privileges, so will protect the fund from the irresponsible behavior of certain participants, but will also act in the interest of the participants if their losses are genuine and are covered by their contribution terms and conditions or policy.

To distinguish from a conventional insurance product, we established that the policyholder is in essence a participant, and the participant contributes to a fund on a voluntary basis under the contract of *tabarru*, and appoints a *takaful* operator as an agent to manage the contribution fund and pay claims to the participant in the event a loss is incurred by the participant. For these services the *takaful* operator is allowed to charge an agency fee, from which the *takaful* operator will manage all its operating expenses, sales commissions, and so on.

The *tabarru* contract will be for a period of one year, and will be renewable at the end of each year, during which period the participant is entitled to protection against specific risks. If the negative event for which the *tabarru* is made does not occur, the participant is not entitled to any refund, and the amount resides in the fund. This excess amount known as a *surplus* is discussed later in this chapter.

The example earlier illustrates a policy covering a vehicle under a *general takaful* plan for automobile accident, theft, or fire. It does not cover for any damage done to a person caused by any other event nor does it cover the participant for damage caused to the person. The customer will have to have a separate policy for coverage for damages caused to their person, under personal accident *takaful* plans. The plan may also cover damages caused to another party's vehicle, and this is known as a *liability coverage*. At times a car accident incident may cause an individual to have a heart attack. This would go into the domain of multiple damages and multiple causes. The expenses for heart surgery would come under medical *takaful* plans or personal accident *takaful* plans. *Takaful* companies would go for the proximate cause, or nearest cause that created the damage or loss, and if that cause is covered by their policy, would compensate the participant for their loss.[4]

PRODUCT MENU

The *takaful* industry is segregated into two broad categories, *Family Takaful* and *General Takaful*. Products are developed to fulfill the need for protection within these broad categories. Family *takaful* traditionally involves life and medical coverage, whereas general covers marine, auto, theft, fire, personal accident, medical coverage, and others. We first examine products under general *takaful*.

General *Takaful*

General takaful offers such plans as accident, fire, theft, medical, and marine *takaful*. These plans are typically short-term plans, with policy durations of one year. Participants intending to continue with their coverage plans are required to contribute to the fund on a rollover basis. The challenge in general *takaful* is to secure enough money in a fiscal year to pay for any expected claims. General *takaful* companies are not interested in any residual surplus other than to strengthen the contribution fund if the operation model is the classic *wakalah fee* model. Conventional insurance companies rely

[4]For a glance through the principles in *takaful* operations, see Bank Negara Malaysia's *Takaful* annual report 2005, www.bnm.gov.my/files/publication/tkf/en/2005/booklet.en.pdf.

on any surpluses for their profits. A general *takaful* plan's process flow is illustrated in Figure 25.2. However, this risk can be mitigated through using modified *Wakalah* model whereby the operator might be awarded a *jualah* "incentive" on achieving a certain required surplus amount.

Participants contribute to a plan that provides protection against auto theft, for instance. Each participant contributes according to the dollar value of the protection they seek and their individual risk profile. The fund accumulates $6,100 in contributions and takes on a contingent liability of $24,000. This is the total dollar amount of protection the fund has committed itself to. The *takaful* operator takes a fee of 2 percent or $480 upfront for organizing the participants and for processing claims. The total claims for the year are $5,780, leaving a surplus of $320 for the fund for the next year. Assuming all participants joined the plan at the beginning of the year on January 1, they have a *takaful* coverage until December 31 even if they did not submit all claims within the period. Any participants wishing to participate in the plan again would have to contribute to the fund for another year with fresh contributions.

Participants file in claims during the year or later. The reader should note that if total claims are greater than the funds accumulated, the *takaful* operator will then provide an interest-free loan "*qard hasan*" to make good the difference from shareholders' funds. This loan shall be paid back to the shareholders' fund when the participants' risk fund starts to make surpluses.

The process illustrates how Participants A, B, C, D, and E pool in their risks together, and contribute to protecting themselves from exposure to particular risks by contributing to a fund whose sole purpose is in fact to cover the risks of the participants from specific events. The *takaful* operator is required to ensure that the fund is solvent enough to pay all claims.

The above process can be applied to plans that cover a wide array of risks. In the category of *general takaful* a participant can be an individual or a company. The category of losses can be numerous as can be the causes.

Automobile *Takaful* Plans

Such plans cover participants against losses caused by a covered accident or the theft of their automobile. Additional losses can be covered, such as the cost of having to rent a car until the claim is settled. Such losses are known as *consequential* losses, but require higher contributions.

Fire *Takaful* Plans

Participants can seek to protect assets from damages caused by fire. Individuals can protect houses, furniture, domestic belongings, and a wide array of assets from damages caused by fire.

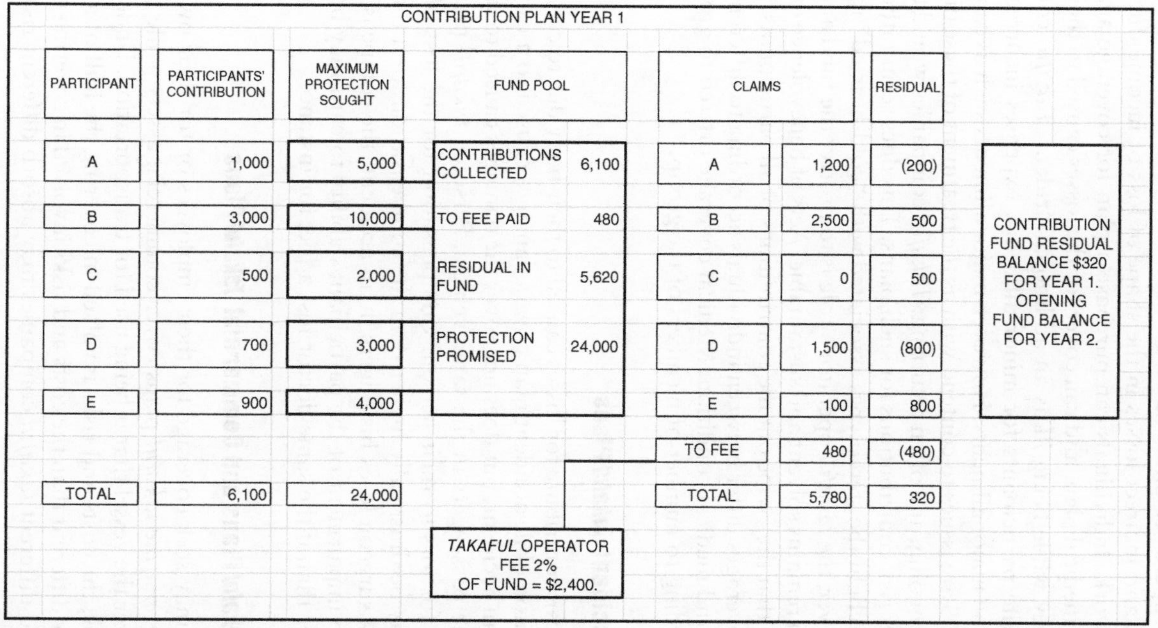

CONTRIBUTION PLAN YEAR 1

PARTICIPANT	PARTICIPANTS' CONTRIBUTION	MAXIMUM PROTECTION SOUGHT	FUND POOL		CLAIMS		RESIDUAL
A	1,000	5,000	CONTRIBUTIONS COLLECTED	6,100	A	1,200	(200)
B	3,000	10,000	TO FEE PAID	480	B	2,500	500
C	500	2,000	RESIDUAL IN FUND	5,620	C	0	500
D	700	3,000	PROTECTION PROMISED	24,000	D	1,500	(800)
E	900	4,000			E	100	800
					TO FEE	480	(480)
TOTAL	6,100	24,000			TOTAL	5,780	320

CONTRIBUTION FUND RESIDUAL BALANCE $320 FOR YEAR 1. OPENING FUND BALANCE FOR YEAR 2.

TAKAFUL OPERATOR FEE 2% OF FUND = $2,400.

FIGURE 25.2 General *Takaful* Process Flow

Medical *Takaful* Plans

Participants experience direct financial losses caused by illnesses in terms of medical bills and indirect losses in the shape of loss of income due to time away from work. Individuals can purchase a plan for coverage against illness under a medical plan, and can cover for the losses caused to their ability to earn money while being ill as an additional "rider." *Takaful* companies can underwrite participants for minor ailments, expenses incurred during pregnancy, and major ailments. However, major ailments such as cancer, diabetes, or AIDS are issues to contend with as the treatment of these diseases is very costly, ongoing, and often recurring. *Takaful* companies would typically charge higher risk contributions for such plans. This does seem rather unfair and brings to light the stereotypes associated with "cold-hearted" insurance plans. However, the *takaful* operator's role is to protect the fund and ensure that the fund remains solvent and sustainable. Acts of benevolence cannot be of such scale that they wipe out the contributions of all participants. Medical plans and coverages differ between individuals according to different factors such as age and medical condition. Medical coverage offered to groups also differs according to number of members of the group.

Personal Accident *Takaful* Plans

Individuals can contribute for losses caused to their body due to certain accidents. An automobile accident plan covers damages caused to a car when it has been in an accident, but does not cover the damages caused to the driver or any of the passengers in the same vehicle. Personal *takaful* plans cover participants for loss to their person. Compensation for the loss of an eye, however, may be drastically higher than the compensation for a thumb, for instance. If a surgeon loses his fingers in an accident, the compensation for losses due to impairment of the participant's ability to earn may be considerably higher than if the same doctor lost a toe, for instance.

Personal *Takaful* Plans and Commercial *Takaful* Plans

Companies may seek coverage for their employees or for their own assets. For instance, *marine takaful* plans cover commercial assets while in transit and also cover the vessel that is being used for transportation. Under marine *takaful* plans, the costs and risks involved in covering the hull of a ship are considerably different than the costs and risks involved in covering the cargo of a ship and different *takaful* companies may absorb different risks in one transaction.

Individuals may be exposed to risks while traveling, for instance. A normal medical plan may cover a participant only in a particular country, so while traveling an individual may have to purchase additional coverage for different countries. Individuals may also purchase coverage for loss of their luggage while traveling and can purchase plans that protect them from losses to a maximum amount.

Here we illustrate another point, *utmost good faith*, which is crucial to the functioning of the *takaful* industry. An individual purchases a *takaful* plan that protects her for maximum losses of $10,000 to belongings while traveling. The individual claims to be traveling to a friend's wedding in another country and is carrying gold jewelry worth $6,000 and clothes worth $4,000. The individual may mislead the *takaful* operator on the true value of the contents and then have her luggage "stolen" at the airport through some means. The participant then files a claim for the damages. Although this is in effect not a case of jewelry theft, in essence the effect is the same as the individual is benefiting from receiving goods worth $10,000 that never belonged to her. The *takaful* operator has utmost good faith in the customer that the latter reveals all required information when applying for a plan, and acts with integrity and honesty.

A candidate seeking medical coverage may fail to disclose the medical history of his family, which includes diabetes, as this would raise their required contributions. Hence it is to be noted that customers are the beneficiaries of *information asymmetry* as they know more about themselves than they choose to reveal to *takaful* operators.

Liability *Takaful* Plans

Modern citizens are surrounded by risks. Imagine a situation where a citizen walking on a street falls down an uncovered pot hole and dies. Who will be liable for the financial losses caused to the family from this event, and who will be liable for emotional trauma caused to family members of the deceased? How could one quantify the inability of the wife of the deceased to earn an income due to the emotional stress caused to her by the loss? These events and the related payouts come under *liability takaful* claims, where one party is liable to another party for losses caused on the original party's property, or due to the negligence of the original party.

A company employee may fall on a slippery tile at the office. Typically if the same event occurred at home, the individual would only have himself to blame, but in a company office, the company can be held liable for damages. Imagine a football player who earns $100,000,000 and falls in the locker room of a stadium because the janitor failed to put a "Wet Floor" sign. The fall causes unrepairable damage to the football player's ankle and his ability to therefore perform on the pitch. Would the stadium owners be liable for this oversight? The more complex our social systems are becoming the more complex the web of risks we are being entangled in on a daily basis.

Imagine a terrible rollercoaster accident that ends with people being killed. Who will be liable for these losses? Can these losses be termed financial losses or just emotional losses? Certainly if a breadwinner dies, the family members will incur a financial loss. Should this family member purchase additional coverage before riding a rollercoaster or going for a parachute jump while on a holiday? A normal company executive who purchases a *takaful* family plan that covers his beneficiaries in the event of loss of life may never have disclosed an appetite for dangerous sports while filling out a *takaful* family form. If the person dies while taking part in a dangerous sport, is he or she not being irresponsible to himself, to his family members, and to the fund? After all, it is the fund that will compensate for any losses and should have a right to regulate the actions of the participant.

GENERAL *TAKAFUL* BUSINESS MODEL

Companies that offer general *takaful* products must maintain separate funds for each type of risk that they undertake.[5] Any contributions obtained for automobile theft must be maintained in a separate fund from contributions collected for fire *takaful* plan. Claims for a fire plan cannot be paid by funds collected under a theft fund, for instance. A deficit in one category of fund cannot be compensated by funds from another category. For instance, if a fire fund runs into a deficit due to an unusually high frequency of house fires in a given year, the general *takaful* company cannot make good the deficit from any surplus in the other funds.

Figure 25.3 shows what a general *takaful* fund looks like.

CONCEPTS RELATED TO *TAKAFUL*

In order to understand the *takaful* industry we need to understand some concepts and the language of the insurance business. We cover some of these concepts here.

Financial Loss and Permissible Interest

A participant can seek coverage for only those assets, damage to which will cause the individual personal financial loss. An individual can seek to cover assets of family members. An individual cannot seek to cover losses incurred by an unrelated party. For instance, an individual cannot seek to cover losses

[5]See IFSB's "Exposure Draft—Standard on Risk Management For Takaful Undertakings," BNM's "Guidelines on Takaful Operational Framework," and Securities and Exchange Commission of Pakistan, "Takaful Rules 2012."

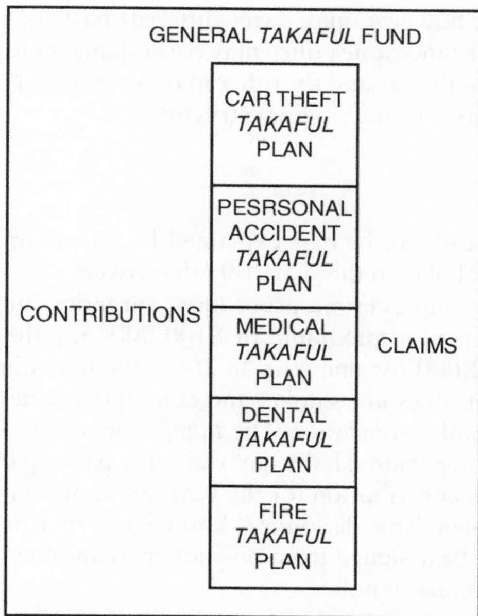

FIGURE 25.3 General *Takaful* Fund

caused to a cruise ship in which he or she has no vested interest and the damage of which will not cause the said individual any financial loss. To be eligible for filing a claim or purchasing a policy a participant must have a permissible and vested interest in the asset at the time of buying the plan or at the time of filing the claim.

Multiple Plans

As general *takaful* plans are plans of indemnity, an individual cannot benefit from them. For instance, an individual owns a Maserati for $100,000, and purchases an accident cover from *Takaful* Operator A for $100,000 and another plan covering the same asset for the same damages for another $100,000. In principle, the customer must reveal to both the companies the intent to purchase two plans to cover the same asset for the same risks. In the event the car is damaged in an accident, both companies will pay a combined benefit of just $100,000. Operator A may pay the full amount and may receive half the amount from B, or both can pay the customer 50 percent each. In either event the customer cannot get $200,000 in claims benefits. The customer cannot claim $200,000 for damage done to an asset of $100,000 and thus benefit from the peril.

The customer, however, may cover different parts of the car under the two policies. For instance, one policy may cover damages to the body, engine, and transmission of the car and the other may cover an expensive set of rims, or modifications done to the original structure.

No Loss Bonus

No loss bonus (NLB) can be best explained by an example. An individual purchases a medical plan in the year 2001 that covers visits to the emergency room, medical checkups, certain procedures, surgeries, and hospitalization. This coverage is up to a maximum of $100,000. Say the contribution for this coverage is $2,000 for one year. In 2001, the individual jogs regularly, watches his weight, does not smoke, and consequently never visits the hospital and does not file any claims. The *takaful* operator as a reward to the participant for good personal habits may give the participant a 5 percent discount on his or her contribution for the year 2002, provided the participant renews the same plan. This discount is known as a *no loss bonus*.

This NLB can be assigned from one policy to another depending on the jurisdiction and company policy.

Deductibles

Deductibles are the first dollar cost borne by a participant and are used to discourage misuse of *takaful* policies. For instance, a participant has an automobile accident coverage plan for $10,000. On the way home the participant carelessly bumps into the gate, scratching his side door. If the plan has a deductible of $500, the first $500 of the damage will be paid by the participant. In future he or she will make sure the gate is wide open. Deductibles are also used to discourage the participant from filing for small losses to reduce operational costs.

THE RIGHTS OF THE FUND OVER THE PARTICIPANT AND THE RIGHTS OF THE PARTICIPANT OVER THE FUND

As the fund is responsible for paying benefits to the participant if certain specific negative events transpire, the fund has some right in principle to regulate the behavior of a participant or expect certain minimum standards of behavior. If losses occur due to negligent behavior of the participant, the *takaful* operator (TO) can opt not to pay any claims.

For instance, a family purchases a fire *takaful* plan for their home, but have in place shabby wiring, or do not care to put lights out before leaving the house, or are careless in operating electric stoves, or place flammable material near electric heaters, for instance. Such acts of negligence can be uncovered during a forensic investigation of a site where a fire occurs and the evidence of negligence on the part of the participants may be to their detriment when filing for claims.

A young officer purchases a new car and finances the purchase using a loan contract. The bank requires the officer to insure the car. The officer, knowing that in the event the car is damaged losses will be borne by the TO, misuses the car, drives at reckless speeds, does not maintain the quality of the tires, for instance, and eventually has an accident. If the TO can discover evidence of misuse and negligence, the young officer may find himself footing the bill.

Certain assets and events are of a complex nature. Ships must follow certain routes from one port to another. These routes are chartered by seamen and typically avoid any areas that have rough weather, or shallow reefs, and so on. If a sea captain does not follow these routes and breaks the protocol of a certain journey possibly because he is intoxicated or such, and causes damage to the ship, and if the TO can uncover that *negligence is the proximate cause*, then the TO does not cover for damages in this instance.

There are certain *conditions* under which claims can be paid, and the participant must *warrant* to maintain and utilize assets as per their required purpose. For instance, if a BMW sedan is used for off-roading, the TO can question the purpose behind the act and deny paying the claim as a TO calculates probabilities of loss based on the normal usage of an asset, not the abnormal usage of an asset.

Participants also have rights over their *takaful* operators. TOs must fully disclose the salient features of the plan they are offering and the risks that are covered and circumstances under which certain risks are covered and circumstances under which certain risks are not covered. TOs must also ensure transparency in their pricing of risk contribution and in their policies on surplus distributions.

Acts of God

An individual walking on the street is struck by lightning. A waterfront property is damaged by a flood caused by excessive rainfalls. These events cannot be statistically predicted nor do they come under the ambit of *takaful* policies, as they are considered Acts of Nature or Acts of God.

Calamities

Calamities are fat-tailed events that happen rarely, but when they do happen, they cause significant financial losses. Imagine a waterfront development project washed out in a tsunami. Imagine whole sections of a city submerged under water due to such a calamitous event. The loss of life is enormous as is the damage caused to private and public property. In such an event, any *takaful* company would be unable to absorb the losses incurred and would require government assistance to cover losses. As such, calamities are not covered by typical *takaful* operators.

Frequency and Severity

Events have a certain frequency and a certain impact level, especially in the context of the financial losses they may cause. "Fender benders" are frequent occurrences when driving cars, especially in countries with traffic congestion issues. But fender benders have little impact in terms of financial loss, with average damages of just $100 per car.

Let us look at an example to illustrate this point. A TO provides coverage to 10,000 cars in a city, for an average contribution of $1,000. Total annual contributions are therefore $10,000,000. The TO "actuary" looking at past data calculates the following:

Probability of fender benders:	10 percent
Average claim:	$150
Probability of bad accidents:	1 percent
Average claim:	$8,000

The severity of a fender bender is an average claim size of $150, whereas the frequency of a fender bender is 10 percent. There is a 10 percent likelihood that a car on the road would get into a fender bender. This describes the frequency of the event.

The severity of a bad accident, however, generates an average claim of $8,000, but happens less frequently. A car on the road has a 1 percent chance of getting into a bad accident.

PRICING GENERAL *TAKAFUL* PLANS

Pricing *takaful* plans is essentially an exercise in pricing risk. The principles behind pricing *takaful* plans can even be used in pricing options, for instance, as each product has a payout of a specific amount linked to a specific event. We cover the general pricing concepts and provide a general overview of the principles behind pricing *takaful* plans.

Measuring and Pricing Risk

Pricing a general *takaful* plan is essentially an exercise in pricing risk. Risk in *takaful* is priced in a manner similar to how other financial products in the financial industry are valued. We observe similarities in how a *takaful* policy is priced and how options are priced or how expected losses are calculated for banks. Pricing risk is of crucial importance to *takaful* operators as it is their responsibility to calculate the correct amount of contribution for an appropriate amount of risk to be covered. In the terminology of *takaful*, the protection sought by the participant is referred to as the *sum assured*, and the contribution amount paid for this protection is referred to as the *risk contribution* (RC).

In order to price risk, *takaful* operators must fully understand the risk they are underwriting, the payouts involved in case a specific event occurs, and the probability of such events occurring. The mathematics behind calculating probabilities is down to a rather specific science in the world of conventional finance, and Islamic finance borrows considerably from the work done in the conventional insurance industry to price its products.

Probabilities are calculated from historical data. Historical data is available in various countries to varying levels of complexity and accuracy. For instance, the United States may have considerable data on car sales, and car theft for a given interval in time, whereas countries like Pakistan may not have accurate data for the same. The ability of *takaful* operators is highly dependent on the data provided to actuaries who are able to study data, extract patterns of human behavior, and determine how those patterns expose the *takaful* company to risks.

Risk Contribution

The risk contribution is comparable to an insurance premium, in effect, but in form it is collected by a *takaful* operator under the contract of *tabarru*. Risk contribution is the contribution made by a participant to a pool of funds known as the *takaful fund*. This contribution entitles the participant to a certain sum of monies, from the fund, if the participant suffers some financial losses due to certain specific events. The mathematical formula for risk contribution is simply calculated as follows:

$$\text{Probability of Event} * \text{Severity of the Event}$$

For instance, if a participant seeks coverage for the theft of an iPhone, the *takaful* operator will assess the probability of the phone being stolen.

The *takaful* operator checks with local retail vendors and discovers that there are 20,000 iPhones sold in a certain area. The *takaful* operator then refers to three local police stations and discovers that 400 iPhones were reported stolen in the past years. Roughly 2 percent of all iPhones sold were stolen, which means the probability of theft of an iPhone is 2 percent. Making adjustments for the participant's life style, such as frequency of using public transportation, and frequency of going to restaurants and other public places, the *takaful* operator assesses that the probability of theft for a particular customer's iPhone is 2.3 percent. The customer in the event of theft will seek a replacement phone that costs $500. Therefore, the sum assured is $500.

The risk contribution for the iPhone will be 2.3 percent * $500 = $11.50. This amount will simply cover the risk for theft and does not provide any fees or income to the *takaful* operator nor for any margin of error. The *takaful* operator may add a 15 percent fee to the offer to adjust for expenses and required rate of return. For a simple general *takaful* policy the formula for the total contribution paid by the participant would be as follows:

$$\text{Total Contribution} = \text{Risk Contribution} + \text{Fees}$$

Using legal terms of the *takaful* industry the formula actually looks something like this:

$$\text{Gross Contribution} = \text{Risk Contribution} + \text{Expenses} + \text{Lambda}$$

Expenses would include the *wakalah* fee of the *takaful* operator. The *takaful* operator would deduct all administrative expenses, sales commissions to company salespeople, and other expenses from this amount. Shareholders would recover their profits from this expense as well.

Lambda is a reserve that a *takaful* operator keeps on their books in case there is a surge in robberies in the area and the probability of theft increases, exposing the fund to more risk than previously calculated.

Importance of Data

We examine how probability tables are calculated by looking at data, as in the example in Table 25.1. A *takaful* company decides to offer auto theft *takaful* in an upcoming suburb. The community is six years old and there seems to be a growing need for theft coverage due to an increase in criminal activity. From various sources the *takaful* operator is able to gather the following data for the past five years.

TABLE 25.1 Data for Five Years

	Cars on Road at Beginning of Year	Cars Sold	Total Cars on the Road	Total Cars Stolen in that Year	Probability of Theft (%)	Average Claim	RC per Car
2009	300,000	40,000	340,000	15,000	4.41	35,000	1,544.12
2010	325,000	65,000	390,000	20,000	5.13	28,000	1,435.90
2011	370,000	55,000	425,000	18,000	4.24	45,000	1,905.88
2012	407,000	60,000	467,000	24,000	5.14	30,000	1,541.76
2013	443,000	30,000	473,000	15,000	3.17	18,000	570.82
Averages	369,000	50,000	419,000	18,400	4.42	31,200	1,378.15

The *takaful* operator carefully assembles the data required to price its products. Data is obtained from car sales outlets, the care registration department, and the police department. The data suggests that between 2009 and 2013, there were on average 419,000 cars on the roads, with on average, 50,000 cars sold per year. Police records show 15,000 car thefts in 2009, 20,000 in 2010, 18,000 in 2011, 24,000 in 2012, and 15,000 in 2013. On average 18,400 cars were stolen per year, which means there is a 4.42 percent probability that a car will be stolen in 2014.

Average claims for the past five years is $31,200. The probability of a claim arising is 4.42 percent, thus the *takaful* operator prices its car theft risk contribution to be 4.42 percent × $31,200 or $1,378.15.

It is the actuary's role to calculate the probability and assess the authenticity of the data as it is an essential component in *takaful* calculations.[6] If actual theft patterns deviate from those revealed in the data above, the *takaful* operator may be exposed to more or less risk in 2014.

The *takaful* operator has not charged in this amount any fee for its *wakalah* fee. The *takaful* operator has to pay from this *wakalah* fee its rent on office space, expenses, costs related to training a sales staff, and commissions that are paid to sales agents who must sell the plans to the public. The *takaful* operator also has to factor in administrative costs of stamps, mailing, check issuances, and so on, and must *also add a factor into the wakalah fee of the required profit the takaful operator wishes to earn.*[7] The *takaful* operator is not in the business to just pay its expenses but wishes to earn some profit from offering its services.

---

[6]Peter Casey, "Supervisory Issues in Takaful: An Overview," ed. S. Archer, R. A. A. Karim, and V. Niesnhaus, *Takaful Islamic Insurance: Concepts and Regulatory Issues* (Singapore: John Wiley & Sons, 2009).
[7]Ibid.

Unlike conventional insurance where expenses can be passed onto the fund, a TO (*takaful* operator) is not able to pass on any expenses to customers or the contribution fund. So, for instance, if the TO feels a candidate for a medical plan requires a medical checkup, the TO will foot the medical bill. This component of expenses we refer to as E. Therefore, up to now, our total contribution for a *takaful* plan includes a risk contribution RC and expenses E. To employ *takaful* industry terminology, the total contribution is referred to as *gross contribution*. The formula for gross contribution (GC) is risk contribution plus expenses.

Expenses are typically expressed as a percentage of gross contribution, so our equation so far looks like this,

$$GC = RC + E$$

Not all customers fit the terms and conditions of generic protection plans. In the earlier example some individuals might be exposed to greater risks of theft because of the nature of their job or travel routines. Certain participants may travel extensively by trains and may leave their cars at public parking lots near commuter stations for extended periods of time, thus adding to the risk of the fund. Other participants may actually lower the risks they pose to the fund, by keeping tracking devices, car jacks, and other such tools that deter theft.

However, to take into consideration those participants that expose the fund to higher risks, *takaful* operators charge what may best be understood as a risk premium or *lambda* λ. Let us express λ as a percentage of RC, and say it is 10 percent. So we have added a 10 percent loading to our gross contribution to cover for, in essence, unexpected losses.

Our equation is looking like this now:

$$\text{Gross Contribution} = \text{Risk Contribution} + \text{Expenses} + \text{Lambda}$$

$$GC = RC + E + \lambda$$

To refer to our earlier example where we computed a risk contribution of \$1,378.15, we make some additional assumptions. We express expenses (E) as 15 percent of gross contributions and lambda (λ) 10 percent of gross contributions. Using simple algebra, the gross contribution for a vehicle to be covered for theft is tabulated to be \$1,837.53. This amount is what the *takaful* operator will charge to price its risk, cover expenses, earn a profit, and maintain a cushion for higher risk exposures.

Armed with such statistical sophistry, the *takaful* operator decides to underwrite 60,000 new cars sold in 2014 for a hefty gross contribution of \$110,251,802.44. The *takaful* operator will deduct 15 percent of this

TABLE 25.2 Surplus Calculation

	Per Car	60,000 Cars
Gross Contributions	1,837.53	110,251,802.44
Expenses	275.63	16,537,770.37
Residual Fund		93,714,032.08
Probability of Claims	4.42%	4.42%
Actual Claims	31,200	82,742,400.00
Surplus		10,971,632.08
Surplus as %		10

amount to cover its costs and earn a profit or $16,537,770.37, which is transferred out of the fund and into the control of the *takaful* operator to run the company and pay shareholders. The residual $93,714,032.08 is retained in the *takaful* risk fund to cover any claims registered by participants. If, as the data suggests, 4.42 percent of the car owners have their cars stolen, during the period of the plan, with an average claim size of $31,200, the *takaful* operator would settle claims worth $82,742,400 for the year and have a surplus of $10,971,632.08, which, accounting for rounding errors, is 10 percent of the gross contribution and equivalent to λ.

Making a simple assumption that all plans are offered at the beginning of a year, and gross contributions are collected in the first month of the year, the *takaful* operator can invest the sums collected in short-term *shariah*-compliant securities and earn a return on these funds till claims start being filed as in Table 25.2.

A crucial question from the *shariah* point of view and from a risk point of view is what is to be done with the underwriting surplus, and who owns the underwriting surplus: the participants or the shareholders?

It would be tempting to divide this surplus between shareholders and the participants, but prudent *takaful* operators maintain reserves for[8]

- Strengthening the fund
- Events that have occurred but are not reported
- Contributions paid in the middle of the year whose tenure will fall into part of the next year

Remember one of the main purposes of a *takaful* operator is first to safeguard the interests of the participants. This is done by paying legitimate

[8] Abdulrahman Khalil Tolefat and Mehmet Asutay, *Takaful Investment Portfolios: A Study of the Composition of Takaful Funds in the GCC and Malaysia* (Singapore: John Wiley & Sons, 2013).

claims and is also done by maintaining the solvency of the fund and strengthening the fund to counter for any future unexpected losses.

Second, certain participants may have experienced a negative event, but are in the process of filing their claim, or have not claimed as yet. These participants are not going to pay any contribution again for covering these losses. *Takaful* operators would have to be mindful of these unpaid claims and would have to maintain reserves from the current year's contributions to pay claims in the following year.

Third, many customers buy into plans in the middle of the year, but they pay the entire year's risk contribution upfront. If a participant enters into a plan in the middle of the year, and at year-end does not file any claim, the participant has until the middle of next year to submit any claims. Therefore, it is prudent for the TO to keep half of such participants' risk contribution in reserves for the next year. These reserves are recorded as liabilities in the *takaful* operator's books.

From the example earlier, the *takaful* operator may retain as much as 50 percent of the surplus of contributions over claims as reserves and distribute the remainder as a surplus.

OBSERVATIONS OF GENERAL *TAKAFUL*

Participants in general *takaful* plans by their very structure are unable to accumulate enough funds in their plans to cover any claims they may file. This is so because, in general *takaful,* there are no accrued balances of unpaid contributions that are held in favor of a participant. In essence, if a participant pays $500 for an auto theft policy with probability of theft of 4 percent and a sum assured of $12,500, if the participant's car is not stolen, the $500 is not returned to the participant. Contribution balances are not rolled over with each policy period.

If on the other hand the participant's car is stolen, then the *takaful* operator will pay from the risk fund, or a pool of funds, which essentially is the contributions of other participants. The *takaful* operator would need a critical mass of at least 25 participants to collect enough funds to pay the first participant's losses, provided no other participants file any claims. Technical analysts refer to this art of managing the funds as cash management. Critics have also likened it to a Ponzi scheme, as a general *takaful* plan is by definition insolvent and it cannot pay for its claims. *Takaful* operators rely on funds of other participants to fund the payouts. The reality is that it is, after all, participants who agree to pay for each other in case a negative event occurs, so the possibility of a Ponzi scheme is eliminated by definition.

FAMILY *TAKAFUL*

Family *Takaful* plans differ greatly from general *Takaful* plans, as participants' contributions do in fact roll over to subsequent years as the plans are typically long term in nature, and at some point a participant's risk contribution can in fact fund the member's own death benefit.

So far we have been talking of *takaful* plans that cover risks alone. There are also *takaful* plans that combine covering risks with investments. These are salient features of family *takaful* plans. These are as expected, long-term plans that have to be renewed every year, and are not contracts of indemnity but contracts of benefit. Here an individual contributes to a plan to compensate his or her family members or beneficiaries in the event he or she expires. There is financial loss to the beneficiaries in terms of loss of income, especially if the deceased is the breadwinner. Family *takaful* plans are contracts of benefit where a sum is paid out to the family members of the deceased. The participant can choose the maximum coverage he or she wishes and pays a contribution accordingly. If a participant wants a death benefit of $1,000,000, he or she may have to pay a contribution of $10,000 per annum. If the participant wants a death benefit of $10,000,000, he or she may have to pay a contribution of say $30,000.

In the event that the participant does not die, and continues to pay all contributions for the life of the contract, the participant will be rewarded by a sum of money equal to the death benefit or exceeding the death benefit as a certain percentage of the contribution would be set aside by the *takaful* operator and invested in long-term assets. Here the contributions of the participants are segregated into a risk fund that is used to pay out a death benefit, and an investment fund, which is used to pay out a benefit as a reward in case they do not die. The *takaful* operators are responsible for managing these funds, and their *wakalah* fees include a service charge for this fund management. However, certain *takaful* models allow the *takaful* operator to share in the returns on investments made through the investment fund.

In family *takaful* plans, therefore, a component of asset management is added as these plans are long term in nature and there is a savings component to the payouts involved. In general *takaful*, if no negative event occurs, participants are not entitled to any refunds or reimbursements; they may get a no loss bonus when renewing the policy in subsequent years. In family *takaful* plans, however, due to the long-term nature of the plan, if no negative event occurs and the participant survives the term of the policy, he or she is rewarded by a payout that often exceeds the amount of the death benefit.

Events in family *takaful* have a low frequency but a high impact, whereas events in general *takaful* typically have high frequencies and low impacts. However, in the case of marine *takaful* the impact may also be severe.

Another unique difference between family *takaful* and general *takaful* plans is that when a participant's family submits a claim to a *takaful* operator in the event of death, and the benefit is paid, at that point the contract is terminated. In a general *takaful* contract, even if within the span of one year a participant submits a claim, the contract is not terminated; in essence the participant can submit several claims in one year if he or she is experiencing a negative event with a high frequency.

Family *Takaful* Process Flows

The diagram in Figure 25.4 shows the process flow for a family *takaful* plan. Participants A, B, C, D, and E contribute to their respective plans by paying a gross contribution every year. After adjusting for expenses a risk contribution payment is divided into a risk fund and an investment fund. Seventy percent of the risk contribution is credited to a risk fund, and 30 percent to an investment fund. Each participant will be rewarded either by virtue of a payout to beneficiaries in the case of death, in the amount known as the death benefit, or by the payment of a survival benefit if the participant lives through the term of the plan. The term *survival benefit* is not an industry term but is useful for illustrative purposes.

The *takaful* operator maintains records of the accrued balances for each participant for his or her respective funds as these are typically long-term relationships. Each progressive year's contributions beef up the participant's balance in the *takaful* fund. If a participant dies, the death benefit is paid from the *takaful* operator's risk fund; any contributions of the participant to the investment fund shall be paid back along with all of its related accumulated profit. For instance, in our illustration, Participant A dies. The participant's own contributions to the risk fund to date were only $98,000, whereas the death benefit was $150,000; the difference of $52,000 is paid by the risk fund. However, the participant's balance of $42,000 in the investment fund with be paid with all of the accumulated profit. Similarly, Participant D actually outlives his plan and is entitled to a survival benefit of $90,000 to be paid from the risk pool. He will also get the balance of the investment fund.

There are several types of family *takaful* certificates, the term *takaful* certificate does not carry any investment part. Therefore the actual contribution paid is less than the other type, which is the investment-linked certificate. Investment-linked certificates have two funds, the risk fund and the investment fund. Some family *takaful* plans carry a survival benefit also, meaning that if the participant survives (stays alive) until the expiry of the certificate, he or she will get the survival benefit sum covered. There is a dispute about the validity of this benefit from *Shariah* point of view.

PARTICIPANT	PARTICIPANTS' CONTRIBUTION CURRENT YEAR	PARTICIPANTS' CONTRIBUTION TO RISK FUND	PARTICIPANTS' CONTRIBUTION TO INVESTMENT FUND	PARTICIPANTS' CONTRIBUTIONS PREVIOUS YEARS	PARTICIPANTS' ACCRUED RISK FUND	PARTICIPANTS' ACCRUED INVESTMENT FUND	TOTAL CONTRIBUTIONS	PARTICIPANTS' RISK FUND	PARTICIPANTS' INVESTMENT FUND	DEATH BENEFIT	SURVIVAL BENEFIT	DEATH BENEFIT CLAIMS	IMPACT ON RISK FUND	INVESTMENT FUND PAYOUTS	IMPACT ON INVESTME NT FUND
A	10,000	7,000	3,000	130,000	91,000	39,000	140,000	98,000	42,000	150,000	225,000	150,000	(52,000)	-	42,000
B	30,000	21,000	9,000	200,000	140,000	60,000	230,000	161,000	69,000	300,000	450,000	-	161,000	-	69,000
C	5,000	3,500	1,500	70,000	49,000	21,000	75,000	52,500	22,500	80,000	120,000	-	52,500	-	22,500
D	7,000	4,900	2,100	53,000	37,100	15,900	60,000	42,000	18,000	60,000	90,000	-	42,000	90,000	(72,000)
E	9,000	6,300	2,700	70,000	49,000	21,000	79,000	55,300	23,700	130,000	195,000	-	55,300	-	23,700
TOTAL	61,000	42,700	18,300	523,000	366,100	156,900	584,000	408,800	175,200	720,000	1,080,000	150,000	258,800	90,000	85,200

WAKALAH MODEL

TO FEE = 2% = $1,220

RETURNS ON INVESTMENTS	15,690
TO'S SHARE	7,845

	JUALA MODEL	WAKALAH MODEL	MUDHARABAH MODEL
TO'S SHARE	77,640	1,220	7,845
	UNDERWRITING SURPLUS	AGENCY FEE	PROFIT SHARING

FIGURE 25.4 Family *Takaful* Process Flows

This graphic illustration demonstrates with clarity how participants benefit from pooling into a fund.

Takaful operators have various sources of income in family *takaful* plans. The simplest source of income is a *wakalah* fee for providing underwriting services, a second source of income is a share in the returns generated by investing funds in the investment fund, and the third source is a share of the underwriting surplus. In our brief illustration above, the *takaful* operator is able to earn $1,220 as *wakalah* fee of just 2 percent, and $7,845 from its share in the returns generated by investments, with a profit-sharing ratio of 50:50, and $77,640 as the share of the underwriting surplus in the risk fund. These income-sharing models are discussed in greater detail later.

BASIC ACCOUNTING ENTRIES FOR *TAKAFUL*

Let us imagine a scenario where a *takaful* company begins from scratch with a capital of $300,000,000. With this capital the *takaful* company leases out certain office space, purchases computers, equipment, hires employees, and trains newly hired staff and further deploys them in the market to go door-to-door to sell automobile *takaful* coverage.

The leasing expenditures will come as expenses as will all other expenses incurred. Let us assume this expenditure totals $10,000,000. The TO pays these expenses from its own capital and this is reduced now to $290,000,000. The TO lends $10,000,000 to the risk fund to cover any premature risks; this loan is under the contract of *qard hasan*.

The product is successful and the company sells 10,000 certificates and earns contribution income of $10,000,000. Each contribution on average is $1,000. The *takaful* operator charges an upfront *wakalah* fee of 30 percent; therefore $3,000,000 is recorded as shareholders' income. The *takaful* operator will maintain separate records of its income and expenses and separate records of the contributions and claims borne by the fund.

During the year, the TO also receives claims of $2,000,000 from various participants. This is recorded as an expense for the TO. This expense impairs the value of the fund, which has a residual value of $8,000,000 at year-end. The TO maintains $1,000,000 of the risk fund as a reserve or liability and records this $1,000,000 as such.

As the TO has set up a new fund, it does not treat the surplus of $4,000,000 it has received in excess of contributions over claims and reserves as a surplus. The fund still owes the TO the seed money of $10,000,000, which it will slowly retire over the years.

We can examine this same company in 10 years' time, where it has launched several new products, including fire, theft, personal accident, and

TABLE 25.3 Accounting Treatment

Takaful Operators Funds	Beginning of Year ($)	Risk Fund	Beginning of Year ($)	
SH funds	300,000,000	Risk fund	10,000,000	Asset
Expenses	−10,000,000	Contributions	10,000,000	Income
Qard to fund	10,000,000	*Wakalah* fee paid	3,000,000	Expense
Wakalah fee earned	3,000,000	Claims	2,000,000	Expense
Commission expenses	−1,000,000		End of Year	
Administrative expenses	−500,000	Risk fund	15,000,000	
Net income	1,500,000	Reserves	1,000,000	Liability
		Risk fund	14,000,000	

medical coverage to participants. The fund has also repaid the *qard ul hassan* obtained from the TO.

At year-end its books look something like this:

Fund at beginning of year:	$300,000,000
Contributions for the year:	$75,000,000.
Claims paid for the year:	$40,000,000
Wakalah fee paid to the TO:	$22,500,000
Surplus contributions over expenses:	$12,500,000
Reserves kept for next year:	$5,000,000
Net surplus	$7,500,000
Income from investments	$ 15,000,000 (Fund at BoY and contributions invested at 4 percent)
Fund at end of year:	$305,000,000

TAKAFUL OPERATOR MODELS

Using the data given in the previous section, we can explore the two different *takaful* operating models.

Wakalah Model

There is a simple *wakalah* model, where the *takaful* operator only earns a *wakalah* fee, which is priced into the calculations of gross contributions as $GC = RC + E + \lambda$. In this instance, the TO would only earn $22,500,000 from the above operation.

Modified *Wakalah* Model or *Wakalah Mudharbah* Model

This model not only allows a *takaful* operator to earn the *wakalah* fee but also allows the TO a share in the returns generated from investments of the fund. In this case the fund earns a return of $15,000,000. If the TO is working on a *mudharabah* model, it can share this income on a pre-agreed ratio. (The TO's share cannot be more than 50 percent.) Let us assume the TO's share is 35 percent of the returns; this would allow the TO to earn an additional income of $5,250,000.

Another more refined model also allows the TO to share in the underwriting surplus (contributions over claims). This surplus is recorded at $7,500,000. The TO can earn a percentage of this surplus under a contract of *joala* or performance-based reward, where if the surplus is in excess of $5,000,000, the TO can have 40 percent of the amount above the $5,000,000 mark. This would allow the TO an additional income of $1,000,000, which will be its share in the underwriting surplus.

Income earned according to the model:

Wakalah model:	$22,500,000
Modified *wakalah* model:	+ $5,250,000
Modified *wakalah joala* model:	+ $1,000,000
Total income:	$28,750,000

The most contentious issues here are of the sharing of underwriting surplus, which is the subject of a separate discussion on *shariah*.

DISTRIBUTION OF UNDERWRITING SURPLUS

This is a contentious issue from the point of view of *takaful* operators and participants alike. Participants contribute to a *takaful* fund on the basis of a unilateral, voluntary contract of *tabarru*. *Shariah* scholars feel that as this contract is one of collaboration with other participants and has an underlying benevolent tone to it, the participants should not profit from it.[9] *Tabarru* is an act of giving a donation, and one cannot benefit from giving a donation. Similarly, the *takaful* operator is compensated for services via the *wakalah* fee, and even shares in the investment returns in the modified *wakalah* model. There is no criteria of effort, capital, or risk that justifies earning a profit from the underwriting surplus.

[9]Humayon Dar, and Umar Moghul, *The Chancellor Guide to the Legal and Shariah Aspects of Islamic Finance* (Miami: Chancellor Publications, 2009).

In various legal jurisdictions, sharing of underwriting surplus is a key factor, with some countries permitting this and others forbidding it. There is unanimous consent that all underwriting surplus should be credited back to the *takaful* fund. This would strengthen the fund, and enable the *takaful* operator to diversify the risk portfolio and earn additional income in the future, which can then be shared both with participants in the shape of investment returns and with TOs in the shape of *wakalah* fees. *Shariah* scholars also feel that were TOs to share in underwriting surplus, the incentive structure would become similar to insurance companies, and participants may suffer at the hand of TOs who earn more income if fewer claims are paid out. The current incentive model of *wakalah* fee and *mudharabah* fee circumvents this conflict of incentives between participants and *takaful* operators.

CONCLUSION

Takaful is quite similar to insurance. The concept allows participants to contribute to a fund that in turn protects them from specific perils. A subtle difference between the *takaful* models and the insurance models is how the operator is rewarded. For most insurance companies the only source of income is underwriting surplus, thus, there is an incentive to try not to pay claims. *Takaful* operators are compensated via an agency fee that is linked to the size of the fund and the contributions collected and not the underwriting surplus. This incentive structure should influence how a *takaful* operator functions and how an insurance company works. Again "the proof is in the pudding" and the *takaful* industry has yet to achieve the critical mass it needs to make a visible difference.

CHAPTER 26

Pricing of *Takaful* Policies and *Retakaful*

We examine some basic approaches to pricing general and family policies in this chapter.

CASE STUDY 1: CORPORATE MEDICAL *TAKAFUL* PLAN UNDER GENERAL *TAKAFUL*

In this case study, we calculate the gross contribution to be paid by a company with 1,000 employees. The company is seeking medical coverage for its 1,000 employees from a *takaful operator* (TO).

The TO analyzes the records of the company and puts together the data in Table 26.1 that reveals certain patterns of behavior among the employees with regard to their hospital visits.

The data reveals that of the 1,000 employees, 605 never visited the hospital last year, 305 visited the hospital once, 76 visited twice, 13 visited three times, and one sorry fellow went to the hospital four times. On average, the 1,000 employees made 500 visits to the hospital. Each hospital visit cost the employer $100. Therefore, the employer paid $50,000 in hospital bills in the previous year.

The actuary then visits the hospital to assess for which treatments the employees on average came. This helps the actuary structure the product offering so that an average claim size is $100 per visit.

Based on this historical data alone, the actuary of the TO comes up with some conclusions in Table 26.2.

The actuary determines that there is a 50 percent chance any one employee will visit the hospital on a given day in the year. On average the

TABLE 26.1 Medical History Table

Medical History of 1,000 Employees for Previous Year				
Number of Employees	Frequency of Hospital Visits	Total Visits	Cost of Each Visit	Total Costs
605	0	0	100	0
305	1	305	100	30,500
76	2	152	100	15,200
13	3	39	100	3,900
1	4	4	100	400
1,000		500		50,000

TABLE 26.2 Data Conclusion

Conclusions Drawn from Data		
1,000 employees visited the hospital 500 times		
Probability of employee visiting the hospital		50%
Average cost of employee visit borne by employer		$100
Total cost to employer of hospital visits		50,000
Frequency	Probability of claim occurring	50%
Impact/Severity	Average claim size/employee	100
	Average risk cost/employee	50

bill will be $100. So for the TO, the cost of risk or risk contribution (*RC*) per employee is as per the formula:

$$\text{Probability of Event} \times \text{Severity of Event (Payout)}$$
$$= 50 \text{ percent} \times \$100 = \$50$$

The average cost of covering the medical bill of an employee is $50. The TO adds to this its *wakalah* fee, expenses as a 15 percent component of the total premium/donation, and adds 1 percent of the total premium/donation to load up for employees like the one who goes four times to the hospital, to cover for additional risk. This is shown in Table 26.3.

The TO calculates a gross contribution as in Table 26.4.

The *takaful* operator presents the policy terms to the company. The gross premium or contribution for 1,000 employees is $59,523. The TO also specifies what ailments are covered under this policy based on the actuarial data.

TABLE 26.3 *Takaful* Data

Employer Decides to Buy a Policy to Cover Medical Expenses for the Year of 1,000 Employees			
Risk contribution	/employee	$.50 \times 100$	50
Risk contribution	/1,000 employees	$= 1{,}000\ (.50 \times 100)$	50,000
Expenses (assume)			15% of GC
Lambda λ (assume)			1% of GC

TABLE 26.4 Premium/Donation Calculation

Policy Premium Calculation for 1,000 Employees

$$GC = RC + E + \lambda$$
$$GC = RC + .15GC + .01GC$$
$$GC = 50{,}000 + 0.15GC + .01GC$$
$$GC - 0.15GC - 0.01GC = 50{,}000$$
$$0.84GC = 50{,}000$$
$$GC = 50{,}000/.84$$
$$GC = 59{,}523$$

This could include:

- One-night stay in the hospital
- Emergency room visit for injuries (assuming this is a mining company)
- Basic x-ray, bandaging, casts for broken limbs

These would be the risks that would be covered under this plan.

The company CEO sees that the policy premium is $59,523, but feels that he has locked in his medical expenses for the year, and anticipates a few more injuries in the coming year. He also now can predict his medical bills for the year, which will help him develop a budget and forecast more accurately. The CEO accepts the policy terms and pays the premium or gross contribution for one year for 1,000 employees.

The TO's actuary, having initially collected the data needed to assess the risk, now has to monitor the behavior of 1,000 employees to see if the risks actually pan out as calculated, and whether the behavior of medical visits corresponds to the previous year's data. If there is variance in the actual behavior of the employees, the actuary will have to modify the pricing for the next year when the TO hopes that the employee will renew the policy.

CASE STUDY 2: CORPORATE MEDICAL *TAKAFUL* PLAN UNDER GENERAL *TAKAFUL*

We can briefly examine another policy as shown in Table 26.5.

Note that the weighted average cost of admissions is exactly the risk contribution, as that is the number the TO must have to cover the medical expenses of 1,000 employees whose medical behavior and the costs associated with that medical behavior are reflected in the earlier data.

The total cost of 1,000 employees is $2,604,000, with a probability of a visit being 50 percent of the time. The risk contribution can be calculated in two ways here.

Method A

The average claim *per visit* is $5,208.

The probability of a claim is the *number of visits by employees/total number of employees* = 500/1,000 or 50 percent. Probability of a claim is 50 percent.

TABLE 26.5 Policy B

Hospital Cost per Admission			Median Cost	Total Admissions	Weighted Average Cost of Admissions
A		B	(A + B)/2	Data	[(A+B)/2] × DATA
	<	4,000	2,000	280	5,60,000
4,000	to	8,000	6,000	130	7,80,000
8,000	to	12,000	10,000	40	4,00,000
12,000		16,000	14,000	25	3,50,000
16,000		20,000	18,000	14	2,52,000
20,000		24,000	22,000	7	1,54,000
24,000		28,000	26,000	3	78,000
		30,000	30,000	1	30,000
				500	26,04,000

The above data suggests that 1,000 employees visited the hospital 500 times and incurred total costs of $2,604,000.
Probability of an employee visiting the hospital is 500/1,000 = 50%.
Average cost of visit is $2,604,000 / 500 = $5,208.
Risk Cost for 1 employee is Probability of Hospital Visit × Average Payout per Visit = 50% × 5,208 = $ 2,604.
Risk Contribution for 1 employee is $2,604.
Risk Contribution for 1,000 employees is 1,000 × 2,604 = $2,604,000.
RC = Weighted Average Cost of Admission.

$$\text{Risk Contribution} = \text{Probability of Claim} \times \text{Severity of Claim (Payout per Claim)} = 50\% \times \$5,208 = \$2,604$$

(This is equal to average payout or claim per employee—two ways of looking at the same thing.)

Method B

The average claim per total employees is *total claims/total employees*, which is $2,604,000/1,000 = $2,604. If the actuary wants a risk reserve to cover medical bills, he can use this calculation as well. This is your *RC* right away.

CASE STUDY 3: CORPORATE FAMILY *TAKAFUL* PLAN

To price family *takaful* plans we must first understand the concept of mortality tables. Mortality tables provide data of a population sample in every age group. They begin with the number of people surviving in each age group and look at how these populations move into subsequent age groups with the passage of every year.

For instance, we look at the number of births in the year 2000. Assuming they are 10,000. We then see how many of these 10,000 babies survive to the age of 1; let us say 9,950 babies survived to the age of 1. This means 50 babies (unfortunately) died between the ages of 0 and 1.

The probability of a baby surviving from 0 to 1 is simply

$$= \frac{\text{Number of Lives at Age 1 This Year}}{\text{Number of Lives at Age 0 to 1 in Previous Year}}$$

$$= 9,950/10,000$$

$$= 99.50 \text{ percent}$$

The probability of a baby dying before reaching the age of 1 is simply

$$= \frac{\begin{array}{c}\text{Number of Babies Who Died Previous Year} \\ (= \text{Total Sample} - \text{Number Who Survived})\end{array}}{\text{Number of Babies in Previous Year}}$$

$$= (10,000 - 9,950)/10,000$$

$$= 0.50 \text{ percent}$$

In family *takaful* plans, TOs are provisioning for the probability of deaths per year as they must make a death benefit payout for every death. TOs are also interested in the probability of life as they must make reserves for those individuals who subscribe to family plans with survival benefit. As each event triggers a different payout, each event has a separate fund. This is why a risk fund is maintained separately to cover for death benefit payouts and investment funds are kept separately to pay for investment returns.

Back to mortality tables and some probability calculations: We must understand that in family *takaful* plans only two things can happen to an individual that are relevant to assessing his or her risk: death or survival. If the participant dies, the *takaful* operator must pay the beneficiaries the agreed death benefit. If the participants survive, they will hopefully renew their policy for another year, which will lead to contribution income for another year.

Infant mortality risks are high in countries with poor hygiene records.[1] In developed countries, data suggests that the risk of death for very young babies and very old people is high. The risk of death for a young child from the ages of 2 to 12 are rather low, as are the risks in teen years right to the ages of 40 or 50, where lifestyle habits such as smoking, drinking, and stress levels begin to impact an individual's risk of death.

The point we are trying to make is that a policyholder presents different levels of risk over his or her life span, but insurance companies and TOs calculate an equal premium for the entire term of a policy. Premiums do not vary with the risk presented by the participant in each age category. If one were to purchase a policy for this infant, the TO will not calculate different premiums each year depending on the probability of death in each segment. The TO will charge one premium for the life of the contract. At times, this premium may be insufficient to cover the risks and at other times the risk contribution would be in excess of the risks covered. Assuming the parents of these 10,000 babies buy *takaful* policies when the baby turns five, the baby has already passed this highest stage of risk. Each year, the risk of death does grow, but the same risk contribution is paid by the parents. This introduces the concept of *dripping*, where in the initial years where risks of death are low, the TO will retain a lower percentage of the risk contribution in the risk fund in early years, and keep the balance in an investment fund and in subsequent years this percentage retained in the risk fund will grow and the amount kept in the investment fund is diminished.

[1]United Nations Children's Fund (UNICEF) (2008), *The State of The World's Children 2008: Full Report Panels*, http://www.unicef.org/sowc08/docs/sowc08_panels.pdf, accessed August 2014.

Policyholders pay only one premium a year. This premium is calculated using probabilities that are weighted over the life of a policy.

DETAILED MORTALITY TABLE FOR LIFE *TAKAFUL*

The mortality table in Table 26.6 is a hypothetical one created by using a generic probability algorithm. It indicates the probability of life and death for each age bracket. The table begins with a population pool of 100,000 lives. We only monitor the number of deaths in this pool and have to remove

TABLE 26.6 Mortality Table

	Probability of Survival	Probability of Death	Age	Death Benefit	Risk Contribution P.A.	Average RC	Excess/ Deficit Over RC
	97.00%	3.0000%	0	100,000	3,000	30,753.37	27,753.37
	98.5000%	1.5000%	1	100,000	1,500.00	30,753.37	29,253.37
1.50%	98.4000%	1.6000%	2	100,000	1,600.00	30,753.37	29,153.37
	98.3000%	1.7000%	3	100,000	1,700.00	30,753.37	29,053.37
	98.2000%	1.8000%	4	100,000	1,800.00	30,753.37	28,953.37
	98.1000%	1.9000%	5	100,000	1,900.00	30,753.37	28,853.37
	98.0500%	1.9500%	6	100,000	1,950.00	30,753.37	28,803.37
	98.2000%	1.8000%	7	100,000	1,800.00	30,753.37	28,953.37
	98.2000%	1.8000%	8	100,000	1,800.00	30,753.37	28,953.37
	98.3000%	1.7000%	9	100,000	1,700.00	30,753.37	29,053.37
	98.4000%	1.6000%	10	100,000	1,600.00	30,753.37	29,153.37
	98.5000%	1.5000%	11	100,000	1,500.00	30,753.37	29,253.37
	98.5000%	1.5000%	12	100,000	1,500.00	30,753.37	29,253.37
	98.5000%	1.5000%	13	100,000	1,500.00	30,753.37	29,253.37
	98.5000%	1.5000%	14	100,000	1,500.00	30,753.37	29,253.37
	98.5000%	1.5000%	15	100,000	1,500.00	30,753.37	29,253.37
	98.5000%	1.5000%	16	100,000	1,500.00	30,753.37	29,253.37
	98.5000%	1.5000%	17	100,000	1,500.00	30,753.37	29,253.37
1.700%	98.3000%	1.7000%	18	100,000	1,700.00	30,753.37	29,053.37
	98.3000%	1.7000%	19	100,000	1,700.00	30,753.37	29,053.37
	98.3000%	1.7000%	20	100,000	1,700.00	30,753.37	29,053.37
	98.3000%	1.7000%	21	100,000	1,700.00	30,753.37	29,053.37
	98.3000%	1.7000%	22	100,000	1,700.00	30,753.37	29,053.37
	98.3000%	1.7000%	23	100,000	1,700.00	30,753.37	29,053.37
	98.3000%	1.7000%	24	100,000	1,700.00	30,753.37	29,053.37
	98.3000%	1.7000%	25	100,000	1,700.00	30,753.37	29,053.37
	98.3000%	1.7000%	26	100,000	1,700.00	30,753.37	29,053.37
	98.3000%	1.7000%	27	100,000	1,700.00	30,753.37	29,053.37
	98.3000%	1.7000%	28	100,000	1,700.00	30,753.37	29,053.37
	98.3000%	1.7000%	29	100,000	1,700.00	30,753.37	29,053.37

(continued)

TABLE 26.6 (Continued)

	Probability of Survival	Probability of Death	Age	Death Benefit	Risk Contribution P.A.	Average RC	Excess/ Deficit Over RC
2.7000%	97.3000%	2.7000%	30	100,000	2,700.00	30,753.37	28,053.37
	97.3000%	2.7000%	31	100,000	2,700.00	30,753.37	28,053.37
	97.3000%	2.7000%	32	100,000	2,700.00	30,753.37	28,053.37
	97.3000%	2.7000%	33	100,000	2,700.00	30,753.37	28,053.37
	97.3000%	2.7000%	34	100,000	2,700.00	30,753.37	28,053.37
	97.3000%	2.7000%	35	100,000	2,700.00	30,753.37	28,053.37
	97.3000%	2.7000%	36	100,000	2,700.00	30,753.37	28,053.37
	97.3000%	2.7000%	37	100,000	2,700.00	30,753.37	28,053.37
	97.3000%	2.7000%	38	100,000	2,700.00	30,753.37	28,053.37
	97.3000%	2.7000%	39	100,000	2,700.00	30,753.37	28,053.37
14.800%	85.2000%	14.8000%	40	100,000	14,800.00	30,753.37	15,953.37
	85.2000%	14.8000%	41	100,000	14,800.00	30,753.37	15,953.37
	85.2000%	14.8000%	42	100,000	14,800.00	30,753.37	15,953.37
	85.2000%	14.8000%	43	100,000	14,800.00	30,753.37	15,953.37
	85.2000%	14.8000%	44	100,000	14,800.00	30,753.37	15,953.37
	85.2000%	14.8000%	45	100,000	14,800.00	30,753.37	15,953.37
14.800%	85.2000%	14.8000%	46	100,000	14,800.00	30,753.37	15,953.37
	85.2000%	14.8000%	47	100,000	14,800.00	30,753.37	15,953.37
	85.2000%	14.8000%	48	100,000	14,800.00	30,753.37	15,953.37
	85.2000%	14.8000%	49	100,000	14,800.00	30,753.37	15,953.37
	85.2000%	14.8000%	50	100,000	14,800.00	30,753.37	15,953.37
27.200%	72.8000%	27.2000%	51	100,000	27,200.00	30,753.37	3,553.37
	72.8000%	27.2000%	52	100,000	27,200.00	30,753.37	3,553.37
	72.8000%	27.2000%	53	100,000	27,200.00	30,753.37	3,553.37
	72.8000%	27.2000%	54	100,000	27,200.00	30,753.37	3,553.37
	72.8000%	27.2000%	55	100,000	27,200.00	30,753.37	3,553.37
39.200%	60.8000%	39.2000%	56	100,000	39,200.00	30,753.37	−8,446.63
	60.8000%	39.2000%	57	100,000	39,200.00	30,753.37	−8,446.63
	60.8000%	39.2000%	58	100,000	39,200.00	30,753.37	−8,446.63
	60.8000%	39.2000%	59	100,000	39,200.00	30,753.37	−8,446.63
	60.8000%	39.2000%	60	100,000	39,200.00	30,753.37	−8,446.63
45.000%	55.0000%	45.0000%	61	100,000	45,000.00	30,753.37	−14,246.63
	55.0000%	45.0000%	62	100,000	45,000.00	30,753.37	−14,246.63
	55.0000%	45.0000%	63	100,000	45,000.00	30,753.37	−14,246.63
	55.0000%	45.0000%	64	100,000	45,000.00	30,753.37	−14,246.63
	55.0000%	45.0000%	65	100,000	45,000.00	30,753.37	−14,246.63
65.0000%	35.0000%	65.0000%	66	100,000	65,000.00	30,753.37	−34,246.63
	35.0000%	65.0000%	67	100,000	65,000.00	30,753.37	−34,246.63
	35.0000%	65.0000%	68	100,000	65,000.00	30,753.37	−34,246.63
	35.0000%	65.0000%	69	100,000	65,000.00	30,753.37	−34,246.63
	35.0000%	65.0000%	70	100,000	65,000.00	30,753.37	−34,246.63
75.000%	25.0000%	75.0000%	71	100,000	75,000.00	30,753.37	−44,246.63
	25.0000%	75.0000%	72	100,000	75,000.00	30,753.37	−44,246.63
	25.0000%	75.0000%	73	100,000	75,000.00	30,753.37	−44,246.63
	25.0000%	75.0000%	74	100,000	75,000.00	30,753.37	−44,246.63
	25.0000%	75.0000%	75	100,000	75,000.00	30,753.37	−44,246.63

TABLE 26.6 (Continued)

	Probability of Survival	Probability of Death	Age	Death Benefit	Risk Contribution P.A.	Average RC	Excess/ Deficit Over RC
80.0000%	20.0000%	80.0000%	76	100,000	80,000.00	30,753.37	–49,246.63
	20.0000%	80.0000%	77	100,000	80,000.00	30,753.37	–49,246.63
	20.0000%	80.0000%	78	100,000	80,000.00	30,753.37	–49,246.63
	20.0000%	80.0000%	79	100,000	80,000.00	30,753.37	–49,246.63
	20.0000%	80.0000%	80	100,000	80,000.00	30,753.37	–49,246.63
90%	10.0000%	90.0000%	81	100,000	90,000.00	30,753.37	–59,246.63
	10.0000%	90.0000%	82	100,000	90,000.00	30,753.37	–59,246.63
	10.0000%	90.0000%	83	100,000	90,000.00	30,753.37	–59,246.63
	10.0000%	90.0000%	84	100,000	90,000.00	30,753.37	–59,246.63
	10.0000%	90.0000%	85	100,000	90,000.00	30,753.37	–59,246.63
	2.0000%	98.0000%	86	100,000	98,000.00	30,753.37	–67,246.63
	2.0000%	98.0000%	87	100,000	98,000.00	30,753.37	–67,246.63
	2.0000%	98.0000%	88	100,000	98,000.00	30,753.37	–67,246.63
	2.0000%	98.0000%	89	100,000	98,000.00	30,753.37	–67,246.63
Totals					2,740,050.00	2,767,803.37	

any addition of new lives to this pool. Collecting this data is an intricate process and extends over a long period of time. In fact, just for this pool of 100,000 it will take 89 years to accumulate the required data. Each age bracket provides a separate risk profile to the TO, and in principle a separate risk contribution is calculated for each age bracket for one individual with a death benefit of $100,000.

These RCs are then summed up to the 89th year of life, after which as per this algorithm the chances of death become greater than 100%. An average RC is calculated for over 89 years. It can be seen that in the early years of the policy, the TO collects an RC far in excess of the risk for the early brackets, whereas in later years the *takaful* operator collects an RC far less than the risk covered in those brackets. In early years, the TO can afford to transfer some of the moneys from the RC to an investment fund and use that money in case the policyholder survives the life of the contract and is paid out a different benefit.

MORTALITY TABLES AND PROBABILITY CALCULATIONS

A company decides to offer family *takaful* plans for 1,000 of its senior executives. Keeping the case very simple, it realizes most of its senior executives are in the age brackets of 35, 36, 37, and 38. A death benefit of $100,000 is computed for all of the executives. The actuary now analyzes the data in mortality tables for the relevant age brackets and obtains the results in Table 26.7.

The probability of an individual dying at the age of 35 is 0.001550 and living to 36 is 0.99845.

The probability of an individual dying at the age of 36 is 0.001670 and living to 37 is 0.99833.

The probability of an individual dying at the age of 37 is 0.001810 and living to 38 is 0.99819.

One can see that the probability of dying increases with each age bracket and the probability of living decreases with each age bracket.

Other more complex scenarios are as follows:

The probability of a 35-year-old living until age 36 and dying at 36 would be:

The probability of surviving to 36 (0.99845) × the probability of dying at 36 (0.001670) = 0.0016674.

The probability of a 35-year-old surviving to the age of 36, then surviving to 37 will be the product of the respective probabilities:

Probability of surviving to 36 (0.99845) × probability of surviving to 37 (0.99833) × probability of dying at 37 (0.001810) = 0.1804. This process can be repeated for each age bracket.

By looking at the number of lives in each age bracket, we can assess the probability of death in each bracket and multiply this probability by the death benefit to reach a risk contribution figure for each bracket, as in Table 26.8.

The RC for a 35-year-old is $155, for a 36-year-old it is $167, and for a 37-year-old it is $181. If the company has 1,000 employees in the following age brackets, the total risk contribution will look like Table 26.9.

The previous calculations are suitable for calculating the RC for one year. In the subsequent year, a different RC would be tabulated depending on how many employees migrate from one age bracket to the next.

We illustrate a slightly complex RC calculation that will cover the 400 employees in the 35-year-old age bracket for three consecutive years, which include the current year, and the subsequent year when 35-year-olds migrate to the 36-year-old bracket and the year after that when the same 35-year-olds (now 36 years old) migrate to the 37-year-old bracket.

TABLE 26.7 Mortality Data

Age Bracket	Number of Lives	# That Died	Probability of Death	Death Benefit	RC	# That Lived	Probability of Living	Combined Probability
	A	B	B/A	C	[B/A] * C		1 – B	
A35	1,000,000	A35 – A36						
		1,550	0.001550	100,000	155	998,450	0.99845	
A36	998,450	A36 –A37						
		1,667	0.001670	100,000	167	996,783	0.99833	0.001667
A37	996,783	A37 –A38						
		1,804	0.001810	100,000	181	994,979	0.99819	
A38	994,979							

TABLE 26.8 Risk Contribution and Probability

Age Bucket	Number of Lives	# That Died	Prob. of Death	Death Benefit	RC	# That Lived	Prob. of Living	Comb Prob.
	A	B	B/A	C	[B/A] × C		1 -B	
A35	1,000,000	A35 - A36						
		1,550	0.001550	100,000	155	998,450	0.99845	
A36	998,450	A36-A37						
		1,667	0.001670	100,000	167	996,783	0.99833	0.001667
A37	996,783	A37 -A38						
		1,804	0.001810	100,000	181	994,979	0.99819	0.00
A38	994,979							

Standalone Probabilities for a given bucket:

Single Event	Prob. of Single Event	RC for Single Event
Probability that a 35-year-old will die between ages 35 and 36	0.00155	= \$100,000 × .00155 = \$155
Probability that a 36-year-old will die between ages 36 and 37	0.00167	= \$100,000 × .00167 = \$167
Probability that a 37-year-old will die between ages 37 and 38	0.00181	= \$100,000 × .00181 = \$ 181

TABLE 26.9 Risk Contribution

Age	# of Employees	Risk Contribution	Total Risk Contribution
35	400	155	62,000
36	400	167	66,800
37	300	181	54,300
Total Risk Contribution			**183,100**

Table 26.10 illustrates this calculation.

The combined risk contribution for all employees is included in Table 26.11.

It can be noted that the age bracket of 35-year-olds contributes the most to total RC because in three years they can move into age brackets with varying probabilities.

Interpreting the mortality table is a key component of the actuarial cycle, and then monitoring the frequency and impact of actual events against probabilities is crucial for making adjustments to policy terms. Note family *takaful* policies are renewed every year, and TOs cannot revise the *tabarru* rate every year. Once the RC is calculated for a policy, it cannot be revised. It is therefore suitable when calculating the gross contribution in our formula of $GC = RC + E + \lambda$, that the *takaful* operator keep some cushion parked in λ for variations in calculations from actual events.

RISK PROFILING

Imagine covering a company of 100 employees for family *takaful* coverage. The details of these families can be combined like in Table 26.12. The death benefit is calculated at 100 salaries irrespective of the scale of the employees or their role in the organization.

The above company is a high-tech company with 100 employees. Its CEO, CFO, and COO are paid rather well, along with the senior executives of the company. These eight employees have a combined salary of $3,200,000 and are all above the age of 50. They pose a combined risk of $320,000,000. It would be advisable that these individuals never fly together on a plane. This senior team constitutes a high-risk bracket referred to as Bracket A.

The second bracket of risk consists of 92 employees consisting of middle-level executives, senior employees, and workers, which are all below

TABLE 26.10 Risk Contribution Calculation

Standalone probabilities for a given bucket		
Single Event	**Prob. of Single Event**	**RC for Single Event**
Probability that a 35-year-old will die between ages 35 and 36	0.00155	= $100,000 × .00155 = $155
Probability that a 36-year-old will die between ages 36 and 37	0.00167	= $100,000 × .00167 = $167
Probability that a 37-year-old will die between ages 37 and 38	0.00181	= $100,000 × .00181 = $ 181
Combined probabilities for one participant migrating from 1 bucket to another		
Combined Event	**Prob. of Combined Event**	**RC for Combined Event**
What can happen to a 35-year-old?		RC for Dying at 35
A 35-year-old may die before turning 36.	0.00155	=.00155 × 100,000 = $155
A 35-year-old may survive to 36 and die before reaching 37.		
Probability that a 35-year-old will survive to 36 and then die before turning 37		
Combined probability of surviving from 35 to 36 and then	0.99845	
dying from 36 to 37	0.00167	RC for Surviving to 36 and Dying Before 37
Combined Probability	=0.99845 × 0.00167 = 0.0016674	= $ 100,000 × .00166741 = $ 166.741

A 35-year-old may survice to 36, then survive to 37 and die at 38.		
Probability that a 35-year-old surivives to 36	0.99845	
Probability that a 36-year-old survives to 37	0.99833	
Probability that a 37-year-old dies at age 38	0.00181	RC for a 35-Yr-Old Surviving Till 37 and Dying at 37
Combined Probability	=.99845 × .99833 × .00181 = .0018042	= \$100,000 × .0018042 = \$180.42
Total Risk Contribution for 3 Years for a 35-Year-Old		= RC (D35) + RC (S35 D36) + RC(S35:S36:D37) = \$155 + \$166.741 + \$180.42 = \$502.16
Risk Contribution for 35-Year-Old for 3 Years is \$502.16. For 400 Employees = \$201,040.		

TABLE 26.11 Combined Risk Contribution

Age	No. of Lives	No. of Deaths	p	q
35	1,000,000	1,550	0.00155	0.99845
36	998,450	1,667	0.001669588	0.998330412
37	996,783	1,804	0.001809822	0.998190178
38	994,979			
35-Year-Old		**Prob.**	**DB**	**RC**
Die at 35		0.00155	100,000	155
Die at 36		0.001667	100,000	167
Die at 37		0.001804	100,000	180
Total RC				502
36-Year-Old		**Prob.**	**DB**	**RC**
Die at 36		0.001669588	100,000	167
Die at 37		0.001806801	100,000	181
Total RC				348
37-Year-Old		**Prob.**	**DB**	**RC**
Die at 37		0.001809822	100,000	181
Total RC				181
		RC	**# Emp**	
35-Year-Olds		502	400	200,800
36-Year-Olds		348	400	139,200
37-Year-Olds		181	200	36,200
				376,200

the age of 40. They have lower probabilities of death and have lower death benefits per employee. The combined death benefit of these 92 employees is $210,500,000.

The total RC for the company will be $2,496,950, of which $2,120,000 is sufficient to cover just the senior team and only $376,950 is sufficient to cover the remaining 92 employees of the company.

The risks of covering this company's employees are highly skewed, with high probabilities of death for the mere eight senior executives coupled with large payouts and low payouts for 92 employees with lower probabilities of death. The TO in this case has to decide on exposing itself to a total risk of payout of $530,500,000 with a total RC of $2,496,950 or sharing this risk with a *retakaful provider. Retakaful* is merely a process whereby a *takaful*

TABLE 26.12 Risk Profiling Data

	Age	Pr. Death	# of Emplys	Salary/ Emply	Total Salary	DB	Total DB	RC		
CEO	60	0.009	1	1,000,000	1,000,000	100	100,000,000	900,000		
CFO	58	0.007	1	850,000	850,000	100	85,000,000	595,000		
COO	55	0.005	1	850,000	850,000	100	85,000,000	425,000		
Senior Execs	50	0.004	5	100,000	500,000	100	50,000,000	200,000	RCA	2,120,000
Risk Bucket A					3,200,000				8	320,000,000
Mid Execs	40	0.003	10	50,000	500,000	100	50,000,000	150,000		
Senior Emplys	30	0.002	25	30,000	750,000	100	75,000,000	150,000		
Workers	28	0.0009	57	15,000	855,000	100	85,500,000	76,950	RCB	376,950
Risk Bucket B					2,105,000	Tot DB	530,500,000	2,496,950	92	210,500,000

company shares risk along with the contribution collected with another company. We cover *retakaful* in subsequent works as we have exhausted the space limit allowed for this book.

CONCLUSION

It would be evident that the quality and accuracy of data is a fundamental component of pricing *takaful* policies. Data helps *takaful* operators to accurately predict the probability of an event occurring and thus pricing the risks attached with that event.

Afterword

I became interested in Islamic finance around 2008. This was a year where banks were announcing losses of unprecedented scale, countries were nearing default on bonds, and just as one crisis subsided another emerged. I happened to be working with Barclays bank in Pakistan at that time and was able to witness much of the turbulence in the banking industry firsthand. It was just not clear to me how the banking system was collapsing, and why so many banks in the United States and Europe had so much exposure to the real estate sector in the United States. I was also curious as to why the financial systems of China and ASEAN countries were not facing the same crisis. What also amazed me is how a credit freeze in the United States and Europe caused companies to cancel orders from factories and put the rest of the world in an economic slowdown. I realized that much of the buying power of the United States and Europe depended on debt, and much of the growth in emerging markets depended on this debt-based buying power.

Since 2008, China began to realign its focus and reduce its dependence on U.S. and European demand and is now cultivating domestic and regional demand. China has not grown alone, and it has helped its regional neighbors grow as well, much like how the United States in the post–World War II era grew in economic might and helped its European allies to do the same.

Amid all the confusion and this transition of economic power, Islamic finance seemed to offer an alternative. The International Centre for Education in Finance offered a comprehensive program, and Mohsin and myself made the most of the opportunity.

Islamic banking and *takaful* rely on the same model as conventional banks and insurance companies. The model pools funds from different sources and uses these funds to either extend financing or make investments. Profits are shared between the banking operator and customers and the participants and the *takaful* operator. Both models depend on all liability customers not calling in their claims at the same time, that all depositors do not withdraw their funds at once, and not all participants file their claims together. Both systems are, however, in a state of perpetual insolvency.

As much as *riba* is an issue of concern, the authors both feel that a banking system based on the concept of a deposit creates the potential for bubble economies as it is a system of money creation. We have explained this is in detail in the chapter on *wadiah*. Therefore, Islamic financial intermediation and *takaful* is vulnerable to the same risks that a conventional financial system presents. The subtle distinctions in nature of contracts employed are a steppingstone. Certainly, Islamic banks cannot compound profit rates as conventional banks do, and *takaful* companies that operate on *wakalah* and modified *wakalah* by definition are not interested in earning revenues from underwriting surpluses. The story of Islamic finance does not end here.

The subject itself has created a platform where scholars from the Muslim world congregate and deliberate on various issues. Let us not forget, the whole ethos of Islamic civilization and its institutions was dismantled by colonial rule. With each Muslim country trying to develop its own institutions, organizations like the Islamic Development Bank is the first initiative where Muslim countries have combined their resources to fund infrastructure projects in the Muslim world. Institutions like AAOIFI and IFSB have created platforms for Muslim countries to develop think tanks by calling in intellectual capabilities from around the Muslim world. Conferences are being held where traders and financiers sit under one roof to discuss possibilities. These conferences are being held in Dubai, London, Hong Kong, Pakistan, Malaysia, Indonesia, Saudi Arabia, South Korea, and Luxembourg.

Thirty years ago Islamic banks were worried about how to raise capital; now they are buying out conventional banks. In 2013–2014, the Abu Dhabi Commercial Bank bought Barclays operations in Dubai. Let us also not forget that Qatar Holdings and Abu Dhabi Sovereign Wealth Fund had injected GBP 8 billion into Barclays in 2008, saving it from the same fate as RBS.

As this book was written, RHB Bank and CIMB Bank in Malaysia are exploring opportunities of a merger to create a mega-Islamic bank that has the necessary paid-up capital to underwrite international *sukuk* issuances. Cities around the world are vying for the top slot and to be the hub of Islamic finance so as to attract billions of dollars into *shariah*-compliant assets.

Mohsin and myself firmly believe that this book could not have been written anywhere other than in Kuala Lumpur. Much of it was written in coffeeshops under the majestic aura of the Petronas Towers in an area that is known as KLCC. We feel Kuala Lumpur is the face of Islamic finance and other Muslim cities should not compete with it but complement it. Just as a mosque requires four minarets, an Islamic economic system requires four pillars, one of finance and capital, another of natural resources, a third of a vibrant and skilled workforce, and a fourth of well-functioning markets. Malaysia has one of the most complex financial systems within the Muslim world and is integrated into international capital markets with well-engineered trading platforms. Having said that, Islamic finance cannot reach its full potential without the combined efforts of all stakeholders, and integrated capital markets within the Muslim world, and a single currency could change the landscape of global commerce.

On a personal note, Mohsin and myself are deemed to be moderate Muslims. We have both been educated in private schools in Pakistan and then in the United States, and have throughout our working years and academic years been cognizant of the fact that the Muslim world has so much to offer to the human race. We hope that Islamic finance sets the stage for the self-actualization process for the Muslim diaspora and global community to crystallize.

We have had several discussions with scholars and practitioners in the industry from Austria, Syria, Saudi Arabia, Bosnia, Pakistan, Algeria, Bangladesh, Indonesia, and the UAE. I have followed the various lectures offered by Sheikh Hisham Kabbani, a scholar of international reputation, who emphasizes that substance is as important as form in human affairs and commercial relationships.

We hope that we have offered non-Muslims and Muslims a clear picture of the precepts of Islamic finance. For critics we can only propose that they come up with better alternatives. The authors can be contacted at huseinkureshi@gmail.com and mohsinhayat@gmail.com.

About the Authors

Hussein Kureshi (Kuala Lumpur, Malaysia) obtained his degree in Business Administration at Stony Brook University in the United States and a Master's degree in Islamic finance in Malaysia. He has extensive experience in consumer banking, credit risk management, loan origination, and monitoring for SME and commercial clients. Hussein has a lucrative banking career spanning over 15 years specializing in banking operations and management with organizations such as Barclays Bank Plc (Pakistan), Bank Al Habib (Pakistan), Union Bank (Islamabad), Emirates Bank International (Islamabad), Standard Chartered Bank, Commerce Bank (New Jersey, U.S.), and Chase Manhattan Bank (New York, U.S.). Hussein is attached to a global Islamic bank as a Knowledge Manager.

Mohsin Hayat grew up in Pakistan and has worked in capital markets across Hong Kong, Singapore, New York, and London. His passion is in being an entrepreneur and investor; he's been a business advisor to start-ups and businesses in Asia-Pacific and worked with new-media start-ups on strategic alliances across 45 countries. Mohsin Hayat has more than 20 years of experience and combines capital management, investment management, and international finance knowledge to contribute to businesses in both emerging markets and international finance hubs.

A graduate from Stony Brook, New York, his technical background is in investment banking, venture capital, SMEs, and real asset management.

As a consultant and advisor he regularly contributes research and ideas to academia, regulators, and private sector investors.

Mohsin Hayat divides his time among Kuala Lumpur, Islamabad, and Hong Kong while living in Kuala Lumpur with his wife and two sons.

Bibliography

Accounting and Auditing of Islamic Financial Institutions (AAOIFI). *Shariah Standard.* 2010. www.aaoifi.com/en/standards-and-definitions/shari%E2%80%99a-standards/.

Accounting and Auditing of Islamic Financial Institutions (AAOIFI). *Shariah Standard.* No. 1, "Trading in Currencies." www.aaoifi.com/en/standards-and-definitions/shari%E2%80%99a-standards.

Accounting and Auditing of Islamic Financial Institutions (AAOIFI). *Shariah Standard.* No. 7, clause 2. http://www.aaoifi.com/en/standards-and-definitions/shari%E2%80%99a-standards.

Accounting and Auditing of Islamic Financial Institutions (AAOIFI). *Shariah Standard.* No 16. www.aaoifi.com/en/standards-and-definitions/shari%E2%80%99a-standards.

Accounting and Auditing of Islamic Financial Institutions (AAOIFI). *Shariah Standard.* No. 23, clause 2/1. www.aaoifi.com/en/standards-and-definitions/shari%E2%80%99a-standards.

Accounting and Auditing of Islamic Financial Institutions (AAOIFI). *Shariah Standard.* No. 30, article 4/5. 2010. www.aaoifi.com/en/standards-and-definitions/shari%E2%80%99a-standards.

Accounting and Auditing of Islamic Financial Institutions (AAOIFI). *Shariah Standard.* No. 30, article 4/6, 4/7, 4/8, 4/9, 4/10, 5/1, 5/2. 2010. www.aaoifi.com/en/standards-and-definitions/shari%E2%80%99a-standards.

Al-'Asqalani, Ibnu Hajar. *Bulugh al-Maram min Adillah al-Ahkam.* Matba'ah al-Salafiyyah, 1928.

Al-Bassam, Shaykh Abd Allah. *Tawdeeh al-Ahkam sharh Bullogh al-Maraam.*

Al-Misri, Rafiq Yunus. *Bai al Taqsit- Tahlil Fiqhi wa Iqtisadi.*

Al-Samarqandi, Imam Ibnu Ahmed. *Tuhfat al-Fuqaha.* Vol. 3. Beirut: Dar al-Kutub al-'Ilmiyah, 1983.

Al-Sawi, Hasyiyah. *Al-Sawi 'ala Syarh al-Saghir.* Vol. 3. Dar al-Ma'arif, 1982.

Al-Zuhaili, Wahbah. *Al-Fiqh al Islami wa Adillatuhu, Islamic Jurispudence and its Proof.* Dar al Wafa, 1989.

Archer, Simon, Rifaat Ahmed Karim, and Volker Niesnhaus. *Takaful Islamic Insurance: Concepts and Regulatory Issues.* Hoboken, NJ: John Wiley & Sons, 2009.

Ash Shawkani, Muhammad. *Nayl al-Awtar Sharh Muntaqa al-Akhbar.* Vol. 5.

Ayub, Muhammad. *Understanding Islamic Finance.* Hoboken, NJ: John Wiley & Sons, 2007.

Bacha, O. I. "Derivative Instruments and Islamic Finance: Some Thoughts for a Reconsideration." *Journal of Islamic Financial Services* 1, no. 1 (1999): 9–25.

Bakar, M. D. "Contracts in Islamic Commercial and Their Application in Modern Islamic Financial System." *Iqtisad Journal of Islamic Economics.* 2003. http:Islamic-world.net/economics/contract_01.htm.

Bank Negara Malaysia (BNM). *Takaful Annual Report.* 2005. www.bnm.gov.my/files/publication/tkf/en/2005/book.en.pdf.

Bank Negara Malaysia (BNM). *Capital Adequacy Framework for Islamic Banks (Risk Weighted Assets)*. 2009. www.bnm.gov.my/guidelines/01_banking/01_capital_adequacy/02_gl_capital_adequacy_framework_islamic.pdf.

Bank Negara Malaysia (BNM). *Shariah Resolutions in Islamic Finance*. 2nd ed. 2010. http://www.bnm.gov.my/microsites/financial/pdf/resolutions/shariah_resolutions_2nd_edition_EN.pdf.

Bank Negara Malaysia (BNM). "Guidelines on the Recognition and Measurement of Profit Sharing Investment Account (PSIA) as Risk Absorbent." No. BNM/RH/GL 007-11, Islamic Banking and Takaful Department. 2011. www.bnm.gov.my/guidelines/01_banking/01_capital_adequacy/06_psia.pdf.

Bank Negara Malaysia (BNM). "Guidelines on Takaful Operational Framework." 2013. www.bnm.gov.my/guidelines/02_insurance_takaful/03_prudential_stds/Guideline_Takaful_Operator_Framework.pdf.

Bank Negara Malaysia (BNM). "BNM: About the Bank." 2013. www.bnm.gov.my/index.php?ch=7&pg=715&ac=802.

Bank Negara Malaysia (BNM). "Guidelines on Ibra' (Rebate) for Sale-Based Financing." 2013. www.bnm.gov.my/guidelines/01_banking/04_prudential_stds/Updated_GL_on_Ibra_Final_Sept2013.pdf.

Bank Negara Malaysia (BNM). "Hibah (Shariah Requirements and Optional Practices) Exposure Draft." 2013. www.bnm.gov.my/documents/SAC/01_Hibah.pdf.

Bank Negara Malaysia (BNM). *Islamic Financial Services Act 2013*. www.bnm.gov.my/documents/act/en_ifsa.pdf

Bank Negara Malaysia (BNM). "Malaysian Financial Sector: Islamic Banking and Takaful." 2014. www.bnm.gov.my/index.php?ch=fs_mfs&pg=fs_mfs_bank.

Bank Negara Malaysia (BNM). "Tawarruq (Shariah Requirements and Optional Practices)." Exposure draft December 2013. www.bnm.gov.my/documents/SAC/13_Tawarruq.pdf.

Bank of International Settlements. "Basel II: International Convergence of Capital Measurement and Capital Standards: A Revised Framework." 2006. www.bis.org/publ/bcbs128.htm.

Bank of International Settlements. "Basel III: Liquidity." 2013. www.bis.org/bcbs/basel3.htm.

Boris, Heinrich. *Institutions, Behaviour and Economic Theory: A Contribution to Classical-Keynesian Political Economy*. Cambridge: Cambridge University Press, 1997.

Casey, Peter. *Supervisory Issues in Takaful: An Overview*. Hoboken, NJ: John Wiley & Sons, 2012.

Choudhry, Moorad, and Irving Henry. *Bank Asset and Liability Management Strategy, Trading and Analysis*. Hoboken, NJ: John Wiley & Sons, 2007.

Dar, Humayon, and Umar Moghul. *The Chancellor Guide to the Legal and Shariah Aspects of Islamic Finance*. New York: BMB Group, 2009.

Ethica Institute of Islamic Finance. *Ethica's Handbook of Islamic Finance*. Dubai: Ethica Institute of Islamic Finance, 2013.

Hadith of Bukhari. Vols. I.II.II & IV.

Hamzah, Z. A., and B. Vizcaino. "Malaysia Tightens Rules on Divisive Islamic bai Inah Deals." 2014. www.reuters.com/article/2014/05/21/us-islamic-finance-malaysia-idUSBREA4K0FM20140521.

Hugonnier, J. and E. Morellec. "Bank Capital, Liquid Reserves, and Insolvency Risk." Technical report. Swiss Finance Institute and EPFL, 2014.

Ibnu Rusyd, Averroes. *Bidayah al-Mujtahid, Distinguished Jurists Primer, a translation of Volume 2, Center for Muslim Contribution to Civilisation*. Ann Arbor: University of Michigan, 1994.

Ibrahim, U. "Securitization of Debts: Bay al Dayn." 2002. Paper presented in Islamic Bonds Colloqium, June 24, 2004. Conference Hall 2, Securities Commission Malaysia.

Imam Hafiz Abu Dawood Sulaiman bin Ash'ath Abu Ammar Qadhi. *Sunan Abu Dawood*. Vols. I to V, Arabic-English. Darussalam, 2008.

International Centre for Education in Islamic Finance (INCEIF). *Risk Management of Islamic Financial Institutions Module Book, IB2002*. Kuala Lumpur, Malaysia: INCEIF, 2006.

International Centre for Education in Islamic Finance (INCEIF). *Shariah Rules in Financial Transactions Course, SH1003*. Kuala Lumpur, Malaysia: INCEIF, 2013.

International Centre for Education in Islamic Finance (INCEIF). *Applied Shariah in Financial Transaction*. Kuala Lumpur, Malaysia: INCEIF, 2006.

International Financial Services Board. "Exposure Draft—Standard on Risk Management for Takaful Undertakings." 2013. http://ifsb.org/docs/IFSB%20ED-14%20Risk%20Management%20for%20Takaful%20Undertakings%20Final%20(01-11-2012).pdf.

International Shariah Research Academy (ISRA). *Islamic Financial System: Principles and Operations*. Kuala Lumpur, Malaysia: ISRA, 2012.

Iqbal, Zamir, and Abbas Mirakhor. *An Introduction to Islamic Finance Theory and Practice*. Hoboken, NJ: John Wiley & Sons, 2007.

Jaffer, Sohail. *Islamic Asset Management: Forming the Future for Shari'a Compliant Investment Strategies*. London: Euromoney Books, 2004.

Kettell, Brian. *Introduction to Islamic Banking and Finance*. Hoboken, NJ: John Wiley & Sons, 2011.

La Porta, R., A. Shleifer, and F. Lopez. "Corporate Ownership Around the World." *Journal of Finance* 54, no. 2 (1999): 471–527.

Lahsasna, A., and L. S. Lin. "Issues in Islamic Capital Markets: Islamic bond/Sukuk." In *3rd International Conference on Business and Economic Research Proceeding*. (2012, pp. 12–13).

Leslé, V. L. and S. Avramova. *International Monetary Fund (IMF): Revisiting Risk-Weighted Assets*. 2012. www.imf.org/external/pubs/ft/wp/2012/wp1290.pdf.

The Majelle Al Ahkam Al-'Adliyyah: A Complete Code of Islamic Civil Law. 2000.

Malaysia International Islamic Finance Centre (MIFC). "Shariah Screening Methodology: Adopting a Two-Tier Quantitative Approach." 2013. www.mifc.com/index.php?ch=28&pg=72&ac=54&bb=uploadpdf.

Martin, Iain. *Making It Happen: Fred Goodwin, RBS and the Men Who Blew Up the British Economy*. New York: Simon & Schuster, 2013.

Middle East Insurance Review. *Shariah Column—Ask Your Scholar: What Makes a Shariah Scholar?* 2012. www.meinsurancereview.com/Magazine/ReadMagazineArticle/aid/10443/Shariah-Column-ndash-Ask-Your-Scholar-What-makes-a-Shariah-scholar

Muslim, Imam Abul-Husain. *English Translation of Sahih Muslim*. Vols. I to VII. Translated by Nasiruddin Al-Khattab. 2007.

Naim, A. "Malaysia-The Tax Haven for Islamic Finance." *Islamic Finance News Magazine* (October 2010).

New York Stock Exchange. 2001. www.NYSE.com/data/transactions-statistics-data-library.

Organization of Islamic Countries (OIC). Fiqh Academy. 7th Session on Installment Sale. 1992. www.fiqhacademy.org.

Organization of Islamic Countries (OIC). Fiqh Academy. 7th session. 1992. www.fiqhacademy.org.

Organization of Islamic Countries (OIC). Fiqh Academy. 16th meeting. 2002. www.fiqhacademy.org.

Organization of Islamic Countries (OIC). Fiqh Academy. Resolution no. 179 (19/5). www.fiqhacademy.org.

Perbadanan Insurans Deposit Malaysia (PIDM). PIDM: Mandate, 2014. www.pidm.gov.my/getdoc/0eb0ff26-c029-490a-985a-257dfff5f6e7/Mandate.aspx.

Poitras, Geoffrey. *Valuation of Equity Securities: History, Theory and Application.* Singapore: World Scientific, 2010.

Pok, W. C. "Analysis of Shariah Quantitative Screening Norms among Malaysian Shariah Compliant Stock." *Investment Management and Financial Innovations* 9, no. 2 (2012): 69–80.

Prins, Nomi. *All the Presidents Bankers: The Hidden Alliances that Drive American Power.* New York: Nations Books, 2014.

Saleem, Muhammad Yusuf. *An Introduction to the Theoretical Foundations of Islamic Transactions.* Kuala Lumpur, Malaysia: Ilmiah, 2012.

Saleem, Muhammad Yusuf. *Islamic Commercial Law.* Hoboken, NJ: John Wiley & Sons, 2013.

Securities and Exchange Commission of Pakistan. "Takaful Rules 2012." 2012. www.secp.gov.pk/notification/pdf/2012/Takaful-Rules-2012.pdf.

Securities Commission Malaysia. "Information Required for the Shariah Compliance Review at Pre-IPO Stage." 2014. www.sc.com.my/wp-content/uploads/eng/html/icm/Pre-IPO_InfotemplateI1.pdf.

Securities Commission Malaysia (SCM). "Resolutions of the Securities Commission Shariah Advisory Council." 2nd ed. 2007. www.sc.com.my/wp-content/uploads/eng/html/icm/Resolutions_SAC_2ndedition.pdf.

Standard and Poor's Dow Jones Indices, Dow Jones Islamic Market Indices: Screens for Shari'ah Compliance. 2014. www.djindexes.com/islamicmarket/?go=shariah-compliance.

Sunan Al-Thirmizi. *Collection of Hadith.*

Taleb, Nicholas Nassim. *Fooled by Randomness: The Hidden Role of Chance in Life and in the Markets (Incerto).* New York: Random House, 2005.

Tijani, I. M. "A Snapshot of Tawarruq In Contemporary Islamic Finance." *International Shariah Research Academy Monthly Publication* (September 2013).

Tolefat, A.R.K. and M. Asutay. *Takaful Investment Portfolios: A Study of the Composition of Takaful Funds in the GCC and Malaysia.* Hoboken, NJ: John Wiley & Sons, 2013.

United Nations Children's Fund (UNICEF). "The State of the World's Children, 2008: Full Report Panels." 2008. www.unicef.org/sowc08/docs/sowc08_panels.pdf.

Usmani, Taqi Muhammad. *An Introduction to Islamic Finance.* Pakistan: Idara Isha'at-e-Diniyat (P), 2005.

Van Greuning, Hennie, and Zamir Iqbal. *Risk Analysis for Islamic Banks.* World Bank, 2008.

Wilson, R. (2008), "Innovation in the Structuring of Islamic Sukuk Securities." *Humanomics* 24, no. 3 (2008):170–181.

Index

Printed and bound by CPI Group (UK) Ltd, Croydon, CR0 4YY